AF600660

Korean Studies of the Henry M. Jackson School of International Studies

James B. Palais, Editor

Korean Studies of the Henry M. Jackson School of International Studies

Over the Mountains Are Mountains: Korean Peasant Households and Their Adaptations to Rapid Industrialization
by Clark W. Sorenson

Cultural Nationalism in Colonial Korea, 1920–1925
by Michael Edson Robinson

Offspring of Empire: The Koch'ang Kims and the Colonial Origins of Korean Capitalism, 1876–1945
by Carter J. Eckert

Confucian Statecraft and Korean Institutions: Yu Hyongwon and the Late Chosŏn Dynasty
by James B. Palais

Peasant Protest and Social Change in Colonial Korea
by Gi-Wook Shin

Origins of the Chosŏn Dynasty
by John B. Duncan

Protestantism and Politics in Korea
by Chung-shin Park

Protestantism and Politics in Korea

CHUNG-SHIN PARK

UNIVERSITY OF WASHINGTON PRESS

Seattle and London

This publication was supported in part by the Jackson School Publications Fund, established through the generous support of the Henry M. Jackson Foundation and other donors, in cooperation with the Henry M. Jackson School of International Studies and the University of Washington Press.

Printed in the United States of America

University of Washington Press
P.O. Box 50096
Seattle, WA 98145-5096, USA
www.washington.edu/uwpress

Library of Congress Cataloging-in-Publication Data
Park, Chung-shin.
Protestantism and politics in Korea / Chung-shin Park.
p. cm.—(Korean studies of the Henry M. Jackson School of International Studies)
Includes bibliographical references and index.
ISBN 0-295-98149-0 (alk. paper)
1. Christianity and politics—Korea—History. 2. Presbyterian Church—Korea—History. 3. Korea—Church history. I. Title. II. Series.
BR1328 .P358 2001 280'.4'09519—DC21 2001027688

The paper used in this publication is acid free and recycled from 10 percent post-consumer and at least 50 percent pre-consumer waste. It meets the minimum requirements of the American National Standard for Information Sciences—Permanence of Paper for Printed Library Materials, ANSI Z39.48–1984. ∞♲

TO FOUR WOMEN:

Sunrae Chin, my late mother;
Arum and Dawn, my daughters;
and Jeongwon, my wife

CONTENTS

ACKNOWLEDGMENTS

Although I am solely responsible for any flaws and errors this book might have, it was made possible by scholarly, moral, and financial support from my teachers, friends, students, and family, as well as from many institutions and organizations. I would like to take this opportunity to express my deepest appreciation to some of them.

James B. Palais of the University of Washington, mentor, friend, and colleague, deserves my heartfelt thanks. For many years at the university and thereafter, he has provided invaluable suggestions, guidance, unceasing aid, encouragement, and care. He is a model scholar from whom I learned academic thoroughness, diligence, and integrity. He read this manuscript several times. Grateful acknowledgment is also due to Kenneth B. Pyle, former director of the Henry M. Jackson School of International Studies at the University of Washington. As a teacher, he shared with me his profound historical knowledge and craftsmanship. I am indebted to him for his attention, advice, wisdom, and concern during my long professional training. I also benefited greatly from the scholarship and friendship of Bruce Cumings, formerly of the University of Washington and now at the University of Chicago. His critical comments, particularly on chapters five and six, greatly influenced the final revision. Professors Kent R. Guy, John E. Toews, and the late Jack Dull—all of the University of Washington—deserve special mention for their teaching and guidance. Along with Professors Palais and Pyle, they read all or part of the original dissertation upon which this work is based and offered valuable comments and criticism.

Special thanks go to my friends and colleagues in the fields of history and Korean studies in North America: Michael E. Robinson of Indiana University, Carter J. Eckert of Harvard University, Donald L. Baker of the University of British Columbia, John B. Duncan of the University of California at Los Angeles, Donald N. Clark of Trinity University in San Antonio, Bruce Fulton of Seattle, and Helga Harriman of Oklahoma State University. They have all gladly, yet critically, read part or all of the manuscript, provided valuable suggestions, and encouraged me to publish the work. I wish to express my thanks also to those anonymous individuals who reviewed this manuscript and endorsed it unanimously for publication.

My teachers and friends in Korea also deserve my gratitude. The late Professors Kim Yangsŏn, Hong Paengnyong, and Im Pyŏngtáe of Soongsil University, and Professors Kang Man’gil, Kim Chunyŏp, and Kim Chŏngbae of Koryŏ University are the teachers who first ignited my passion for historical studies. I am also very grateful to Lew Young Ick, professor of Korean Studies and director of the Institute for Modern Korean Studies at Yonsei University. He has shared with me his profound wisdom and scholarship. Professors Yi Manyŏl of Sungmyŏng Women’s University, Ch’a Sangch’ŏl of Ch’ungnam National University, Yi Sangsŏn of Sŏngsim Women’s University and Yun Kyŏngno of Hansŏng University were always available when I needed them in Korea. Ch’oe Ŭnju, Han Myŏnggŭn, and Kim Kwŏnjŏng of Soongsil University also deserve my special thanks. As long-time friends and students, they have always encouraged my endeavors.

Research for this book was greatly facilitated by the splendid resources, librarians, and staff of the East Asian Library at the University of Washington, Soongsil University Library, Yonsei University Library, and the Edmond Low Library at Oklahoma State University. Yoon-whan Choe of the University of Washington not only familiarized me with the library’s excellent collection, but also gathered valuable materials for my research.

On this score, my family in Korea also deserves my deep gratitude. My father, the Reverend Myŏngsu Park, former moderator of the Jesus Presbyterian Church in Korea and former board member of various Korean institutions for Christian education and evangelism, including the Christian Broadcasting System and Ch’ongsin University and Theological Seminary, and my mother, Sunrae Chin, who passed away without seeing this book, shared with me their valuable personal recollections and experiences in Korean church politics, as well as their private collection on Korean church history. They particularly deserve my love and appreciation. I am very grateful to my older brother, Professor Yong-shin Park of Yonsei University. A sociological theorist and Korea specialist, he has been my closest colleague, my most discerning critic, and most of all, my greatest cheerleader.

At various stages in my professional training and research for this book I was supported by a number of sources: a Beatrice Ross Scholarship from the University of Washington, a research assistantship from the Henry M.

Jackson School of International Studies at the University of Washington, a National Resource Fellowship from the United States Department of Education, several Dean's Incentive Grants and Summer Research Grants from the College of Arts and Sciences at Oklahoma State University, a research leave and funds from the Department of History at Oklahoma State University, a visiting professorship from Soongsil University, a guest professorship from Yonsei University, and a fellowship from the Korea Foundation. Special thanks go to the Social Science Research Council and the American Council of Learned Societies. Their Advanced Research Grant facilitated the completion of this book. A research grant from the Oklahoma Humanities Council helped me to concentrate on the final revision of the manuscript for publication.

In addition, I am grateful to the University of Washington Press for its interest in the manuscript. Executive editor Michael Duckworth was most helpful in guiding this book to publication. I am particularly grateful to Bruce Acker, my copy editor, for the effort, care, and skill he displayed in editing my manuscript. Of course, all errors and mistakes are my own.

Lastly, I wish to express my love and gratitude to four ladies: again, my late mother Sunrae Chin, my two daughters, Arum and Dawn, and my wife, Jeongwon. A minister's wife, my mother worked on behalf of Korean women and children, who had been at a disadvantage in Korea's male- and adult-dominated society, until her death in 1988. From her I learned endurance, humility, and love. Arum and Dawn sacrificed their playtime with their father at an age when they most needed it. It was they who encouraged and "supervised" me most as I wrote this book. "Daddy! You're writing a book! A thick book!" they often said proudly. This work could not have been completed without the support, patience, and love of my wife, Jeongwon. The book is dedicated to these four wonderful ladies.

Protestantism and Politics in Korea

INTRODUCTION

On a spring day in 1984, a motorcade of hundreds of vehicles proceeded along the highway connecting Inch'ŏn, a port city, to Seoul. Spectators lining the road would break into applause every once in a while. If Horace N. Allen, Horace G. Underwood, Henry G. Appenzeller, and other Protestant missionaries who had traveled the very same path about one century previously could have reappeared to witness the procession, they would have been astonished. They would have learned to their amazement that the occasion was the centennial anniversary of the first Protestant evangelistic effort, undertaken by none other than themselves. It had been one hundred years since Horace N. Allen, an American physician and the first Protestant missionary, had arrived in the "Hermit Kingdom" to "Christianize" the Koreans. The motorcade was part of the festivities organized by Korean Protestants to celebrate the successful expansion of Protestantism in their country in numbers and influence.[1]

By 1984, Protestant Christians had come to number some 25 percent of the population in South Korea. In 1990, there were 11,888,374 Protestant Christians among 43,520,199 South Koreans.[2] Churches are everywhere—in cities, towns, and even small villages. The capital, Seoul, is filled with church buildings and signs of the cross, and has been called "a city of churches."[3] Ironically, the largest Protestant church in the world is found not in America, which introduced Protestantism to Korea one century earlier, but in Seoul.[4] Church-related schools, publishing houses, newspapers, broadcasting stations, and a variety of outreach institutions such as the YMCA, the YWCA, Campus Crusade for Christ, and so forth are found in major cities. The Protestant church has indeed reached a point where it is a social force to be reckoned with in South Korea.

Martin Marty, an internationally renowned theologian and church historian, declared that already in 1930 South Korea "was well on its way to being the most Christianized nation in Asia."[5] A "miracle" that no one had anticipated in 1884 happened in South Korea in a short period—the incredible growth of the Protestant church in numbers and influence. The spread of Protestantism in modern Korea is unparalleled in comparison with its growth in other Asian countries such as India, Japan, and China.[6] Allen and the other missionaries might well wonder how the seeds they had sown on the soil of the Confucian kingdom could have grown to such stature.

How did this religion from the West grow so steadily and rapidly in a land steeped in Confucianism and xenophobia? Why has Christian evangelical activity been successful in Korea but not in other Asian countries? What is the historical meaning of the unbelievable growth of the Western religion in late Confucian and colonial Korea?

THE PROTESTANT CHURCH, REFORM, AND NATIONALIST ACTIVISM, 1884–1945

Unlike its evangelical activity in other Asian countries, the Protestant church movement in Korea was closely allied with a progressive reform movement in late Confucian Korea (1884–1905) and with nationalist activism in the colonial era (1905–1945).[7] Not only did the Western religion introduce to Koreans new values and concepts such as freedom, rights, equality, and democracy, but in late Confucian Korea it also fostered progressive social and political movements, such as the Independence Club Movement, that were affiliated with churches and mission schools. During the early Japanese colonial period, almost all nationalist activities occurred in and around the Protestant religious community, and most of the major personalities behind these movements, whether they were moderate culturalists or militant socialists, were members of the Protestant church or products of this religious community.[8] How could it be possible that Protestant Christianity, which came ashore in the wake of Western imperialism, established a strong ideological and organizational relationship with the Korean nationalist movement?

During the period between its introduction and the outbreak of the March First Movement in 1919, the Protestant church's position was unique in Korean society. It had been the largest center of progressive reform activities in late Confucian Korea. And the religious community, which was allowed to function when all political and social organizations and activities were banned, served as a forum for political discussion, a political training ground, and a clearinghouse for political information in early colonial

Korea. Koreans cleverly used this religious community and its programs for their social and political activities. Therefore, Protestant communities became the center of Korean social and political endeavors, including the March First Movement.[9] The religious community served as a rallying point for fervent nationalists striving for independence. Church leaders enthusiastically supported those nationalists who used the religious community as a base of operations; some even initiated anti-Japanese activities.

Although Protestants continued to participate in a variety of nationalist activities to bring about the end of Japanese rule, their involvement became individual and moderate during the late colonial period. A great change occurred in the organizational and ideological relationship between the Protestant church and Korean nationalists after the March First Movement of 1919. Previously the largest organized social and political community for the colonized Koreans, the Protestant church and its leaders began to retreat from their dominant position in nationalist politics. The church's role in Korean nationalist activities was transformed from the core to a peripheral position in terms of ideology, organization, and leadership.[10]

What made the Protestant church and its leaders act as they did in the post–March First Movement era? Although some historians have tried to understand this retreat of the Protestant Christian community in purely theological or political terms, their explanations are unpersuasive because they tend to be emotional and apologetic.

Certain historical developments are primarily responsible for the change in the Protestant church's political role during the late period of Japanese rule. Right after the March First Movement of 1919, the Japanese colonial government abolished all militaristic practices and adopted a more conciliatory approach. Limited freedoms of the press, assembly, and association were granted to soothe wounded Korean feelings and improve the damaged image of Japanese imperialism abroad. During the period of this so-called cultural rule, Koreans formed thousands of small social and political organizations outside the religious communities. Naturally, the church's role as the center of nationalist activity was greatly diminished, and the church was no longer the sole center of nationalist endeavors.

Although these changed historical circumstances should not be ignored, it is much more significant that Protestant Christianity went through a very interesting metamorphosis, moving from a religion defiant toward both Confucianism and the colonial regime to an established religion. Its leaders were now conservative in tenor and sought comfort and security within the establishment. How can one explain this metamorphosis? Was it due to the church's conservative fundamentalist theology and doctrine, as some historians argue? Or was it a result of the transformation of Protestant Christian belief within its social and political context?

PROTESTANTS IN POST–WORLD WAR II SOUTH KOREA

Another interesting historical phenomenon is that Christians came to assume leadership positions in politics and society immediately after the 1945 liberation from Japan. Yŏ Unhyŏng, Kim Ku, Kim Kyusik, Hŏ Hŏn, Syngman Rhee, and other prominent leaders in the South, and Cho Mansik, Hyŏn Chunhyŏk, Kang Yang'uk, Yun Hayŏng, and others in the North were church leaders who emerged as national leaders.[11] According to a pioneer work on the Korean ruling elite, Christians occupied some 40 percent of political leadership positions, even though they constituted less than 10 percent of the South Korean population at the time.[12] As might be expected, Christian ceremonies were widely adopted in public functions, Christmas became a national holiday, and a chaplain system was established in the military.[13] Thus, many historians believe that all the signs in post-Liberation South Korea pointed to the beginning of "a Christian era."[14]

Was the emergence of Protestant Christians as national leaders simply a product of the U.S. occupation because Americans recruited Christians for leadership positions, as some have argued? Or was it simply a result of the rise of Syngman Rhee, a church elder, to the presidency?[15] Or was it due to specific features of evolving Protestantism in Korea in the context of liberation from colonial rule and confrontation with communist challenge from the north?

PREVIOUS SCHOLARSHIP ON PROTESTANTISM IN KOREA

The history of Protestantism in Korea—how this Western religion was grafted onto Korean society and why it succeeded, what role it played in the historical changes peculiar to Korea, and what change this religious community itself underwent in the process—is indeed an intriguing subject for study. There is a multitude of fragmentary works on Protestantism in modern Korea. However, most of them were written by missionaries and in-house church historians. They describe Korean Protestant church history in terms of providence, divine grace, or God's workings, and they usually eulogize the church's contributions and achievements. These writings approach history on an ad-hoc basis, using the Independence Club

Movement, the March First Movement, the controversy over Shinto-shrine worship, and so forth to emphasize the church's positive role in the development of modern Korea.[16] They fail to evaluate the church's proper place in history or its relationship to society. This perspective emphasizes only the church's bestowal of favors on Korea: it ignores the interaction, conflict, and mutual change that occurred in the encounter between Protestantism and Korean society.

Others, however, have presented the church only in a negative way, arguing that Protestant Christianity in Korea was a product of the West's expansion into Asia. Christianity, they say, was an instrument of Western imperialism. They have denigrated the church by limiting their studies to Horace N. Allen and others of mundane leanings, the missionaries who, consciously or not, cultivated friendly relations with Japanese authorities during the colonial period, and so forth.[17] What they have ignored is the fact that even though Christian missionaries might have acted as the vanguard of Western imperialism, circumstances in Korea pushed Protestant Christianity in a direction the missionaries might not in fact have intended. These scholars have not appreciated the fact that the imperialist enemy in Korea was Japan, not the West. The Japanese threat induced Korean nationalists to join the religious community to obtain modern education, spiritual solace, a sense of association, and political solidarity.[18] In this sense, Friedrich Engels was right when he said that history never turns out exactly the way historical actors intended.[19]

One-sided approaches which have ignored the overall Korean context have led serious scholars astray. Studies that have focused on separate incidents or brief periods of time have ended up either praising the role of the church or condemning it. It is mandatory, therefore, to provide an inclusive and systematic view of the history of Protestantism in Korea since its introduction in the late nineteenth century. It will also help us to obtain a clear picture of the subtle changes that have taken place over time in both the goals and methods of this religious community. For example, the change in the church's political position—one of the major questions to be raised in the following chapters—cannot be fully explained by studying an event or a short period, for the Protestant community, which at first was defiant toward the secular Confucian regime, less than fifty years later sought comfort and security within the social and political establishment. This transformation can be explained only by considering the whole century of Protestant Christianity in Korea.

Those who discuss the social and political position and activities of a religious community usually focus on its theology and doctrine. This is because religion is usually thought of as a creed based on a system of beliefs around which its adherents rally. Such a perspective is strongly evident in all writing on the political position and role of Protestantism in Korea. The usual argument is that during the 1970s and 1980s most Christians who were socially committed and critical of the government adhered to a liberal, radical theology, whereas the majority who remained indifferent to social and political issues belonged to conservative, fundamentalist denominations. This argument implies that different theologies motivate different social and political behavior.

This idealistic explanation has some justification, because most participants in clerical activism against the three authoritarian regimes of Pak Chōnghŭi (Park Chung-hee), Chōn Tuhwan (Chun Doo Hwan), and No T'ae'u (Roh Tae-woo) in the 1970s and 1980s were liberals, while conservative Christians ignored social and political affairs. However, pietist fundamentalists also performed political activities for or against the government depending on circumstances and their position in society.

Prior to 1945, the defiant position of fundamentalist Protestantism toward the Confucian establishment resulted primarily from the hostile atmosphere toward the new religion and the social and political position of church members—a small number of young elite with political grievances and commoners left out in the cold by the Confucian establishment. Their theology justified and reinforced their actions, which challenged old values and attempted to consolidate their position against the old order. The conformist position of fundamentalist Christians in South Korea after 1945 was produced by the favorable atmosphere toward the church and the social and political position of church members. Many lay as well as clerical leaders had arrived financially and socially at positions that moved them in that direction. These Christians were now themselves part of the ruling establishment in South Korea, and in the interest of maintaining their social standing they affirmed realities as they were and lent passive or active support to the system. Their theology was invoked to justify a progovernment position, just as it had earlier sanctified opposition to the government. Therefore, this study will view the functional role of theology in modern and contemporary Korean history—that is, the role it played in Christian political activism for or against the government—instead of perceiving theology as the immutable cause or motive for Christians' action.

Looking at the growth of Protestant Christianity in Korea together with the church's political involvement, one can detect a pattern in which challenge to authority gradually changed to acceptance of and finally identification with authority. It is from this perspective that I will discuss the history of Protestant Christianity as a social institution.

This book is organized into two parts. Part 1 is written for a general and structural understanding of Protestantism in Korea—that is, the religion's growth, theological orientation, and organization as a social institution—in order to provide a background for Christian involvement in politics. With this structural understanding, part 2 discusses the relationship between Protestant Christians and politics during the last century to see how Christians behaved sociopolitically and why they acted as they did.

PART 1

PROTESTANTISM IN KOREA: A SOCIAL HISTORY

1 / The Growth of Protestantism

History and Meaning

The growth of Protestantism in Korea was exceptional—to some observers a miracle. Recent statistics show that more than 25 percent of the population in South Korea is Protestant.[1] The Protestant church is still growing rapidly: according to some observers, in the 1980s, six churches were established every day in South Korea.[2] Several of the largest Protestant congregations in the world, including the largest one, Yŏŭido Full Gospel Church (Yŏŭido sunbogŭm kyohoe), are found not in the Western world which introduced Protestantism to the so-called heathen countries in Asia, but in Seoul.[3] In 1984, Korean churches sent 3,232 missionaries to thirty-six countries throughout the world, and 1,093 Korean churches were also founded in twelve other countries, including the United States, Japan, Egypt, Germany, and Australia.[4] Church adherents and institutions have reached such proportions that they present a social force to be reckoned with. South Korea is indeed one of the most Christianized countries in the non-Western world.[5]

Christianity, both Catholicism and Protestantism, generally has met strong resistance in non-Western countries, since the Western religion has spread throughout the world on the waves of aggressive Western expansionism. Missionaries have been regarded by natives as agents for Western aggrandizement. It has been difficult, if not impossible, for Western missionaries to convert hostile indigenous people such as Indians, Japanese, Chinese, and others to their religions.[6] The early history of Protestant Christianity in the "Hermit Kingdom" was no exception. Indeed, the circumstances under which Protestantism was introduced, one could say, were even more anti-Western and anti-Christian than elsewhere in Asia, because the bloody persecution of Catholic priests and Korean converts in the eighteenth century had left a grim legacy.[7]

Nevertheless, Protestantism made unparalleled strides in Korea in the late nineteenth and early twentieth centuries. The lack of success elsewhere in Asia by missionary movements that had enjoyed significantly greater funding and staffing makes the Korean case even more surprising. Examining the unusual growth of Protestantism provides a unique opportunity to understand the social and political structure and emergence of modern Korea.

Although many scholars have touched upon this phenomenon, they have not presented a persuasive explanation for it. Scholars addressing this issue can be divided into three groups representing different viewpoints. The first group, comprised mostly of those who study comparative religion, theology, and folklore, has tried to explain the unusual growth of Protestantism in terms of the religious affinities between Protestant Christianity and Korean folk cults. According to this school, Koreans were familiar with the concepts of God (*Hananim*, *hanullim*, *hanŭllim*, and *hanŭnim*), the Trinity (*Hanung*, *Hwanin*, and *Tan'gun*), and heaven and hell (*Ch'ŏndang* and *Chiok*) in their own traditional beliefs. Because of these conceptual affinities, this school argues, Koreans could easily accept Protestantism without a strong theological burden.[8]

This argument would be very persuasive if Catholicism, which had been introduced a century earlier than Protestantism and which also shared those above-mentioned religious concepts, had grown like the latter did a century later. Catholicism, however, had not been successful, despite the so-called theological affinities. One is forced to ask why such theological affinities did not play any positive role for Catholicism during the eighteenth century, but worked well for the remarkable expansion of Protestantism during the late nineteenth century.[9]

The second group of scholars has tried to explain the expansion of Protestantism in relation to Christian social and political activism. They put forward numerous points: the church's initiative for modern education, social programs, and political reform in late Confucian Korea; its nationalist activism against the Japanese regime in colonial Korea; and its promotion of human rights, social justice, and democratization in the 1970s and 1980s. All these activities, they argue, earned public sympathy and confidence and brought many Koreans into the church community. This school even says that the church grew rapidly when its social and political participation was intense, but slowly when it lacked such activism.[10]

This argument is partly ahistorical and certainly not accurate for the entire period from the 1880s to the present. The church continued to grow at a steady pace after the March First Movement of 1919, even though the religious community retreated from front-line nationalist activity against Japanese colonial rule. Moreover, during the 1970s and 1980s, only the conservative churches, which opposed social and political activism against authoritarian military regimes, grew explosively, while the activist liberal churches were remarkably slow in their growth.[11] Contemporary Korean Christians themselves have indicated that their church grew not because of its social and political activism against dictatorial rule, but because of its purely religious functions of spiritual solace and security amid rapid industrialization and political unrest.[12] The rapid social change caused by industrialization and urbanization prompted Koreans to long for a community that would fill their psychological emptiness and give them a sense of belonging.

A third school of thought has seen the exceptional expansion of Protestant Christianity as a result of the early missionary method, which centered on indirect missionary programs such as educational, medical, and social services rather than direct proselytizing. The method was effective, this school has argued, not only because missionaries could avoid and gradually weaken the hostility and suspicion of Koreans, but also because they could contact and sometimes convert Koreans through those educational, medical, and social services. Indeed, this indirect missionary method seemed to work well since small Protestant church communities began to form around mission schools and hospitals.[13]

However, this explanation is insufficient and needs some clarification.[14] The "indirect missionary" schema was practiced almost universally by Westerners for the "opening up" of evangelical work.[15] Indeed, a method similar to that applied to Korea had been practiced in China earlier by Protestant Christians, but their success was not as spectacular in China as it was in Korea. Missionaries in early Meiji Japan also carried out medical and educational services and achieved "a spectacular growth" in Protestant Christianity during the 1880s and early 1890s. For example, church membership jumped from 32,354 in 1889 to 43,273 in 1899. Additionally, in both China and Japan there was greater funding and staffing than in Korea. However, the program faltered and did not produce any positive results after Japan came into political conflict with Western powers and the Japanese developed strong anti-Western nationalistic sentiment.[16] As they came to see Protestant Christianity as a cultural and religious arm of Western expansionism, the Japanese naturally became antagonistic toward the religion from the West. One wonders, then, why scholars have kept searching for the primary cause of the unusual growth of the Protestant church in Korea

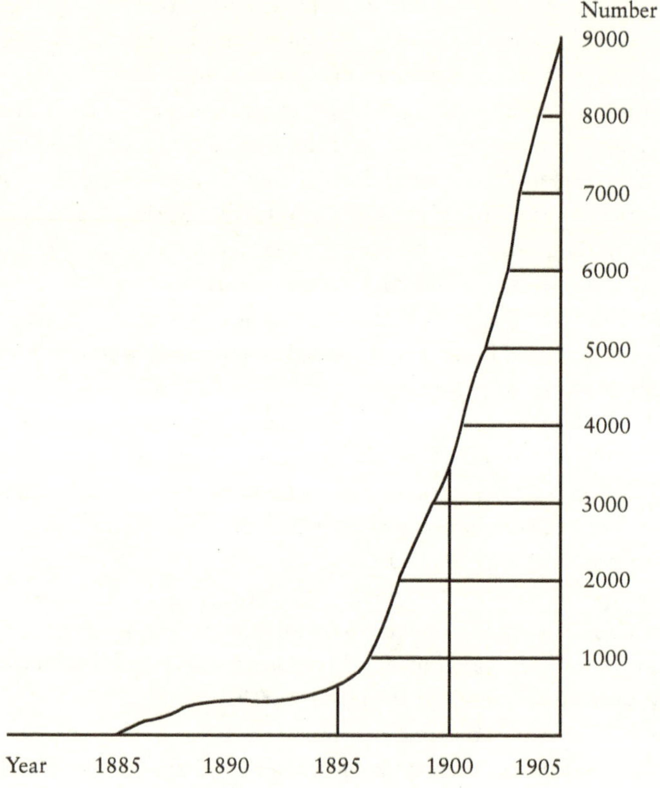

FIG. 1.1. Number of baptized members of the Presbyterian Church in Korea (1885–1905).

SOURCE: Roy E. Shearer, *Wildfire: Church Growth in Korea* (Grand Rapids, Mich.: William B. Eerdmans Publishing Co., 1966), p. 543.

in such universally practiced missionary methods. One should rather ask why such methods worked so well in Korea.

Although Protestantism was introduced in 1884, it grew very slowly until the mid-1890s when it took off, as Figure 1.1 shows.

Why did Koreans begin to respond positively to the religion from the West and its missionary programs? What made Koreans, who had previously been suspicious and hostile toward Western countries and their religion, suddenly so receptive? How could we explain this dramatic shift in the Korean attitude toward Protestantism? If the same missionary methods and programs were practiced before and after the mid-1890s, but if the results were different, it is logical and desirable to consider the particular historical context in which the sudden expansion of the religion took place.

Modern Korea developed differently than did other Asian countries such as India and Japan. Although the Western countries that brought Christianity to Asia were the main imperialist powers, leading to resistance to Christianity by natives, it was Japan, a non-Western, non-Christian country, that emerged as the chief enemy of Korea within a decade of the introduction of Protestantism. The emergence of Japanese imperialism and later Japanese colonial rule helped to eliminate Korean hostility toward the Western countries and Protestant Christianity. Rather, Japanese colonial rule contributed greatly to the remarkable growth of Protestantism in Korea. The helpless Koreans joined the religious community in large numbers for spiritual consolation and for political maneuvering against Japan.

The liberation from Japan in 1945 opened up a new prospect for Protestant Christianity in Korea. The United States, whose missionaries had extensively promoted the religion since the late nineteenth century, now came as the "liberator" from Japanese aggression. Native church leaders, many educated at American-founded mission schools and some in America itself, assumed social and political leadership.[17] Pro-American and pro-Christian social and political sentiment peaked in South Korea, especially during and after the Korean War, and the church expanded its numbers and influence. The Protestant church continued to grow explosively in the 1960s, 1970s, and 1980s, when Koreans, who longed for spiritual solace and fellowship in the process of industrialization and urbanization, joined the church in great numbers.

The unusual growth of Protestantism in Korea, therefore, should be explained in the context of modern and contemporary Korea's unusual historical development. Only by accepting this approach can one grasp the historical meaning of the rapid spread of Protestantism in modern Korea.

THE ACCEPTANCE OF PROTESTANTISM IN THE LATE CHOSŎN PERIOD, 1880S–1905

Modest Beginnings, 1884–1893

Horace N. Allen arrived in 1884 as the first Protestant missionary in the Hermit Kingdom to "Christianize" the Koreans[18] just eight years after the opening of Korea by Japan in 1876 and two years after the beginning of diplomatic relations with the United States in 1882. Nevertheless, Allen and the other missionaries who arrived after him could not openly preach their religion in anti-Western, anti-Christian Korea. Allen was even introduced to King Kojong not as a missionary but as a United States legation doctor.[19] Early Protestant missionaries, one may argue, found a more anti-Western, anti-Christian atmosphere in Korea than in other Asian countries. Many historical factors combined to produce these unfavorable conditions for evangelism.[20]

First of all, the politico-cultural structure of the Chosŏn dynasty produced an anti-Western political atmosphere. At its founding in 1392, the Chosŏn dynasty proclaimed Neo-Confucianism as its ideological orthodoxy and a Sinocentric tributary relation as its international policy. Sinocentric politics were strengthened by the domestic power structure—the symbiotic relations between weak monarchs and powerful aristocratic *yangban* families. The domestic power structure and strong Chinese influence in ideology and politics contributed to the dynasty's longevity and stability, but also handicapped the regime. The Korean ruling elite was culturally and politically immersed in Sinocentrism to the extent that its members could not do anything independently from Beijing; they had to wait passively for the Chinese to move or issue orders. Thus they reacted to the West ideologically, but not practically, during the late nineteenth century. In other words, this ruling class could accept neither culturally nor politically the existence of the West. Most of its members even regarded Westerners as barbarians and Western values as heresies. This was the historical atmosphere that Allen and other early missionaries encountered in Korea.

Second, the factional politics of the dynasty also strengthened the anti-Western, anti-Christian attitude of the Koreans and made them keep away from Westerners and things Western. For example, some Koreans came into contact with Western civilization, including Catholicism, through China—the only doorway to the outside world in the eighteenth century.[21] Eventually they accepted Catholic Christianity as their religion; Korean converts numbered tens of thousands by the beginning of the nineteenth century. Unfortunately, however, the early history of Catholicism in Korea was deeply colored by the vortex of factional politics. Most early Catholic converts were the so-called *namin* elite (southern faction) and the commoners around them. Their political rivals, in attacking them, branded Catholicism as a heretic Western religion that challenged the Confucian foundation of the dynasty. The result was an intense persecution of Catholic converts that made most Koreans afraid of being associated with both Westerners and Christianity.[22]

Equally responsible for the Koreans' anti-Western, anti-Christian attitude was the aggressive activity of Western powers such as France and the United States. Prior to 1876, Western warships frequently appeared on the shores of the Hermit Kingdom to demand the opening of trade and explanations for the persecution of Catholic priests and native converts. In 1868, Westerners senselessly irritated the ruling elite in the so-called Ernest Oppert Incident. They bragged that they had desecrated the tomb of the royal ancestors in retaliation for the murder of Catholic priests. They also demanded the opening of Korea to trade and diplomatic relations. The Korean government, which had seen the Opium War and the occupation of Tientsin, China, in 1860 by an Anglo-French force, itself experienced the French occupation of Kanghwa Island, the General Sherman Incident, and other threats to its sovereignty. These aggressive activities by Western powers only strengthened the xenophobia of the Confucian officials in particular and the Korean people in general. Most Koreans came to identify Christianity with Western expansion.

Lastly, Catholic converts themselves were also responsible for the strengthening of Korea's xenophobia. For example, they were behind the so-called Hwang Sayŏng (Alexander Hwang) Incident. The Confucian officialdom found in 1801 that Hwang, a Catholic convert, had prepared a letter addressed to the French bishop in Peking. In the letter, Hwang proposed that foreign powers intervene diplomatically, as well as militarily, to exact a guarantee of freedom for Korean Catholics. The result of his efforts was not religious freedom, but organized persecution by the Confucian officials who took the position that Catholicism was an open challenge to Confucian orthodoxy and the authority of the throne.[23]

Again, in 1868, the converts participated in the previously mentioned Ernest Oppert Incident. They guided Westerners to the royal burial site where a lamentable desecration of the tomb of the Taewŏn'gun's father was attempted. Such incidents strengthened the anti-Western, anti-Christian attitudes of the Confucian elite and commoners alike. Even after Korea opened its doors to the outside world in 1876 and signed a series of treaties with Western countries, this anti-Western, anti-Christian attitude did not disappear. The Korean government did not change its views and then voluntarily establish diplomatic relations with Western powers. The Chosŏn government carried out its new policy reluctantly under pressure from and inducement by China, the suzerain state, which wished to check the increasing influence of Russia and Japan in East Asia.

Nevertheless, the opening of the country and the beginning of diplomatic relations with the West gradually weakened Korea's militant, chauvinistic exclusionism. For example, Li Hung-chang, who dominated Chinese political and foreign affairs at the time, pressured the Korean government to accept his so-called treaty system diplomacy. *Strategy for Korea* [Ch'ao-hsien ts'e-lüe], written by Huang Tsun-hsien, a Chinese legation official in Japan, appeared in 1880. It described the United States and Protestant Christianity as follows:

> What is practiced in America is Protestant Christianity, a sect different from Catholic faith although both have a common origin. . . . Protestant Christians by doctrine stay out of political affairs; many of them are good upright people. The record shows that since China opened trade [with the West], missionaries were frequently murdered but it does not mention a single case of Protestant Christians. What is central to this religion is enjoining people to be good. Would it not be, then, that Protestant Christianity is far better than the way of Prince Chou and Confucius? . . . If that is indeed true what harm can possibly come from letting them continue their missionary work?[24]

Although this single pamphlet could not immediately change the attitudes of the Korean government and people, it is certain that it influenced some Koreans, especially the *kaehwa* (enlightenment) adherents, who had been searching for a better way to solve their country's problems. Most important, the document distinguished the United States from France and Protestantism from Catholicism. In other words, there began to appear slowly some cracks—forced though they were—in Korea's cultural exclusionism and militant xenophobia after the opening of the country and the beginning of diplomatic relations with Western powers.

The conservative elite, who had strong ties with China, still dominated court politics even after the opening of the country, but they also had to adjust to the new era. In 1881, for example, the "gentlemen's excursion group" (*sinsa yuramdan*) was dispatched to Japan to observe the Meiji modernization effort.[25] Some of young *yangban* elite who accompanied the official mission chose to stay behind for further observation of reform and modernization measures undertaken by the Japanese. They contacted such leading pro-Western Meiji intellectuals as Fukuzawa Yukichi and Nakamura Masanao.[26]

In 1883, Min Yŏng'ik, the first Korean envoy to the United States and one of the most powerful figures in Korea, met the Reverend John F. Goucher, president of Goucher College, Baltimore, by chance on a train to Washington. They discussed Protestant Christianity and the opening of missions in Korea.[27] Furthermore, just prior to the 1884 attempted coup, Kim Okkyun, one of the coup leaders, met in Japan with Reverend Robert S. Maclay, the superintendent of the Methodist mission in Japan. They discussed the establishment of mission schools in Korea. Kim later introduced the Reverend Maclay to King Kojong and persuaded the king to permit the establishment of a mission school and a hospital in Korea.[28] Some Korean merchants, who made frequent trips to Manchuria, met Western missionaries there and converted to Protestant Christianity.[29] These examples show that before the arrival of the first Protestant missionary, but after the opening of the country, some converts and sympathizers had appeared among the progressive elite and commoners as well.

Protestantism in Korea reached a turning point in 1884. That year, the progressive *kaehwa* elite, aided by a Japanese military contingent, staged a palace coup and removed the pro-Chinese conservative Min faction. The new regime immediately launched a sweeping reform program; however, the revolutionary government lasted only three days before it was overthrown by Chinese troops. The conservative Min faction returned to power, and the ousted *kaehwa* elite, branded as pro-Japanese traitors, were executed or managed to flee to Japan.[30]

Following the coup attempt, China's strongman, Li Hung-chang, sent Yuan Shih-kai to Korea to protect Chinese interests and to block the growing Japanese influence on the Korean Peninsula. For Protestant evangelism, the failure of the 1884 palace coup, which seemed to create an unfavorable political situation, was actually a great fortune.

Dr. Allen had arrived in Seoul just before the coup. As mentioned above, he was introduced to the king not as a missionary but as a United States legation doctor. He could not even think about any missionary work in the anti-Western, anti-Christian land. But he was invited to treat Min Yŏng'ik, a high-ranking official of considerable influence, who was seriously wounded during the 1884 coup. Through his medical skills, Allen established a personal relationship with the powerful Min family, King Kojong, and other court officials—a relationship that was probably a "bridgehead" for the Christian mission at the time, as Allen himself believed.[31] As a matter of fact, Allen was able to open a modern hospital, the Kwanghyewŏn (later renamed the Chejungwŏn), in Seoul in April 1885 with support from King Kojong and the Min family.[32]

Because of personal relationships, Allen and other missionaries, including Horace G. Underwood, Henry G. Appenzeller, John W. Heron, and Mr.

TABLE 1.1
Mission Schools Founded, 1886–1890

Year	*Name*	*Founding Denomination*	*Place*
1886	Paejae	Methodist	Seoul
1886	Ihwa	Methodist	Seoul
1886	Kyŏngsin	Presbyterian	Seoul
1890	Chŏngsin	Presbyterian	Seoul

SOURCE: Based on Yi Kwangnin, *Han'guksa kangiwa* [Roundtable discussions of Korean history], no. 5 (Seoul: Ilchogak, 1983), p. 543.

and Mrs. William Scranton, who arrived from America in 1885, were able to establish additional mission hospitals and schools (see Tables 1.1 and 1.2). These organizations became the first places where missionaries could contact Koreans and influence them to change their anti-Western, anti-Christian views. By providing Koreans modern medical treatment and education, the early missionaries began to establish a good image among them.

Although missionaries came into contact with many Koreans in and around these missionary hospitals and schools, they could neither preach Christianity openly nor convert Koreans themselves to the Western religion immediately. According to a report by Allen, which was sent back to his Presbyterian mission board, he and other missionaries recognized that it would take time to assure the Koreans what the missionaries' real interest was.[33] Thus, while they worked in hospitals and schools, they took care to instruct themselves in Korean language and customs. While waiting for favorable social and political conditions, Allen said, it would be a prudent and practical strategy for missionaries to contact Koreans in hospitals and schools and to make a good impression on them.[34]

Under such circumstances, medical and educational work proved to be the best method for proselytizing. Those Koreans who were treated in mission hospitals naturally came into contact with missionaries. The number of patients grew rapidly to the point of requiring expanded facilities to accommodate them. Especially since the early missionaries treated patients equally regardless of their social status, and even provided free or inexpensive treatment for poor Koreans, they were able to change the Korean view of missionaries, as well as of Protestant Christianity.[35] In the field of education, Henry G. Appenzeller was permitted to open the first modern school for boys, Paejae School, and Mrs. Mary F. Scranton opened the first modern school for girls, Ihwa School, in 1886. Soon after, two more mis-

TABLE 1.2
Number of Patients in Mission Hospitals, 1892

	Southgate	*Women's*	*Chŏngdong*	*Total*
In-Patient	542	51	1,000	1,593
House Visit	9	110		119
Operation	43			43
Out-Patient	1,636	3,831	2,224	7,691
Total	2,230	4,092	3,224	9,446

SOURCE: Based on the statistics presented at the eighth annual meeting of the Methodist Episcopal Mission. See *The Korean Repository*, vol. 1, no. 8 (August 1892), pp. 286–87.

sion schools were founded. All four were located in Seoul. The immediate result was less spectacular than in medicine. According to an 1892 report, for example, Paejae School had a total enrollment of fifty-three, Ihwa School only twenty-nine.[36]

In a word, through these mission hospitals and schools, the early missionaries were able to contact the hostile Koreans and even to convert some of them to Protestant Christianity. In fact, a small Protestant Christian community began to form in and around these institutions.

Nevertheless, one should not overemphasize the success of the early indirect missionary methods in explaining the unparalleled growth of Protestantism in Korea. In a sense, the medical and educational work was remarkable because it was achieved in spite of the strong cultural chauvinism and xenophobia, language and cultural obstacles, and the difficult psychological problems faced by the isolated missionaries in a strange foreign land. Compared with its growth in neighboring countries, the spread of Protestantism in Korea was not spectacular between 1884 and 1894, the year of the outbreak of the Sino-Japanese War.

The Changing Order in East Asia and the Dramatic Growth of Korean Protestantism, 1894–1904

As noted earlier, Protestantism began to grow sharply only after the mid-1890s (as Figure 1.1 shows). Only four mission schools were founded in Seoul from 1884 to 1893. However, from 1894 to 1904, nineteen mission schools were opened in rapid-fire succession throughout the country (see Table 1.3). Why did Koreans begin to respond positively to the religion from the West and its missionary programs after 1894? Of course,

TABLE 1.3
Number of Mission Schools Opened, 1894–1904

Year	*Number*	*Place*
1894	3	P'yŏngyang(2) and Yŏngbyŏn
1895	1	Tongnae
1896	2	Seoul and P'yŏngyang
1897	3	Seoul, P'yŏngyang, and Inch'ŏn
1898	3	Seoul, P'yŏngyang, and Chaeryŏng
1903	3	P'yŏngyang, Wŏnsan, and Mokp'o
1904	4	Wŏnsan (2), Kaesŏng, and Haeju

SOURCE: Based on Yi Kwangnin's *Han'guksa kangiwa,* p. 534.

the number of missionaries had increased and the Koreans' view of the West and Protestantism had become more favorable. But most of all, a sense of national crisis developed before and after the Sino-Japanese War of 1894.

The war destroyed the Sinocentric order in East Asia, allowed the Japanese to compete with other powers for leadership in the region, and weakened Korea's centuries-long cultural and political dependence on China. Japan now came to play the dominant role in the Korean Peninsula.[37] At the same time, the war gave a great shock to the Koreans. Having seen China beaten by the Japanese, who had learned Western values and practices, some Koreans began to believe that all things Western were superior. For example, Yun Ch'iho, who converted to Christianity in exile in China after the 1884 palace coup, attended Vanderbilt and Emory Universities, and later became the president of the Independence Club, observed the transformation of Nashville from, as he put it, "the hunting ground of Indians" to the "Athens of the South" as a result of "Christianity, good government, and an enlightened people."[38] And he came to believe that in order to make the Koreans survive as "the fittest" in a Darwinist world of competition, they should accept Christianity, which had made Western countries powerful and wealthy, and he even declared "Christianity is the only salvation to Corea [Korea]."[39] The war awakened some educated Koreans to search, like Yun Ch'iho, for a new way to build a rich and powerful nation like Meiji Japan. These Koreans began to long for the introduction of Western values and practices into their country.[40]

The Sino-Japanese War of 1894–1895, and later the Russo-Japanese War of 1904–1905, which also resulted in a Japanese victory, gave rise to anti-

Japanese sentiment and softened the anti-Western attitude among Koreans. As Japan, long a distrusted neighbor, emerged as the chief imperialist power in Korea, not only did many Koreans change their hostile attitude toward the West, but they also became eager to establish a deeper relationship with Western countries and to seek help from them. For example, some *kaehwa* elite such as Yun Ch'iho and Sŏ Chaep'il, who had been prominent Japan admirers and pro-Japanese reformers at the time of the 1884 palace coup, became anti-Japanese, pro-Western reformist leaders and formed the core of the Chŏngdongp'a, a pro-Western political group.[41] Even King Kojong came to seek help from the "Christian countries" such as the United States, believing naively that since those nations were far from the peninsula they would not colonize but rather would help the desperate Koreans stand up against powerful Japanese expansionism.[42] Anti-Japanese sentiment dominated in Korea to the extent that many Koreans opposed any modernist reform if it suggested Japanese involvement. Lillias H. Underwood, a missionary, summed up the changed political mood in Korea after the Sino-Japanese War:

> The favor with which all Americans were regarded by Korean authorities . . . [was] due perhaps to the fact that we belong to a large and powerful nation which had no object in interfering in Eastern politics in any way to the detriment of Korea, and which might become an efficient ally and defender.[43]

In other words, according to Underwood, the Koreans, including King Kojong and his court officials, alarmed by Japanese imperialist moves, began to think of the United States as "an efficient ally and defender" of Korea.

By this time, a favorable view of the United States was spreading widely among the desperate Koreans. According to Lew Young-Ick's recent study, newspapers such as *Hansŏng sunbo* [Hansŏng ten-daily], *Tongnip sinmun* [Independent], and *Taehan maeil sinbo* [Korea daily news] frequently introduced the United States as "a nation of wealth," "a nation of strong military power," "a nation of benevolence and righteousness," "a nation of truthfulness," "a brotherly country," "the nation who can restrain the Japanese oppression in Asia," and, most of all, "a Christian nation."[44] A strong pro-American sentiment prevailed among Koreans even after the United States adopted a pro-Japanese policy in Asia. Lew calls it a one-sided love (*tchak sarang*).[45] It was important for the growth of Protestantism in Korea that most Protestant missionaries came to the peninsula from America.[46]

The rise of anti-Japanese sentiment drew Koreans with a passion for reform to the Protestant church community in great numbers. As we shall see, the new converts came forward not exclusively out of religious motives, but also because of their discovery that the Western church could be a handy vehicle with which to advance their political and social reforms.[47] As Song Ch'anggŭn, a prominent church leader and theologian, commented in 1934:

> Some of our people are failing to tell the difference between the truth itself and what we refer to as the civilization of the West. . . . One sometimes wonders if some of the first Christians did not place the political movement ahead of evangelism. Not only Korean church leaders but foreign missionaries as well went to some length turning the prevailing public sentiment to account and stepped up their evangelical activity.[48]

When the Koreans had to keep their eyes on Japanese imperialism and at the same time reform their country, they sided with the United States, which they regarded as the only available source of power and wealth. As Song Ch'anggŭn observed, missionaries and early church leaders made good use of this "prevailing public sentiment" for the expansion of the new religious community. Consequently, socially and politically motivated conversion became readily apparent after the Sino-Japanese War and more so after the Russo-Japanese War, which made Japan the leading imperialist power in the Korean Peninsula and at the same time strengthened anti-Japanese sentiment there.[49]

Explanation of the Dramatic Growth

How should we interpret the unusual growth of Protestantism in late Confucian Korea? If it was a product of Korea's historical development, it should be analyzed within a historical context, including political events and the social composition of the religious community.[50]

The first Koreans to heed the teachings of Western Protestant missionaries were for the most part *sangmin* (commoners)—drawers of water, hewers of wood, tillers of soil, and artisans of cheap, everyday ware—and *ch'ŏnmin*—butchers and other social outcasts, including some slaves.[51] Because commoners and outcasts did not enjoy high social positions or special privileges, they benefited little from the Confucian establishment. They lost little—politically or economically—by becoming Christians. The rigid status structure made the conversion of the upper stratum, the *yangban* class, more difficult than that of the non-*yangban* population. Members of elite circles had a lot to lose by becoming Christians.

Church growth in the northwestern provinces, P'yŏng'an and Hwanghae, is a case in point. According to one study, although earlier Western missionaries followed similar missionary policies throughout Korea, the northwestern provinces were unusually ripe for Protestant Christianity.[52] Among the factors in this unusual receptiveness to Protestantism was the fact that throughout the period of the monarchy, residents of this region had been subjected to a discriminatory policy that restricted opportunities for upward social mobility by appointment to regular government posts and rapid promotion, even though the government took measures to allow them to take the civil service examinations. This discriminatory policy had effectively blocked northwesterners from career advancement.[53] Put into socioeconomic terms, they were forced to fend for themselves as independent farmers and traders. William M. Baird, a Presbyterian missionary, wrote of the residents in the northwest in 1897:

> The Traveler is impressed in the North by the independent, manly spirit of many of the mountain people. A man seems to be more of a man in the North than in the South. In looking for the causes of this I find it in the marked absence of the so-called "gentlemen" [*yangban*] class. In the South the independent middle class is apt to be crushed out between the upper and the nether mill stones, between the strutting, conceited "yangban" and the obsequious, cringing serf. The North is brighter with hope because of the predominance of an independent middle class, who have to work for their own living and as a result have more muscle and more brain.[54]

Although we do not know what Baird's "middle class" means exactly, it is clear that there were not many *yangban* in the northwestern part of the country and that residents there were more alienated by and more independent of the central government and its guiding philosophy of Confucianism. If they were not openly defiant of central authority and ideology, it is certain that their ideological and political commitment to the Confucian system was less secure. The more alienated they became, the more enthusiastic they were about the new religion that came with Western civilization. When Protestant Christianity arrived in late Confucian Korea, the commoners in the northwest, who had little to lose by converting, constituted a majority in the early Protestant church.

According to George L. Paik, a pioneer on church history in Korea, outcasts such as butchers were particularly attracted to Protestantism. As outcasts, they were forbidden to marry outside of their social class. By the mid-1890s, there were some thirty thousand butchers on the peninsula. Paik remarked that when the first of them was converted to the new religion:

> the first convert of the butchers became instrumental for spreading Christian liberty as well as social freedom among his caste. It is reported that a large number of butchers became Christians, but there are no precise records.[55]

Commoners and outcasts entered the new religious community because it preached equality and freedom in a hierarchical Confucian society.

Protestantism also attracted the attention of some of the upper stratum in Confucian society. The so-called *yangban* converts were, understandably, much smaller in number than the non-*yangban,* but they exercised far-reaching influence in the propagation of the faith. Though committed to Confucian values and institutions, they also sought solutions to the problems of inept government, administrative abuse, worsening social inequity and unrest, and aggressive foreign (particularly Japanese) intervention in Korean affairs. Most of them, however, were intellectuals in seclusion or young men who felt their opportunities for positions and promotion were limited by court politics which were dominated by the Confucian conservatives.[56] In the face of foreign challenges in the late nineteenth century, these so-called *kaehwa* elite thought about adopting Western methods and institutions in order to build a nation of wealth and power like Meiji Japan. To this end they championed an outward-looking policy for Confucian Korea. Some of them even argued that it would be necessary to adopt the West's technology, as well as its values and practices, because the former was derived from the latter.

Although there had been some converts and sympathizers among the *kaehwa* elite before the failed palace coup of 1884, these pro-Western, pro-Christian reformers grew in number after the coup. Not only did they form a pro-Western (American) political group, the Chŏngdongp'a, but they also changed their strategy for reform. They began to advocate a gradual yet radical reform from below, partly because they had learned from the coup attempt that an effort to reform from above would be doomed to failure. They had also witnessed how American missionaries provided educational, social, and medical services as part of their successful evangelistic endeavor in Japan.[57] To many in this progressive elite, Protestant Christianity was just the kind of Western institution they had been waiting for. Some of them even came to regard the Protestant Christian movement as the only possible means for progressive reform in late Confucian Korea.[58] Such men as Yun Ch'iho and Sŏ Chaep'il joined the Protestant church to promote reform. This was just the beginning of the association between Protestantism and progressive elites in late Confucian Korea.

In short, reform-minded Koreans—commoners and outcasts who were estranged from the Confucian society and the progressive elite who desired to transform it—joined the early Protestant church. The social composition of the early church determined its social and political orientation and role. As we will see later, the early Christian church community was, therefore, destined to play a prime role in social and political reform in late Confucian Korea.

THE EXPANSION OF PROTESTANT CHRISTIANITY DURING THE COLONIAL PERIOD, 1905–1945

In 1905, flush with its victory over Russia, Japan forced a treaty which made Korea its protectorate. Then in 1910, a treaty of annexation was signed that made Korea part of the Japanese empire. As Table 1.4 shows, the churches and their memberships doubled from 1905 to 1907. How was the Japanese colonization of Korea related to the growth of the Protestant church?

As mentioned, missionaries and church historians have pointed out that Koreans joined the religious community at this time for a number of reasons: they saw the church as providing livelihood, protection, and modern education. Through the church, Koreans also could engage in political activ-

TABLE 1.4
The Growth of Protestant Christianity, 1905–1907

	Churches	*Stations*	*Baptized Adherents*	*Probationers*
1905	321	470	9,761	30,136
1907	642	1,047	18,964	99,300
Percent Increase	200	222.3	194.2	329.5

SOURCE: Horace G. Underwood, *The Call of Korea* (New York: Fleming H. Revell, 1908), pp. 146–48.

ity for reform and independence.[59] Although it is true that these factors contributed to the sudden growth of Protestantism, they do not fully explain its remarkable expansion in late-nineteenth and early-twentieth-century Korea. Nor, insofar as can be judged, was this remarkable increase caused by any acceleration of missionary work or any particular missionary strategy. As one missionary reported in 1906:

> Last year in our station of Syechun [Sŏnch'ŏn] we had 6,597 adherents; this year there are 11,943. From whence the 5,436 conversions during the twelve month period? . . . an average of 453 per month. Could this be the result of our small band of missionaries? Could it be from the $72 spent on local evangelists during the year?[60]

Seeking Consolation and Political Rights through the Church

As the 1906 report clearly shows, the sudden expansion of Protestantism in the early colonial period should not be understood as the result of missionary effort. Rather, it should be explained by the particular historical conditions, that is, the coming of the Japanese as the main imperialist "enemy" and the hopelessness felt by the colonized Koreans. The Koreans, who had long been humiliated by foreign powers, were frustrated and angry when their country became a protectorate, later a colony, of neighboring Japan. Their despair and helplessness led them to search for psychological consolation and a source of new hope.

The new religious community accommodated these popular feelings. The church's language of consolation, political teaching, and organization were enough to win over the Koreans, who were deprived of all freedom of speech, association, and assembly—especially after the Japanese annexation in 1910. The Protestant church, many Koreans felt, would fill their psychological and political needs.

As noted, King Kojong and some of the progressive elite had tried to side with the "Christian countries" such as the United States, which, they naively believed, would help the desperate Koreans against powerful Japanese imperialism.[61] Yet those Christian nations ignored the expectations and appeals of the Koreans and continued to pursue their own interests under the name of neutrality and noninterference.[62] The United States, the country from which King Kojong and many other Koreans expected so much, secretly approved Japan's colonization of Korea in return for its promise not to interfere with American colonization of the Philippines. This understanding was agreed to in the Taft-Katsura Memorandum, a secret pact between President Theodore Roosevelt and the Japanese.[63] At the time, however, no Korean knew about this, and most still held on to a "one-sided love" (*tchak sarang*) with the United States.[64]

American missionaries were sympathetic to the helpless Koreans and critical of Japan before 1905, even though the U.S. government strongly advised them to be politically neutral. Even after 1905, some missionaries personally sided with the Koreans.[65] But most missionaries, in order to stay in Korea to proselytize, chose reality over morality and announced officially their cooperation with the Japanese colonial government. On the other side of the coin, the Japanese found it necessary to cooperate with the missionaries who controlled the Protestant church, probably the largest organized Korean community at the time, in order to rule the peninsula effectively. For their mutual benefit, the missionaries and the colonial government began to establish a friendly relationship. Itō Hirobumi, the Resident-General, established especially good relations with missionaries.[66] The missionaries recompensed the colonial government for its support by announcing that Japanese rule would be beneficial for the Koreans and by teaching Korean Christians that religion should be separate from politics. They cooperated, at least officially, with the colonial government and even persuaded the politically minded Christians to acquiesce to Japanese rule. They tried to cool Korean anger against foreign rule.[67]

This friendly relationship between the missionaries and the colonial government stimulated antipathy and resistance by the colonized Koreans toward Protestantism, and could have been detrimental to the expansion of the new religion from the West. Indeed, it was at this time that some young Korean Christians became critical of the pro-Japanese or politically neutral attitude of missionaries; some even physically attacked missionaries, and others left the religious community.[68]

It is interesting to note that before and after the Japanese annexation, a religious revival movement prevailed in Protestant churches across Korea.[69] A nationwide campaign of revival meetings, conducted independently or jointly by churches and denominations, began in 1907. Preachers argued from the pulpit that the humiliating loss of national independence was brought on by Koreans themselves; that Korea had sinned as a nation; and that independence would not be regained until Korea repented its sins. Korean Christians blamed not the Japanese, but themselves first. The activity was not seen as outwardly political, but inwardly religious. The preachers talked about some indefinite future, not the "here and now." This way of reacting to Japan's protectorate and annexation was encouraged by the missionaries, who wished to avoid an open clash with the Japanese authorities, and was welcomed by the colonial government, which also desired peace with the missionaries. To the missionaries and the colonial authorities as well, these revivals seemed purely religious on the part of Christian Koreans.[70]

In spite of the intention of the missionaries and the seemingly apolitical nature of the revival movement, it produced an unintended result. The church grew to be the largest and most cohesive Korean community to defy the colonial government. What brought about this unintended result? As the revival movement was sweeping the country, Koreans who were seeking consolation and a community of their own joined the church in larger numbers. Through these emotional gatherings, these Christians came to share the following belief about the yoke of foreign rule which they had to endure:

> All ye that grieve over lack of freedom and equality, if you do grieve, accept Protestant Christianity. If you are in sorrow over your plight, adhere to Protestant Christianity. If you muster enough Christians in the country to demand your legitimate rights by proper means, no evildoers can silence you![71]

These words were typical of the message conveyed to Protestant Christians at the various revival meetings. They were convinced that if the majority of Koreans embraced Protestant Christianity with firm conviction, the "Satan" Japan would retreat.[72] The religious community not only grew rapidly, but also became more cohesive and militant after the emotional revival movement.[73]

The Protestant churches filled the psychological and political need for a community where Koreans could gather to share their frustration, a sense of crisis, and a feeling of solidarity, and to discuss the future of their country. Since the protectorate government had prohibited them in 1907 from participating in any organizations and activities except for religious ones, colonized Koreans who were searching both psychologically and politically for a community of their own had to choose among Buddhism, Confucianism, Ch'ŏndogyo (a nationalistic folk religion), and Christianity.[74] Some Ch'ŏndogyo leaders had discredited themselves by engaging in pro-Japanese activities. Many patriotic Koreans had already lost faith in the traditional religions of Confucianism and Buddhism. It seemed as if Christianity was the only option for many. Since they were looking for a com-

TABLE 1.5
Number of Presbyterian Churches, 1910

Seoul	11
Hamgyŏng	31
P'yŏng'an	260
Hwanghae	103
Kyŏnggi	56
Ch'ungch'ŏng	25
Chŏlla	76
Kyŏngsang	125
Total	687

SOURCE: Yi Kwangnin, *Han'guksa kangiwa,* p. 541. Yi's table is based on *Chosŏn Yesugyo changnohoe sagi* [A historical record of the Jesus Presbyterian Church in Korea], comp. Ch'a Chaemyŏng (Seoul: Chosŏn Yesugyo changnohoe, 1910).

munity and at the same time modern education, Protestantism was especially attractive.[75] It was under this historical circumstance that colonized Koreans joined Protestantism in great numbers.

Thus, the annexation of Korea by Japan, a non-Western and non-Christian nation, encouraged many Koreans to join the Protestant community. In 1910, twenty-five years after the opening of its mission, the Presbyterian denomination alone had 687 churches throughout the peninsula (see Table 1.5). According to another source, however, just one year later the Presbyterian denomination had 1,448 churches.[76]

If churches of other denominations, such as Methodist and Anglican, are included, the number is even larger. Already in 1910, there were some 200,000 Christians in Korea, including 144,261 Presbyterians and 37,722 Methodists.[77] In addition, there were also more than 755 church-related schools and hundreds of private schools founded by Korean church leaders,[78] with more than 20,131 students enrolled.[79] At the time, Protestant denominations also published newspapers and other religious and social pamphlets.[80]

As Koreans joined the church in larger numbers, the religious community underwent a significant change. For example, in 1907 the Korean Presbyterian churches, which were established by four different Presbyterian mission societies and were not connected closely in terms of organization and church administration, were reorganized into one denomination, the Presbyterian Church of Korea.[81] This meant the development of a full and close liaison around 1910 among more than one thousand Presbyterian churches, nearly 150,000 adherents, and some one hundred schools and other outreach agencies across the country. The Protestant church thus emerged as the largest organized Korean community, with its own hierarchy as well as a nationwide organizational and communication network.

At the same time, native Korean leaders began to share responsibility and power in church administration and politics that missionaries had formerly assumed themselves. For example, thirty-three foreign missionaries and thirty-six Korean elders joined to form the Presbytery of the Presbyterian Church of Korea on September 17, 1907.[82] Afterwards, Korean church leaders assumed positions such as moderators, treasurers, and secretaries. This meant not only that Korean Protestant leaders established their voice in church administration and politics as the missionaries' influence declined, but that they were able to contact Christians across the country through the church's organizational and communication networks. The Protestant church was gradually becoming a Korean community, moving away from the missionaries' control.

In short, the missionaries and the colonial government did not achieve their intended goal—the apoliticization of the Protestant church community. The church kept growing, in fact faster than before the annexation, because repressive Japanese policies intensified the sympathy and confidence of Koreans toward Protestantism, and gave them little choice but to join the only available organized community. The *Korea Daily News* [Taehan maeil sinbo] summed up in 1907 the cause for the rapid growth of Protestantism:

> Over the years the people of Korea have felt bewildered and helpless under government oppression and Japanese maltreatment. As a result, more and more have been converted to the faith of the West. Lately their numbers keep growing even more, and it now seems that Korea as a whole, rebounding from oppression and maltreatment, may well turn into a Christian nation. If so, the oppression and maltreatment will have done great service to Protestant Christianity.[83]

This community of colonized Koreans obviously bore an anti-Japanese political coloration. The colonial government accordingly began surveillance and suppression of it.[84] However, the more the colonial government suppressed the Western religion, the more Protestantism earned the sympathy and confidence of the Korean people and the more rapidly it grew.

Although the church's organization, programs, and teachings were not structured particularly for anti-Japanese Korean political activism, the colonized Koreans joined the religious community under the particular circumstance of colonialism and reshaped it for their own uses. The association between the church and Korean anti-Japanese sentiment and activity—the primary cause of the rapid growth of Protestantism during the early colonial period—was established unintentionally, not by the church, but by colonized Koreans who joined the religion and colored it politically.

Church adherents and institutions reached such proportions that they presented a social force to be reckoned with on the eve of the 1919 March First Movement. In 1918, Yi Kwangsu, the foremost Korean novelist of the period, testified that the church had grown to such numbers and influence as to show "the appearance of a state" vis-à-vis the colonial government. At the time, 300,000 people—that is, one-fiftieth or one-sixtieth of the total population, but a well-organized and well-educated segment—were Christians. Korean citizens, according to Yi, expected the church to lead them not only in religious matters but also in social and political affairs, because it had leadership, organization, membership, and a communication network.[85] At the time, an organized Korean community comparable to the Protestant church did not exist.

It is therefore no surprise that Christian leaders initiated the March First Demonstration for independence and that stern and ruthless punishment was meted out to Protestant churches and their membership as a result.[86] But in the long run, this retribution only served to increase Korean sympathy and confidence in the religious community and to reinforce the church's growth. The case of the Presbyterian Church of Korea is illustrative. There were 1,778 churches with 160,919 members in 1918, while the numbers decreased to 1,705 churches and 144,062 members in 1919 (see Table 1.6). It seems clear that the Protestant church, which was targeted directly by the colonial government, began to stop growing right after the March First Movement, mainly because many Koreans witnessed the persecution of Christians and tried to distance themselves from the religious community for the time being. However, the church bounced back quickly. The Presbyterian Church of Korea established 115 new churches in 1919, 184 in 1920, and 267 in 1921. As Table 1.6 shows, from 1920 the denomination began to grow again and in 1921 it surpassed the pre–March First Movement level in terms of numbers of churches and adherents. The Protestant church continued to grow steadily until the beginning of the 1940s.

TABLE 1.6
The Growth of the Presbyterian Church before and after the 1919 Uprising

Year	*Churches*	*Newly Established Churches*	*Adherents*
1917	1,648	52	149,526
1918	1,778	102	160,919
1919	1,705	115	144,062
1920	1,738	184	153,915
1921	1,879	267	179,158

SOURCE: Kim Yangsŏn, *Han'guk kidokkyosa yŏn'gu* [A historical study of Korean Christianity] (Seoul: Kidokkyomunsa, 1971), p. 123.

The Declining Political Role of the Church in the Last Years of Colonial Rule

The religious community began to decline after that (see Table 1.7). What was the primary cause of this lack of growth in the last years of colonial rule? If the church's association with the rising desire for reform in the late Chosŏn period and then the anti-Japanese sentiment were the primary causes of the growth of Protestantism up to the early 1920s, it is logical to explain its stagnation also in terms of its relation to the Korean nationalist movement in the second half of the colonial period. Following the crushing blow dealt by the Japanese authorities in retaliation for Protestant church involvement in the events of 1919, the church gradually edged away from being the center of nationalist activity. In the last decade of colonial rule, the religious community came to show little interest in nationalist politics.[87] Since this subject will be addressed in detail in later chapters, it is sufficient here to mention three important developments in the second half of the colonial period.

First of all, out of a careful calculation, the colonial government relaxed its strong-arm rule and granted limited freedom of the press and assembly in order to improve its damaged image abroad and soothe wounded Koreans.[88] Responding to this relaxed colonial policy (the so-called *bunka seiji*, or cultural politics, policy), Koreans formed thousands of social and political organizations outside the church community.[89] The sudden emergence of these organizations brought about a significant change in relations between the Protestant church and the Korean nationalist movement.[90] Nationalist activity, which had formerly taken place under the aegis of religious communities such as Ch'ŏndogyo and Protestantism, now spread

TABLE 1.7
Church Membership

Year	*Adherents*
1937	374,085
1939	370,462
1941	332,607
1943	208,758

SOURCE: Based on the statistics in Kim Tŭkhwang, *Han'guk chonggyosa* [A history of Korean religions], (Seoul: Haemunsa, 1963), p. 436.

widely throughout the new organizations. This meant the beginning of the diversification of the Korean nationalist movement in terms of ideology, strategy, and organization. These new organizations began to encroach on the church's role in Korean nationalist politics and diminished its leadership position.

Second, the Protestant church as a social institution and the social status of its leaders had undergone a change that also altered the church's involvement in and influence on the nationalist movement. Christians, who had led new social and political movements since the late nineteenth century, retreated gradually, not suddenly, from the main intellectual current after 1919, when socialist and communist ideas began to appeal strongly to Koreans.[91] Initially, Christians were open to socialist and even communist ideas. Many church leaders, such as Yi Tonghwi, Yŏ Unhyŏng, Pak Hŭido, Yi Taewi, and Kim Pyŏngjo, were leaders of or sympathizers with leftist movements and continued to lead the nationalist movement.[92] But these leaders became disaffected from the more conservative church community.

To explain more persuasively the main reason for the church's dissociation from the nationalist movement in general and from its radical segments in particular, it is necessary to go beyond ideological considerations. The Protestant church was established as a social institution, and already by the 1920s, it was operated by well-educated and well-positioned Koreans.[93] As they enjoyed a secure living as religious professionals even in the colonial situation, they began to seek security rather than risk political action.[94] This was a major factor in the church's dissociation from the nationalist movement in the second half of the colonial period.

Lastly, the Protestant church began to cooperate with the colonial government and later became a Japanese religious institution, whether or not it wished to do so.[95] When Japan invaded Manchuria in 1931 and envisioned war with such Western powers as Great Britain and the United States as it carried out its plan to defeat China, it felt an increasing need to silence any antiwar sentiment that might assert itself in the ranks of liberals and pro-Western elements in Japan. Under the watchword of rallying national morale toward spiritual mobilization, the Japanese began psychological preparation on two levels: rallying popular sentiment behind the throne as the symbol of total national unity and good—that is, things originally and intrinsically Japanese—and elimination of all "evil," such as antiwar and pro-Western elements.[96]

Pressure was brought to bear on Korea and particularly on the Korean Protestant church community. As the largest organized Korean community, it not only had a strong connection with the United States, but it also had a lingering tie with Korean nationalist activism.[97] During the late 1930s, a visit to a Shinto shrine became a requirement on all occasions of national significance. Homage was regularly paid by a ceremonial bow in the direction of Tokyo, where the Japanese emperor resided. As a step toward turning Koreans into full-blown imperial subjects, the assimilation policy was upgraded to one of "imperialization." Adoption of Japanese-style family names was officially encouraged (and enforced in practice), use of the Korean language was forbidden in public places, and the use of Japanese in the privacy of the home was vigorously "encouraged."

Compulsory worship at a Shinto shrine struck Korean Christians close to home.[98] Shrine visiting aroused anger among most Protestant Christians, who saw emperor worship as unmistakable idolatry, an abomination admitting no compromise. There was a heated debate in the Protestant church community between those for and against emperor and shrine worship. Although the majority of church opinion was against Shinto-shrine worship, under coercion the Korean church decided to condone this as a national rite in 1938.[99] Although some Presbyterian church leaders stood militantly against such worship after 1938 and suffered imprisonment or exile until the liberation of 1945, most Christians followed, probably reluctantly, the government order.[100]

In addition, the colonial government separated the Korean church from the missionary influence and the Western world. Western missionaries were ordered to leave the Korean Peninsula in 1940. Later that year, 219 missionaries departed to their home countries, and the remaining 99 Western missionaries left Korea in 1941. The Korean church lost "a protecting tent" (*poho mak*) of Western missionaries.[101] The following year, the Japanese colonial government maneuvered to bring churches of all denominations under government control by merging them into one Christian group, the Korean Branch of the Japanese Christian Church (Ilbon kidokkyo Chosŏn kyodan), which in turn was made part of a national group comprising Japan proper and colonial areas. Kim Kwansik, a Presbyterian minister, was appointed president by the Governor General.[102]

These developments contributed to the decline of church growth in Korea. As Table 1.7 clearly shows, conversions to Protestant Christianity were negligible in the late 1930s and early 1940s as church membership decreased from 374,085 in 1937 to 208,758 in 1943. During this period, nationalists, whether they were socialists or culturalists, began to criticize the church's noninvolvement in sociopolitical issues.[103] They were incensed that some church leaders even were involved in Japanese war-mobilization activities.[104] When Protestant Christianity officially became a Japanese religious institution, many members were outraged. Many Koreans had joined the church or had become sympathizers because the Protestant community had been a place for psychological consolation, social association, and political discussion. Now they began to lose faith in the church community, and left. This was the main cause for the decrease in church membership in the last ten years of the colonial period, the first such decline in the history of the Protestant church in Korea.[105]

THE EXPLOSIVE GROWTH OF PROTESTANTISM IN SOUTH KOREA, 1945–1980S

In August 1945, troops of the United States and the Soviet Union arrived in Korea for the purpose of disarming and repatriating Japanese troops. A line was drawn at the 38th parallel to mark the boundary between the zones of occupation of the two foreign armies. This temporary division was the beginning of hostile relations between Soviet-controlled North Korea and the U.S.-administered south. The two separate regimes that soon emerged fought each other in the Korean War of 1950–1953, but the tension and hostility between the two Koreas did not end after the armistice. During this tragic period of division, a significant change occurred in the history of Protestantism in Korea. As Figure 1.2 shows, there was an explosive growth in Protestant Christianity in the south, whereas the religious community existed only by name in the north, where it had been quite strong before the liberation of 1945.[106]

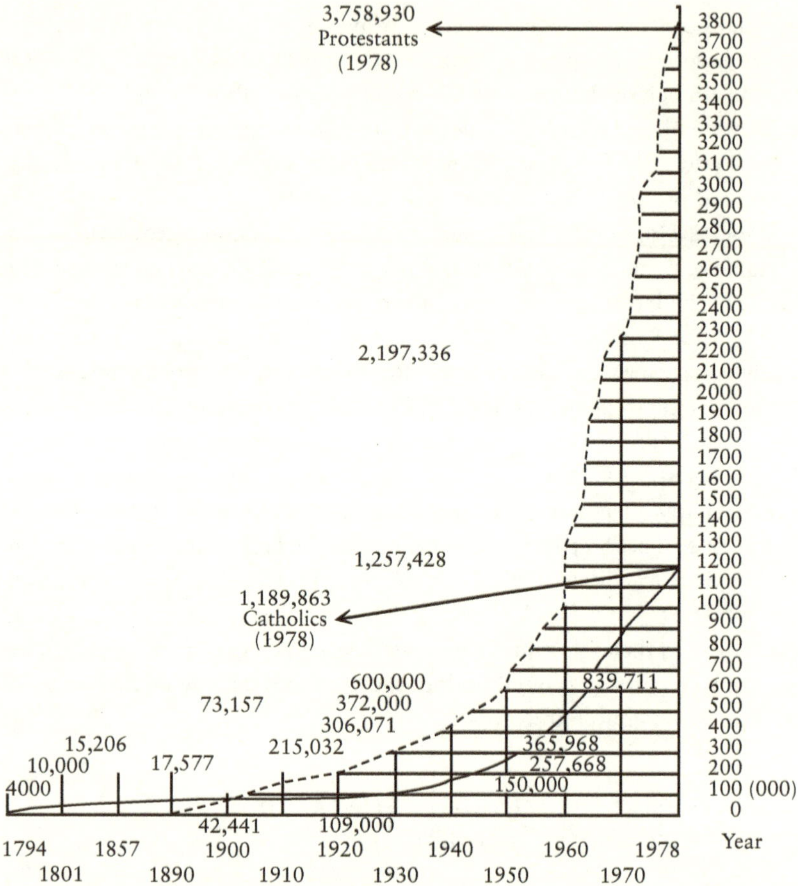

FIG. 1.2. Number of Christian adherents in Korea

SOURCE: "Han'guk kyohoe sŏngjang t'onggye (purok)" [Statistics on the growth of the Protestant church in Korea: Appendix], Han'guk kidokkyo sahoe munje yŏn'guwŏn, *Han'guk kyohoe paengnyŏn chonghap chosa yŏn'gu: pogosŏ* [A comprehensive study of the Korean church during the last century: A report] (Seoul: Han'guk Kiddokyo sahoe munje yŏn'guwŏn, 1982), p. 144, table II-4.

The Division of the Peninsula and the Explosive Growth of Protestantism

Opinions vary on what factors attracted people to the Protestant church in South Korea. As noted, some have argued that Koreans entered the church in order to seek spiritual solace and security amidst sociopolitical disturbance and unrest. They say that a series of tragic events such as the division of the country and the Korean War, as well as the social and political unrest in the process of industrialization and urbanization during the 1960s, 1970s, and 1980s, led Koreans to join the religious community in larger numbers.[107] Yet this argument does not explain why Koreans chose Protestant Christianity over religions such as Buddhism and Ch'ŏndogyo, whose membership declined.

Just as any study on the history of Korea after 1945 should begin with the division of the country, one who intends to explain the explosive growth of Protestantism in South Korea after 1945 should also start with the division of the peninsula. The division itself was one of the main causes for the church's explosive growth in South Korea.

In the south, religious persecution and discrimination toward the Western religion disappeared. Rather, under the U.S. military government and the Syngman Rhee regime, a favorable social and political atmosphere for the Protestant church community developed.[108]

In sharp contrast, tension and conflict characterized relations between Protestants and the USSR, and later the Kim Il-sung regime in the north.[109] The USSR, ideologically hostile to religion, held a strong antipathy toward the Korean Christian community, in part because the United States, its rival in the south, had promoted the religion in Korea since the late nineteenth century. Most of all, the USSR and the Kim Il-sung group, which maneuvered for the establishment of a pro-Soviet, anti-American regime in the north, saw the religious community as a major obstacle. Church leaders such as Cho Mansik, Yi Yunyŏng, O Yunsŏn, and Yun Hayŏng had already assumed political leadership in the north before the arrival of Soviet forces and Kim Il-sung's guerrillas in 1945. The northwestern region had been a stronghold for Christians, and P'yŏngyang had been called "the Jerusalem of the East."[110]

In dealing with the Protestant community, which had the largest, most long-standing organization of any Korean community, the USSR and Kim Il-sung arrested church leaders and put them under constant surveillance. As Protestants continued their struggle to survive, the government systematically eliminated Christian elements in the north by confiscating all church properties, putting all church leaders under a government-sponsored Christian League, and cutting down the number of churches and clergymen.[111] Whatever caused the conflict and the religious persecution, it produced a huge "religious migration" of North Korean Christians to the south that peaked during the war of 1950–1953. Donald N. Clark has called it a "spectacular exodus."[112]

According to Bruce Cumings, "a steady, massive stream of refugees from

TABLE 1.8
Number of Students Who Fled to the South

School	*Total*	*Christians*	*Percent*
Sŏnch'ŏn High	20	10	50
Sŏnch'ŏn Commercial	7	4	57

SOURCE: *A List of Sŏnch'ŏn Middle School Students Who Fled to the South* and *A List of Sŏnch'ŏn Commercial School Students Who Fled to the South* in *Sŏnch'ŏnchi* [Records of Sŏnch'ŏn County, North P'yŏng'an Province], 1946–1947, compiled by Amerasian Data Research Service, Inc., 1985. No page number is available. This is a compilation of valuable historical documents such as surveys, intelligence reports, and statements which were prepared by the communist authorities.

the north" was caused by a variety of historical factors, such as people returning home after the Liberation, the land reform of 1946, and bad harvests. There is no available data on the exact number of refugees from the north going south or from the south going north, but according to Cumings, there were far fewer refugees from the south than from the north. This was, Cumings argues, mainly because the North Korean authorities "encouraged" the migration to the south in order to cause troubles with "food supplies" and "relief facilities" in the south. They hoped that a massive population increase would bring about social and political disorder. Pointing out that many landlords in the north migrated to the south before and after the land reform of 1946, which deprived them of their property, Cumings concludes that the massive stream of refugees was a class realignment "on a north-south basis."[113]

This interesting argument is certainly valuable for our understanding of the migration that took place after Liberation. However, if the migration was truly a class realignment, one may wonder why peasants and workers in the south did not migrate north in larger numbers to benefit from the introduction of communism. Moreover, Cumings overemphasizes class theory to explain a complicated historical phenomenon and neglects the "religious migration" caused by the political tension and conflict between the Protestant community and the Kim Il-sung regime. According to a document written by the North Korean authorities in 1946, many migrants to the south were Christians whom the communist regime had put under constant surveillance (see Table 1.8). At the time there were some 300,000 Christians in the north. The data are sparse, but they show the nature and degree of the migration toward the south before the Korean War.

Whatever caused the massive migration to the south, it became one of

TABLE 1.9
Increase in Baptized Members of the Presbyterian Church

Year	*Baptized Members*
1952	231,473
1957	599,111

SOURCE: Hyŏndae sahoe yŏn'guso, *Han'guk kyohoe sŏngjang gwa sinang yangt'ae e kwanhan chosa yŏn'gu,* Table I-3, p. 26.

the main causes for the explosive growth of Protestantism there. First of all, these Christian migrants joined the churches in the south or established new churches composed primarily of refugees from the north.[114] Second, the religious migration from the north strengthened the favorable social and political atmosphere toward Protestantism in the south because the South Korean government, which was already "pro-Christian," treated the refugees, especially Christian refugees, very well to use them against the North Korean regime.[115]

Not only did Christian refugees establish new churches in the south, but most non-Christian refugees joined the churches, whether their motive was religious or social. According to Roy E. Shearer, the refugees, who suffered the most socially, economically, and psychologically during the war, entered the "refugees' churches" founded by clergymen from the north for solace and social association.[116] According to Presbyterian data, the number of baptized members increased by almost 300 percent from 1952–1957 (see Table 1.9). Although these data are not fully accurate because of wartime conditions, other information supports them. For example, the number of baptized adherents in the region of the Southern Presbyterian Mission grew from 14,818 in 1948 to 40,781 in 1958. The church membership in this region also increased by nearly 300 percent from 1948 to 1958.[117]

It is not adequate to say without qualification that the war caused the refugees and other Koreans to join the church in larger numbers for spiritual solace and security. This does not explain why they chose Protestant Christianity to ameliorate their social and psychological insecurity and anxiety. Why did they not choose other religions, such as Buddhism or Ch'ŏndogyo, to do so? As mentioned, a favorable social and political atmosphere toward Christianity developed in South Korea because of the U.S. occupation and the emergence of Syngman Rhee. In particular, U.S. participation in the Korean War and in the rehabilitation of the war-torn country strengthened not only U.S. influence but also the favorable atmosphere

TABLE 1.10
The Growth of Christianity, 1960–1990

	1960	*1970*	*1980*	*1990*
Protestant	623,072	3,192,621	7,180,627	11,888,374
Catholic	451,808	953,799	1,321,193	2,632,990
Total	1,074,880	4,146,420	8,501,820	14,521,364
Total Population			37,436,000	43,520,199

SOURCE: Korean Overseas Information Service, *Statistical Data on Korea* (1982), Column 50; Kyŏngje kihoekwŏn chosat'onggyekuk, *Han'guk t'onggye yŏn'gam,* p. 39; Yonhap News Agency, *Korea Annual, 1981* (Seoul: Yonhap News Agency, 1981), p. 211; and Han'guk chonggyo sahoe yŏn'guso, *Han'guk chonggyo yŏn'gam,* p. 208.

toward the Protestant church in the postwar era. Many Koreans who wished to join a religion chose the Protestant church over other religions in this pro-Christian social and political atmosphere.

In addition, the Protestant church's programs were different from those of other religions. Undoubtedly, we must agree that Protestant church gatherings attracted Koreans who sought spiritual solace and security. Through regular gatherings, such as Sunday worship, Sunday and Wednesday evening prayer meetings, and daily dawn prayer meetings, the refugees from the north met their fellow refugees to share their feelings and exchange practical information. The church also held special group activities for students, youth, women, and men. The church functioned as a religious community as well as a social community for the Koreans, particularly the refugees in the post–Korean War era.[118] This is one of the main causes for the explosive growth of the so-called "refugees' churches" such as Yŏngnak Church, Ch'unghyŏn Church, and Sŏngnam Church. Other churches also grew rapidly by providing the Koreans with the religious and social fellowship they longed for after the war.

But there are other reasons for church growth. The Protestant denominations attracted Koreans by providing a tremendous amount of material relief during and after the war. The Protestant community, which had ties with the global Christian community, particularly the churches in the United States, received and distributed money and goods. Koreans during and after the war needed the tents, food, medicine, and clothes distributed by the church. For example, the Methodist Church received some $120,000 as well as 143,850,000 Korean won in cash by the end of 1951 for relief.[119]

TABLE 1.11
Programs That Should Be Strengthened

Program	*Percent*
Worship	2.4
Dawn and overnight prayer	10.1
Bible study	28.1
Church education	12.9
Fellowship	19.5
Pastoral visits	4.8
Sectional prayer meetings	3.2
Revival meetings	3.9
Mission outside the church	13.1
Other	2.0
Total	100.0

SOURCE: Hyŏndae sahoe yŏn'guso, *Han'guk kyohoe sŏngjang gwa sinang yangt'ae e kwahan chosa yŏn'gu,* Table II-16, p. 57.

In 1952 alone, American churches sent the Methodist Church in Korea 1,538,505,500 won.[120] In addition, the Korean Methodist Church received a tremendous amount of tents, clothes, food, and medicine.[121] Since these relief monies and goods were distributed preferentially to clergymen and Christians, it was natural for the Koreans who needed them to join the church in greater numbers.

The Protestant church also continued sustained growth during the Park Chung-hee era (1963–1979) and after.[122] As Table 1.10 shows, the Protestant church grew rapidly during this period. What caused this continuation of the explosive growth of Protestantism? Some scholars have argued that the church grew rapidly during this period due to its stand for human rights, social justice, and democratization against the dictatorial regimes of military generals. These positions earned it public sympathy and confidence.[123]

Nevertheless, all available evidence refutes this interpretation. The conservative Christian denominations such as the Hapdongp'a and the Koryŏp'a that opposed Christian political activism grew impressively—by over 70 percent from 1974 to 1979—while a liberal church group like the Kijangp'a, which led Christian activism against Park Chung-hee, grew a mere 11 percent from 1971 to 1977.[124] A survey by liberal Christian scholars also coun-

TABLE 1.12
What Christians Wanted to Obtain in the Church

Needs	*Percent*
Warm human relationships	16.4
Self-confidence to live	24.9
Blessings for family and business	5.9
Hope for the world after death	3.3
Concern about neighbors	6.3
Concern about social justice	1.6
Other	1.6
Total	100.0

SOURCE: Hyŏndae sahoe yŏnguso, *Hanguk kyohoe sŏnjang gwa sinang yangt'ae e kwahan chosa yŏn'gu.*

ters this interpretation. The survey, conducted in the early 1980s, showed that 52.3 percent of Christians had a negative view of activist trends,[125] and joined the Protestant church not because of its political activism. Other factors must have caused the growth of conservative churches.

More than 90 percent of Korean Christians were attracted by such programs as Bible study, revival meetings, and dawn and overnight prayer meetings—the conservative church's major programs.[126] As Table 1.11 indicates,[127] most thought such programs should be enhanced, while only 13.1 percent argued that the "mission outside the church," which the liberal congregations emphasized, was more important. The conservative churches' programs appealed to Koreans more strongly than those of the liberal churches, so most Korean Christians did not affiliate with the Protestant church because of its social and political activism.

Why, then, did Koreans prefer the conservative church's apolitical teaching and programs? As Table 1.12 indicates, they sought identity, association, fellowship, material blessings, and hope for spiritual salvation. Certainly the division of the country and the Korean War were factors in bringing about this mentality. However, rapid social change and political unrest in the 1960s, 1970s, and 1980s were the primary contributing factors.

Amidst rapid industrialization, unbalanced economic growth, urbanization, frequent military coups, dictatorial regimes, and a series of violent demonstrations, Koreans became "identity seekers" or "community seekers."[128] To them, the conservative church's teaching about the afterlife and programs for fellowship were more attractive than the liberal church's social and political activism. As the rapid expansion of Yŏŭido Full Gospel Church clearly shows,[129] the explosive growth of the Protestant church from the 1960s to the 1980s should be explained in the context of the social pathologies of the period.

CONCLUSION

With the exception of the last ten years of colonial rule, Protestantism in Korea has shown a consistent pattern of growth throughout periods of change and flux—a dynasty fallen, old ways replaced by modern ways, sovereignty lost and later restored, the division of the country, war, rapid economic growth and urbanization, and authoritarian dictatorship. Students of religion argue that theological affinities between the Korean folk cults and Protestant Christianity are the main cause for the remarkable growth of Protestantism. Missionaries and church workers have ascribed this spectacular expansion to their missionary methods and strategies. Politically conscious liberal Christians have argued that the success of Protestantism in Korea was due primarily to the church's social and political activism.

As we have seen, none of these theories is persuasive. Similarities between local beliefs and Christianity have been found in cultures where the religion did not spread. Indeed, the preliminary evangelical work in Korea likewise brought relatively unfavorable results. Koreans joined the religious community sometimes because of its political activism and sometimes because of its spiritual solace and charity.

The cause of Protestant Christianity's remarkable development must be put in the context of modern Korean history. Protestantism came to Korea toward the end of the nineteenth century, when the old order built on Confucian values and a China-centered world view began to collapse. A small number of Korean intellectuals, who saw the strength and wealth of the Western powers, keenly felt the need for modernization. They tended to identify Christianity with the source of Western power and wealth. These reform-minded Koreans adopted Protestantism as a means for reform and self-strengthening. In addition, commoners, the downtrodden, slaves, and others who had been alienated from the old Confucian regime and saw the strength of the West, were attracted to the new religion from the West because they thought it would bring them a better life. Once the new doctrine took hold, the church served as a vehicle to spread and sustain patriotic nationalist sentiment, which contained an added urgency before the steady advance of Japan. In the process, many Koreans came to join the religious community for spiritual solace and security as well as for the opportunities it offered for political activity on behalf of independence. The church provided them with leadership and organization, in addition to a sense of community vis-à-vis Japanese colonial rule.

In 1945, when Korea was freed from Japan but was divided in two, a new social and political setting developed for the expansion of Protestantism in South Korea. In the north, where Protestantism had been particularly strong, a political conflict developed between the church and the Soviet administration and later the Kim Il-sung group. The political conflict and the persecution of Christians caused a massive religious migration toward the south, where a pro-Christian social and political atmosphere developed primarily because of the U.S. occupation and the emergence of Syngman Rhee. The "religious migration" and the massive number of refugees caused by the Korean War produced the sudden growth of Protestantism in the south. It was in the 1960s, 1970s, and 1980s, however, that the Protestant church grew like "wildfire." The social changes and political disturbances caused by dictatorial rule and the resistance to it; by rapid economic growth and unbalanced distribution of wealth; and by urbanization and social anomie made Koreans seek a community where they could obtain spiritual solace, security, identity, and fellowship. It seems that the Protestant church will continue to grow, despite the conclusion of one scholar in 1972 that "the period of the dynamic growth of Christianity is past."[130]

What does the growth of Protestantism mean in the history of modern Korea? Protestantism, an unaccepted religious sect from the West in the nineteenth century, became an accepted religion by absorbing those Koreans who had lost faith in the foundering Confucian system in the late nineteenth century and who were hopeless and helpless during the Japanese colonial period. It was a community of poor, alienated, and defiant Koreans in late Confucian Korea, and it became the largest organized community of colonized Koreans during the period of Japanese colonial rule. As the Protestant church grew rapidly to become the largest organized Korean community, its influence in politics and society increased accordingly.

As Protestantism was becoming an accepted religion, especially as its leaders came to enjoy higher social, economic, and political positions after the 1920s, particularly in South Korea after Liberation in 1945, the religious community began to move away from controversial social and political issues and toward cooperation with the government. This tendency was greatly accelerated in the post-Liberation era in South Korea. With the elevation of the status of church leaders and members, the attitudes of this religious community changed toward matters of society and politics. Therefore, the history of the remarkable growth of Protestantism in modern Korea is a history of the metamorphosis of the religion from a foreign, Western faith to an accepted Korean religion, and from a minority religion of the poor and ignored that defied established society and power to a larger religious community that adopted a conformist position toward the authorities and the status quo.

2 / The Theological Orientation of the Protestant Church

Its Formation and Transformation

Divergent theological or doctrinal opinions may be advanced as an attempt to rationalize individual interests or gloss over underlying personal conflicts, which often result from regional clashes of loyalties or divergent goals based on self-serving motives. However, since a church is a religious institution in which members share a common theological and doctrinal system, its theological orientation deserves close attention. There has been a tendency to view a church's social and political position in terms of its support for a conservative or liberal theology: that is, conservative Christians are generally thought to be disinterested in political and social issues, but liberals more concerned.[1] Therefore, it is necessary to discuss the theological orientation of Korean Protestant churches in order to understand their political activism.

Han Wansang, a politically active Christian sociologist during the 1970s, lambasted his fellow Christians who had conservative leanings and avoided political involvement. He criticized conservatives for blithely ignoring sociopolitical realities while singing the praises of pure faith (*sunsu sinang*) and individual salvation (*kaein kuwŏn*). The conservatives, Han said, believe that "so long as salvation of 'I' and entry into the Kingdom of Heaven after death are ensured, nothing else much matters." He went so far as to say that the conservatives, by retreating into "abstract" theology, were indirectly strengthening the "authority of the Caesars of this world."[2]

Following the Western liberal theological tradition, liberal Christians in Korea during the 1970s and 1980s seemed more concerned than their conservative counterparts about sociopolitical affairs. According to them, since developments in modern science and technology had brought far-reaching changes in society, the church needed to make an about-face in its traditional theology, which was concerned only with individual salvation. If the church's chief concern was the salvation of humanity, they argued, it should be concerned with people and society, and set up a new mission to guide people in this changing society. Christians should be more concerned with the here-and-now than the afterlife. The way to know God is through one's neighbor, and the other world can be approached through this world. In other words, not only spiritual salvation but also the union with invisible God can be obtained through concern and love for neighbors. Therefore, the church should divert its concern from God to people, from the Heavenly Kingdom to this world, and from spiritual salvation to social salvation. The followers of this liberal theological teaching urged greater involvement in social and political issues.[3]

To counter liberal criticism, Pak Hyŏngnyong, the leading conservative Protestant theologian in Korea, and his followers condemned the political activity of liberal Christians. They claimed that focusing on this world would automatically nullify the transcendence of God, which in turn would subvert the authority of the Bible and the church. Liberal theology was nothing but a self-serving misuse of the Bible; immersed in social and political issues, liberal advocates lost sight of the other world. Pak and his fundamentalist conservative followers opposed all the liberal theological trends, including Christian concerns with worldly issues.[4]

Although there is some justification for studying the church's social and political activism in terms of theological differences, it is important to avoid stereotypical thinking. It is worth remembering that the attitudes of a church, fundamentalist or otherwise, toward political issues do not remain consistent. Theology alone does not determine how a church will react to a sociopolitical issue at a given time. The same theology may play a "liberal" role in one period and a "conservative" role in another.[5] The theological orientation of a church should be seen in its historical context: how it came about, how it evolved as circumstances and its followers' social status changed, and how the programs of the church were affected as a result.

Although the early missionaries and Korean converts were theologically conservative fundamentalists,[6] they were determined to turn Confucian Korea into a Christian nation. They were thus devoted to winning new converts and to reforming social customs to conform to Christian ethics. Korean converts, who had long searched for some means by which to overhaul Confucian society, discovered in Protestantism an appropriate answer and began to make changes according to the teachings of Christianity. As a result, conservative fundamentalist theology worked not as a force for conservatism, but as a force for social reform and change in nineteenth-century Korea.[7]

Fundamentalist theology came to emphasize millenarianism and eschatology as Japan tightened its hold on Korea. As hopes for independence were dashed and despair deepened, Korean Christians tried to look beyond the here and now. This millenarian and eschatological emphasis in theology was taken by many scholars simply as an escape from painful reality, a serious failure of nerve.[8] They argued that Christians, faced with troubled times, were giving up on their struggle for freedom and independence. These scholars took the seemingly otherworldly theology literally. However, they did not consider it in its particular historical context, and they failed to see its functional significance. In particular, the millenarian and eschatological strains in fundamentalist theology continued to draw Koreans to the church; and the church continued to grow as a community of colonized people after 1905. Paradoxically, this seemingly otherworldly theology strengthened the political activism of those who longed for a deliverance from Japanese colonial rule. To those Christians, who participated in the March First Movement of 1919 and the Anti-Shrine Worship Campaign during the late colonial period, it functioned as a "theology of hope."[9]

This conclusion does not deny that millenarian and eschatological theology could function also as an otherworldly escapism. During the late colonial period after the March First Movement, this theology justified the inaction of some church leaders against foreign rule and their moderate line toward the Japanese authorities. At the time, there was a change in the social position of church leaders, who had come to enjoy a comfortable life as religious and cultural professionals—preachers, schoolteachers, and functionaries in church-related agencies. They also enjoyed social prestige, which they had earned by leading social and educational movements and by participating in nationalist activities. As their position in society changed from that of outcasts to that of recognized professionals, church leaders tended to avoid any militant stand against Japanese rule which might destroy their position. They now taught their followers the same otherworldly theology, but stressed longing for "paradise" in the afterlife in order to make their followers ignore the painful colonial reality.[10]

The liberation of 1945 marked a sea change for Christians in Korea. Rising from relative obscurity, they moved in great numbers toward the center of public life; government offices throughout the hierarchy from lowest to highest were theirs for the taking, and they filled key positions in public organizations.[11] As a result, Protestant Christian leaders soon became part of the political establishment and openly identified with the powers that be.

Fundamentalist theology was invoked to bless a secular regime and emphasized only ecclesiastic activity. Voices of criticism, if any, were definitely a minority.[12]

After Syngman Rhee passed from the political scene in 1960, criticism of Christians grew and came out into the open as Park Chung-hee persisted in his antidemocratic rule. At the same time, within the church fundamentalist theology itself came under attack for its lack of social and political concern. Some preferred to associate political activity only with liberal theology, conveniently ignoring the fact that fundamentalists themselves had participated in earlier political activism. One cannot therefore view fundamentalist theology as less conducive to political consciousness and activity than liberal theology. It was only after 1960 that church leaders of more liberal theological leanings became vocal in criticizing the political reality, while those with a fundamentalist outlook tended to approve it. Until then such liberal church leaders had not been particularly active in voicing their political concerns.

We have seen that the theological orientation of the Korean Protestant church remained constant, but that the church's response to political concerns fluctuated throughout the decades. Thus theology should be discussed in conjunction with the historical context in which it functioned.

EARLY PIETIST FUNDAMENTALISM IN LATE CONFUCIAN KOREA

In 1919, Arthur J. Brown, executive secretary of the Board of Foreign Missions of the Presbyterian Church, U.S.A., summed up the theological outlook shared by early missionaries in Korea:

> The typical missionary of the first quarter century after the opening [of missionary activity] was a man of the Puritan type. He kept the Sabbath as our New England forefathers did a century ago. He looked upon dancing, smoking, and cardplaying as sins in which no true followers of Christ should indulge. In theology and biblical criticism he was strongly conservative, and he held as a vital truth the premillenarian view of the second coming of Christ. The high criticism and liberal theology were deemed dangerous heresies. . . . The church must be composed of men and women of clean lives; but efforts to clean up the community and bring about better social conditions are regarded as a use of time and strength that could be more usefully employed in other ways.[13]

Missionaries brought Korea the Puritan pietist ethic and a conservative fundamentalist theology in the late nineteenth century. Following the theology of their home church, they viewed the Bible as the word of God revealed to man, an immutable law by which to steer one's faith and life. Faith was an exclusively personal experience, and life with faith was to be achieved through direct communion with God. Typical American fundamentalists at the time looked inward toward personal salvation and were quite unconcerned about making the world over or building the kingdom of heaven on earth. Rather they militantly defended the historic faith against churchmen who attempted to adjust it to the needs of the new age by liberalizing their theology and emphasizing the social aspects of the gospel. Higher criticism or historical criticism, which was gaining ground among liberal theologians in the early nineteenth century, was held to subvert faith itself. A Christian position in favor of involvement in social and political issues was objectionable as long as faith was understood as an intense personal experience; a "social gospel" was a contradiction in terms.[14]

William D. Reynolds, an early missionary who taught systematic theology at the P'yŏngyang Presbyterian Theological Seminary, also expressed opposition to tampering with scripture:

> I look upon the relationship between religion and Scripture as absolute. For this I may be considered ultraconservative, but I cannot change my conviction. . . . Change Scripture, and the religion too will change. One must not change words or phrases, or ignore the underlying spirit, or bend meaning to suit one's purpose. The Bible must be kept in its original form and its spirit upheld as originally revealed.[15]

It was only to be expected that students taught by these professors came to embrace fundamentalist theology. Thus, apolitical conservative fundamentalist theology came to prevail in the Korean Protestant church.

But once adopted by Koreans, this conservative fundamentalist theology played a different role. In Korean minds, Protestant Christianity was a new cult from the West, the land of advanced civilization and modern ways. Embracing Christianity meant accepting modern Western lore and ideas. So eager were some Koreans to seek social and political reform and to infuse new life into a stagnating society that they found themselves capable of discontinuing the age-old memorial services for ancestors, a pivotal rite typifying the Confucian family system and the symbolic foundation of a whole system of morality.[16] In this way, fundamentalist theology presented itself in a new garb, which was reminiscent more of liberal theology in its attitudes toward social renovation and moral regeneration.

The pietist missionaries of the early years made the gate "straight" for Koreans who desired to pursue the "narrow way" leading "unto life." They called for nothing less than a clean break with the conventions of the Confucian outlook and morality. These conventions, they warned, were none other than the "wide gate" and the "broad way" that "leadeth to destruction," as the Bible admonished. In other words, they regarded everything "heathen" as the work of evil. Such pietist fundamentalist teachings played an almost revolutionary role at the time, as one missionary witnessed:

> [The convert] finds he is called upon to step aside from the religious path followed by the entire mass of his countrymen, and espouse a system whose followers as yet are but a handful, and these of humble origin. To his friends he seems as one who has not only apostatized from the views decreed by public opinion, a serious offence the world over, but as also having cast off all allegiance to his parents and ancestry and thus violated one of the fundamental precepts of ordinary morality.[17]

The early Protestant church's doctrine and theology, though conservative fundamentalist in nature, made Korean Christians more hostile toward Confucian ethics and practices, and thus truly revolutionary.

The Protestant missionaries made no attempt to compromise with the Confucian tradition: Rather they aggressively denounced Confucianism as a form of paganism.[18] As mentioned above, they insisted on the abolition of ancestor worship. The early church's demand that its members discontinue all Confucian rites was a direct challenge to the ideological foundation of Confucian Korea. For example, "On the Salvation of the World" (Kuseron), a missionary pamphlet of the time, taught this lesson to Korean Christians in the style of catechism, as the following excerpt reveals:

> QUESTION: Is it right to hold ancestor worship rites or not?
> ANSWER: It is not right.
> QUESTION: Is it right for Christians to hold ancestor worship rites or not?
> ANSWER: It is not right, and we are not allowed to do that at all.
> QUESTION: Why isn't it right?
> ANSWER: Since our ancestors have already passed away and are not able

to eat any food, it is useless. And also since it violates the Christian commandment, we can not even do that on the sly.

QUESTION: If you do not hold ancestor worship rites, how can you express your reverence to your ancestors?

ANSWER: We can express our heartfelt reverence, by loving them dearly, remembering their teachings, doing what they asked us to do, and remembering them as long as we live.[19]

Not only did the early church emphasize the difference between Confucianism and Christianity on the issues of social status and value of life, but it also demanded from its followers a total commitment to Christian doctrine. A document of 1898, for example, clearly shows that early missionaries taught Korean Christians that all men and women were equal:

> The [Confucian] sages of Korea taught the nation that woman is inferior to man. Christianity flatly contradicts this, and there is a clash. The sages taught that some men are better than other men, and again we have discord.[20]

Furthermore, early American missionaries even taught that Confucian society was "evil" or "heathen" and that it should be Christianized.

> The evil of this [Confucian] custom is that it denies the right of every man to freedom and creates a class standard of blood and ancestry instead of merit. It shuts up the cooly to that development of his faculties which would fit him to fill a higher status in life. It places the low man at the mercy of his superior which would put him in prison in the States and yet the cooly can obtain no redress. It cheapens human life, while custom secures the noble the possession of his goods, immunity from fortune and a regard for his person, not so the luckless low man. . . . This cheapens [*sic,* cheapness] of human life and disregard of the sacredness of the human body is, after all, not so much a result of caste as a different effect of heathenism itself.[21]

Such uncompromising fundamentalist teachings, whether or not they contained a Western bias, had a singular appeal for those who were eager for change. To be a Christian meant to reject Confucian values and practices and thus to act progressively. The minimum requirement for church membership was abandonment of everything Confucian. Therefore, every action by the pietist fundamentalist church community was a direct challenge to the Confucian establishment in Korea, in a way that it could never be in the United States and most other Western countries.

Early missionaries and Korean Christians sought to build a church community of "men and women of clean lives" who renounced smoking, dancing, cardplaying, and concubinage. This community was totally divorced from "heathen" society, which was regarded as an "enemy of Christianity." The new ethics dictated by pietist fundamentalist missionaries moved the converts willy-nilly in the direction of social and eventually political reform.[22]

Another significant feature of this fundamentalist march toward social reform was the idea of the equality of the sexes. Women were traditionally expected to obey their husbands and follow them in all ways. Thus Sŏ Chaep'il, who had been a radical reformist member of the *yangban* elite in the failed palace coup in 1884 and later himself converted to Protestant Christianity, said in 1896, "Korean women are the most pitiful in the world. Today we address ourselves to the people of our country in support of women. . . . Being weak, Korean women are without freedom and are treated like prisoners." Sŏ then proclaimed that "men and women are created equal by God" and preached this teaching through newspaper articles and public lectures to the people of his country. The early missionaries and native church leaders taught that all Christians should follow this teaching of equality as "the God-given rule."[23] They did not just teach the new ethics and ideas; they were determined to practice them. In this sense, the pietist fundamentalist theology played a progressive role for social reform in Confucian Korea.

The fundamentalist theology had an enormous impact on the new religious community. One Korean *yangban*'s reaction to Christian teaching and practices was typical of the Korean experience of conversion at the time:

> Four months ago I was ashamed to be here at the sarang [guest room], and when the congregation bowed down to pray I felt very queer, and sat up straight, but after a little while I began to bow down too, and the feeling of shame was all gone, God has given me a believing mind. My friends say I am crazy, and they don't come to see me any more, but it is not a sign of craziness to worship the true God. To be sure, I am a *Yang Ban* [*yangban*], but God did not make one man a *Yang Ban*, another a

> *Sang Nom* [*sangnom*, common fellow]. Men have made that distinction. God made all men equal.[24]

While commoners, women, and children did not have any voice and were treated unequally in the hierarchical Confucian society, things were quite different in Protestant congregations. Nobles and commoners, men and women, old and young sat together in one place as equals to hear sermons, sing hymns, read the Bible, and discuss matters of religion. And then they left the church community to preach these social teachings in Confucian society. The "social gospel" of Christian fundamentalism spread across late Confucian Korea through churches, church-related schools, hospitals, church-connected newspapers, and other outreach agencies. In addition to teaching egalitarian ethics, the early Christians participated actively in such social and political movements as the Independence Club movement and the campaign for modern education, which challenged Confucian values and practices.

How, then, could Arthur J. Brown and other scholars indicate that the early fundamentalist missionaries and Korean Protestant Christians ignored the social application of the gospel? How could they fail to see the reform-oriented nature of early pietist fundamentalist theology in late Confucian Korea?[25] Without a doubt, fundamentalist theology in late-nineteenth and early-twentieth-century America was concerned more with the salvation of individual souls than with improving social conditions. It is also true that the fundamentalist theology opposed the social gospel then being preached in America. Even in the face of a collective change in Korean Christians' lifestyle and outlook on life, certain missionaries refused to admit to the social changes unexpectedly wrought by theological conservatism.

Though it was fundamentalist theology that was being delivered from the pulpit, Korean congregations, eager for change and reform, accepted it as the way of the West. The reform and change prompted by this theology pointed away from the traditional Confucian values and practices. The missionaries condemned Confucian beliefs and customs as heathen to reinforce their teachings, which served to push early Korean Christians further away from their age-old social and political values and practices. Conversion to the Western religion itself was indeed a revolutionary act at the time. The early converts, though small in number, had experienced a clash between the old beliefs and the new religious teachings and had finally determined to follow the latter. Their conversion was a total commitment to face the scorn and condemnation that was sure to follow. Through their lonely determination to convert and become members of a new religious community, the early converts came to have a strong sense of the special role that the multitude was incapable of playing.

In this historical context, the teachings and activities of pietist fundamentalist missionaries and native Christians were identified with reform. Many Koreans came to believe that for reform and modernization to take place, it was essential to educate men of ability. In order to develop educated leaders, it was necessary to convert their countrymen to Protestant Christianity. For example, Yun Ch'iho, an early convert and a prominent leader in the reform movement at the turn of the century, identified Christian evangelism with reform activities. Believing that "Christianity is the only salvation to Coreans [Koreans]," he led the evangelistic endeavor and the social and political movement as if they were identical.[26] According to Yun:

> There is no other means but Christianity to help along education in our country and restore spirituality to our people. In working for the country or for reform, my aspiration is to serve the Savior up above with all my heart and mind and gain for my soul perfect happiness here below.[27]

Yun and other reform activists, who saw the incompetence of a *yangban* elite enslaved by Confucian values and practices, accepted the religion from the West as a source of power and wealth that they perceived in Western Christian countries in the late nineteenth century. Since the form of Christianity introduced to Korea imbued converts with a sharp dichotomy between good versus evil, Christian versus Confucian, and Christian nation versus Confucian society, it induced them aggressively to "Christianize" Confucian Korea. In this context, pietist fundamentalism acted as an ideology of reform in nineteenth-century Korea because reform-minded Koreans adopted it specifically in a period of social and political conflict between Confucian traditionalists and pro-Western reform forces.

The early missionaries initiated new religious, educational, medical, and other humanitarian undertakings in order to propagate Christianity, and thereby aided Korean Christians to reform Confucian Korea. According to the field manual prepared by the Council of Missions in Korea in 1893, these works were directed mainly for the benefit of disregarded, oppressed, and poor people. Early missionaries and Korean converts thus tried to convert common people, especially women and youth, more than the upper classes. To communicate with the less educated, they wrote everything in the Korean vernacular, reducing their use of Chinese characters, which were difficult for the uneducated women and commoners to understand. As a result, the disadvantaged in society became the first Koreans to receive a modern education, medical treatment, and other social services from Protestant denominations. Of course, the early fundamentalist missionaries adopted these principles as an effective means for communication and the rapid propagation of Christianity. But at the same time they trained the lower classes to lead the new religious community and their native society as well. As a result, many early Korean converts became leaders in social and political movements in the late nineteenth century.[28]

Early pietist fundamentalist theology was a far cry from the position of the fundamentalists after the liberation from Japan in 1945. The pietist fundamentalists in the post-Liberation era addressed themselves to the middle- and upper-class segments of society. Their aloofness from controversial social and political issues in fact had a political impact—by making their followers ignore social and political affairs, by teaching them to be satisfied with reality, and even by supporting dictatorial regimes.[29] In sharp contrast, the early fundamentalists forwarded a "social gospel" (which they really did not condone) by virtue of their opposition to the conditions existing on the peninsula in their time. Oddly enough, the true heirs of these early fundamentalists are the Christian liberals who are concerned with socioeconomic issues in South Korea today.

APOCALYPTIC ESCHATOLOGY IN COLONIAL KOREA

The Second Coming Tied to Political Liberation

The fear that Korea might lose its independence, a concern for the last quarter of the nineteenth century, became a reality in 1910. In the years leading to the disaster, there was a growing sense among Christians that justice might not be obtained within the foreseeable future after all, that Japan would never allow freedom and independence for Korea. It was a depressing thought, one that led to a change of attitude toward spiritual salvation. Arthur J. Brown noted in 1919 that

> the thought of the Korean churches is fixed on the next world. The present world is regarded as so utterly lost that it cannot be saved in this dispensation, nor is it believed that the Divine plan contemplates such an end. The duty of the church now is to preach the gospel "for a witness" to gather out the elect, and to leave the world till Christ shall return.[30]

The earlier fundamentalism gradually came to emphasize millenarianism and apocalyptic eschatology with otherworldly theological language and symbols. While Japan was proceeding toward annexation, the Christians among the frustrated, humiliated Koreans began to pin their hopes on the second coming of Christ, and were enjoined to await the day of glory that was sure to come.

Revivals were frequent during the early colonial period. One prominent leader of the revivals was the Reverend Kil Sŏnju, who declared:

> The prophets of the Old Testament gained their salvation not by obeying the Law but by believing in the coming of the Messiah as promised. . . . Brothers and sisters, the very basis of our faith is not the blood shed by Christ on the cross but resides in a hope that will not change or perish but will endure forever, the hope that the Lord will return to earth to build a paradise of peace. I want you to keep awake and ready, to stand fast in faith, and to wait in hope and joy for the coming of the Lord.[31]

Brown and some others viewed this otherworldly trend as the religious escapism of Korean Christians who found Japanese pressure more than they could bear. They argued that these Christians, having shut out the troublesome political and social realities, seemed to be seeking individual salvation in the quietude of communion with the Divine.[32]

These scholars, however, understood the theological tendency of Kil Sŏnju and his contemporaries only in a literal sense without relating it to the historical context.[33] It would be erroneous to infer that the position of Kil Sŏnju and other revivalists toward the political realities of the day was one of escapism simply because the language of revivalism was ostensibly concerned more with what was to come than with what was. As the preceding quotation clearly shows, Kil cautiously started his theological persuasion by relating symbolically the colonial reality of Korea to the history of the Hebrews. He referred to the old prophets "believing in the coming of the Messiah" to deliver the Hebrews from oppression. As a matter of fact, Kil had his feet firmly planted on the ground, concerned with what was happening to Koreans around him, although never losing sight of what was to come in the end. He preached that "this earth will turn into a paradise" and the paradise would be in "this world."[34] Even in a literal sense, Kil's theology was not a religious escapism that longed only for an otherworldly paradise. His "paradise of peace" was designed not for the next world but for this world, which the promised Messiah would come to build. His concept of "hope" did not mean doing nothing until Christ's second coming, but was rather a call "to keep awake and ready, to stand fast in faith, and to wait with hope and joy."

Kil and others began to preach these biblical symbols and phrases to the Koreans who were searching for a new hope, who were seeking the meaning of life at a time of foreign rule. Church leaders preached that Japan's seizure of Korea did not signify that God had forsaken the Koreans, but that He wanted them to repent of their sins and undergo a period of tribulation. In other words, they demanded a total separation from the previous Confucian values and practices and the beginning of a pietist life with hope as the most important prerequisite for the coming of the promised Messiah. This was the central theme in the revival meetings they led. Therefore, historians should ask why Korean Christians used such otherworldly symbolism, and what it meant to them during the colonial period, rather than understanding this theology literally.

Kil Sŏnju's theological language and symbolism should be understood in relation to his life and the times in which he lived. Born into a poor family in 1869, Kil began his education in Chinese classics in a *sŏdang* (traditional elementary school) according to the convention of the time. He had to cut his education short to support his family by keeping a small store, which did not succeed. He then retreated to the mountains for some soul-searching, as young men of the time frequently did before deciding what career to pursue. He became afflicted with a serious eye problem which plagued him throughout his life. Such were his circumstances when he embraced Protestant Christianity. By 1902, he had been named an elder of a Presbyterian church; in 1907, he graduated from P'yŏngyang Presbyterian Theological Seminary and was ordained as a minister. The Reverend Kil became one of the most successful revivalist preachers in the Korean Protestant church during the great revival movement. His personality inspired sympathy and trust, and he consecutively occupied various leadership positions in church politics. He died in 1935 while delivering a sermon.[35]

Kil Sŏnju, a most otherworldly preacher, was also active, with An Ch'angho, in non-church political organizations such as the P'yŏngyang branch of the Independence Club.[36] His first son, Kil Chinhyŏng, who was presumably influenced by his father's concern with social issues, was also very active in nationalist movements, including the New People's Association. Kil Chinhyŏng died young from imprisonment and severe torture.[37] Kil Sŏnju was one of the thirty-three signatories to the Declaration of

Independence in 1919. When the Korean Youth Association (Sinhan ch'ŏngnyŏndang) in Shanghai, China, secretly dispatched Sŏnu Hyŏk to Korea, the first person he met was Kil Sŏnju, because he was the foremost church leader at the time. Sŏnu persuaded him to initiate a mass demonstration through church organizations. Kil readily accepted and exercised his good offices to organize a secret meeting with other church leaders. Sŏnu and other nationalists could not ignore Kil. He readily became one of the earlier "political ministers" in Korea. Members of the Kil family indeed were politically active Christians against foreign rule at the time.[38] The confluence of religion and politics in Kil's life clearly shows that the revival movement he led was not simply religious escapism and that the millenarian and eschatological theology behind it was not apolitical at all.

A number of articles in *Taehan maeil sinbo* [Korea daily news], a newspaper closely related to the church community, clearly indicate Protestants' inclination during the revival movement toward action to change this world. One article read:

> If we hold God to be supreme, if we set Christ over us as commander-in-chief and press on with courage, the Spirit our sword, faith our shield, who would refuse to plead guilty and who would defy our orders?[39]

In the church, Christians would spend days at a time sharing these religious yet political themes. Soon after the revival movement, the Protestant church became the most cohesive Korean community, organizationally as well as emotionally.

A Sunday school lesson from the early colonial period shows how these Christians interpreted biblical passages and how they perceived the colonial reality. The Protestant church taught that "God, with his power, saved the people of Israel from suffering and enslavement, and made them the people who enjoyed glorious freedom." In other words, God, whom these colonized Christian Koreans believed was "the Savior," was the one who liberated Israel from Pharaoh. This Sunday school lesson stated that:

> Egypt is the shadow of the power of sin just as Japan represents a symbol of evil in their [the Koreans'] situation. Just as the people of Israel got acquainted with the power of evil and sin, the Korean people are learning about the nature of evil; just as the people became aware of God, the Korean people are getting to know God; and this is one of the strong reasons they preach the Gospel to the people of Korea, because they know

> about the God who is just and powerful. Thus Christian belief, for Korean Christians, is the power with which the people can be saved. Just as the people of Israel prospered because of God's help, the Korean people can prosper even under Japanese rule, if God helps. . . . The Book of Exodus teaches that the enemy of justice persecutes the people of God and oppresses them, but it cannot ruin the witness to the truth, nor can it prevent it.[40]

Korean Christians had thus began to perceive colonial reality through biblical symbols. They identified their painful reality with that of Israel's bondage in Egypt, and longed for the liberation Israel had won. The people of Israel banded together under Moses' leadership believing firmly in the promise of Yahweh and thus finally attaining freedom from Egyptian rule through the Exodus. Likewise, if Koreans were to unite in a firm belief in God as their spiritual savior and political liberator, no one could ruin their community, "even under Japanese rule," and finally Korea would experience a figurative exodus from Japan. Korean Christians became more cohesive by sharing this revival theology.

The revival movement was a collective religious experience: people stayed together for several days and nights, singing hymns, praying, and studying the Bible.[41] Korean Christians not only shared biblical teachings, but also gained a sense of togetherness through the revival movement. The Protestant church, soon to become the largest organized Korean community, now came to have an ideologically as well as emotionally cohesive membership.[42] For this reason, the Japanese colonial authorities never relaxed their vigilance over the Protestant Christian community; no other major religion, such as Confucianism or Buddhism, ever came under similar scrutiny. At the time Arthur J. Brown commented:

> As the Japanese police note the multitudes of Christians flocking to the churches, they irritably wonder why these Christians met so often and what they were doing. . . . Their suspicions were roused as they heard the great congregations sing with fervor such hymns as: "Onward, Christian Soldiers, Marching as to War!" "Stand Up, Stand Up for Jesus, Ye Soldiers of the Cross!" . . . and then listen to a stirring sermon which perhaps personified the forces of evil in the heart, as Paul did, and summoned the believer to cast them out. One of the missionaries, Mr. George S. McCune, . . . expounded the narrative of David and Goliath, emphasizing the conventional lesson that the weak man whose cause is just and

> whose heart is pure can overcome the strongest. This was promptly reported to the authorities as treasonable, since Mr. McCune must have intended to teach that David symbolized the weak Korean and Goliath the strong Japanese. One pastor is said to have been arrested because he preached about the Kingdom of Heaven; he was told that there was "only the kingdom of Japan." The Japanese police in Korea got it into their heads that the great organization of the Korean church was the hotbed of revolutionary opportunity, and they jealously watched it. The so-called "Million Evangelistic Campaign" in 1910 and 1911 intensified these suspicions. . . . [They] feared that such an enormous reinforcement would make the leaders of the church overshadow the [Japanese] civil authorities still more. The police accordingly redoubled their activities.[43]

The revival theology born in the historical context of colonization played an influential role in nationalist politics as a theology of hope, at least in the early colonial period.

Followers of revival theology actively participated in Korean nationalist activities such as the Educational Society of Hwanghae Province (Haesŏ kyoyuk ch'onghoe), the New People's Association (Sinminhoe), and the March First Movement of 1919. Above all, their participation in the March First Movement of 1919 clearly tells us that they were not at all otherworldly escapists. Kil and other revivalist church leaders became "political ministers" for Korea's independence, not just spokesmen for their religious beliefs. As a radical socialist described it, the Protestant Christianity of the revival movement was "not a mere spiritual religious institution" but would be "the mother of Korean independence."[44]

One should consider the revivalists' theological rhetoric together with their political action. They taught an apocalyptic eschatology that gave the colonized Christian Koreans hope and meaning for living. Furthermore, they identified the time the promised Messiah would come to build a paradise with the time of national independence. Christian Koreans, who had longed for "the time" or "the day," took the 1919 uprising as "the day" that was "rarely given" by God and vigorously participated in it—believing that to do their "part" was "an order" from God the liberator.[45]

In the second half of the colonial period, however, this otherworldly theology no longer functioned strongly as a political impulse for the independence movement against Japan. Rather, it came to weaken or block political activism in the Protestant church community. As we have seen, theology played a major role in Christian activism for reform and independence by providing them with an alternative value system, consolation, political symbols, and a romantic, optimistic vision for a "paradise" in their land. After the March First Movement, the same theology became in fact a type of religious escapism and lost its strong political coloration.[46]

Post 1919: The Shift from Political to Personal "Liberation"

Many factors combined to bring about the transformation in the political role of the otherworldly theology. First of all, in the wake of the abortive uprising of 1919, a general tenor of disillusionment, frustration, and despondency set in. As we have seen, Koreans placed their cherished desire and fond hopes in the uprising to throw off alien rule. However, instead of obtaining national independence, they brought on violent suppression, from which they suffered severely. The "fervor that once spurred them on" was gone, and they began to retreat from painful reality and to look for personal security and consolation.[47] Christians were among those Koreans who shared the disillusionment that followed the 1919 uprising. If they suffered from the violent suppression more than other Koreans (since they played the most influential role in the uprising), Christians also were more in need of security and consolation. Their otherworldly theology came to play a quite different but necessary role—one that gave them a sense of security and consolation. It became a religious justification for their escapist political stand, an escapist theology for those Christians who wished to avoid painful reality.

Second, as we have noted, otherworldly theology itself performed a dual function—political activism with an eschatological hope and escapism. Otherworldly symbols such as the kingdom of heaven, eternal life, and the coming of the promised Messiah could be understood in various ways depending on followers' different intentions and the circumstances in which they had to live. For example, while some believers could interpret the kingdom of heaven as a paradise to reach toward on earth, others could take it as a paradise to follow this worldly life. While some could take the exodus from Egyptian rule as a political liberation from foreign oppressors, others could interpret it simply as a spiritual salvation from a sinful world. Korean Christians generally took this otherworldly theology as a secular and political, as well as a spiritual, teaching in the early colonial period. However, they tended to interpret it solely in spiritual terms in the second half of the colonial period, when they looked for consolation and security in the present world.[48]

Third, a change in the socioeconomic position of Korean Christians, especially church leaders, occurred after 1919. As we will see in the next chapter, church leaders, who were formerly common people or alienated *yangban*, came to establish their position in society as a "cultural class" (*munhwa kyegŭp*) of clergymen, church-related schoolteachers, and functionaries in other church agencies. They even attained social and political prestige by leading a variety of educational, social, and political movements, such as the Independence Club, educational campaigns, and, most of all, the March First Movement. Members of this so-called cultural class suffered the most following the 1919 uprising. By the 1920s, they were seeking security rather than risking political action, which would destroy their means of making a living and their established position in society. In other words, this cultural class, which numbered some five thousand by the mid-1920s, formed an interest group that tended to protect their position in society. They made good use of this otherworldly theology not only for psychological consolation, but also for justifying their moderate political stand during the late colonial period.[49] As their followers' social position and intentions changed, their otherworldly theology came to function almost as a religious escapism. Having once made good use of this theology in their political activism, this cultural class utilized it to justify their political inaction after the March First Movement.

After 1919, the Protestant church, criticizing its previous activism on behalf of reform and independence, devoted itself solely to religious activities and spiritual preparation for salvation in the afterlife. In so doing, the Protestant church came to function as a political community by default in that it supported the colonial reality simply by taking no action at all. This metamorphosis was clearly discernible in the so-called political ministers such as Kil Sŏnju, Chŏng Ch'unsu, and Kim Insŏ, who had previously been active in social and political movements. As Kil, for example, avoided controversial issues after the 1919 uprising, his otherworldly theology, previously oriented to a political activism, became a religious rhetoric of escapism.[50] The Reverend Chŏng Ch'unsu, one of thirty-three signatories to the Declaration of Independence in the 1919 uprising, came to criticize the church's involvement in social and political activities, as did Kim Insŏ, an influential church journalist and a former political prisoner. Kim not only criticized the church's participation in nationalist politics, but also rejected even its moderate activities such as educational and social services. "Do you follow Christ for a nationalist cause?" he asked. "Leave him!"

"Do you follow Christ as a means to improve society? . . . Forsake Him!" he warned. He argued that "one who loves his nation more than Christ is not fit for Christ."[51]

Although this conformist position under the Japanese occupation prevailed in the Protestant church community in the second half of the colonial period, there were also those who took the otherworldly theology differently. In the late 1930s, they inherited the political activism of their predecessors as they rejected Japanese-mandated Shinto-shrine worship.[52] Since we will discuss this subject in chapter five, it is sufficient here to mention briefly. The Korean church was officially forced to accept Shinto-shrine worship in 1938, but some church leaders in the otherworldly fundamentalist faction, such as Chu Kich'ŏl, Han Sangdong, Yi Kisŏn, and Pak Hyŏngnyong, chose to organize their followers against it. These otherworldly and apocalyptic church leaders rejected the Japanese nationalistic religion and even organized a religious and political campaign against it. In this sense their theology should be regarded as a theology of hope or a political theology.

In sum, if one understands this otherworldly theology during the colonial period solely in terms of textual analysis, it might seem purely escapist. But the conduct of some of its believers shows that it was also a theology of political action, at least in the early colonial period and to some extent later. As we have seen, Protestant Christians perceived the colonial reality by identifying symbolically with the history of Israel, and thus never lost hope for a figurative "exodus" from Japan. Through this religious symbolism and the revival movement, the Protestant church continued to be the largest cohesive Korean community. The otherworldly fundamentalist Christians actively participated in nationalist movements.

Nevertheless, this otherworldly theology came to function clearly as religious escapism in the late colonial period, for the social position of its followers, especially the church leaders, had changed. Church leaders, who suffered the most both physically and psychologically from the violent repression that followed the 1919 uprising, came to feel a threat to their established position as a cultural class. They tried to protect their personal and group interests by avoiding controversial issues. They made good use of the otherworldly theology to justify their apolitical, purely religious stance for security in this world. In other words, they assumed this-worldly political conformity as much as an otherworldly escapism. Although the anti-Shinto-shrine worshipers in the late 1930s inherited the tradition of political activism associated with otherworldly theology, most Protestant church leaders tended to avoid activist politics in the second half of the colonial period.

LATE PIETIST FUNDAMENTALISM IN SOUTH KOREA

Fundamentalist Theology Challenged

There was no change in the Protestant church's theological outlook after the liberation of 1945; it held to its fundamentalist tenets as firmly as ever. In 1953, Pak Hyŏngnyong, the most prominent fundamentalist theologian at the time, said in his address on assuming the presidency of the Korean Presbyterian Theological Seminary in Seoul:

> In response to the surge of theological self-awareness now sweeping through our church, we will press forward with building a theology befitting the Korean church. By building a theology I do not mean that we should seek to establish some new theological system. Far from it. What I mean is the kind of theology that preserves the orthodox faith of the apostles, the theology we accepted seventy years ago when our church was established. This means that this theology should be made secure for good as belonging to our church.[53]

Ten years later he gave the same message in the preface of his major theological treatise:

> The true intention of the author is to accept orthodox Calvinist theology and pass it on, not to create something else. For it is the author's cherished desire to pass on to the new generation the correct theology, just as Western missionaries brought it to this land eighty years ago.[54]

Pak's desire was not to establish a new theological system but to deliver intact to the new generation "the correct theology"—that is, the pietist fundamentalist theology that missionaries taught in the late nineteenth century. That students taught by Pak in the largest denominational seminary came to embrace fundamentalist theology was only to be expected. Most Korean clergymen were theologically influenced by Pak, either as his students or as his fellow ministers.

After the liberation from Japan, however, the fundamentalists could not immediately control the only Presbyterian seminary existing at the time, the Chosŏn Theological Seminary (Chosŏn sinhakkyo). This seminary had been established in Seoul by a small number of liberal theologians in 1940 after the fundamentalists closed the P'yŏngyang Presbyterian Theological Seminary in 1938 because of its campaign against Shinto worship. The fundamentalists had been imprisoned or exiled in the early 1940s. Coming out of prison or exile after the Liberation, however, they attempted to take over control of theological education from the liberal theologians. Using their personal popularity and reputations, which were unstained by cooperation with the Japanese because of their exile and religious purity, these fundamentalists maneuvered to take back the institution for theological education, which liberal non-northwesterners controlled. The northwesterners were not happy with the Chosŏn Theological Seminary, whose influence was growing. Church leaders mostly from the northwest began to attack the Chosŏn Seminary faculty. In church politics, control of the seminary was important, not only because the controlling group could influence the theological orientation of future clergymen but also because seminary teachers could establish personal ties with the new generation of church leaders. Although the northwesterners held hegemony in church politics at the time, they saw a dark future unless they took back the seminary. They could not rest until they saw the old P'yŏngyang Presbyterian Theological Seminary fully restored in Seoul under their control so that their fundamentalist orientation would prevail in the South Korean churches. They maneuvered to take over the Chosŏn Theological Seminary or to withdraw the denominational certification from it and then found a new seminary.

In April 1947, fifty-one students at the Chosŏn Theological Seminary submitted a petition for the creation of a fundamentalist seminary, accusing some faculty members of being excessively liberal:

> The Old and New Testaments are the works of God, providing the only infallible law to govern our faith and deeds. . . . Afire with the sense of having been called, we have been studying the Bible and theology at the Chosŏn Theological Seminary for more than a year. . . . But now we find our faith from our childhood days and our view of the Bible shaken down to the foundations. . . . We deplore modern theological thought and higher criticism. We refuse to have anything to do with liberal theology and rational theology.
>
> The [faculty] try to defend higher criticism and liberal theology as not weakening faith, but what's the use of this when in fact faith is being destroyed? Because of such trends in thought, the age is gradually headed for faithlessness. . . . Therefore, even if the whole world is swept along

> by the current of liberal theology, we will not be ashamed to challenge the world as warriors of pure evangelism.[55]

This petition criticized the liberal view of the Scriptures held by Chosŏn faculty such as Kim Chaejun and Song Ch'anggŭn. Most of the faculty members indeed taught higher criticism and rational theology, which they had learned in Japan or the United States. The liberal theology, called *sin sinhak* (new theology) or *kŭndae sinhak* (modern theology) in Korea, originated in the eighteenth-century Enlightenment in Europe. It is difficult to define liberal theology because it did not advocate a new creed or doctrine. It was a "fluid theology" that questioned the credence of the fundamentalist theology and the meaning of the traditional Christian creed in the new era of science and rapid social change. Liberal theology was characterized by the use of scientific, historical, and social methods in understanding Christianity and the Bible as it attempted to adjust Christianity to the needs of human beings in a changing society. Not only did liberal theologians argue that the Bible should be understood historically (scientifically), not literally, they also declared that it should be reinterpreted for solutions to a variety of secular problems facing humans. They believed in the Bible's symbolic value.

The fundamentalists responded by defending the traditional faith against the liberal theologians. They believed that the Bible was literally inspired by God and totally free of error or deviance, that it allowed no room for variant interpretation or free criticism; different views of the Bible were not deemed appropriate subjects for academic pursuit. They also criticized the liberal theologians for attempting to adjust their religion to the needs of the new age by liberalizing their theology and emphasizing the social aspects of the Bible.[56]

Ever since Protestant Christianity reached Korea late in the nineteenth century, fundamentalist theology had been the official theology of the Korean Presbyterian Church, the largest Protestant denomination in Korea, and no one had challenged it seriously.[57] After the fundamentalists closed the P'yŏngyang Presbyterian Theological Seminary in 1938, the Chosŏn Theological Seminary became the only seminary to produce clergymen for the Presbyterian Church. Through this seminary liberal theology began to take root in the Korean Presbyterian Church, and liberal theologians increased their influence.[58]

Pak Hyŏngnyong, former faculty member at the P'yŏngyang Seminary, was the prime mover among the northwesterners who maneuvered to found a new fundamentalist seminary or to take over the Chosŏn Theological Seminary from the liberal theologians. His intentions were displayed in his five principles issued by the Christians released from prison (*ch'urok sŏngdo*) in 1945. It was in this context that fifty-one students of the Chosŏn Theological Seminary submitted their previously mentioned petition for the creation of a fundamentalist seminary in 1947.[59] It is difficult to determine whether the fundamentalists from the northwest incited those students, as Kim Chaejun claimed, because such plots usually occurred behind the scenes. In any event, Pak and other fundamentalists used this petition to attack liberal theologians at the Chosŏn Seminary and to make public their intention to recapture the seminary or to withdraw its certification.[60] Here again the great theological controversy between the fundamentalist majority and the liberal minority took the form of the personal contest between Pak Hyŏngnyong for the fundamentalist camp and Kim Chaejun for the liberal group.[61]

We can gain great insight into late pietist fundamentalism in South Korea by considering the life and thought of Pak Hyŏngnyong. A native northwesterner, Pak had studied under fundamentalist missionaries in mission schools such as Sinch'ŏn School and Sungsil College. He then attended Chinling College in Nanking, China, Princeton Theological Seminary, and the Southern Baptist Theological Seminary in Louisville, Kentucky. After returning to Korea, he became a faculty member at the P'yŏngyang Presbyterian Theological Seminary, where he became the leading fundamentalist theologian of the Korean Presbyterian Church. As a student at Princeton, he had observed the fundamentalist-liberal controversy in the late 1920s. He was a follower of radical fundamentalist theologians such as J. G. Machen, Charles Hodge, and B. B. Warfield. Pak even has been called "the Machen of Korea." He became the leading fundamentalist critic of liberal theology in Korea, using the same theological rhetoric and method that American fundamentalists used. He later became president of the Koryŏ Presbyterian Theological Seminary in Pusan, the Presbyterian Theological Seminary in Seoul, and the Ch'onghoe Theological Seminary in Seoul. He passed away in 1979, leaving twenty-two volumes of writings, most of them examining other theological opinions and denouncing liberal theological views.[62]

Along with the earlier fundamentalist Christians, Pak was also active in the reform and independence movements. As a student at Sungsil School in P'yŏngyang, he led student movements to enlighten youth and farmers. He was even arrested by Japanese authorities because of his political sermons against foreign rule. Most of all, he became a "political minister," opposing Shinto-shrine worship and being exiled to Manchuria in the late 1930s, whereupon he relinquished his professorship at the P'yŏngyang Presbyterian Theological Seminary, his only means of livelihood.[63] After Liberation, however, he spent all his energy defending fundamentalist theology and turned away from his previous concern with social and political problems.

In the twenty-two volumes of his work, one can readily identify his two major concerns: his fundamentalist belief in the Bible as the literal and infallible word of God, a theme modern higher criticism tended to undermine, and his militant defense of traditional Christian doctrine, which liberal theologians tended to adjust to human needs in a rapidly changing industrial society. In other words, he opposed all the liberal trends that began to appear during the Enlightenment and were accelerated by advances in science. His intention was not to establish a new theological system but to preserve the old theology and deliver it to the new generation.[64] He was radical, and his method was clear and simple. His favorite apology for fundamentalism had to do with the original Greek meaning of the word *orthodoxy* (right opinion) in contrast with word *heterodoxy* (other, different opinion). He argued that since there can be only one "right opinion," any other opinion was bound to be wrong and heretical.[65] In other words, he tried to make the Korean church return to the beliefs introduced by American fundamentalist missionaries in the late nineteenth century—denouncing the liberal trends that Kim Chaejun and his Chosŏn Theological Seminary colleagues had brought to Korea.[66]

Pak condemned David Strauss and Ernest Renan, who in the late nineteenth century began to interpret Jesus as a great human being and historical figure, but not the Son of God. Pak was particularly harsh on the German Romanticist school, represented by Friedrich Schleiermacher, for turning Christian dogma into interior experience. Schleiermacher stressed individual meditation and self-consciousness, which would lead to union with God, and repudiated the traditional view that Christian theology consisted of a number of fixed doctrines that must be accepted on faith. Union with God, he claimed, is obtained not by dogmatic ideas but by the individual feeling of dependence on God. This individual, subjective union with God could not be criticized or judged on the basis of fixed doctrines. Since this subjective union with God could differ from person to person, there would be different experiences or feelings. Thus began a theology of tolerance.[67] After

Strauss, Renan, and Schleiermacher, there appeared a variety of theological views that differed from fundamentalist doctrines. But Pak believed that the truth revealed in the Bible was infallible and immutable. Any new interpretation arising from advances in knowledge and understanding of the origins of the Bible and the concept of the Son of God was a deviation from truth, a wrong opinion—and wrong opinion posed a genuine threat to the Christian faith.[68]

Emil Brunner, Martin Buber, Rudolf V. Bultman, Paul Tillich, Reinhold Niebuhr, and Dietrich Bonhoeffer all came under fire from Pak for their endeavors to "demythologize" the Bible and their belief in taking biblical truth existentially, socially, culturally, and politically rather than literally. Twentieth-century theologians such as Harvey Cox, P. Van Buren, and John Robinson were, of course, not spared either.

Pak's criticism of Cox and Robinson is particularly pertinent to an understanding of his fundamentalist theology. In *The Secular City,* Cox urged an about-face in the traditional concepts of the church and theology, which were concerned only with individual salvation. Developments in modern science and technology had brought far-reaching changes in society. If the church's chief concern was the salvation of humanity, Cox argued, it should be concerned with people and society. The church should set up a new mission to guide people in this changing society. It was time, he argued, that Christians become more concerned with the here-and-now than with the afterlife. Cox's theology of today was to be "the theology of social change."[69] Robinson, for his part, advocated an "incarnational theology" in his extremely controversial book *Honest to God*. The way to know God was through one's neighbor, and the other world could be approached through this world. In other words, according to Robinson, not only spiritual salvation but also the union with invisible God could be obtained through concern and love for neighbors. Therefore, the church should divert its concern from God to people, from the Heavenly Kingdom to this world, and from spiritual salvation to social salvation.[70]

Pak felt that focusing on this world would automatically nullify the transcendence of God, which in turn would subvert the authority of the Bible and the church. Pak concluded that secular or incarnational theology was nothing but a self-serving misuse of the Bible, and that by focusing on this world its advocates lost sight of the other world.[71] Pak, a consistently radical fundamentalist, had once been committed to social improvement and national independence, but by now he had abandoned all his political and social concerns in order to vindicate his theological stand.

Fundamentalist Defense of the Authoritarian Government

Another "doctrine" of Korean fundamentalists has been that communism is an anti-Christian ideology and in turn Christianity is an anticommunist religion. Therefore, to support an anticommunist regime, they believed, was not a political activity but a religious mission. They criticized liberal Christian activism against the anticommunist yet dictatorial Korean government as a dangerous political activity, relating it to the World Council of Churches (WCC), which, they claimed, had supported leftist guerrilla activities in Africa and Latin America. Such an accusation had begun to appear by the time of the liberation from Japan, but it became a fixed doctrine before and after the Korean War. Song Sangsŏk, an influential fundamentalist clergyman, leveled the following charges against the church liberals in 1951:

> We are appalled that the Korean National Council of Churches [KNCC] . . . should have affiliated with the World Council of Churches, an organization which favors and encourages communist policies, and that the KNCC representatives attended the East Asian Conference of the WCC. Just as appalling is the fact that the KNCC has been receiving relief in goods and money from the WCC.[72]

This charge was contained in a pamphlet circulated by Yi Kyugap, a clergyman and national assemblyman, and twenty-four other Christian national assemblymen and fundamentalist church leaders during the Korean War. The pamphlet, *Kidokkyo wa yonggong chŏngch'aek* [The church and the procommunist policy], cited the USNCC's demand to recognize the People's Republic of China, the participation in the WCC of churches in communist countries, and the WCC's moral and financial support for radical movements in Africa and Latin America.

In 1958, Pak Hyŏngnyong also criticized the WCC:

> Certain church personalities from communist countries use the WCC conferences as a forum for communist propaganda in the free world. The WCC shows signs of fraternizing with communists. Some members of the WCC from communist countries have been decorated by communist governments; others are being paid out of political funds to engage in espionage full time. . . . [This organization] strikes a bargain with communism and is committed to merciless struggle, and is influenced by communist propaganda. . . . This is simply ridiculous. One may defend the WCC by saying that church representatives from a communist country are Christian

> after all, so these people may be shown kindness while discussing church affairs at the same table. But such excuses cannot hold water. These representatives are communist and they are there to take and act only with the approval of their government. How can they be true Christians? Would not the true believers in these churches in the communist country be the ones persecuted by a red regime, in danger of martyrdom and excluded from the privilege of attending an international conference?[73]

To Pak, even Martin Luther King Jr. was "a believer who often supported communist-sponsored activities." He hid behind the slogan of nonviolence, Pak charged, inciting rioting and arson. Hubert Humphrey was "an extremist liberal," and leading antiwar singer Joan Baez "a notorious communist."[74]

Such openly political polemics were music to the ears of Christians from the north who had fled south and survived the Korean War. The fundamentalists whose political interests were now aligned with those of the Seoul government used the WCC connection of the liberals to condemn them. To the fundamentalists, whether the government was authoritarian or democratic did not matter so long as it was anticommunist. The fundamentalists stopped just short of identifying liberalism with communism itself. Ch'ae Kiŭn, a fundamentalist minister working on a Christian newspaper, portrayed communism in particularly vile forms in the 1970s:

> Our church sees communists as enemies of Christ, as Satan personified; they are enemies of Christian faith. . . . One should realize that if we do not oppose communism there can be no freedom for the church or the world. . . . We should denounce the procommunist policies pursued by the WCC and let the churches of the world know of the communist strategy of infiltrating the WCC; we should not only urge the WCC to remedy this situation but also demand that all affiliated churches [in Korea] withdraw from the Council.[75]

This political charge occurred at a time when Christian liberals, who had affiliated with the KNCC and the WCC, voiced grievances against the authoritarian Park Chung-hee (Pak Chŏnghui) regime. A common view and interest soon developed between the fundamentalists and the government as both were squarely opposed to communism and both disliked liberalism and free criticism. The fundamentalists defended the government as a bulwark against the evil of communism, and the government in turn supported the fundamentalists' activities.

From a somewhat simple-minded affinity between church and government, which had occurred primarily because Syngman Rhee was Christian himself, the fundamentalists went a long way toward developing a sophisticated symbiosis with the state. Kim Ŭihwan, a popular fundamentalist theologian at the Ch'onghoe (Assembly) Theological Seminary in Seoul, operated by the largest of the Presbyterian denominations, developed a sophisticated theological justification for the ruling establishment in the name of church neutrality in matters of politics.

> In the name of patriotism the church has been making mistakes by leaving its own realm. Nor can the church in its own name involve itself in political matters. . . . The church registered its opposition, on its own behalf, to the restoration of diplomatic relations with Japan. That should not have been done. It was wrong again for the church to speak for or against the change in government. Christ's church should not become involved in politics. . . . Render . . . unto Caesar the things which are Caesar's; and unto God the things that are God's.[76]

He even claimed that the church should not have been concerned with any patriotic activity directed against Japanese authority during the colonial period.

The fundamentalists, however, did not confine themselves to criticizing liberal political activism, but developed a theological justification for authoritarian regimes. When the liberal Christians criticized the dictatorial government during the 1970s and 1980s, Kim Ŭihwan and other fundamentalists argued that the Bible teaches Christians to pray for the secular powers and to obey them. At the same time, they themselves actively defended the authoritarian regimes. For example, they argued that the power General Park held was ordained by God in order to fulfil civic rule meant for this world. Power, they said, whether held by General Park or someone else, was God's doing. The fact that power was entrusted specifically to Park, they believed, was also ordained by providence. The reasoning led to a startling conclusion:

> It follows then that Christians cannot insist only on a democratic form of government. One ought to obey higher powers, be they Roman or of some other empire.[77]

Their argument had thus come full circle. They started by calling for separating church and state but ended by giving absolute obedience to the rulers—absolute because it was in the name of God and predestination.

The government returned the favor to these unquestioning servants of the state. In the 1960s and 1970s, when liberal criticism of the authoritarian government was becoming vocal, pastor Kim Chun'gon and other conservative church leaders would conduct regular prayer breakfasts at an exclusive hotel in Seoul. On hand were national assemblymen from the government party, high officials, and business magnates. The meetings were occasionally honored by the presence of the president or the prime minister. Because the government's reputation had been tarnished by its repressive domestic policies, which included harassing liberal church leaders and interrupting their religious gatherings, the government wanted to improve its image at home and abroad by showing it was enjoying the support of the majority of Christians.

There was no change in the church's theological outlook after the liberation of 1945. What did change, however, was the church's attitude toward the political powers that be. As we have seen, the church stood in an adversarial relationship with the government under the Confucian monarch and the Japanese rulers. The religious community adapted or collaborated with the colonial power in the last several years of colonial rule, but it did so reluctantly, under oppression. During these years the church viewed Confucianism and Shinto as heathen and evil, and it intended to abolish those beliefs and to build a Christian country. Many Christians became involved in the reform and nationalist movements as activists or sympathizers. After Liberation, however, the church willingly associated with the government in South Korea. Keeping in step with the government in matters of administration and policy, the church soon became an unofficial agent of the government. The pietist fundamentalist theology that had previously bolstered the church's adversarial political stand toward the secular powers came to provide religious justification for the church's progovernment position, as well as for government policies and actions. As we have seen, Kim Ŭihwan, who replaced Pak Hyŏngnyong as the foremost fundamentalist spokesman during the 1970s, declared that people ought to obey "higher powers," whoever they were.[78] The fundamentalists even came to say that their predecessors were wrong in resisting Japanese power. Only by repudiating the earlier fundamentalists could the fundamentalists of today support the postwar government and condemn liberal activism against it.[79]

Motivations Driving Church Support for the Secular Regime

What caused this transformation in the political attitude of the church and in the political role of fundamentalist theology after 1945? Liberals have tended to view the fundamentalists as disinterested in political or social issues. They infer that participation or nonparticipation was caused mainly by theological and doctrinal differences. There is some justification for this view because most of the participants in the critical political activity against the secular powers during the 1970s and 1980s were liberal Christians and most nonparticipants—that is, those whose political position accommodated the regime—were fundamentalists.

Nevertheless, this liberal school is missing several significant points. First, these scholars do not fully explain why the earlier fundamentalists did participate in political activism against Confucian rule and the colonial regime. Second, they try to explain the motive for a complicated political action exclusively with references to theology. Yet, theology alone does not determine how a church or a Christian will react to an issue at any one time. Third, as we have seen in the case of Kim Ŭihwan, the fundamentalists were not absolutely apolitical; they supported the secular powers, whether dictatorial or democratic. The change in the functional role of fundamentalist theology in the post-Liberation era should be discussed in relation to social and political circumstances and to the position of Christians, particularly church leaders, in society and politics.

A social and political atmosphere favorable toward Protestant Christianity developed in South Korea. It began with the U.S. occupation and the emergence of Syngman Rhee, a Christian who ruled South Korea for twelve years. From 1945 to 1948, Christians, many of whom had studied in mission schools and in the United States, were appointed to military government offices. Many Christians also enjoyed other leadership positions under Syngman Rhee. In short, after Liberation, the position of church leaders in society rose in South Korea as a pro-Christian atmosphere developed. The church soon became a "political" community that actively supported the establishment, and church leaders enjoyed exercising their influence in politics and society.[80]

The Cold War, the "north-south" division and confrontation—and in particular the Korean War—made the Korean church into a strong anticommunist community that supported a South Korean government that stood firmly against communism. Just as Washington's Cold War policies shaped the South Korean regime, so the influence of American fundamentalist churches contributed to the Korean church's anticommunist position. In addition, a great number of Christians from the north who moved to the south before and after the Korean War because of religious persecution by the communist regime not only came to enjoy the pro-Christian social atmosphere but also supported the anticommunist government. The South Korean Christians, mostly fundamentalists, tended not to criticize but to protect the anticommunist government as a religious mission, and the South Korean church soon became an anticommunist church (*pan'gongjŏk kyohoe*).

LIBERAL THEOLOGY AND POLITICAL ACTIVISM IN SOUTH KOREA

The Emergence of Liberal Theology and the Establishment of a New Presbyterian Denomination

Since it did not advocate a new creed or doctrine, the liberal theology is difficult to define. As mentioned, it was a new theological trend that emerged with scientific advances and industrialization in the West. In Korea, this liberal theological trend had begun to appear by the 1930s. As it emerged, it began to raise questions about the credence of the fundamentalist theology—the orthodoxy of the Korean church. Some Korean clergymen began to question the doctrine that the Bible was literally inspired by God and totally free from error or deviancy.

Early in the 1930s, the Reverend Kim Ch'unbae wrote an article in a Christian newspaper about the biblical view of women:

> "Let the woman learn in silence. . . . I suffer not a woman to teach" says the Bible. As I see it, this is not an immutable truth but an admonition addressed to or a custom prevailing in the special circumstances of a local church some two thousand years ago.[81]

At the time, the Korean Protestant church followed the fundamentalist doctrine that women could not assume any governing positions, such as minister or elder, because the Bible, the fundamentalists believed, said so. Kim Ch'unbae argued that women should also be allowed to occupy those governing positions. In other words, Kim challenged the fundamentalist belief in the Bible as the literal and infallible word of God.

Kim Yŏngju, another Presbyterian minister in Seoul, expressed his doubts about the authenticity of the theory that Moses was the author of the Book of Genesis.[82] He and Kim Ch'unbae bravely followed the new theological trend of understanding the Bible not literally (lower or textual criticism) but scientifically and historically (higher or contextual criticism). They created strong repercussions in the Korean church, which the fundamentalists dominated numerically and politically. These two liberal clergymen were tried in the church in 1934, and the General Assembly of the Korean Presbyterian Church adopted the report on the matter prepared by two fundamentalist theologians, Archibald Campbell and Pak Hyŏngnyong. The report recommended that the General Assembly chastise the two liberal ministers, who had "interpreted the Bible in accordance with the current thought of the times," and relieve them of all church responsibilities. The matter was settled, however, when the two made public apologies.[83]

Then in 1935, a translation of the *Abingdon Bible Commentary* incurred fundamentalist ire. American theologians F.C. Eiselen, Edwin Lewis, and D.G. Downey had edited this commentary, which was based on the so-called higher criticism, and had published it in 1929. Although Yu Hyŏnggi, a Methodist theologian, was the editor of the Korean translation, several Presbyterian theologians of liberal leanings, such as Ch'ae P'ilgŭn, Song Ch'anggŭn, Kim Chaejun, and Han Kyŏngjik, had assisted with translation. The Presbyterian Church banned the translation as liberal and heretical. When the Presbyterian translators were called to account, they explained their position on an academic level, and finally submitted to the church's decision so as to forestall any escalation of the controversy.[84] The liberal challenge to fundamentalist theology seemed to end without success. With the increasing pressure following the Shinto shrine worship controversy in the late 1930s, the church was hardly in a position to carry the liberal-fundamentalist feud to a conclusion. This was not to come until after liberation in 1945.

As we have already seen, a handful of liberal theologians, assisted by a private donation, founded the Chosŏn Theological Seminary in 1940 in Seoul and increased their influence in the largest Presbyterian denomination until 1953.[85] As the sole Presbyterian seminary of its kind, the Chosŏn seminary drew many young men who wished to enter the Presbyterian clergy. From 1940 to 1953, the seminary became the cradle of liberal theology in Korea. If liberal theologians of the 1930s were too weak in influence and too small in number to openly challenge the entrenched fundamentalists, the liberals in the 1950s were a different breed altogether because they had produced followers at the Chosŏn Theological Seminary for more than ten years.

What the Chosŏn Theological Seminary stood for is shown in its instructional guidelines, issued in 1940. The liberals declared that they would introduce to their students different theories of theology, including the method of higher criticism, and that they would train their students to have their own evangelistic faith through free, independent thinking. It is clear that since the liberals had experienced the doctrinal pressure of the fundamentalist church leadership, they wished to build up their seminary on the spirit of "freedom" and "autonomy."[86] As a matter of fact, the liberals' educational philosophy posed a challenge to the fundamentalist church establishment.

Although the Chosŏn Theological Seminary was the only Presbyterian seminary in Korea, it still could not match the influence of the defunct P'yŏngyang Presbyterian Theological Seminary. The P'yŏngyang Seminary had produced clergymen from 1907 through 1938, many of whom were well established in the church, especially in the northwest. The latent rivalry between the two wings of the Presbyterian church finally flared up over the petition of the fifty-one students of the Chosŏn Theological Seminary in 1947. As we have seen, the students protested what they believed to be the overly liberal orientation of the instructional policy and theological position of the seminary.[87] The liberal wing was inspired by its strong commitment to freedom of thought, but it was at a disadvantage in the size of its following and in its organization. The outcome of this clash, as we have seen in the previous section, was the dismissal from the pulpit of Kim Chaejun, the central figure among the liberals. In 1953, he and his followers founded the Christ Presbyterian Assembly in the Republic of Korea (Han'guk kidokkyo changnohoe), a separate denomination.[88]

The controversy that was brought into the open by the students' petition revolved around the central belief in the Bible as the literal and infallible word of God, a theme modern higher criticism intended to undermine. In order to act on the students' petition, the Presbyterian leaders decided to question Kim Chaejun in a formal church trial. At the inquest Kim began with a gesture to soothe the ruffled feathers of the Presbyterian conservatives when he said, "Refusing to acknowledge the authority of the New and Old Testaments is to deny the authority of the Bible as the word of God." But he also explained that

> the primary object of the Bible is not to teach chronology, scientific facts, or ethnography. The Bible does not pay as much attention as it might to these matters; it is not without inaccuracies. . . . To insist on the infallibility of the Bible would be to repeat the folly of the monk who pronounced Galileo's heliocentricity to be a heresy. Does this mean that I

> do not believe that the Bible is without error? No, I am convinced that the Bible is without error, but only insofar as it concerns "faith and deed."... Those who are behind a literal adherence to the tradition mistakenly hold to tradition itself, replacing the role of a medieval inquisitor with the pride and stubbornness of a Pharisee.[89]

In the face of the danger that he might be ousted from the church, Kim Chaejun had the audacity to challenge a major tenet of the fundamentalists—that the Bible was free of any and all errors.

When the liberals formed a separate denomination, they made a public declaration of their theological outlook and their liberal faith.

1. We reaffirm that we reject Pharisaism in all forms in favor of freedom of evangelism and salvation through belief in the living Christ.
2. We reaffirm freedom of faith and conscience as we go about building a sound church.
3. We reject the attitude of slavish dependence and seek to uphold the spirit of self-reliance and self-help.
4. Nevertheless, we are wary of narrow isolationism; we rededicate ourselves to the spirit of churches of the world in which Christians of the whole world work together.[90]

What distinguished this group from other denominations was its openness to ideas, freedom of explanation, and independent thinking.

Kim Chaejun had been the central figure in the liberal theological movement in Korea since its emergence in the 1930s.[91] Born into a poor family in a remote village in Hamgyŏng Province in 1901, Kim had almost no formal education until he was twenty. In 1920, he moved alone to Seoul and was converted to Christianity while going through a simplified high school course. He went to Japan and graduated from the Theology Department of the Aoyama Gakuin, where he was profoundly impressed by the completely free intellectual climate. He then proceeded to Princeton to continue his theological studies, later transferring to the Western Theological Seminary at Pittsburgh. He had to suspend his studies there in 1932 because of the Depression, and returned home to teach at Christian schools in P'yŏngyang and elsewhere. In his contributions to the *Sinhak chinam* [Presbyterian theological review], a journal of the P'yŏngyang Theological Seminary, he cautiously introduced an outlook different from that of orthodox fundamentalism. He was also one of the translators of the *Abingdon*

Bible Commentary, which as noted engendered considerable theological controversy. When the fundamentalists maneuvered to take over the Chosŏn Theological Seminary and responsibility for theological education in 1945, Kim Chaejun and his followers stood their ground firmly, and finally founded a new denomination after he was dismissed from the pulpit.[92] Kim continued as the leading liberal theologian, and also became the most prominent leader of Christian political activism in the 1960s and 1970s.

The Christ Presbyterian Assembly in the Republic of Korea came to prevail among liberal intellectuals in church circles, and gradually the majority of liberal intellectuals as a whole were represented by, or closely associated with, this group. Through its close relations with churches worldwide, the new denomination was alert to new theological trends and church movements abroad and often served as a conduit of new ideas.

These liberal Christians became articulate critics of government policy and social evils in the 1970s and 1980s. Kim Chaejun, Mun Ikhwan, Mun Tonghwan, Pak Hyŏnggyu, An Pyŏngmu, and other leaders and intellectuals in the denomination, together with the new church's youth and students, actively participated in the democratization campaign directed against the dictatorial regimes of Park Chung-hee, Chun Doo Hwan (Chŏn Tuhwan), and Roh Tae-woo (No T'ae'u). They were also instrumental in opposing the move to amend the constitution to allow for a third term for Park Chung-hee and Chun's military coup of 1980, and in promoting human rights, social justice, and democracy under the of Park, Chun, and Roh regimes.[93]

While the fundamentalists spared no effort to bless the dictatorial regimes, Kim Chaejun and his fellow liberal Christians were raising their voices against military leaders and their regimes. At the same time, the liberals also criticized the fundamentalist church's lack of concern with politics and society.

> The church has thus far been looking away from society with the notion that it can preserve its sanctity by divorcing itself from the world, particularly from politics. Such an attitude has done much to corrupt democracy in Korea. . . . It is essential for the church to become an organization of strength, awakening each citizen to a sense of sovereignty and letting him speak out with the church as his forum.[94]

Contrary to the fundamentalist teaching that Christians should not be concerned with matters of government and society, the liberal Christians argued that the church could not and should not be separated from politics and society, and the church should serve people as their social and political "forum."

The liberal Christians pointed out that the distinction between the things that are God's and the things that are Caesar's is not always clear. Rather, they argued that it is in this world that the church operates in history and in society, and surely not somewhere outside it. Because it exists within a particular society, they held, the church ought to confront problems that the society forces upon it. The ultimate reason for the church's existence is to spread the gospel (multi-dimensional evangelism in a complicated society). The church should be capable of growing to meet the demands of society, the liberals argued. Since the world is the place where God accomplishes His providence, the church in this world should actively participate in worldly affairs.[95]

Kim Chaejun explained more about the relationship between the church and the secular world in 1971:

> To escape from history into mysticism, to sublimate oneself from reality into abstraction, or to retreat from the secular world into the church. . . is to take a passive direction, not a creative or positive or aggressive one. A creative spirit of love must prevail in material civilization—this is what the Christian doctrine of incarnation teaches. If poverty wrecks man we must fight poverty. If wicked power and unjust legislation warps and shrinks man we must do our best to remove them.[96]

Unlike the conservative theologians, who tried to turn Christians' attention from society to the church and from this world to the afterlife, the liberals taught their followers to be concerned with matters of politics and society in this world. The essence of Christianity, the liberals argued, is the "incarnation" in which God came to the human world to liberate people from repression and exploitation. Therefore, Christians should not only be concerned with matters of politics and society of this world, they should also try to "remove" its repressive and exploitative structure. Liberals have been actively involved in politics since the mid-1960s because they believe it is "part of the church's mission task."[97]

Social and political concerns were a new phenomenon in the Korean Protestant church community, where the apolitical teachings of the conservative fundamentalists have prevailed at least since 1945. After forming a new denomination and freeing themselves of the doctrinal pressure and political interference of the conservative majority, the liberal theologians participated in the activities of the world Christian community, particularly the WCC, and imported a variety of new and radical theologies.[98]

In the new theology, known by designations such as liberal theology, neoorthodoxy, or Christian existentialism, the human rather than divine aspect of the personality of Jesus was stressed. The gamut of Christian legend—the virgin birth, a life full of miracles, and the significance of the crucifixion and resurrection—was demythologized. Thus, Jesus was portrayed as an exemplary human being. Traditional Christian theology focused on Jesus as savior of the soul, and fostered the belief in life after death. The conventional theologians were thus concerned about the afterlife and their theologies were abstract and metaphysical. Liberal theologians now considered Jesus to be an exemplary man in history doing the will of God. It was natural that the new theologians should become even more concerned about the problems of humankind in this world—poverty, war, class conflict, racial strife, and other social and political injustices.

This humanistic theology, a continuation of nineteenth-century liberal theologies in method and perspective, came to be radicalized by new voices in the third world in the postwar years. In the early postwar years, many of the countries that were freed from colonial rule joined the United Nations and came to speak often as a group, since they shared a wide community of interests and views on world politics. The World Council of Churches, formed in Amsterdam in 1948, played a role in church circles similar to that of the UN. Church leaders and theologians from the third world also participated in the WCC and raised their shared theological views and concerns. Because of this input, both theological outlook and Christian concerns in the world Christian community were radically transformed.

The Development of Radical Theologies in the Third World

When political leaders from the third world raised their frustration and discontent with the world order established by the United States and the Soviet Union, third-world church leaders began to argue that Christianity was strongly imbued with ideas of white superiority, if not supremacy, and its theologies were "white" theologies of dominance and otherworldly salvation. Whereas the conventional (fundamentalist) theology was racist, they argued, the new (liberal) theology was one of a humanistic bystander. Together with some Western theologians, they tried to formulate a new theological system based on the perspective of the oppressed, the poor, and the downtrodden in non-Western countries. As a result, a variety of schools appeared that included political theology, theology of hope, black theology, theology of liberation, and doing theology.[99]

From the liberal school of theology these radical theologies inherited a humanistic concern about a variety of social and political shackles restricting human beings. But radical theologians argued that Christians not only should be concerned about human problems, but that they also should act to solve them. Since radical theologies were born in human anguish, suffering, and oppression, they emphasized action to remove those problems.

Consider the case of Dietrich Bonhoeffer, a German Lutheran pastor who was imprisoned by the Nazis for his political activity against Hitler's regime. He died in a prison cell at the age of thirty-nine. His correspondence from prison, published as *Letters and Papers from Prison*, greatly influenced the perspective and method of radical theologies in the postwar years. In one of his letters from prison, he also emphasized Christian participation in the suffering of God in the life of the world.

> Man is challenged to participate in the sufferings of God at the hands of a godless world. He must therefore plunge himself into the life of a godless world, without attempting to gloss over its ungodliness with a veneer of religion or trying to transfigure it. He must live a "worldly" life and so participate in the suffering of God. He may live a worldly life as one emancipated from all false religions and obligations. To be a Christian does not mean to be religious in a particular way, to cultivate some particular form of asceticism . . . but to be a man. It is not some religious act which makes a Christian what he is, but participation in the suffering of God in the life of the world. . . . [Participating in the suffering of God] is what makes a man a Christian.[100]

A famous German theologian, Jurgen Moltmann, declared that Christianity is the "church for the world" as well as the "church of God," because God works to fulfil his will in this world. The "church for the world," Moltmann argued, does not have to serve humankind in order that this world may remain what it is, but in order that it may transform itself and become what God wishes. Moltmann's "church for the world" is the "church for the Kingdom of God," which acts to ensure justice in this world.[101] All radical theologians shared the argument that Christians and churches should act to remove the human structure of oppression and exploitation and to establish a just society in this world. James H. Cone, a black American theologian, even claimed that Christianity is the gospel for political, social, and economic justice, and Christians are the "strugglers" whom God has sent to bring it to pass.[102] Going beyond the argument of previous liberal theologians that Christians should be concerned not only with their spiritual salvation but also with worldly affairs, radical theologians in the mid-1960s came to deny the theological separation of spirit from flesh and church from politics. They declared that to talk about God is itself a political discussion, because God works for the fulfillment of His will in this world. The church, they claimed, is not a place just to debate the liberation of people (exodus) idealistically and abstractly, but a political institution founded for their actual exodus in this world. Meeting God, they declared, can be achieved through participation in social and political activity by establishing the just society that God demands.[103]

The Influence of Radical Theologies on Liberal Korean Christians

As we have mentioned, the liberal theologians of the Christ Presbyterian Assembly in the Republic of Korea, which joined the WCC in the 1960s and has participated actively in a variety of conferences sponsored by the WCC since then, had introduced to Korea this radical new Christian concern with society and politics that had emerged in the world Christian community. The Korean liberals disseminated a new theological trend and a new evangelistic movement mostly through the monthly *Kidokkyo sasang* [Christian thought]. The periodical was founded in 1957 by the Christian Literature Society of Korea, which was run by liberal theologians and clergy. Bonhoeffer's *Letters and Papers from Prison*, Moltmann's *Theology of Hope*, Harvey Cox's *The Secular City*, John Robinson's *Honest to God*, and other major works of radical theologians abroad were introduced in the monthly or translated by the Christian Literature Society of Korea.[104]

This small group of Christian liberals had been banished from the conservative church establishment. Deprived of a congregation and forum, they had to look elsewhere for willing ears. Challenging the conservative line with newly imported liberal and radical theologies, they were able to appeal to church members who had become aloof to or estranged from the more conservative elements in the Protestant denominations. To justify their stand and to establish their voice in the church community, they began to criticize traditional Korean Protestantism from within the church.

The liberals eventually enlarged the scope of their attacks on the old church to include social and political critique. They began to raise their voices against the authoritarian government in the mid-1960s at a time when the parent church supported it. Consequently, non-church groups alert to injustice and undemocratic practices in society and politics allied with this liberal Christian group. It was at about this time that international church groups such as the WCC became outspoken in criticizing political and social injustice. No doubt their criticism encouraged the liberal Christians in Korea who had joined the WCC movement. In 1966, the WCC held a conference on "Church and Society" attended by representatives of the liberal church in Korea. The following year, the Christ Presbyterian Assembly set up a Committee on Church and Society to work out the denomination's social programs.[105] The timing of these two events and the phrase "Church and Society" employed in both is not coincidental. The radical theologies and social activism in the world Christian community had influenced the political activism of Korean liberal Christians.

Even prior to 1967, some Christian leaders began to believe that they could not be isolated from political events. In the early 1960s, South Korea experienced a series of political upheavals: the student uprising of April 19, 1960; the collapse of the Syngman Rhee government; the birth and downfall of the Second Republic; and Park Chung-hee's military coup of 1961 and subsequent dictatorial rule. In particular, liberal and moderate Christians, who had been exposed to the world Christian community and influenced by radical theological currents and church movements, began to raise their political voices. In 1964, they organized a campaign to block negotiations leading toward diplomatic relations with Japan because of what they regarded as excessive concessions to the Japanese. This was the first collective political action that Christians had undertaken since 1945.[106]

Liberal Christians continued their political activism for human rights, social justice, and democratization, as we will see in chapter seven. They denounced election irregularities in 1967; strongly registered their resistance to the constitutional revision allowing Park's third term as president; vigorously supported Kim Daejung's (Kim Taejung) run for the presidency against Park; called continuously for the repeal of the Restoration (Yusin) Constitution, which allowed Park to establish a garrison state and permanent rule; and fought for democracy against Chun Doo Hwan and Roh Tae-woo throughout the 1980s. These liberal Christians gradually became the core element in the so-called democratization campaign. Through these political activities, liberal Christians established their voice in the Korean church community as well as in the general society.

Their participation in social and political affairs, the liberal Christians said, was not political activism but a major mission activity. In the 1973 *Theological Declaration of Korean Christians* [Han'guk kidokcha sinang sŏnŏn], liberal Christian activists confessed that they were compelled to speak out and take action on the following grounds:

1. We are under God's command to be faithful to His Word in concrete historical situations. . . . We are commanded by God to speak the truth and act in the present situation in Korea.
2. The people of Korea are looking up to Christians and urging us to take action in the present grim situation. . . . We are urged and encouraged to move on this course of action . . . because we are moved by their agony to call upon God for their deliverance from evil days.
3. We stand in a historical tradition of such struggles for liberation as the independence movement by Christians against Japanese colonialism. . . . We are determined to seek our theological convictions from the historical traditions of our church.[107]

An Pyŏngmu, a prominent liberal theologian and political activist, has persuasively explained the background of the shift toward Christian political activism. During the late 1960s and early 1970s, as Park Chung-hee was establishing permanent rule through constitutional revision, he suppressed opposition forces, including students, some university professors, a group of journalists, and critical politicians. There was virtually no political force that could play a critical role against his dictatorial regime, even though there were frequent student demonstrations and proclamations. In such a police state, An Pyŏngmu explained, liberal Christians, who were greatly influenced by social and political theologies and by the new evangelistic movement in the world Christian community, began to be involved in political activism against Park's rule.[108]

In the 1970s and 1980s, when freedom of the press, assembly, and association were curtailed, criticism of the dictatorial government was usually raised by the opposition forces just mentioned, since they had an available, albeit restricted, forum and audience. However, the activity of these opposition groups was not and could not be a movement based on a grass-roots organization with networks for communication at home and abroad.

Their activity was limited to a series of student demonstrations and political statements in Seoul and some other urban areas.

By the mid-1960s, the political activism of liberal Christians had begun to change the nature and scope of the so-called democratization campaign in South Korea. Christian activists connected the democratic forces such as students, intellectuals, and workers outside the church to the church community, which had an incredible organizational strength. Although the church was infiltrated by government agents and its clergymen frequently subjected to harassment and arrest, it was an institution that was relatively free from government control and had a variety of domestic and international networks. The religious community also had tens of thousands of highly educated elite who could contact the people directly through regular services and in the name of evangelistic activities. This was one of the reasons why the democratic forces outside the church community turned to the liberal Christian activists.

In addition, the democratic forces outside the church, which needed an organizational network, protection, and leadership, followed the Christian liberals because the latter had a sophisticated political language and plans for action. With a sense of mission and a spirit of martyrdom, liberal Christian leaders were the first elite group to register resistance against the Yusin Constitution. They could provide young radical students, scattered intellectuals, and other democratic voices an organizational base, a political forum, and a leadership willing to sacrifice. The influx of radical theology into Korea provided an occasion for Korean churchgoers, especially liberals, to reconsider the meaning of the church, its position in society, and its relation to the government. The new theology and evangelistic zeal learned from the WCC functioned to consolidate Christian political activism in the 1970s and 1980s.

Nevertheless, that very strength of Christian liberalism also was a weakness in the peculiar position in which Korea found itself. The dictatorial government, for example, attacked the theological basis of Christian activism against the government, and in doing so was supported by fundamentalist Christians who had coexisted uneasily with the liberals in church politics.[109] Given the constant threat from the northern part of a divided land, liberal Christians were vulnerable to accusations that they were too accommodating toward or had ties with the communists through the WCC. Christian liberals thus had the additional burden of proving they were in no way allied with or speaking for the communists.[110]

Emphasizing security concerns, the government and fundamentalist Christian leaders launched a campaign to discredit church liberals, whose influence had by the 1970s grown into a force to be reckoned with. Examples of government-inspired propaganda included such publications as *Ch'onghwa wa yusin* [General harmony and the restoration] by Kim Kyŏngnae and Hong Chiyŏng;[111] *Sanŏp sŏn'gyo nŭn muŏsŭl norinŭn'ga* [What is the Urban Industrial Mission after?] by Hong Chiyŏng;[112] *Haebang sinhak kwa tosi sanŏp sŏn'gyo* [Liberation theology and the Urban Industrial Mission];[113] and *Taehak kwa sasang* [College and thought] by *Kyŏnghang sinmunsa* [Kyŏnghyang daily news].[114] All declared that at a time when national unity was crucial because of the security problem posed by North Korea and because of the need for economic growth, Christian liberals in the name of evangelism were spreading subversive propaganda in every walk of life. Furthermore, the government and the Christian fundamentalists tried to connect church liberals' thoughts and activities with communism. A *Kyŏnghyang sinmunsa* article remarked in 1981:

> Liberation or revolutionary theologians derive their authority for evangelizing urban labor from the theology of social salvation advanced by Rauschenbush, an American Catholic theologian, and Moltmann of Germany, a Marxist, both of whom interpret the Bible in terms of communist theory. Such evangelistic activity can rightly be seen as a new form of the labor movement couched in terms of Christianity. . . . The new form of the labor movement with assistance from abroad proposed to overthrow the political establishment and create a socialist society in renunciation of the capitalist system.[115]

Such government propaganda greatly influenced Koreans who had experienced the division of their country, the Korean War, and the constant tension between the two parts of the peninsula.

In addition, the government, never happy with the Christian activism against it, sought to isolate liberals within the church and outside by allying with the fundamentalist Christians. For their part, fundamentalist church leaders reasserted their theological justification for the government by maintaining that Christians should uphold church-state separation and Paul's teaching on obedience to civil authority. As mentioned, they held that Christians ought to obey the secular powers, whether democratic or authoritarian. Since the absolute majority of Christians were under fundamentalist influence, liberal activists were seriously challenged to find support among rank-and-file churchgoers. They had to persuade Christian fundamentalists that Christians had to participate in political activity against the government.

CONCLUSION

The functional role of theology in the Korean Protestant church was transformed mainly by changes in historical circumstances and its followers' social status. This is contrary to the conventional argument that fundamentalist theology has given rise to aloofness from sociopolitical issues, while liberal theology itself has been at the bottom of the Christian activism against the government. The existing views on Christian activism have been concerned exclusively with the literal content of theology, but not with the historical context in which theology functioned. Surrounded by a stagnant Confucian order, fundamentalist theology inspired social reform in the late nineteenth century. As the Confucian order began to disintegrate, some reform-minded Koreans who had been alienated politically from and exploited socioeconomically by the old establishment searched for some means by which to change Confucian society. These Koreans joined the new religion from the West, which emerged as a new source of power and wealth, and adopted the fundamentalist Protestant teachings that Confucianism was "heathen" and "evil." Early fundamentalist theology thus functioned politically and positively for the Korean reform movement at the time.

The theology became more apocalyptic and eschatological when alien powers threatened to impose their yoke on Korea, and finally Japan, a non-Western and non-Christian country, came to rule the peninsula for forty years. Contrary to the conventional theory that the otherworldly theology during the colonial period was apolitical escapism, it functioned, at least early in that period, as a theology of hope for freedom for the colonized Koreans. This millenarian and apocalyptic tone proved effective in drawing the colonized people to the church community. As a community of colonized people, the church led the early nationalist movement, and its messianic theology provided the population with a hope for liberation and a spirit of martyrdom. The theological orientation did assume a strong political coloration, not a religious escapism from the painful reality, at least in the early colonial period.

That same theology, however, functioned as an otherworldly escapism in the late colonial period mainly because of the change in the social status of church leaders. Emerging as a religious and cultural class, church leaders gradually tended to avoid a militant stand against the colonial government and to engage only in moderate activity. The otherworldly theology was used by these church leaders for justifying their changed political stand and made their followers long only for "paradise" after this world, not a promised heavenly kingdom on earth.

In an entirely different environment following Korea's liberation from Japanese rule in 1945, fundamentalist and otherworldly theology did not provide occasion for criticizing injustice, iniquity, and inequity at the hands of the government in South Korea. Instead, it came to function as a theological justification for authoritarian dictatorship. The Rhee government, supported by church leaders such as Ham T'aeyŏng, Yi Yunyŏng, Pak Yŏngch'ul, Yi Kibung, and Hwang Sŏngsu, identified itself as Christian. Many Christians indeed came to enjoy social and political influence. As part of the political establishment, church leaders tended to maintain their position as well as the pro-Christian social and political atmosphere. Fundamentalist theology functioned to bless the secular regime.

A small group of Christians became politically active against the dictatorial regimes of Park Chung-hee, Chun Doo Hwan, and Roh Tae-woo from the 1960s through the 1980s. These liberal Christians had been isolated from and finally dismissed by a church establishment controlled by the fundamentalists, especially from the northwestern part of the country. The liberal Christians, who had sought a role in the church, became free from the fundamentalists' pressure and interference after their dismissal in 1953. They freely imported new theological trends and evangelistic concepts from the world Christian community, and in particular from the World Council of Churches. With this new theological language they could justify their minority position against the fundamentalist majority. They launched a church movement that rejected any doctrinal control and advocated freedom of faith. It was a challenge to the parent denomination. The socially concerned theology and the hostile relations of the liberals with the fundamentalist majority pushed the liberals not only to criticize the parent church, which directly or indirectly supported the authoritarian regimes in the name of God, but also to register their resistance against the dictatorships on behalf of human rights, social justice, and democracy—also in the name of God.

3 / The Korean Protestant Church as a Social Institution

In the 1970s and 1980s, the Korean National Council of Churches (KNCC) was quite vocal in advocating democracy and social justice and criticizing violations of human rights, but the organization did not represent all Protestant groups.[1] The KNCC represented a mere six of between seventy and one hundred denominations and other groupings within the Korean Protestant church in the 1970s, and its membership accounted for less than half of the church's total membership.[2] More important, KNCC affiliation did not necessarily entail full endorsement of the organization's political stand by its members. Liberal ministers not assigned to a church but employed in church-related institutions such as radio and television stations, seminaries, the YMCA, and the KNCC itself were the most vocal clergymen politically. Therefore, the clerical activism of the KNCC in the 1970s and 1980s was not organizationally based on the whole Protestant church community or even the churches affiliated with the KNCC.

As mentioned in the previous chapter, most scholars have discussed Christian political activism in Korea solely in terms of theology.[3] There is some justification for this approach, because most participants in clerical political activity have been liberals, while conservative Christians have tended to ignore social and political affairs. But these scholars have not explained why most liberal churches and pastors have not participated in the political activities of the KNCC. The reason is to be found not exclusively in theological differences but in the structure of the Protestant church in Korea. It is historically true that denominations, whether conservative or liberal, have not followed political actions initiated by other denominations because relations among Korean Protestant groups have traditionally been hostile. Furthermore, conservative and liberal ministers alike have tended not to be involved in controversial activity that was not supported by their congregations. Most of all, since the Korean Protestant church became a religion of the social establishment, it has tended to avoid controversial issues and actions.

These structural aspects of the Korean Protestant church created a situation hardly conducive to political activity. To fully understand Christian political activism in Korea, it is important to examine the structural aspects of the Korean Protestant church as a social institution, including such factors as regional and denominational divisions, organizations and modes of functioning, tensions and conflicts between clergy and laity, and the upward social mobility enjoyed by many church members.

Throughout its history, the Protestant church of Korea has been divided. As a Korean organization, it seems, the church was no exception to the fissiparousness that beset the politics of the Chosŏn period. Opinions diverged over fine doctrinal points or minor differences in theological interpretation, and each group went its own way in the name of integrity and devotion to faith. The usual pattern has been that a theological or doctrinal dispute develops and the contending parties carry it on until they split into two irreconcilable groups. Fractiousness rather than cooperation and accommodation has been the rule.[4]

The Korean Presbyterian churches have always outnumbered other denominations and exercised greater influence: other denominations, such as the Methodist Church and the Full Gospel Church, have tended to follow the example of the Presbyterian Church.[5] In the Presbyterian system, church elders—not the pastor, as in the Methodist Church—decide matters of management and finance. This had a particular appeal to reformers and active nationalists in late Confucian and early colonial Korea who sought to attain a position of influence in the church. In other words, the Presbyterian hierarchical system appealed to Koreans because it provided them with not only churchly, but also social and political status. This was especially true during the early colonial period, when the Japanese did not allow social and political organizations and activities, and also in South Korea after the 1945 Liberation, when rising to a higher position in the church meant increasing one's social and political influence.

Since the elders usually have the final say in appointing or dismissing a pastor in a Presbyterian church, they exercise restraint on his performance. Korean Protestant churches were originally managed by missionaries, but by 1907, when the Korean Presbytery declared itself independent of the missionaries in church management, the voice and power of elders grew visibly. They were now the main source of finance within their church communities and leaders of opinion in society more broadly. Elders were usually chosen from among church members who had high economic and social status. The office of pastor had symbolic value because he was picked from the outside, not from the congregation itself. Should he involve himself in a dispute with the elders, who spoke for the congregation, he might have to leave the church—a situation hardly conducive to his engaging in political activity not condoned by his flock.[6]

The church's social composition, especially the social status of church leaders, changed gradually as the religious community grew. At the beginning, the new religious community was composed of a small number of reform-minded *yangban* elite and alienated commoners, but by the 1920s, it was becoming a religious community which was operated by socially and economically established Koreans. Although most members were still poor, its leaders secured positions in society as a cultural and religious class. Already in the second decade of the twentieth century, some educated Koreans regarded the Protestant church as a religious community for established individuals and labeled church leaders as a new *yangban.*[7] Under the U.S. military and Syngman Rhee governments, the once-defiant church now became very much a part of the ruling establishment, openly espousing government policy. All edges of critical thinking were blunted; what controversy there was in the church remained purely internal. The church's social and political role and meaning were dramatically transformed, both by new historical circumstances and by the change in the social status of church members.

Denominationalism and regionalism, the Presbyterian mode of functioning, and the social position of church members all combined to create a context in which liberal and conservative pastors refrained from political activity outside the church. In addition to the theological orientation of the Korean Protestant church, these structural features restricted the Christian nationalist movement in late colonial Korea and liberal clerical activism in the 1970s and 1980s.

DENOMINATIONALISM AND REGIONALISM

Soon after Horace N. Allen, representing the Northern Presbyterian Church in the United States, introduced Protestantism into Korea, missionaries from other denominations followed. These included the Methodist Episcopal Church in the United States, the Anglican Church, the Southern Presbyterian Mission in the United States, the Canadian Presbyterian Church, and the Australian Presbyterian Church.[8] Operating out of their respective mission stations, they helped form Korean churches along denominational lines. The number of denominations and sects in Korea has continued to grow. Division has become a major characteristic of the Korean Protestant church. Interdenominational cooperation has been at a minimum; strong partisanship and rivalry have been the rule since the early days of missionary endeavor.

Some have ascribed the bitter rivalry among the different denominations and groups to the fact that Protestantism was a religion grafted onto Korea, carrying with it all the differences that existed among churches in the home countries.[9] This explanation is not entirely wrong, but it does not go far enough to explain why Korean denominations have been so hostile toward one another.[10] Admittedly, denominational differences have been a feature of Protestant churches, homegrown or transplanted, but in Korea they have assumed an unusual virulence and persistence.

Presbyterian missionaries formed the United Council of Missions in Korea in 1889 in an effort to avoid duplication of missionary activity and economize on their limited resources. They later expanded this council, absorbing all mission societies that practiced the Presbyterian form of government, and renamed it the Council of Missions in 1893. The organization of the coordinating body was designed to achieve cooperation and unity among different churches within the denomination, including the Northern Presbyterian Mission, the Southern Presbyterian Mission, the Canadian Presbyterian Mission, and the Australian Presbyterian Mission. Methodist missionaries also cooperated with the Council. Not only did these foreign missionaries plan to establish one (nondenominational) church on the peninsula through this council, but they also divided the country into several regions and assigned a separate region to each mission in order to avoid conflict (see Table 3.1).[11]

Assigning missions to particular regions had an unforeseen effect, however. Churches in different regions came to have their own identities under different missionary societies. This effect began to be magnified as the church identities became colored by different theological teachings, regional interests, loyalties, and sentiments. The best illustration is provided by the schisms that erupted into bitter feuds after liberation in 1945, when positions of responsibility in the church had gained some substantial meaning in South Korea. Most of the new denominations that appeared after Liberation were formed along regional lines (see Table 3.2).[12]

Though theological differences were proclaimed as justification for secession from the parent church, aggrandizement of personal and regional power

TABLE 3.1
Comity Arrangement among Missions

Mission	*Regions*
Northern Presbyterian	P'yŏng'an, Hwanghae
Southern Presbyterian	Chŏlla
Australian Presbyterian	Kyŏngsang
Canadian Presbyterian	Hamgyŏng and Kando (Chientao)
Methodist	Kyŏnggi, Kang'wŏn

SOURCE: Soltau, *Korea*, p. 21 (map).

was often the primary motive. Referring to a dispute that threatened the parent Korean Presbytery along doctrinal lines, Kim Chaejun, who was once involved in another such dispute, pointed out that "the issue is not a surfacing of any difference in theological thought or confession of faith, but a 'north-south' fight for power in church leadership coming into the open."[13]

By the "north-south" fight, Kim was referring to the disagreement between the northwesterners and the non-northwesterners in the Protestant church. It seems that denominational division was an unforeseen effect of the "territorial division" policy designed to avoid competition and conflict within the Presbyterian missionary community. To be sure, theological arguments within the Presbyterian Church occurred among regional leaders. But such doctrinal and theological disputes masked their desire to promote their own interests and to justify themselves as leaders.

In 1907, a Korean Presbytery was established independent of foreign missions. With two-thirds of the Korean Presbyterian Christians located in the northwestern part of the peninsula, leaders from that region carried considerable weight in the new presbytery; major church meetings and activities all centered in P'yŏngyang rather than in the capital city of Seoul. For example, the Presbyterian institution for theological and clerical education, P'yŏngyang Theological Seminary (P'yŏngyang sinhakkyo), was opened in P'yŏngyang, not in Seoul. Indeed, the northwestern region was the first to accept both modern culture and Protestant Christianity. Because it was there that enthusiasm for modern education was strong, leaders from that region had led a variety of new movements since the nineteenth century, including Protestant Christianity.[14]

The northwesterners' dominant position in church politics created discontent among church leaders from other regions. In the 1930s, for example,

TABLE 3.2
The Post-Liberation Schism in the Presbyterian Church

Year	Denomination	Mission Society	Province
1953	Kidokkyo Changnohoe (Kijangpa)	Canadian Presbyterian Mission	Hamgyŏng-Kando (Chientao)
1954	Yesugyo Changnohoe (Koryŏp'a)	Australian Presbyterian Mission	South Kyŏngsang
1959	Yesugyo Changnohoe (T'onghapp'a)	Northern and Southern Presbyterian Mission	South and North P'yŏng'an South and North Chŏlla North Kyŏngsang
1959	Yesugyo Changnohoe (Hapdongp'a)	Northern and Southern Presbyterian Mission	Hwanghae North Kyŏngsang South and North Chŏlla

SOURCE: Kim Yangsŏn, *Han'guk Kidokkyo haebang simnyŏnsa.*

Song Ch'anggŭn and Kim Chaejun from the Hamgyŏng-Kando (Chientao in Manchuria) region, despite their academic credentials, were not allowed to join the faculty of the P'yŏngyang Presbyterian Theological Seminary because they did not belong to the northwest church establishment.[15] Starting in the mid-1930s, the outsiders sought to weaken the leading clique's hold or to dislodge it from a position of power, but with little success.[16]

The northwesterners' dominance was shaken in the late 1930s when the Japanese colonial government declared worship at Shinto shrines to be a mandatory patriotic rite and decreed installation of a miniature shrine on all altars. Protestant Christian opinion was divided: the "accommodationists" accepted the argument that it was a mere national rite required of all imperial subjects, while the "nonconformists" spurned the decree on the grounds that the Christian God would not allow worship of any other deity. The Presbyterian Church, led by the northwesterners, did not achieve unanimity on this question. At the General Assembly of the Presbyterian Churches in P'yŏngyang in 1938, it was decided that the order for shrine worship would be complied with, on condition that the act be regarded as a national ceremony and not as a religious act. The decision went against the prevailing sentiment within the Presbyterian Church, which was under police surveillance and coercion. But in contrast with this official decision made by the northwestern leadership, the northwesterners also closed the P'yŏngyang Presbyterian Theological Seminary and other church-related schools, such as Sungsil College and Sungŭi School.[17] Rather than give in to the Japanese, church leaders chose to close the seminary and other schools, and to go into exile or to prison.

The northwest leadership in the Presbyterian Church, which was responsible for this contradictory stand, subsequently lost its credibility. Its decision to conform to Shinto-shrine worship was criticized as unpatriotic, un-Christian, and indecisive. While the conformists supporting this policy continued to control the Presbyterian Church, the nonconformists lost their base of operation. They gave up their responsibility for leadership, even though they were praised as patriots and genuine Christians. There was thus a vacuum of effective leadership in the Presbyterian Church. Non-northwesterners such as Kim Chaejun and Song Ch'anggŭn attempted to fill the vacuum and assume responsibility. As mentioned previously, Kim and Song, from the Hamgyŏng-Kando region, in 1940 established a new theological seminary in Seoul, the Chosŏn Theological Seminary. They and their colleagues thereupon began to produce new clergymen and expand their intellectual influence and political power in the Presbyterian Church.[18] Since the P'yŏngyang Presbyterian Theological Seminary, the only institution for theological and clerical training, had been closed, non-northwesterners, especially the Hamgyŏng-Kando group, in fact assumed total responsibility for theological training in the Presbyterian Church. Thus, Presbyterians had two groups of clergymen: the older P'yŏngyang Theological Seminary graduates and those from the new Chosŏn Theological Seminary.

Soon after liberation in 1945, however, a new campaign got under way, led by some fundamentalist Christian ministers from the northwest joined with those from South Kyŏngsang Province. They wished to recapture the leadership they had relinquished seven years before. The core group included the clergymen who had gone to prison or into exile in Manchuria after refusing to worship at Shinto shrines in 1938. Using their personal popularity and their reputations, which were unstained by cooperation with the Japanese, the so-called *ch'urok sŏngdo* (Christians released from prison) argued that since almost all church leaders, including pastors and elders, had worshiped at Japanese shrines, they should undergo a period of repentance before they resumed their assignments in the church. Such disciplinary action, to last at least two months, would be undertaken voluntarily. During the suspension, deacons or other lay members would conduct worship services. Principles for rebuilding and resuscitating the church would be disseminated nationwide. Finally, they called for the P'yŏngyang seminary to be restored to train people for church work.[19]

This program for settling the matter of shrine worship was well regarded, but the way it was carried out was not, especially because the U.S. military government and Syngman Rhee ignored the issue in secular politics. Rhee maneuvered to make the Protestant church community his political base and sided with those church leaders under attack. The popular argument in the Protestant community at the time was that Christians should unite behind Rhee and other Christian leaders as they maneuvered for political power. As a result, the housecleaning campaign launched by the *ch'urok sŏngdo* gradually became a minority endeavor.

Another cause for the failure of the campaign was the division within the *ch'urok sŏngdo*. One group, composed of militant fundamentalists from the northwestern and southeastern regions, pushed vigorously for the purging of former accommodationists who were still in power. The northwesterners, however, soon joined the former accommodationists, who themselves were mostly from the northwest, and avoided their fellow fundamentalists from the southeast. They charged that the southeasterners were too self-righteous and radical to be in the same group with them. Therefore, the fundamentalists and the *ch'urok sŏngdo* from the southeastern region later founded the Koryŏ Presbyterian Church, a splinter denomination, justifying their separation from the parent Presbyterian Church as the only way they could maintain their pure faith.

The northwesterners attempted to take back control of theological education. As we have already seen, the fundamentalists from the northwestern region, who had been forced to abandon the P'yŏngyang Theological Seminary in 1938, were not happy with the Chosŏn Theological Seminary in Seoul controlled by liberal non-northwesterners (largely from the Hamgyŏng-Kando region). They maneuvered to take over the Chosŏn seminary or to withdraw the denominational certificate from it and then found a new seminary. After recruiting fifty-one Chosŏn Theological Seminary students to criticize liberal faculty members, the northwesterners and other fundamentalists themselves criticized the seminary's liberal theologians. Kim Chaejun, the foremost liberal theologian from the Hamgyŏng-Kando region, was put through something of an inquisition and his tenets impugned.[20] Finally he was ousted by the northwesterners. Kim and his followers founded a new Presbyterian denomination in 1953.[21]

Kim's ouster, however, was not the end of division. As we have seen in

Table 3.2, the southeastern group, who felt betrayed by fellow fundamentalists from the northwestern region during the housecleaning campaign against collaborators, also formed in 1954 its own Presbyterian denomination, the so-called Koryŏp'a. The parent Presbyterian Church divided once again in 1959 into two groups—Hapdongp'a (the United Group) and the T'onghapp'a (the Integrated Group). Leaders in the former group came mostly from Hwanghae Province, while those in the latter group were largely from P'yŏng'an Province. Church leaders from other regions, such as Chŏlla, Ch'ungch'ŏng, and Kyŏngsang Provinces, followed either the Hwanghae group or the P'yŏng'an faction. Some of them established small Presbyterian groups independent of the Hapdongp'a or the T'onghapp'a. The splits clearly occurred along regional rather than doctrinal lines, although arguments were invariably cloaked in theological language. The regional factions, such as the northwestern group, the Hamgyŏng-Kando faction, and the South Kyŏngsang group, divided into separate Presbyterian denominations when times were no longer favorable to them in church politics.[22]

One sees an ironic parallel between Christian factionalism and the political feuding that had darkened the Chosŏn court. As Christians claimed to act in the name of purity of faith and correct reading of the Scripture in order to acquire power and other interests in church politics, so Confucians had fought in the name of orthodoxy over fine points of ritual and ceremony in order to obtain the same goals. Christians were jockeying for church leadership positions, and Confucians in their day pursued royal favors and political power. In both cases the battle lines followed a regional pattern.[23]

Division at the leadership level led immediately to a scramble for numerical superiority in membership as a means of obtaining legitimacy and power in church politics. The favorite tactic was to send representatives from factional headquarters to local churches. It was the general rule that if a local church pastor sided with the opposition faction, factional representatives would first try to persuade the local pastor to change his position. Failing that, they then would contact elders of the church to pressure the pastor to change his position. Should exhortation prove ineffective, the congregation was incited to call for an ouster of the pastor or to divide the church into two separate congregations.[24] At this stage, the whole procedure turned into one of personal recriminations and even physical combat. As Kim Chaejun recalls:

> For public worship a minister of one's own group is sent to preside and preach. Resenting intrusion, youths shout him down. And if the person

> refuses to step down, he is physically forced off the pulpit. Among the congregation are elders and lay members in sympathy with the other group. Thus the two opposing groups go right ahead and sabotage the ceremony: one group offers a prayer while the other group will start singing a hymn.[25]

Such behavior only increased the strong hostility among the divided denominations and sects. One could not expect any cooperative spirit from them. If one denomination issued a political statement, others either ignored or criticized it.

Hostile denominationalism in the Korean Protestant community was neither a transplanted structural aspect nor simply a result of theological and doctrinal differences. It was a historical by-product of age-old Korean regionalism and political culture. Although such divisions began to occur after the 1945 liberation from Japan, their theological, doctrinal, and regional foundations had already developed in the 1930s, as many contemporary church publications witness.[26] Under the name of Protestantism, there are today more than one hundred denominations and sects; and the Presbyterian Church alone has split into some seventy denominations and groups.[27] They remain individualistic and hostile toward each other.

PRESBYTERIAN DOMINANCE

In membership, the Presbyterian churches have outnumbered all the other major denominations by two to one. The numerical edge has been consistent since the denomination first established itself in Korea in the late nineteenth century. The Presbyterian supremacy has thus been one of the structural characteristics of Protestantism in Korea.[28]

The arrival of Presbyterian missionaries ahead of those representing rival denominations meant a head start, but that alone, of course, could not have sustained the kind of prosperity enjoyed by the Presbyterians. Methodist missionaries, who came to Korea almost as early as the Presbyterians, have not been as successful, perhaps because they emphasized educational and medical work while the Presbyterians concentrated on evangelical work.[29]

Presbyterians, especially in the Northern Presbyterian Mission, operated in the northwestern region, which witnessed a rate of growth surpassing evangelic endeavors in other parts of the country. According to one study, although earlier missionaries followed similar missionary policies throughout the peninsula, the northwestern provinces were unusually ripe for

Protestantism.[30] Among the factors explaining this receptiveness to Protestant Christianity was the fact that throughout the period of the Chosŏn dynasty residents of this region had been barred from government service (though not from taking civil service examinations for appointments). This discriminatory policy effectively blocked northwesterners from the avenues of upward social mobility that could be gained by attainment of high office.[31] This discrimination against northwesterners became a major source of social discontent and frustration. For example, Hong Kyŏngnae and other discontented, poor *yangban* in this region plotted a rebellion in 1811 demanding the end of discrimination against them. Forced to fend for themselves in making a living, northwest elites were thus more alienated and independent from the central authority and its guiding philosophy, Confucianism, as we have seen in chapter one. Naturally they were more enthusiastic about the new religion that was imported with other Western ideas in the late nineteenth century.[32]

The receptive attitude of northwesterners toward Western civilization is revealed in the number of modern schools founded in the north. As of 1910, for example, there were 2,250 such schools throughout Korea, of which no fewer than 1,130 were located in the three northwestern provinces, North P'yŏng'an, South P'yŏng'an, and Hwanghae.[33] Because they were more receptive to Western civilization and accepting of modern education than other Koreans, beginning in the late nineteenth century northwesterners had been at the forefront of new cultural and social movements. In the case of Protestant Christianity, they had held supremacy in numbers and influence, as we have seen in the previous section.

The northwestern region was assigned solely to the Northern Presbyterian Mission by the 1892 comity arrangement. Churches and church-related institutions such as schools and hospitals in this region, which had previously belonged to other missions, were handed over to the Northern Presbyterian Mission. It is also important to note that the 1892 comity arrangement made Seoul, the capital city, open to all missions. The fact that the Northern Presbyterian Mission was assigned the most receptive region in the country and also was allowed to work in Seoul with other missions is one of the primary causes for the Presbyterian predominance in Korea.[34]

The Presbyterian form of church government also worked positively for Presbyterian dominance in Korea. Riding on the tide of the enlightenment movement before Japan's annexation, reform-minded youths, both noble and common in social status, desired some kind of organization by which to press ahead with their ideas. The newly formed church offered them the kind of organization and forum they were seeking. As the Protestant churches became centers of reform activity, church leaders spearheaded the reform movement. In this context, the Presbyterian form of governance especially attracted people of the commoner stratum who had been alienated from the Confucian establishment. On both psychological and political grounds, they naturally desired to have higher social status and influence. The Presbyterian church, which encouraged the participation of laymen in its management and church politics, was a good place for commoners and some enlightenment elite to pursue their political and social goals.[35]

During the early colonial period, when all social and political organizations except for religious ones were outlawed by the Japanese, the Christian churches became centers of patriotic activity dedicated to the regaining of national independence. In other words, at a time when politics and social activities were prohibited, Koreans joined the Protestant church and practiced "Korean politics" in the church community. The Presbyterian form of church organization attracted politically active Koreans more than other forms did because it encouraged the participation of lay members in its pastor-elder sessions, presbyteries, and general assemblies. Lay members who could rise in this hierarchy gained increased influence in the church—the largest organized Korean community—and the opportunity to use its organizations effectively in the larger world.

In 1945, the situation became more favorable for the Christian church in South Korea. Relations between the secular government and the church became closer than ever before. Church leaders now filled influential positions in South Korean politics and society. The American military government and the national government showed special favor to Christians, and the Protestant church was politicized to the point of endorsing the government. At that time, rising in the church hierarchy meant advancing in politics and society. The Presbyterian Church in particular continued to attract many politically and socially ambitious Koreans because its hierarchy was open to lay members. Its mode of organization continued to contribute to Presbyterian supremacy in Korea.[36]

A Presbyterian pastor usually avoids taking the initiative or openly insisting on his own views, because antagonism can quickly disturb the congregation's harmony and sometimes lead to his termination. The pastor is always procured from the outside, while elders are chosen as the church's "representatives" by a vote of the congregation. They are usually influential individuals with independent means in the community. Relations between the pastor and elders can be cooperative, but usually they are tense, because the pastor comes from outside the congregation and his livelihood depends largely on the church's treasury. Although the pastor has many avenues for independent action, such as preaching, teaching Scripture, guiding the congregation on matters of faith and conduct, and manipulating the congregation during election of elders, he is always subject to pressure and restraint from the congregation.[37]

Relations can be cooperative when both parties agree on the congregation's goals. When the Protestant churches were centers of the progressive reform movement in the late nineteenth century, a pastor who was active in social and political affairs was respected by the congregation. This was true partly because the pastor and the members were converted to Protestant Christianity for similar reasons and partly because the new religious community was cohesive at that time. During the early colonial period, pastors who were active nationalists had no serious trouble with their congregations. Instead, they were morally and financially supported by the church.[38]

On the other hand, the Christian activism of the 1970s and 1980s against the authoritarian governments of Park Chung-hee, Chun Doo Hwan, and Roh Tae-woo was led not by pastors but by the *kigwan moksadŭl*, clergymen in church-related institutions such as the KNCC, denominational offices, and seminaries. These so-called *kigwan moksadŭl* did not experience the pressure from congregations that pastors did. Even liberal pastors sometimes could not participate in antigovernment activities because of pressure from their congregations to abstain from political action.

For example, Pak Hyŏnggyu of the Cheil Church in Seoul, one of the leading participants in the clerical activism of the 1970s and 1980s, was under congregational pressure not to engage in political activity. Because he did not give up this involvement, elders and deacons began to call him "a communist sympathizer," "a political minister," or a minister not concerned with his congregation. Finally, lay leaders tried to expel him from the church by obstructing him from leading worship and even by using violence. He was hospitalized as a result.[39] By way of contrast, Kang Wŏnyong, the pastor of the Kyŏngdong Church in Seoul and another leading Christian activist of the 1970s, suddenly became a leading collaborator with the Chun Doo-hwan regime. According to a well-informed church source, one of the lay leaders in his congregation, Hwang Yŏngsi, a four-star general who participated in the military coup with Chun, persuaded Kang to do so. Whether it was the influential lay leader's pressure or persuasion, Kang Wŏnyong changed his political position.

TABLE 3.3
Laymen's Attitudes toward the Church's Political Activity

	No	*Better Not*	*Occasionally*	*Should*	*No Response*	*Total*
Number	335	687	765	140	44	1,991
Percent	17.8	34.5	38.4	7.0	2.2	100

SOURCE: Han'guk kidokkyo sahoe munje yŏn'guwŏn, *Han'guk kyohoe paengnyŏn chonghap chosa yŏn'gu: pogosŏ,* pp. 109–116, especially see p. 110.

In addition to the fact that professional pastors attempted to avoid conflicts with wealthy and influential lay leaders who were generally quite comfortable with the status quo, a majority of church members did not approve of antigovernment activity on the part of pastors. As the survey in Table 3.3 shows, 1,022 out of 1,991 church members (52.3 percent) were definitely opposed to political activism against the government. Under these circumstances, the Presbyterian form of church government functioned to weaken clerical activism against the authoritarian government during the 1970s and 1980s.

While the ostensibly democratic system of governance in the Presbyterian Church encouraged the participation of laymen in decision-making, it also had a more conservative political result because the laymen selected to those positions usually were socially and economically well established. The structure of the Presbyterian Church was one of the reasons why a minority of clergymen—those not directly under the pressure of laymen—acted on social and political issues in South Korea during the 1970s and 1980s.

CHANGE IN THE CHURCH'S SOCIAL COMPOSITION

From the beginning, Protestantism in Korea met with hostility from Confucian scholar-officials and a generally Confucian public. But since Confucianism was well in decline and could not offer any meaningful resistance to opposition, Protestant missionaries found some listeners among commoners and downtrodden people, who had not received any benefits from Confucian rule, and among some *yangban* elite who were disillusioned with the government and old values.[40] According to church historian George L. Paik, "A large proportion of the first Christians" were economically motivated poor Koreans, who worked for missionaries as "household servants, language teachers, colporteurs, teachers in schools who received compensation or salary," and mission school students, "who were entirely supported" by missionaries. The Protestant community began to find root among these poor Koreans, who were sometimes called "rice Christians."[41]

It was after the Sino-Japanese War in 1894 that some Korean intellectuals joined the new religious community. Of these Koreans, Paik once remarked:

> The victory of Japan over China made a great impression. The Koreans had respected China as the source of power and civilization; now she was beaten to her knees by the eastern islanders who had learned the arts of war and government from the West. The people began to believe that everything of the West was superior and best, and they were ready to accept the religion of the Westerners.[42]

To these Koreans, Protestantism meant a new way to associate themselves with powerful and wealthy Westerners and to reform the Confucian government.

According to Yi Kwangnin's study in 1979, many independent middle-class people (*tongnipchŏk chungsanch'ŭng*), mostly those who engaged in commercial activity, had suffered discrimination from the Confucian establishment and joined the new religious community in late Confucian Korea.[43] While it is not entirely clear what Yi meant by "independent middle class," they were probably those traders and shopkeepers who earned their living through small-scale commercial activity.

A more recent study seems to confirm Yi's conclusion for the early colonial period. In the absolute majority of cases, church members were still poor and of common social background, and received disdainful treatment socio-politically under alien rule. According to the "Catechism of Saemunan Church Members" (Saemunan kyo'u mundapch'aek), between 1907 and 1914 most church members were small shopkeepers, peddlers, unskilled laborers, or unemployed (see Table 3.4). During the period, among 363 out of 657 church members who disclosed their occupation, 84 were small shopkeepers who dealt in such commodities as soy sauce, vegetable oil, rice and other grains, and, strangely for Protestant Christians, *makkŏlli* (Korean rice liquor). Twelve manufacturers were small printing-house owners, small-scale tailors, and others. In addition, there were 62 unskilled laborers, 15 peasants, 141 students, 43 professionals, and 6 with unidentified occupations. Among the 43 professionals were 2 medical doctors, 16 schoolteachers, 2 lawyers, and 2 journalists. The rest were not strictly professionals,

TABLE 3.4
Socioeconomic Status of Members of the Saemunan Church in the Second Decade of the Twentieth Century

Merchants	84
Manufacturers	12
Peasants	15
Laborers	62
Professionals	43
Students	141
Others	6
Total	363

SOURCE: No Ch'ijun, *Ilcheha Han'guk Kiddokyo minjuk undongsa yŏn'gu,* pp. 107–113.

but served as office workers. The 294 church members who did not disclose their occupation probably were unemployed or partially employed.

Observations of church membership in the 1920s showed no change in socioeconomic composition. Given the difference between rural and urban churches, it is significant that most of the clergymen in rural areas were still poorly paid in the 1930s, according to a recent study.[44]

Nonetheless, Protestant churches had become institutionalized and were operated and controlled by paid religious and cultural professionals. At the beginning, the religious community was small and coherent. All social stratification vanished in the church, and its members called each other "brothers and sisters," displaying a spirit of unity. As it grew, the religious community came to need clergymen, staff personnel, and teachers for managing numerous churches, church-related schools, and other church-affiliated institutions such as the YMCA, the YWCA, and church newspapers. As a result, by the 1920s thousands of religious and cultural professionals had been hired by the Protestant church community.[45] In 1924, for example, the Presbyterian and Methodist Churches alone had 1,266 pastors and 1,846 church workers.[46] There were also some 3,000 teachers in church-related schools by the 1920s.[47] Thousands of religious and cultural professionals hired by the church attained respectability and a relatively secure living by capitalizing on their new knowledge and cultural occupation.

I do not argue here that the Protestant church was composed totally of prosperous individuals or that most church members became socially and economically well established in the 1920s and 1930s. The absolute majority of church members in late colonial Korea were still poor and were sociopolitically disadvantaged. Generally put, one cannot see a great change in the church's socioeconomic composition in the 1920s and 1930s. What I suggest here is that church leaders, particularly those who operated larger churches in cities, church-related schools and hospitals, and the church's outreach agencies came to be socioeconomically well-established individuals. One should sense here a metamorphosis of the Protestant church from a religious community of the poor and the alienated to a well-established religion which was distancing itself from the disadvantaged.

It was after liberation in 1945 that the Protestant church community became an apparent part of the ruling establishment in South Korea. With the end of colonial rule, the church reasserted itself without any constraint from the government. To the contrary, the American military government welcomed the participation of Christian leaders—many of whom had an American education and could communicate in English. Many Christians assumed leadership positions in almost all spheres of South Korean society. The influx of Christians into government and public circles continued until the church as a whole was integrated into the ruling establishment. Being a leader in the church now automatically carried commensurate social influence as well.

Many established individuals joined the church for secular as well as religious motives when church affiliation came to provide a social and political advantage. In the early 1980s, Kim Chaejun, the prominent liberal theologian, witnessed the change in the social composition of the Korean Protestant church. Rich and powerful Koreans filled church hierarchies as elders and deacons, and the "middle class" constituted the majority of its membership, Kim said.[48] For example, according to a 1980 church source, eleven out of fourteen elders of the Huam Church (Huam kyohoe), a medium-size church in Seoul, were college graduates (at least five among them had studied abroad). Vocationally, they included a reserve general who held various cabinet positions under Park Chung-hee, a university president and later vice–prime minister, at least three medical doctors, and others who ran their own business or held other professional occupations.[49]

As the Table 3.5 shows, church clerics also enjoyed lucrative emoluments, with the added advantage of social prestige. Nearly 80 percent of 787 clergymen surveyed indicated that they enjoyed a middle-class lifestyle. The survey does not indicate how many pastors, associate pastors, and assistant pastors responded. If we assume that many associate and assistant pastors did so, we can reasonably argue that the economic situation of pastors

TABLE 3.5
The Standard of Living of Clergymen: A Subjective Evaluation, 1982

	Socioeconomic Class				
	Upper	*Middle*	*Lower*	*No Response*	*Total*
Number	18	615	132	22	787
Percent	2.3	78.1	16.8	2.8	100

SOURCE: Han'guk Kidokkyo sahoe munje yŏn'guwŏn, *Han'guk kyohoe paengnyŏn chonghap chosa yŏn'gu: pogosŏ*, pp. 32–37, particularly Table I-16 on p. 37.

was much higher than this, because associate and assistant pastors were temporary church employees and their salaries were much lower than those of pastors. In addition, more than 90 percent of clergymen received higher education (see Table 3.6). The well-established economic and social position of pastors in South Korea was one of the reasons why many graduates of prestigious universities tried to enter theological seminaries to be church ministers in the 1970s and 1980s. As a young scholar remarked in 1994:

> These days graduates from prestigious universities enter theological seminaries through fierce competition, even taking the entrance examination twice or three times. But even if they fail to enter certain theological seminaries, there are other choices, because there are not many native theological seminaries which reject those people who are willing to pay money. Most theological seminaries enroll students far beyond the number fixed [by the Ministry of Education]. These seminaries produce the so-called sham masters or doctoral degrees (*ŏngt'ŏri sŏksa, paksa hagwi*), which the affiliated denominations recognize but the Ministry of Education does not. But this is nothing. A tremendous number of ministers come out of unaccredited theological seminaries (*mu in'ga sinhakkyo*).[50]

According to a 1984 church source, there were then 186 theological seminaries. Among them only 28 were recognized by the Ministry of Education as institutions for higher education and 57 were approved by various denominations, but there were more than 100 private institutes for theological education which were recognized neither by the Ministry of Education nor by major Protestant denominations.[51] These so-called *mu in'ga sinhakkyo* prospered and produced "a tremendous number of ministers." Socially and economically, the ministry had become one of the most popular professions in South Korea.

TABLE 3.6
Educational Level of Clergymen, 1982

	College and Above	*High School and Below*	*Total*
Number	735	52	787
Percent	93.4	6.6	100

SOURCE: Han'guk Kidokkyo sahoe munje yŏn'guwŏn, *Han'guk kyohoe paengnyŏn chonghap chosa yŏn'gu: pogosŏ*, p. 31.

Together with well-established lay leaders, these clerical leaders managed Protestant denominations in South Korea financially and administratively. The Korean Protestant church thus became a community that tended to avoid controversial issues in society.

As the social composition of congregations, especially their leadership, gradually changed from poor and downtrodden people to religious and cultural professionals, the Protestant church's position in society and politics was accordingly transformed from a major force that challenged Confucian, and later colonial, authorities to a huge organization which came to dispense a sense of security and comfort and avoid controversial issues that were not church-related. By the late colonial period, the Protestant church community thus had lost its dynamic as a social force.

PART 2

PROTESTANT CHRISTIANS AND POLITICS

4 / The Protestant Church and Early Nationalist Politics, 1880–1919

In the late nineteenth century, a desire for reform and modernization on the part of some Koreans coincided with the arrival of Protestant evangelism, and Protestantism and the progressive nationalist forces were brought together under these unique historical circumstances. The rapid growth of Protestantism at the time, therefore, meant not just an increasing number of converts and churches, but also an organizational and ideological expansion of Korean progressive and nationalist forces.

When Korea was made a Japanese protectorate in 1905 and a Japanese colony in 1910, Koreans realized the value of nationhood. What little national consciousness had been felt before was sharpened by the annexation. Throughout the Japanese colonial period from 1905 to 1945, a period in which tension and conflict was inevitable between the colony and the colonial power, Koreans constantly tried to free themselves from foreign rule. Particularly during the early colonial period, from 1905 to 1919, when they were not allowed any political organization and action, Koreans cleverly used religious communities and ceremonies for their social and political activities.[1] The Protestant church came to serve as a place for solace, a political forum, a communication network, and an organizational base for Korean nationalist activities. As the largest organized Korean community, the Protestant church exerted great political influence; church leaders emerged as national leaders; and the Western religion continued to grow rapidly as a Korean one during this period.

Examination of the social and political link between the religious community and the progressive and early nationalist forces is therefore critical to an adequate understanding of Korean reform activities in late Confucian Korea and of the independence movement during the early Japanese colonial period. Nevertheless, those who have studied these subjects have developed their interpretations without connecting events with the Protestant church community. They have failed to consider the social and political linkage between Protestantism and progressive reform politics and, later, early Korean nationalism. Consequently, historians have described what happened, and what reform activists or nationalists said, but they have not been able to explain how those social and political movements occurred, who initiated them, what social and political bases the reform activists and nationalists relied on, and so forth.[2]

The Protestant church was a leading ideological and organizational base for Korea's early nationalist movements. Therefore, an examination of the general historical context under which Protestant Christianity and social and political movements were connected will help to explain why and how the specific social, organizational, and even ideological linkages were formed between the religious community and the progressive sociopolitical movement in late Confucian Korea and anti-Japanese nationalist movements in early colonial Korea. This chapter will look closely at the Protestant church and politics between the 1880s and 1919.

PROGRESSIVE REFORM POLITICS, 1880S–1905

The Decaying Chosŏn Dynasty: Conservative and Progressive Responses

Already before the arrival of Protestantism, the Confucian monarchy of Chosŏn Korea was well on the road to decay and was beset with more problems than it could solve. The powerful *yangban* elite were fragmented into factions drawn along family and regional lines. Eventually, a small number of *yangban* families dominated the factional struggle, monopolized political power, and alienated most of the Confucian elite from the government. The majority of the elite retired in the countryside as "fallen *yangban*" and began to criticize the Confucian establishment. This serious schism within the ruling elite was accompanied by disorder and corruption in the central and local governments. One result was that the peasantry, the backbone of the agrarian Korean society, became a mere target of exploitation, heavy taxation, and social harassment by the Confucian government and the elite. Most peasants became tenants with precarious means of survival or landless wanderers who could easily join bandit groups. A series of natural disasters, including drought, struck the country in late Confucian times. This added to the hardship experienced by the rural communities. A rash of popular revolts broke out. In 1862 alone, there were some seventy uprisings.

Along with these internal conflicts, foreign powers attacked the small East Asian country in powerful waves. British, American, French, and Japanese merchant ships appeared off the coast frequently. They even briefly seized Kanghwa Island in 1866 and in 1871. Japan, however, opened Korea to outsiders in 1876. Afterwards, unprepared Korea was forced to sign a series of unequal treaties with Western powers, including the United States, Great Britain, France, Russia, and Germany. These powers increased their pressure on Confucian Korea to obtain more economic and political concessions, while aggressive foreign merchants penetrated deeply into the nascent Korean market. In this urgent situation, Confucian Korea badly needed political leadership which could initiate social, economic, and political reform, and at the same time deal effectively with aggressive foreign powers.

Two ideological and political forces appeared on the scene: the *ch'ŏksa wijŏngp'a* (a conservative group that pushed for the defense of Confucian orthodoxy and rejection of heterodoxy) and the *kaehwap'a* (a progressive group for "enlightenment"). The conservatives, who included most high-ranking government officials and traditional Confucian scholars, continued to try to shore up their sagging house by emphasizing Confucianism, while the progressives, who comprised some alienated young *yangban* elites and a small number of pragmatic government officials, attempted to solve problems by promoting modern Western civilization. The former advocated that Chosŏn Korea guard its own traditional culture and system, believed to be superior to those of the West. These chauvinistic Confucian scholars called for Western "barbarians" to be expelled. On the other hand, the progressives argued that "Westernization" such as had occurred in Meiji Japan would be the only way for Chosŏn Korea to survive. Naturally, there developed an intense ideological and political conflict between the forces of reform and conservatism. The declining royal house and the faction-bound ruling elite could neither provide leadership to solve this ideological and political schism nor initiate a viable reform effort. Without serious preparation, Chosŏn Korea was forced to open its door to outsiders.

A Sense of Mission and an Organizational Base for Reformers

In this historical context, Protestantism was introduced by Western missionaries, who were predominantly American. When the first missionaries arrived in Korea in 1884, Protestantism already had some converts and sympathizers among the progressive reform activists, who desired to adopt Western values and practices, as discussed in chapter 1. In 1884, Kim Okkyun, the leader of the reform group, asked Robert Maclay, a Methodist missionary in Japan, to open a mission in Korea because he felt it would be helpful for the reform effort. In 1885, Sŏ Chaep'il accepted Protestant Christianity, and in 1887, Yun Ch'iho also converted to the religion. It expanded, slowly yet steadily, by converting those Koreans who had been estranged from the Confucian establishment. In other words, an association between the Protestant church and the progressive reform movement developed at the very beginning of Protestant evangelism. The early Christian church community, which was composed of reform-minded Koreans, thus came to play a leading role in the progressive reform movement.

As we have seen, the early missionaries instructed Koreans in Christian ideas: their teaching was not abstract theology, but rather dealt with specific matters of daily life. Their approach to Confucianism was to denounce it as a form of paganism.[3] They insisted on the abolition of the practices of ancestor worship, such as revering ancestors at the grave site on special occasions, holding memorial services on the anniversary of the ancestor's death, and paying frequent homage to the ancestral tablet enshrined at home. The Protestants' demand that members discontinue these Confucian rites was a direct challenge to the basic beliefs of Chosŏn society.[4]

The Protestant missionaries made no attempt to arrive at a compromise with the Confucian tradition. They emphasized the difference between Confucianism and Christianity concerning social status and values. They taught Korean converts that Confucian society was "evil" or "heathen" and that it should be Christianized.[5] Not only did such fundamentalist teachings have a singular appeal for those who were eager for change, but those teachings also made Korean converts experience "a clash" within themselves and in society.[6]

In fact, every action by this new religious community was a challenge to the Confucian establishment, and a series of clashes developed in and around the religious community. Nobles and commoners, men and women, old and young sat together in one place as equals to hear sermons, sing hymns, read the Bible, and discuss matters of religion.[7] They called each other "brothers" and "sisters."[8] Before the congregation assembled in a small room, the *yangban* would confess that all people were equal before God and denounce the man-made status system from which he himself benefited.[9] The emergence of the Protestant church community in the Confucian society thus meant a serious challenge to Confucian values and practices.

Protestant missionaries taught their followers to act differently from

Confucians and to form a community distinctly different from Confucian society. The members of the new religious community were enjoined to abstain from smoking, drinking, gambling, and concubinage, all of which were widely practiced at that time.[10] The minimum requirement for church membership was abandonment of everything Confucian. Thus the early converts had to make a total commitment to face the scorn and condemnation that was sure to follow.[11] Conversion to Christianity itself at that time was indeed a revolutionary act. The early converts, though small in number, were those who had experienced a clash between the old beliefs and the new religious teachings and had finally determined to follow the latter.

Through their dogged determination to accept the Western religion and become members of a new religious community, the early converts came to have a strong sense of privilege and mission. They felt that they were social pioneers who had to initiate programs to reform a Confucian country. For example, Yun Ch'iho, a nobleman by birth and a beneficiary of power and wealth under the Confucian system, embraced Christianity soon after the 1884 palace coup (in which he participated). In doing so, he chose to face ridicule and even persecution. Out of psychological conflict he came to have a sense of mission as an evangelical as well as a social pioneer.[12] While Christian teaching did not provide specific guidelines in matters of reform, it did provide the early Christian reformers with inspiration and encouragement. The reformers' desire to overhaul Confucian society was imbued with a sense of religious mission.[13] Once accepted into the fold of the church community, the new converts felt an exhilarating sense of being set apart for a special role that the multitude was incapable of playing. Reforming Confucian society was identified with "Christianizing."[14]

At a time when Chosŏn Korea was beset with intellectual and political conflict between the Confucian conservatives and the progressive forces, it is no wonder that the foreign religion was embraced by progressives who were critical of the Confucian establishment. Progressive elements within the Protestant church now had a ready-made base from which to launch a reform movement. Their new base signified a challenge to established society and at the same time constituted a source of different, modern ways of doing things. The Protestant church also provided these progressives with a sense of mission.

All social movements need ideas, activists, and organization. The reform movement in Korea was no exception. Many historians tend to overemphasize ideas as the motive for action rather than the reformers' social background and their organizational base. In Korea, the Protestant church served

TABLE 4.1
Number of Modern Schools, 1910

Public	80
Semipublic	73
Subtotal	153
Private	1,325
Religion-related	755
Subtotal	2,080
Total	2,233

SOURCE: *Chōsen sōtokufu, Kyō hankoku kanpō*, pp. 997–98.

not only as a source of inspiration and encouragement, but also as an organizational base, because most of the reform workers were themselves church members or sympathizers. Ch'oe Myŏngsik, a reform activist, recalled that:

> There was in the Anak district only one primary school managed by the Anak Church if one is to name an organization representing the new cultural movement. . . . Christian churches were in fact the only places where Koreans could come into contact with new Western culture, and thus where people could readily assemble for meetings.[15]

Because there were virtually no civic organizations for reform endeavors and also because many reform activists were members of the religious community, enlightenment ideas spread naturally throughout churches, church-operated schools, and other institutions affiliated with the church. These religious institutions were also meeting places and training agencies for reform activists.

One significant achievement of the time was the establishment of Western-oriented schools. As Table 4.1 shows, in 1910 there were 153 public and semipublic schools compared to 2,080 private schools (755 of the latter were church affiliates).[16] According to a recent study, many of these non-church-affiliated private schools were founded by native Christians on the model of, and with stimulation from, successful church-related schools.[17]

The organizational strength of the Protestant church is indicated by the number of its churches on the peninsula. In 1910, the twenty-fifth year after the opening of its mission, the Presbyterian denomination alone had 687 churches.[18] If churches of other denominations, such as Methodist, Anglican,

Baptist, and Holiness, are included, the number is even larger. Churches, schools, hospitals, and other church-affiliated institutions such as church newspapers and periodicals, the YMCA, the YWCA, and the Christian Literature Society had more than just religious or educational significance. Church members and organizations should be included in assessing the political strength of the reform movement.

These church organizations and institutions criticized Confucian values and practices and spread new ideas and practices throughout the church community. The status system was denounced and the idea that all people are equal before God was taught. It was through the Protestant church, for example, that Korean women took a momentous step forward. At the time of the arrival of Christianity in Korea, strict segregation of women was the social convention. Women were not even free to be seen on the streets. Now women were admitted to the church, where they could sit in plain view of men, and girls were allowed to go to mission schools.[19]

The curriculum of mission schools included such liberal arts and sciences as history, geography, English, mathematics, physics, and chemistry.[20] But the long-range goal of missionary education was to liberate Koreans from the Confucian status system. As Henry G. Appenzeller, missionary and founder of Paejae haktang, a mission school in Seoul, noted in 1892, missionaries did not aim to produce technical men in their schools, but desired to educate Koreans to be free and independent so they could initiate something for themselves and society.[21] The new education went a long way toward loosening the rigidities of a status-based society.

Protestant groups also played the role of training agencies for activists. Members were encouraged to participate in a variety of special activities, such as debating or speech meetings.[22] Through these activities not only were they awakened politically, they also learned democratic procedure. For example, in 1896 students of the Paejae haktang formed a student society, the Hyŏpsŏnghoe, with the guidance of Sŏ Chaep'il.[23] This society, which had only 13 members in 1896, grew to some 200 members within a year.[24] The society had a debating group that met every Saturday to discuss topics such as Korean writing in mixed script, educating wives, sisters, and daughters, freeing slaves, making roadside speeches to the public, and refraining from getting married until the age of twenty.[25] Although these topics themselves influenced participants, through such programs they learned the art of public debate and public address. These political techniques were not limited only to the Paejae haktang. They were practiced in all churches and mission schools at that time.[26]

In the church, early converts were urged to lead prayers, to read aloud from the Bible before the congregation, to conduct worship, and to participate in a variety of church activities. The secret ballot was introduced, and orderly discussion was practiced. Even for minor matters such as repairs to church buildings, church members formed committees composed of missionaries and "elected" Korean converts to make decisions.[27] These were the beginnings of democratic procedure that had not been known in the pre-Christian period. Church members came to be concerned with matters of politics and society through such activities. Henry M. Robert's *Pocket Manual of Rules of Order for Parliamentary Assemblies* was translated in 1898 to meet the demand for this new political training in the Protestant church community.[28] Whether *yangban*, *sangmin* (commoners), *ch'ŏnmin* (lowly people), or slaves, church members acquired new knowledge and new political training in the Christian community earlier than other Koreans. Members of the church community were trained to debate, discuss, and organize, and to lead social organizations.

In 1896, the editor of *The Independent* remarked on the values of church organizations and institutions as agencies of reform:

> [Students of mission schools] look down on those who are neither honorable nor patriotic; they realize that the strength of a nation lies in the united effort of the people of the whole nation; and above all, they understand the necessity of reforming the political and social customs of their country.
>
> A few days ago, we witnessed the procedure of the new Debating Society of the Paichai [Paejae] School students. The orderliness of the members, strict enforcement of the rules of parliamentary usage, the earnestness of discussing the question before the meeting, the eagerness of taking part in the procedure by every member present and the fearless manner in which they expressed their views were quite pleasing to the hearts of those who wish for Korea's welfare. We suggest that the members of the Council of State take a few lessons from these boys in parliamentary practices.[29]

The Protestant churches and church-affiliated institutions served as reform agencies that not only provided members with new knowledge and information, but also trained them in new political ideas and practices. Because no other groups rendered such services, the Protestant church community was the sole organizational center for reform endeavors in the late nineteenth century.

The Independence Club

In the years before Japan's annexation of Korea in 1910, the Independence Club (Tongnip hyŏphoe)—with Protestant Christians as its leading members—played a significant role as the largest umbrella organization for reform in a variety of areas.[30] The Independence Club was founded in Seoul in 1896 by Sŏ Chaep'il, Yun Ch'iho, and others upon their return from the exile that began when they fled the country in 1884. They returned as fresh Christian converts with extensive study in the United States. Sŏ Chaep'il was a physician trained in Western medicine,[31] and Yun Ch'iho had a broad liberal arts background.[32] According to Sin Yongha, a leading historian on this subject, Sŏ and Yun formed the Independence Club as a "social club" whose members included a small number of higher government officials and some prominent intellectuals.[33] The nature of this club was transformed, according to Sin, when the "*sin chisik ch'ŭng*" (new intellectual class) and the "*tongnyu ŭi sahoe ŭisik ŭl kajin tasu ŭi minjung*" (many ordinary people who shared a same kind of social consciousness) joined it.[34] The organization underwent four stages of development, Sin claimed: (1) origin as a social club of elites; (2) admission of commoners and some new intellectuals; (3) assumption of leadership by the awakened ordinary people; and (4) adoption of a program for popular struggle.[35] After the initial stage, the club became a political organization for reform. The popularity of the Independence Club movement increased greatly; in 1898, its leaders established chapters in eight cities at the request of the local residents, according to Sin's study.[36]

Sin Yongha attempted to see the Independence Club from the perspective of social history, focusing on the organizations and personalities involved. He did not rely very heavily on the ideas expressed by the reformers, as so many Korean historians did. Nevertheless, we are left to wonder about the "many ordinary people who shared a same kind of social consciousness" and the "new intellectual class." Sin did not fully identify them, nor through what cultural and intellectual agents they received new knowledge and were "awakened" socially and politically, nor why the residents in eight cities requested the establishment of chapters earlier than those in other cities. Sin's work left these socio-historical questions unanswered, because like most scholars he did not address the linkage between the Protestant church community and progressive forces in late Confucian Korea.[37]

Ch'oe Myŏngsik's memoirs help to resolve these questions.[38] Ch'oe recalled that Protestant Christians of the early twentieth century were none other than those who keenly felt the need for reform, and the members of the "new intellectual class" were many of those who had received modern education in mission schools and assumed leadership roles in the Protestant church.[39] Many "new intellectuals" were either church leaders or sympathizers.[40] As we have seen, membership in the Protestant churches was growing rapidly at the time. Although Ch'oe recalled reform activities which commenced a little after the Independence Club movement, his recollection helps establish the tone of enlightened circles before the annexation.

According to Ch'oe Myŏngsik, the Society for the Pursuit of Knowledge (Myŏnhakhoe) was organized in 1906 by a Christian activist, Ch'oe Kwang'ok in Anak, Hwanghae Province, and in 1909 it expanded into the Society for the Promotion of Education in the Northwest (Haesŏ kyoyuk ch'onghoe) for the purpose of establishing one school in each township (*myŏn*).[41] Ch'oe Kwang'ok, who had graduated from the Sungsil School in P'yŏngyang founded by the Northern Presbyterian Mission Society, contacted Christian students and youth with the help of church organizations in the province in order to form this society.[42] The society, contemporaneous but not directly affiliated with the Independence Club, deserves special mention, for the two organizations reveal a pattern common to reform societies of the time. They both attracted Protestant Christians who made up the "new intellectual class," and who were largely the "ordinary people who shared a same kind of social consciousness."

Socially and politically awakened individuals began to join the Independence Club movement in 1897, the twelfth year of the Protestant mission in Korea. They came mostly, if not solely, from the church community, because at that time church members were the only ones to practice such things as debating. In fact, the debating society that originally attracted the socially and politically awakened individuals to the club movement was the Hyŏpsŏnghoe at the Paejae haktang. It was not mere chance that the first debating society outside Seoul was founded in Songch'ŏn (Sorae), where the first Protestant church had been established.[43] Teachers at Paejae haktang such as Sŏ Chaep'il, Yun Ch'iho, and Chu Sigyŏng were either founders or leaders of the Hyŏpsŏnghoe, and they and their students such as Yi Sŭngman (Syngman Rhee), Sin Hŭng'u, Yang Hŭngmuk, and Yi Chunil were activists in the Independence Club movement.[44] Kim Kyusik and An Ch'angho, students at another mission school, the Kyŏngsin hakkyo, and their teacher, Chŏng Tongmyŏng, were also active in the Independence Club movement.[45] Thus, many awakened individuals and new intellectuals who joined or led the Independence Club came from the Protestant church community.

Furthermore, the Independence Club movement was strong in the geographic areas where Protestant Christianity grew rapidly. For example, by 1898, the Independence Club had established branch chapters in eight cities—Kongju, P'yŏngyang, Taegu, Sŏnch'ŏn, Ŭiju, Kanggye, Mokp'o, and Pukch'ŏng.[46] All these chapters were established in response to requests by local inhabitants, according to Sin Yongha.[47] The first local branch, the Kongju chihoe, was established at the request of Yi Sangjae and Chi Sŏggyŏng. Yi and Chi, leaders of the Independence Club in Seoul, were prominent Christian sympathizers at the time, but soon converted to Protestant Christianity.[48] Although we do not know much about how other local chapters were established, we do have an important clue in the regional distribution of local branches in 1898. Four out of eight local chapters (P'yŏngyang, Kanggye, Sŏnch'ŏn, and Ŭiju) were established in the northwestern region, where Protestant Christianity was growing much faster than elsewhere.

As we have seen, people in the northwestern region converted to Protestant Christianity earlier than did those in other regions. They acquired modern education and political training sooner as well. Apart from the northwestern region, a local chapter of the Independence Club was established in Taegu, where Protestant Christianity was also growing rapidly. Therefore, at least six of the eight local chapters were established either by Christian leaders (as in the case of Kongju chihoe) or by people in areas where Protestantism was growing rapidly. The P'yŏngyang branch was established by seventeen Christian leaders, including Kil Sŏnju and An Ch'angho. Kil and An addressed a gathering of some 4,000 people at the opening meeting.[49] It is reasonable to assume that the people were mobilized through church organizations and meetings in the city. The pattern of the establishment of the P'yŏngyang branch can be applied to other branches, because Protestant Christianity was also strong in Sŏnch'ŏn, Ŭiju, Kanggye, and Taegu.[50]

With a nationwide supporting community including the Protestant church and local branches in major cities, the Independence Club launched a campaign of public education through a debating forum and a daily newspaper *Tongnip sinmun*, published in pure Korean (*Han'gŭl*) with an English edition, *The Independent*. Through these vehicles, leaders attempted to educate the public about foreign interference in Korean politics, corruption and incompetence in the Korean government, a new style of education, and a radical agenda for social and political reform. The leaders initiated a popular rights movement which, they believed, would bring about a democratic political system. They even staged the *manmin kongdonghoe* (public association), a mass demonstration in early December 1898, demanding the establishment of a constitutional government, the reorganization of the Privy Council into a quasi-legislature, and the rule of law. King Kojong initially promised to put the demands of the Independence Club into effect. However, the conservative Confucian elements in government called in troops and thugs from the Peddlers Guild to suppress the mass meeting.

The Protestant church served as the main supporting community for the mass demonstration. Not only did Christians participate, but their churches and church-related schools also functioned as the primary organizations through which activists contacted one another and mobilized Christians and students for the meeting. A threatening letter issued by the leaders of the Peddlers Guild to Paejae haktang and other mission schools clearly showed that Christians were considered the "main evils" (*changgui*) among participants in the mass demonstration and that the Protestant church was behind this collective action.[51] In fact, Christians at the time frequently staged public gatherings, criticizing government policies or protesting the corruption and wrongdoing of government officials.[52] Naturally, many Protestant Christians were beaten by police and peddlers; their leaders were imprisoned; and the Independence Club was dissolved in late December 1898.[53] The Independence Club movement, a Protestant Christian political reform movement, failed.

Many Christians supported the Independence Club movement, partly because it was established and led by Christian leaders. However, the primary reason the Independence Club movement was active where Protestant Christianity was strong can be found in the general pattern of reform activities at that time. The Protestant church was the main community aiming to change the Confucian establishment and to provide modern education and new political training. In this religious community, members and sympathizers were politically awakened and trained to be evangelicals and social reformers as well. Church members were initiators, activists, participants, and sympathizers for reform endeavors before the Japanese annexation of 1910. In short, the Protestant church and Korean reform activities were interrelated in terms of leadership, membership, ideology, and organization, and their aim was to change the Confucian society.

THE EARLY INDEPENDENCE MOVEMENT, 1905–1919

After Japan established a protectorate over Korea in 1905 and annexed the peninsula in 1910, anti-Japanese sentiment increased sharply among Koreans, who tried to throw off the colonial yoke. However, it was very difficult, if not impossible, for Koreans to initiate political activism against the colonial power, since Japan administered its colony on a militaristic basis. Although the colonial government proclaimed that Koreans would enjoy equal treatment under a common law, it ruled the colonized Koreans with a strong-arm policy. In 1910, for example, the colonial government had 6,222 military and civilian police, and by 1922, the force increased to 20,771. The Japanese colonial government attempted to intimidate the colonized Koreans, as the increasing number of imprisoned Koreans showed clearly (See Table 4.2).[54] The Japanese colonial government, especially between 1910 and 1919, adopted "the hardest and most relentless form" of rule, as one Western missionary observed.[55] During this so-called Dark Age, Koreans were not allowed any political organizations or activities.

During this period of strong-arm rule, the political and social meaning of the Protestant church for Koreans was enormous. In 1928, James E. Fisher correctly observed:

> With practically nothing in the way of organized religious institutions in the country, the church, with its community organization, its opportunities for meetings, and its services, made a direct appeal to the tendency to get together, organize, and do something which seems to be universal.[56]

It emerged as the largest, if not only, organized Korean community. As a matter of fact, it served as a place for solace, a political forum, a communication network, and an organizational base for social and political activists. Because the Protestant church exerted great social and political influence, the foreign religion not only continued to grow rapidly, but it also became a truly Korean religion during this period.

Koreans could gather in church at least several times a week.[57] Particularly at that time, Protestant churches held frequent revival meetings in which members stayed together at one place several days and nights. These religious gatherings were significant to the colonized Koreans, who were deeply saddened and frustrated after the 1905 protectorate and the 1910 annexation. The revivals gave them opportunities to share their feelings. This

TABLE 4.2
Number of Koreans Imprisoned

	Convicts	*Awaiting Trial*	*Total*
1911	7,342	9,465	16,807
1912	9,652	9,842	19,494
1913	11,652	10,194	21,846
1914	12,962	11,472	24,434
1915	14,411	12,844	27,255
1916	17,577	15,259	32,836

SOURCE: McKenzie, *Korea's Fight for Freedom,* p. 192.

regular, organized contact was itself a consolation, especially because Koreans were banned from social and political organizations and activities.

The Protestant church's organizational potential at the time was useful for Korean nationalists, but dangerous for the colonial government. The church contained thousands of pastors and church workers who led some 200,000 adherents and more than 2,000 churches in the peninsula.[58] There were almost one thousand church-affiliated schools,[59] and Protestants published their own newspapers and periodicals.[60] These organizations were arranged in a hierarchy, and thus were connected closely in terms of organization and church administration.[61] The Protestant church provided a nationwide communication network. According to Ch'oe Myŏngsik, a political activist at the time, Korean patriotic activities indeed proceeded in and through churches, and the Protestant church was the best meeting place and political forum for nationalist activities.[62] It is natural that a Korean nationalist leadership was formed in this religious community.

For example, the Sangdong Church of Seoul opened an academy called Sangdong Young Men's Academy (Sangdong ch'ŏngnyŏn hagwŏn) to educate young Koreans.[63] Like other churches, the Sangdong Church and its academy became meeting places for patriotic Koreans. Christian and non-Christian social and political activists used churches and church-related schools across the country, and churches and related educational and social institutions became communication networks and rallying points.

The New People's Association (Sinminhoe), the largest patriotic organization, was formed in 1907 by church leaders and Christian political activists such as the Reverend Chŏn Tŏkki of Sangdong Church, Yun Ch'iho, Syngman Rhee, and Yi Tonghwi, who later became an early Korean socialist.

Also involved were various non-Christian nationalists such as Yi Chun and Yi Sangsŏl, who were sent in 1907 to The Hague in the Netherlands to enlist help from the Western powers in recovering Korea's sovereignty.[64] This clandestine association can be characterized as a second Independence Club.[65] Some of its founding members, including Yun Ch'iho, Yi Hoeyŏng, and An Ch'angho had participated in the previous Independence Club movement as leaders and young activists.

At the time, the Sinminhoe was often regarded by many Korean political activists as a reappearance of the Independence Club under the mask of a new name.[66] It was no accident that the Sangdong Church of Seoul was its secret headquarters and many Christians joined this secret society. According to a recent study, like the previous Independence Club movement, the Sinminhoe branches were actively established in the northwestern region where Protestant Christianity had been growing rapidly since its introduction. Teachers and students of mission schools such as Sungsil hakkyo and of Christian-founded schools, including Taesŏng hakkyo, Ilsin hakkyo, and Yangsil hakkyo, and church leaders such as Yun Wŏnsam, Yi Tŏkhwan, Sŏnu Hyŏk, and Yi Myŏng'yong were active organizers and leaders in the Sinminhoe movement in the region.[67]

As we have seen in chapter two, the biblical language and symbols offered by the Protestant church not only consoled frustrated, grief-stricken Koreans, but also gave them hope and a desire to be liberated from the colonial yoke. In addition, the Protestant church interpreted the Scripture deliberately to reflect the current political situation. The church taught that the exodus of the people of Israel from Egypt could be likened to the need for Koreans to free themselves from Japan. This was an instance of political language in the guise of religious teaching. Themes often repeated from the pulpit included Israel's bondage to Egypt and the Babylonian captivity of the Old Testament and the coming of the Messiah in the New Testament.[68] Paek Nakchun (George L. Paik), a pioneer in studying church history in Korea, who lived through the Japanese colonial rule, commented:

> When looking at the languages and deeds of Christians, they profess that the people of Israel under the oppression of Egypt succeeded in their exodus for national independence and liberation under God's help and under the leadership of Moses. They teach the biblical story that during the war with another nation the people of Israel were vindicated by David, the Apostle of Justice who destroyed the giant Goliath.[69]

Also, it was not without significance that Korean Christians during the colonial period sang such militant hymns as "Onward, Christian Soldiers" and "Stand Up, Stand Up for Jesus, Ye Soldiers of the Cross."[70]

Some scholars have regarded such hymns and teachings as otherworldly and apolitical, but they overlook the historical context in which such hymns were sung and such teachings were repeated.[71] The songs and teachings were a great help in rendering Korean Christians more militant toward Japan. Korean Christians shared these militant expressions and symbols with the general public. One reader wrote to a newspaper and inquired: "Will devotion to Christianity make the country stronger?" In an editorial response, the newspaper said that as long as Koreans marched under Christ as "commander-in-chief," fortified with the Holy Spirit as their sword and faith in God as their shield, there would be none to resist them.[72] The Protestant church was accepted by despairing Koreans who needed such language and symbols for solace and to encourage them toward patriotic action.

The general public also placed its hope in the church's regular meetings and its organizations. A newspaper editorial of 1905 said of the Protestant church:

> As we look at the way things are in Korea, we see that she never had any physical strength to speak of but that her spiritual strength remains not entirely hopeless. Adherents of Christianity now are numbered in the hundreds of thousands. In defiance of death they have pledged themselves not to let national independence slip from them: they pray to Heaven and urge their countrymen [to have the same hope]. This forms the very basis of Korea's independence. . . . We are convinced that in a matter of years we will see a remarkable display of the efficacy of Protestant Christianity.[73]

It seems that this editorial took a pessimistic view of "the way things are in Korea," but what we notice here is that Koreans placed great hope in the Protestant church because of its growing membership, its regular meetings, its nationwide organization, its religious yet political language, and its members' determination to achieve national independence "in defiance of death." There was a consensus among Korean patriots that it would be safer for their activities to be carried out in and through the Protestant church community, because it had an organizational network and a membership that welcomed such dangerous activities.[74] Even Kim San, who became a leftist guerrilla after 1919, could agree with his teacher who praised the church's position in patriotic activities:

> Christianity will be the mother of Korean independence. In Korea it is a symptom of revival, not a mere spiritual religious institution. In the name of religion many great historical happenings have been brought to pass.[75]

In fact, Christians and their religious community acted for national independence "in the name of religion." One local Christian activist in 1919 explicitly professed his nationalistic motive in converting to Christianity and his sense of religious mission for national independence:

> To be apprehended while engaged in the independence movement is like falling as a hero while fighting for one's country. In fact, we accepted Christianity for we hoped [the way to] independence lay in the church. It is only through Christ's intervention that an opportunity at hand is before us. This is an order, rarely given, which no one under the sun can afford to disobey.[76]

Another Christian activist in 1919 remarked in similar fashion: "The day we Christians have been looking forward to has now arrived. Now is the time for us Christians to hold ourselves ready to lay down our lives doing our part in the Movement to the fullest."[77] Undoubtedly, the Korean Christians identified "the time" of the Messiah's coming with national independence.[78]

The Japanese authorities were not blind to the Protestant church's organizational potential, its religious yet political teachings, and the events unfolding in the Christian community. According to a contemporary Japanese document, for example, the textbooks used in Korean church-related schools were, on the whole, overly critical of colonial government policy and fulminated against protectorate policy. Since many of these textbooks were regarded as little different from "political pamphlets," the Japanese felt that such political education would only breed a rabble of perpetual grumblers and disturb "the peace and order of society." The document concluded that if religious education were turned into "full-time political debate" and agitation, the colonial government would be left with no choice but to bring private schools under its full control.[79] The Japanese authorities could not ignore the language, stories, symbols, programs, and patriotic tone taught in the largest organized community of Koreans.

As one Western observer noted, the colonial authorities noticed "multitudes of Christians flocking to the churches" and wondered "why those Christians met so often and what they were doing." Worrying about the powerful organization of the Protestant church, the authorities already considered the religious community a "hotbed of revolutionary opportunity."[80] A secret Japanese document confirms this impression.[81]

However much the Japanese colonial officials wished to crush the patriotic forces represented by the Protestant church, they felt obliged to play their hand carefully. The Japanese wished to be seen as civilized, and persecution of any religion might have had adverse repercussions at home and abroad. Thus, at least initially, the colonial government tried to conciliate the religious community by conferring frequently with missionaries and Korean church leaders, by inviting them to Japan, and even by supporting church work financially in hopes that the religious community would devote itself only to purely religious activities.[82]

Eventually, however, the colonial government had to change its conciliatory policy and put the Protestant community under constant surveillance. When a plot to assassinate Prime Minister Yi Wanyong, chief signatory to the protectorate treaty, was uncovered in 1909, Yi Chaemyŏng and twelve others were implicated. With the exception of Chŏn T'aesŏn, who was forty three, the conspirators were in their twenties or younger. Seven of the thirteen were Christians, and one belonged to the influential nationalist folk religion, Ch'ŏndogyo.[83] Judging from the frequency and incidence of the revival meetings of those days and from the fact that over half of those indicted were Christians, it would be safe to assume that the plot to assassinate Yi Wanyong was discussed in the church gatherings, where nationalist leaders at the time usually recruited and contacted activists.[84] The assassinations of Itō Hirobumi and D. W. Stevens, an American adviser to the colonial government, were also carried out by Christian patriots in 1908. When the enthusiastic Patriotic Enlightenment Movement prevailed in Korea after the 1905 protectorate was established, the colonial government observed that Protestant Christian leaders and other Korean intellectuals initiated it, and churches and church-related institutions such as schools provided its organizational and communication network. The Protestant church community became a handy vehicle for clandestine nationalist activism, as we have seen earlier in the cases of the Society for the Promotion of Education in the Northwest (Haesŏ kyoyuk ch'onghoe) and the New People's Association (Sinminhoe). Therefore, the colonial government sent spies to watch the Protestant religious community and increased measures to repress it.[85]

The surveillance, however, earned public sympathy and confidence for the church. More patriots joined the church, reinforcing its nationalist orientation and enhancing its attraction to Koreans still outside the religious community. In short, the more the Japanese repressed the religious community, the more it grew.[86] The colonial government then found it necessary to trump up charges against a group of 105 men in order to separate the Protestant church from patriotic activities.[87] Police authorities alleged that a group of Koreans had conspired to assassinate Count Terauchi, the first governor-general of Korea, with weapons smuggled from Manchuria. In the so-called Terauchi assassination plot of 1911, some 500 persons were rounded up across the country, and 105 of them were charged. According to a recent study, 91 were Protestant Christian; 2 were Catholic; 2 were Ch'ŏndogyo; and 10 had no church affiliation.[88] Most were, of course, members of the Sinminhoe. Even though this case was concocted by the colonial authorities, the Protestant church was obviously a hotbed of patriotic activities in the early colonial period.

Church activism moved inexorably toward the dramatic March First Movement of 1919, a nationwide demonstration for independence.[89] Sixteen of thirty-three "national representatives" who signed the Declaration of Independence were church leaders. Along with the Ch'ŏndogyo followers, Protestant Christians played a major role in the mass demonstrations. Of 7,835 major participants in the movement, 1,719 (22 percent) were Protestant; 1,209 (15 percent) were adherents of Ch'ŏndogyo; 3,808 (43 percent) lacked religious affiliation; and the affiliations of the remaining 1,099 (20 percent) were not identified. The Presbyterian church alone experienced the arrest of 3,804 church leaders and followers.[90]

Much that has been published about the March First Movement is emotional in tone. Written largely by Koreans, this literature generally focuses understandably on the events surrounding the mass demonstration of 1919 and on the excessive punishment (frequently, arbitrary execution without trial) meted out by Japanese authorities in putting down the rebellion.[91] We are not concerned here with statistics of victims and descriptions of Japanese cruelty, which are well known. It is more important to examine how the leadership of the movement was formed, how the leaders managed to muster local groups across the country, and through what sorts of organizations the movement was popularized.

During the early colonial period, a variety of groups discussed the country's future. At the time, President Woodrow Wilson of the United States advanced the principle of national self-determination as a guideline for determining national boundaries, and nationhood for different ethnic groups in Europe as part of the peace settlement following World War I. Some Korean leaders saw an opportunity in the enthusiasm for nationhood thus aroused, and decided to strike for national freedom. Leaders in the Protestant church, leaders of Ch'ŏndogyo, Korean exiles in China, and Korean students in Japan independently held secret conferences seeking a way to publicize to the world the desire of Koreans to throw off their colonial yoke.[92] Since these various groups were separately preparing to declare national independence, it would be meaningless to argue about which group was the first to plan the March First demonstration.

The important questions are how those independent activities were unified and through what sorts of organizations the planning for the demonstration proceeded. The March First Movement passed through three stages: (1) the formation of the central leadership; (2) the recruitment of initial agitators and local organizations; and (3) collective action. In these three stages, the Protestant church community played the most significant role in mobilizing people for a nationwide mass demonstration by providing leaders for the movement, activists, and an organizational base throughout the country.

The Sinhan ch'ŏngnyŏndang (New Korean Young Men's Society), known in English as the Korean Revolutionary Party, played a significant role in the initial stage of recruiting leaders and activists.[93] The party was formed mostly by Protestant Christians who had been exiled to China after the attempt to assassinate Governor-General Terauchi in 1911 (also referred to as the "Sinminhoe incident"). The party sent out representatives to secretly contact different groups scattered over wide areas. To ensure unity of action, it sent Chang Tŏksu to Japan to observe political developments and to meet Korean students there. Kim Kyusik went to Paris to enlist international support for the cause; Sŏnu Hyŏk and Sŏ Pyŏngho returned to Korea to work with church leaders; Kim Ch'ŏl took charge of liaison with Ch'ŏndogyo leaders.[94]

Sŏnu Hyŏk was able to win over three major figures in the northwestern region: the Reverends Kil Sŏnju and Yang Chŏnbaek, and Elder Yi Sŭnghun, who were to be three of the thirty-three signatories of the Declaration of Independence. This trio, together with a few others, became the core group around which an ever-widening circle of participants and sympathizers rallied. Through the good offices of the Reverend Kil, Sŏnu also met other local clerical and lay leaders, including Pyŏn Insŏ, Kim Sŏndu, To

In'gwŏn, Kim Tong'wŏn, and Yun Wŏnsam.[95] Sŏnu successfully urged them to hold a mass demonstration. Winning the support of local church leaders meant securing local leadership, agitators, organizational bases, and mass participation in the demonstration. Sŏ Pyŏngho performed the same tasks in Seoul, and Kim Ch'ŏl contacted Ch'ŏndogyo leaders.[96]

Yi Sŭnghun, a prominent nationalist leader at the time, was particularly instrumental in unifying a variety of independent nationalist groups in the church community and in forming the united front with Ch'ŏndogyo.[97] Yi was briefed by Sŏnu Hyŏk on the international situation and urged to organize a mass demonstration. It was after this secret meeting with Sŏnu that Yi worked for a united front with the Ch'ŏndogyo group. Meanwhile, he did not neglect for a moment the task of gaining support from local Protestant leaders. Yi consolidated the organization of local church leaders whom Sŏnu had contacted and expanded local organization for the demonstration by making frequent trips between Seoul and the northwestern region, the stronghold of Protestantism. Without the work of Yi and Sinhan Ch'ŏngnyŏndang in organizing local church leaders and organizations, the declaration of the "33 national representatives" would not have touched off the March First Movement, a truly nationwide mass demonstration.[98]

Pak Hŭido, a Christian activist, was another important figure in the March First Movement.[99] A graduate of Sungsil hakkyo, a mission school, Pak worked as a YMCA director for student and youth affairs at the time. Using the YMCA organization and activities, he had independently recruited students and youths for the nationalist movement. These young people then organized a secret group of activists at their schools. Pak also formed a subordinate group composed of high school student leaders, who informed other students and the general public of the planned demonstration at Pagoda Park.[100] The students and youths recruited by Pak and other church leaders throughout the peninsula made the 1919 nationwide demonstration possible.

Along with Ch'ŏndogyo and other available organizations, churches and church-related agencies also served as a major organizational base for the nationwide demonstration of 1919. First, church organizations provided clandestine meeting places and communication centers for event preparation. As we have seen, Sŏnu Hyŏk, Yi Sŭnghun, and Pak Hŭido all operated through the network of churches to keep different groups in touch with one another.[101] All of the secret activities of local church leaders and YMCA students and youths were also processed through church organizations.[102] Even the revolutionary Kim San, who was disillusioned with the pacifistic approach of the church in the independence movement and thus parted with it after 1919, recognized that church congregations exhibited a strong sense of solidarity and played the initial role in touching off mass demonstrations across the country.[103]

In sum, the Protestant church, though not a primarily political institution, came to function as a political community for Koreans in the early colonial period. The church grew rapidly by being both a place for spiritual solace and a political forum, and consequently the new religious community came to be emotionally and organizationally associated with the patriotic activity of the colonized Koreans. Neither the frustration and grievances of the Koreans nor the economic exploitation by the Japanese automatically brought about a nationwide mass demonstration. There had to be leadership, activists, and organization for such a collective action to occur. For the 1919 demonstration, the Protestant church provided all three.[104]

During the 1919 independence movement, the Protestant churches in Korea showed remarkable unity in organization and action. There was no deviation from their singleness of purpose, no flagging of enthusiasm for the cause, no distraction arising out of internal disputes in spite of relentless repression and attempts at conciliation by the colonial government. Leaders and members alike were united in their desire to throw off foreign rule. In addition, there were no serious conflicts within the Protestant community. Although the beginnings of conflict could be seen between clergy and laity and among clerical leaders as the religious community grew in size, it was too early in the organizational history of the church for any serious jockeying for positions of influence to develop. Any early signs of conflict were readily subordinated for the good of the greater cause. At that time, as yet unharnessed national energies were directed almost exclusively into the Protestant church as a channel of political activism.

5 / Protestant Christians and the Late Nationalist Movement, 1919–1945

In the wake of the abortive uprising of 1919, a general tenor of disillusionment, frustration, and despondency set in. In his magazine *P'yehŏ* [Ruins], poet O Sangsun gave an apt account of the prevailing mood of the post–March First Movement era:

> Our land of Korea is in ruins. These are times of sorrow and agony. Saying this will wrench the heart of our youth. But I must, for it is a fact that I can neither deny nor even doubt. In ruins lie all our defects and shortcomings, inside and outside, physical as well as mental: emptiness, grievances, discontent and resentment, sighs and worries, pain and tears—all these evils will lead to extinction and death. As we stand before the ruins, darkness and death open their fearsome, cavernous mouths, threatening to gobble us up. Again, we are struck by the feeling that the old ruins spell extinction and death.[1]

The cherished hopes of throwing off alien rule were dashed. Not surprisingly, there were no serious nationalist activities immediately after the March First Movement. As novelist Yi Kwangsu remarked, "Gone is the fervor that once spurred them on; people are beginning to think only of themselves" and their families.[2]

Nevertheless, there were sporadic efforts among Koreans to revive their shattered hopes and resume the march toward nationhood even in this period of despair. The Korean aspiration to throw off foreign rule was actually expressed in the language of defeat, frustration, extinction, and death. In fact, an editorial associate of *P'yehŏ* declared, "A new age is on us." He asked the people not to grieve over "the setting sun" or give way to "sorrow by the grave," but to look to the horizon of "a new age." He urged the people to "watch a new plant grow out of the ruins and come to bloom so that we can enjoy in full its lasting fragrance." Instead of standing by the grave, looking wistfully to a past that was gone forever, and indulging in endless reminiscences, Koreans should devote themselves to creating this "new age." According to the editorial, Koreans needed to sow a seed even in the land of ruins rather than give up their hope to throw off the colonial yoke, no matter how remote national independence seemed to be.[3]

Born in despair, Korean patriotic activity after 1919 was different from that of the previous period. Before the abortive uprising, patriotism was somewhat naive and emotional, and it was based on existing religious communities, most particularly on Christianity and Ch'ŏndogyo, and loosely united for the goal of independence under a coalition of religious leaders. Now, having learned from the failure of the March First Movement, Korean nationalists realized that a successful struggle for independence demanded a viable political leadership and central coordination, not a naive, nonviolent religious leadership and loose organization. Thus, in April 1919 they formed the Provisional Government in Shanghai, China, an umbrella organization that attempted to create a well-directed and coordinated strategy at home and abroad to revive efforts for independence.

Korean nationalists not only had to adjust their activity to the altered situation brought about by the general mood of defeatism, but also to the new colonial policy. The Japanese colonial government, realizing that a strong-arm policy caused alienation among its colonized subjects, now showed a more conciliatory attitude to soothe wounded Korean feelings and improve its cruel image abroad. The colonial government thus granted to Koreans limited freedom of the press, assembly, and association.[4] In this new atmosphere, Korean nationalists, who sought a more effective leadership, strategy, and ideology for regaining independence, formed thousands of social and political organizations, using the new guidelines of the so-called cultural policy (*bunka seiji*).[5] Thus a variety of small nationalist groups appeared with different views and strategies. Their politics ran the gamut from left to right. Additionally, using the new guidelines, various small nationalist groups published their own journals and initiated a variety of activities. These organizations and publications were reviving the temporarily lost Korean desire to be free from Japanese colonial rule. A new era seemed to be coming after the March First Movement, and some historians call the period "the dawn of the nationalist movement"[6] or the period of "the nationalist renaissance."[7]

Nevertheless, no single individual or organization, including the Provisional Government in Shanghai, provided viable leadership and coordination for the ideologically diversified and organizationally fragmented groups of Korean nationalists. Unified action became especially difficult because the new Russian regime after the 1917 Bolshevik Revolution frequently stated its anti-imperialist and anti-Japanese position and declared its determination to liberate the oppressed people of the Far East. Socialist and communist ideas penetrated rapidly into the hearts of colonized Koreans. Socialism was particularly popular among those Koreans who became disheartened by the failure of the March First Movement and disillusioned by Western liberalism.[8] It is true that the Korean nationalist movement became more sophisticated after 1919, but it represented a divided struggle for liberation from Japan, a struggle primarily between cultural nationalists and nationalistic socialists.

Of course in this era of diversified, fragmented nationalist activity, Koreans attempted to form a unified movement for national liberation. Thus, the New Korea Society (Sin'ganhoe), a united front, was born in 1927.[9] It was a product of the political needs of both uncompromising cultural nationalists and nationalistic communists. Cultural nationalists, who desired to have a mass base through which they could expand and lead a mass national liberation movement, needed a united front with the leftists whose influence was growing rapidly among the people. Socialists and communists, who were divided into various factions and under harsh Japanese repression, needed a legal front which cultural nationalists could provide. The Sin'ganhoe received a great response from Koreans, and it rapidly grew. In 1930, for example, there were 386 branches with 76,939 members.[10]

Socialists and communists used this united front well for protecting themselves from Japanese repression and organizing peasants, factory workers, and students. They came to control almost all local branches, adopted a militant strategy, and posed a great political threat to both the moderate nationalists and the Japanese colonial government.

However, during and after the 1929 Kwangju Student Movement, when many militant socialists and communists were arrested, the Sin'ganhoe seemed to move to the right ideologically and strategically. Communist leaders began to urge withdrawal from the united front or its dissolution. Korean communists were keenly aware of Chiang Kai-shek's betrayal in the "Shanghai massacre" of leftists in 1927, and in fact never trusted moderate bourgeois nationalists. Finally in 1931, the communists successfully maneuvered to dissolve the Sin'ganhoe. The united front was dismantled after four years of political mud-slinging.

It is intriguing to discuss the political position of the Protestant church in these altered circumstances. Prior to 1919, when the Japanese colonial government allowed only religious organizations and activities, the Protestant church achieved a unique position. As the largest organized community, it was always at the front line of reform and nationalist activity. It functioned as a forum for political discussion, a political training ground, and a clearinghouse for political information for colonized Koreans. In the period following the March First Movement, the religious community found itself retreating from the front line of nationalist activities, and its political role became marginal.

Of course, Protestant Christians continued to be involved in nationalist politics. They led groups that ranged ideologically from socialism to capitalism and strategically from gradualism to armed resistance. Protestant Christians such as Yi Tonghwi, Kim Ku, Kim San, and Pak Yongman favored armed resistance and direct action. Other Christians, such as Syngman Rhee, Kim Kyusik, Yŏ Unhyŏng, Chŏng Han'gyŏng, and Sin Hŭng'u, opted for persuasion through diplomatic channels. An Ch'angho, Pak Hŭido, Yŏ Unhyŏng, Yi Taewi, Kim Wŏnbyŏk, Hong Myŏnghŭi, Kim Kyusik, and Pak Yongman favored or tolerated socialism. Yi Sŭnghun, Syngman Rhee, and other Christians opposed radical ideas and activities. Church leaders such as Yi Sangjae, Hong Myŏnghŭi, and Cho Mansik also actively participated in the Sin'ganhoe. Its opening ceremony was held at the YMCA in Seoul on February 15, 1927: Yi Sangjae, a prominent Christian and moderate nationalist, became its first president; Hong Myŏnghŭi, a Christian teacher at Osan School, founded by prominent church elder Yi Sŭnghun, was elected as its vice president; and 255 clergymen actively participated in the movement.[11] Nevertheless, the Protestant church's role in Korean nationalist activities was transformed from a core to a peripheral position in terms of ideology, organization, and leadership after the March First Movement.

THE PROTESTANT CHURCH AND THE EARLY SOCIALIST MOVEMENT

The Protestant-Socialist Nexus

Although individual Protestant Christians made a substantial contribution to a variety of nationalist movements even after 1919, the religious community as a whole came to stand aloof from nationalist politics, particularly from that of socialists and communists, whose influence was growing rapidly.[12] Even church sources admitted that most patriotic activity and direct action was carried on by leftists. A poll of 152 students in 1932 showed that 67 percent favored the socialists, 4 percent each supported either communists or rightist conservatives, and 25 percent preferred the neutral-to-moderate line.[13] Although not a comprehensive sample, this poll indicates that socialism was becoming the most popular ideology among students and youths during the second half of Japanese rule. The observer who reported the above percentages wrote that "[t]he names of Marx and Lenin are on every tongue."[14] As a matter of fact, socialism and Christianity were the two leading forces in Korean thought at the time.[15] To properly appreciate the political position of Protestant Christianity following the March First Movement, therefore, it is important to discuss how this religious community reacted to the political activity led by socialists and communists.

As briefly mentioned above, some prominent Protestant Christians tolerated leftist ideas and even initiated early socialist and communist movements. For example, Yi Tonghwi, a former Christian evangelist in the Hamgyŏng and Kando region, and Yŏ Unhyŏng, a former associate pastor of Sŭngdong Church in Seoul, played the leading role in organizing the Koryŏ kongsandang (Koryŏ Communist Party) and the Chosŏn kongsandang (Korean Communist Party) to promote the struggle for national independence.[16] It is a well-known fact that Kim Kyusik, a church elder and prominent nationalist, and Yŏ Unhyŏng went to Moscow to attend the First Congress of the Toilers of the Far East as "representatives" of the League of Korean Christians (Chosŏn kidokkyodo yŏnmaeng) in 1922.[17] Hŏ Hŏn, a prominent Christian lawyer, and his daughter, Hŏ Chŏngsuk, became socialists in the 1920s.[18] At the time, the Reverend Kim Pyŏngjo, the Reverend Kang Mae, and Yi Taewi of the YMCA began to introduce socialist ideas, as did Pak Hŭido, formerly a theological seminary student and executive secretary for youth affairs at the YMCA. In 1922, these Christian intellectuals began publishing *Sinsaenghwal* [New life], one of the earliest socialist journals in Korea. It is interesting to note that without the wholehearted support of Protestant missionaries such as Horace G. Underwood and Arthur L. Becker at Yonsei University, a mission institution in Seoul, Pak Hŭido could not have obtained a permit from the colonial government to publish the magazine. The two missionaries even participated in this socialist literary enterprise as board members.[19] When this journal was becoming very popular among Koreans and the editors were planning for expansion, the Japanese colonial government arrested Pak Hŭido and others associated with *Sinsaenghwal*. This is considered to be the first legal case against socialists in Korea.[20]

Yi Taewi[21] and other Protestant Christian intellectuals also used the existing YMCA journal *Ch'ŏngnyŏn* [Youth] to introduce socialist ideas and even to attempt incorporating socialism into the Christian faith. Indeed, some Protestant Christian leaders considered socialism as a new, viable thought for social reform and national liberation after 1919.[22] Yi Taewi pointed out that Christianity began as "a social movement of sorts" and that Jesus was looked upon as "a savior come to the oppressed commoners." He mentioned that like Jesus Christ, Karl Marx also launched "a kind of proletarian movement."[23] Thus he believed that Jesus, who stood against formalism and the distinction of classes, worked vigorously for "social revolution."[24] Yu Kyŏngsang, another Protestant intellectual, came right out and called Christ "a socialist."[25] In 1923, Yi Taewi argued:

> As we undertake to create a new world to our liking in repudiation of the present one, full of grievances and inequalities, we realize Christian thought and socialism are alike. For both not only discern abuses of all varieties in the present world, but also propose to remedy them.[26]

It seems clear that Yi Taewi and his associates at the time emphasized the similarities in the goals of Christianity and socialism. Yi further wrote:

> As the whole is for the individual, so the individual is for the whole. What the individual ultimately hopes for from the whole, and indeed the very meaning of society, is to care for the weak and helpless. . . . [socialism], in repudiating ruses and cruelty, calls for justice. . . . nothing that socialism seeks to achieve does not fit in with that which Christianity envisages.[27]

Many Protestant Christian intellectuals, including Yi Taewi and Yu Kyŏngsang, could point out differences between Christianity and socialism: where Christianity sought to reform the individual first and realize social reform as a result, socialism sought to reform society first in order to achieve reform of the individual. However, they did emphasize the similarities rather than differences between the two dogmas.

Underneath this intellectual current, it seems, there was a nationalist desire to create cooperation rather than confrontation between the two most influential ideas in the second half of Japanese rule. This trend in Christian thought was clearly shown in the writing of Yi Taewi:

> [There are different trends of thought in Korea.] Of these the greatest in influence and the highest in their ideals must be Christianity and socialism. What I do not understand is why Christianity today ignores socialism, and socialists find Christianity so strange.[28]

In order to prevent an ideological and organizational schism within the struggle for liberation from Japan, these Christian intellectuals attempted to reconcile seemingly opposing thoughts and activities. Thus, Yi argued that Christians and socialists would do well to put an end to all the mistrust and animosity between them. In order to do that, he continued, the church should be socialized (*kyohoe nŭn sahoehwa*), and socialism should be Christianized (*sahoejuŭi nŭn kidokhwa*).[29] Only after this could there be cooperation between them—through which many problems plaguing Korea under alien rule could be solved.

Unlike the *Sinsaenghwal* group, which was orthodox Marxist-Leninist, Yi Taewi, Yu Kyŏngsang and other *Ch'ŏngnyŏn* writers were much more flexible in their socialist views. To orthodox scientific socialists, these Christians were utopian socialists or naive pastoral humanists at best. At worst, their critique of capitalism and their concerns with labor and other social issues came out of their "sham concerns" (*saibi kwansim*) long held by Christian liberals.[30] Their criticism never failed to mention a strong Christian identity which, the Marxists implied, could not make them "true socialists."[31]

Perhaps, it is understandable that some of the so-called Christian socialists, who had previously believed that socialism and Christianity could work together for social reform, were gradually becoming apologists for Christianity and eventually would turn antisocialist. For example, Kim Ch'angje argued in 1926 that Christianity was not an aristocratic religion, a protector of capitalism, or an opiate of the people, which orthodox socialists claimed at the time. Instead, Kim argued that Christianity was a religious movement of the poor and weak, Christ was never submissive and nonresistant, and socialists should not denounce it but consider it their religion.[32] Just a year later however, Kim came out to criticize leftist thoughts:

> Is there anyone who was so blinded as to be sucked in by Marxist ideas and movements injudiciously? Is there any friend who stuck dangerously to the wicked stateless attitude? . . . Is there any mad fool who despicably became crazy and frantically cried for that ruinous socialism? We should explode its fallacy for the sake of national unity.[33]

Initially, some Christian socialists and liberals criticized capitalism, and considered socialism as a handy ideological vehicle for curing its diseases, but they became critical about socialism especially after the socialists denounced Christianity as a religion of the well-to-do.[34] Some Christian socialists even committed apostasy (*chŏnhyang*), and one devout Christian socialist, Kim Kyŏngsik, confessed that "no one can operate in today's society without Christ's sharp scalpel."[35]

In Meiji Japan, one great socialist, Kagawa Toyohiko, was a devout Christian. Not only did he criticize capitalism and the single-minded materialistic modernization of Meiji Japan, but he also worked to "cure" the diseases of Meiji Japanese society.[36] As a matter of fact, Korean Christian socialists translated the works of Kagawa Toyohiko into Korean and published them in Christian newspapers and periodicals.[37] Presumably, those Christians believed that they could be socialists without any theological or ideological incompatibility. Be that as it may, the point here is not to judge whether those Christian socialists were scientific socialists or not, but to understand how and why these Christian intellectuals and nationalists reacted to the arrival of such radical thoughts after the March First Movement.

As we have seen, some Protestant Christians were open to socialist ideas and participated actively in leftist intellectual and political activities within and outside the religious community. Just like other socialists, these Christian socialists went through a period of trial and error. Along with Christian liberals, they attempted to work together with non-Christian socialists for national independence and social improvement, and they actively participated in the Sin'ganhoe movement. However, as the united front movement failed, socialists denounced Christianity as a tool of capitalism. Christian socialists and liberals began to work for national independence and social reform in their own way. For example, for ailing rural Korea, Christians vigorously launched educational programs and cooperative associations.[38] By this time, it seems, Christian socialists and liberals were becoming advocates of a "social gospel" approach.

Weighty Opposition to Political Involvement

But it is also true that all these intellectual and political efforts made by individuals exerted little influence on the Protestant church. Rather, the religious community was becoming a leading antisocialist community, as Song Ch'anggŭn, a liberal theologian said in 1933.

> The church is not a place to discuss issues of society, labor, peace, or international affairs. Nor is it a place to exchange smatterings of knowledge or fragments of philosophy. What is essential for our church is the gospel of our Lord Jesus Christ.[39]

Song refused to have anything to do with socialist trends, rejecting even moderate educational and social activities. Kim Insŏ of *Sinang saenghwal* [Christian life], an influential Christian monthly, wrote that he was disturbed over attempts to rally the congregation behind political causes or social projects.[40]

> Let church leaders reply. . . . Do you follow Christ for a nationalist cause? If so, the day will come when you leave Him. One who loves his nation more than Christ is not fit for Christ. Do you follow Christ as a means to improve society? If so, the day will come when you forsake Him. One who loves society more than Christ is unfit for Christ.[41]

Protestant church leaders went so far as to declare that any Christian interested more in political causes or social issues was unfit for the church. Like Song, they believed that the church was not "a place to discuss issues of society, labor, peace, or international affairs." A leading pastor in the northwestern region, Ch'ae Chŏngmin, firmly remarked in 1936:

> My Lord and Savior, Jesus, did not make His church an institution for production. . . . He did not order His church to create a secular movement. Then, why do church ministers today try to make stones into bread? Do today's churches desire to be institutions for production? The day when the church becomes an institution for production, it will be a den of robbers.[42]

To repudiate those Christians who worked to improve Korean society through church organizations, Ch'ae used the biblical story about the confrontation between Jesus and the Devil in the wilderness.[43] Ch'ae even argued that the church should abolish its agency for rural improvement.[44] Some Protestant Christians in the era following the March First Movement continued to participate in a variety of nationalist struggles for independence, and some of them were open even to socialist ideas and activities, but the main current in the Protestant church community was opposed to political involvement.

It is interesting to note that earlier Christians joined the Korean church with hopes of reforming Confucian society, receiving new knowledge, and realizing their nationalist dreams for independence. As a result, from its introduction in the late nineteenth century until the 1919 mass demonstration, the more social-reform minded and nationalist oriented the church became, the more attraction it exerted on Koreans. But after 1919, the Protestant church was retreating even from moderate patriotic endeavors, emphasizing pure faith (*sunsu sin'ang*) instead. Activists left the religious community to resume political and social activities elsewhere. There began to appear an ideological and organizational schism between the Protestant church and the nationalist camp in general, and between the religious community and the leftist camp in particular.

THE RETREAT FROM KOREAN NATIONALIST POLITICS

How can one explain the Protestant church's retreat from its central position in progressive reform efforts and nationalist politics? Why did the religious community, which previously had served as a rallying point of fervent patriotic activity for social reform and national independence, come to condemn such social and political activity?

One may regard the church's new position in politics as a direct result of the relaxed policy toward the press and assembly. The colonized Koreans, who had refrained from engaging in politics under the militaristic regime prior to 1919, now emerged to form thousands of social and political organizations outside the religious community (see Table 5.1).[45] They also began to publish newspapers and magazines such as *Chosŏn ilbo* [Chosŏn daily], *Tong'a ilbo* [East Asia daily], *Kaebyŏk* [Creation], *Tonggwang* [Eastern light], *P'yehŏ* [Ruins], and *Sinsaenghwal* [New life] that were independent of religious organizations. Nationalist activity that used to proceed under the aegis of the church was now spread widely over these new organizations and publications that sprang up like weeds. As these organizations and publications began to encroach on the role that the Protestant church had monopolized in the previous period, the church's social and political role became marginal, and the religious community was no longer the sole center of nationalist endeavors.

Was the new role of the church simply due to the changed historical circumstances brought about by the relaxed colonial policy and the sudden emergence of thousands of new political and social organizations? If so, how can we explain that Protestant church leaders could not tolerate even moderate

TABLE 5.1
Korean Organizations, 1922

Political and intellectual	19
Labor	81
Youth	488
Church youth	217
Religious	1,245
Tenant	28
Children's	25
Academic	114
Industrial	195
Health	1
Anti-drinking	76
Self-improvement	84
Recreation/social	146
Women's	29
Savings and purchasing cooperatives	20
Others	185
Total	3,002

SOURCE: Chōsen sōtokufu keimukyoku, *Chōsen chian jōkyō,* p. 76.

educational, cultural, social, and political activities and instead attempted to make the church a purely religious community unconcerned with social and political affairs? In order to explain the Protestant church's retreat from the front line of nationalist activities, it is important to explain why many nationalists, bitterly disillusioned over the failure of the 1919 uprising, left the religious community to resume their activity for national independence elsewhere.[46] Of particular significance was the phenomenon—unprecedented in Korea—that the Protestant church became the target of intense criticism.

Kim San, a young Christian nationalist who turned to the leftist guerrilla movement after 1919, provided a vivid description of the general attitude toward the Protestant church after the 1919 mass demonstration. He had thought the church to be "the mother of Korean independence" "the best institution in Korea" for the nationalist movement.[47] He became disillusioned with the religious community, however, after the events of 1919, and lost trust in the value of the church as a practical instrument for achieving independence. Kim said:

> After this debacle [the March First Movement] my faith is broken. I thought there was certainly no God and that the teachings of Christ had little application for the world of struggle in which I had been born.[48]

Kim was especially disillusioned with the religious community's retreat from Korean nationalist activities and its teaching that God was punishing Korea and that independence would not come until the nation atoned for its sins. He then wondered why Korea should be the only nation to practice Christian ethics, when others did not "turn the other cheek." He was not happy that the church taught its followers not to hate their enemy but rather to repent.[49]

Kim San was also disillusioned by the church's former strategy for regaining independence. As he saw it, talking, praying, and initiating peaceful demonstrations for independence were the only methods the Korean church utilized in the March First Movement. He declared that "only to pray was to ensure failure" but "to fight was to gain victory."[50] He said that the failure of the movement revealed the church's naivete, fragility, and limited capacities in the real world. Thus Kim San and many other young Koreans left the church to engage in guerrilla activities after 1919.

Another serious reappraisal of the Korean church in the post–March First era—that of Sin Ch'aeho—also indicates why the nationalists did not continue their affiliation with the Protestant church community. Sin, a prominent nationalist historian at the time, had declared in 1910 that Christianity "does deserve to be the new religion of Korea" because of its value in promoting the "new nation."[51] However, after the 1919 demonstration, he became very critical of the religion. For example, in a 1928 statement he criticized Protestant Christianity in the following way:

> By his false teaching that the blessed are the suffering and the persecuted, Christ misled a nation without a state and a public without property into overlooking the real enemy and dreaming of the Kingdom of Heaven, and by doing so he made the job easier for those who rule and lord it over you. But this time he came to a tragic end. An awakened public, working hand in hand with organized non-Christian youths, delivered the coup de grace to the moribund Christ. He is dead for good, never to become resurrected.[52]

Having criticized Christianity as a religion for the haves, Sin desired to see "a tragic end" to Christ. He was very emphatic about the church's support for the colonizer and the haves against the colonized and the have-nots. He disapproved of the Protestant church for shifting to less controversial educational and cultural activity and for concentrating mainly on matters of religion. The leftist critique of the Korean church was turned even into a political and physical attack on the religious community in the late 1920s.[53]

Such outcries were not limited to leftist groups. The moderate *Tong'a ilbo* was also very critical of the religious community. This newspaper said in an editorial of 1922 that church leaders concentrated their attention only on ceremonial activities. Since the church looked away "from the way poor laborers live" and hoped "to receive donations from the rich," it failed to sympathize with the feelings of the maltreated and ingratiated itself "into the good graces of the ruling classes." The editor demanded that if church leaders could not "come down from the pulpit and into the streets" of the starved, the maltreated, the beaten, and downtrodden, they should "cast off [their] clerical robes, step down, and repent."[54]

As early as the 1920s, many educated Koreans began to accuse the Protestant church of clearly becoming a community of, for, and by established people. Already in 1917, Yi Kwangsu lamented that church leaders such as ministers and elders came to behave like "*yangban*" and treated the majority of laymen like "*sangnom*" (a pejorative term for commoners).[55] Even Kim Insŏ of *Sinang saenghwal*, who stood firmly against the church's involvement in social and political activity, observed that while clergy and laymen were "like equal brothers" in rural churches, there was increasingly a strong sense of class distinction in urban churches where power, influence, and interests were concentrated and determined.[56] A Christian journalist, Kim Ch'angje, pointed out that the Korean Protestant church had gradually turned toward the "upper classes."[57] Even a Christian nationalist, Kim Wŏnbyŏk, called the Korean church a religion of the rich and powerful. In 1923, Kim criticized church leaders:

> Listen! Those whose mission is to propagate the ideas and faith of Christ! When did Jesus ask you to protect the rich and oppress the poor? When you discussed important church affairs, had you ever squelched the view of the rich and adopted the opinion of the poor?[58]

These unprecedented criticisms of the Protestant church emerged when the church ceased to be of political use. It no longer was strongly committed to political and social issues.

The inertia and ineptness of the Protestant church was brought on by the change the church itself had undergone as a social institution. Over the decades, the church saw its leadership and staff grow as its membership increased. As the religious community grew, it needed more clergymen, staff personnel, teachers, doctors, and functionaries for managing numerous churches, church-affiliated schools, hospitals, and other social and cultural institutions. By the 1920s, the Korean Protestant church had come to contain a considerable number of paid employees (*ponggŭp chang'i*). In 1924, the Presbyterian and Methodist churches alone had 1,266 pastors and 1,844 church workers.[59] The number of teachers and staff personnel in church-affiliated schools increased from 1,517 in 1919 to 2,789 in 1926.[60] In 1933, the Korean Presbyterian Church alone had 1,103 paid ministers and evangelical workers, 1,608 paid school teachers, and 1,170 unpaid volunteers in church-affiliated schools.[61] Thousands of religious, educational, and cultural professionals hired by the various denominations attained a relatively secure living, and middle-class respectability, by capitalizing on their new knowledge and their position in the religious community. They came to enjoy a semblance of intellectual superiority over other members and the public as well. The religious community now tended to avoid controversial issues in society and in nationalist politics. It is in this context that the church's retreat from its central position in Korean social and political activity should be examined.

Additionally, there was a metamorphosis of the Protestant church from a religion of the alienated, the poor, the maltreated, and the oppressed to a religion which was separating itself from these groups. Church leaders became established sociopolitically and professed "pure gospel" rather than onerous social commitment. In fact, the attitude of looking away from the realities of poverty, starvation, and injustice became typical of Christians. One secular newspaper, the *Tong'a ilbo*, was moved to criticize the religious community and its leaders. Church leaders, it said, were busy insinuating themselves into "the good graces of the ruling classes," but they ignored "the feelings of the maltreated."[62] It is clear that the church, growing in numbers, was becoming a religion of established individuals.

As we have seen in chapter three, it is true that the absolute majority of church members were still poor, and most clergymen, especially in rural areas, remained poorly paid.[63] Nonetheless, the Protestant church had become an institutionalized religion which was operated and controlled by paid religious and cultural professionals. As it grew rapidly and consequently became institutionalized, differences based on position and function within the religious community emerged. In a phenomenon that often occurs as churches grow within a given society, out of the division of labor there emerged in the Korean Protestant denominations two distinct status orders: the clergy, who had "functions: ruling, teaching, ministering to the members," and the laity, who lived in the world and "occupied within the church a position of tutelage."[64] In the Presbyterian Church, lay leaders called elders shared the functions of the clergy.[65] Along with well-to-do lay leaders, religious professionals, especially in urban areas, operated the Protestant denominations.

Another important, if not novel, development in the church was its internal politics, which was characterized by fighting over positions, vested interests, and regional interests. In the earlier period, with faith still strong, there was little room for dissension and strife because a small number of converts were fighting for survival in the midst of a Confucian society and later an alien rule. As the religious community grew, however, a more sophisticated organization led to the creation of various positions of influence in the religious community and in society as well. Consequently, friction among church leaders came to the surface and was reflected in references in various publications to a power struggle. We read about "northwestern hegemony," "anti-northwestern church establishment," "the north-south confrontation," and "a thesis on prohibiting factions." These expressions, used in articles and their titles, appeared frequently in church newspapers and periodicals during the late 1920s and the early 1930s.[66]

If a church is an institution of interrelationships among its members, the Protestant church in late colonial Korea was beginning to suffer from its rapid growth and institutionalization.[67] Following the March First Movement, conflict began to emerge between religious professionals and lay members. In sharp contrast to earlier times, some lay members openly began to dispute the authority of the clergy.[68] Some young church members, dissatisfied with the decisions and policies of well-established religious and cultural professionals, showed signs of setting up a new church.[69] As Kim Insŏ pointed out in 1933, the main cause of this conflict was that "class consciousness [had become] strong between clergy and lay members."[70] Some young Christians began to question not only the authority of clergymen, but also that of wealthy and influential lay leaders, who ignored social and political issues and involved themselves in church politics solely for personal interest and influence. By this time, the unethical behavior of clergymen was frequently reported, and it certainly helped to damage their moral authority.[71]

Also, conflict emerged among church leaders themselves over hegemony in church politics. There were many positions of interest and influence in the Korean denominations, which had schools, hospitals, publishing houses, and other outreach agencies. Whoever controlled church politics could fill those positions. As we have seen earlier, two-thirds of Korean Christians were located in the northwestern region: in North P'yŏng'an, South P'yŏng'an, and Hwanghae Provinces. Leaders from this region had controlled politics in the Presbyterian Church since 1907 when a Korean Presbytery was established. This so-called northwestern dominance in the Korean church gradually created discontent among leaders from other regions. This is the main reason why the Presbyterian church, the largest denomination in Korea, was almost split into two: the northwestern faction and the non-northwestern group.[72] In other words, as the church became institutionalized and its leadership positions carried influence, the earlier communal consciousness began to disappear in the church community. Instead, church leaders began to jockey for leadership positions, its members lost confidence in them, and the church became a target of public criticism.

The Protestant church was no longer a dynamic institution in politics and society in large part because it was in constant internal conflict. As clergymen asserted themselves as professionals, there was bound to be friction between them and lay members. This development caused dissatisfaction with the clergy's behavior. Consequently, the clergy felt themselves pressured by their congregations, a circumstance that tended to discourage overt political activity by clergymen who might otherwise have been inclined in that direction. Especially in the dominant Presbyterian Church, a clergyman, who usually came from the outside and depended on the treasury of his congregation for his livelihood, was naturally very sensitive to the lay leaders. Many clergymen thus pursued their own interests simply by following the wishes of their congregation and its lay leaders.

In the beginning, the church in Korea grew with an ever-heightened feeling of patriotism, to the point where the religious community itself came to symbolize patriotic ardor and action. But as the religious community became institutionalized, there appeared a very different class of preachers and other professionals who had little enthusiasm for social and political activity outside the religious community. Following the crushing blow dealt by the Japanese authorities in retaliation for Protestant involvement in the events of 1919, the church edged away from the center of nationalist activity. In the late 1930s, Christian political commitment seemed to reemerge when a minority of fundamentalist church leaders took an uncompromising stand against the colonial government's order to worship at Shinto shrines. To Christians, it was a serious issue because they had to observe the Ten Commandments and could not recognize other deities. The Reverends Yi Kisŏn, Chu Kich'ŏl, and Han Sangdong and their lay followers stood firmly against the Shinto-shrine worship. For example, when the police questioned the Reverend Chu Kich'ŏl about whether he placed his God, Jehovah, above the emperor of Japan, Chu's answer was an emphatic yes, and that sealed his fate. Chu and others believed that "the present suffering is only the death of our mortal body but the future glory will be in a body of everlasting glory like the resurrected body of Christ."[73] These anti–Shinto-shrine worshipers could accept severe suppression because of their belief in God, who would order them not to worship other gods and would bestow eternal glory on His sincere followers. The Reverend Yi Kisŏn, another church leader in the Anti–Shinto-Shrine Worship Campaign, confessed:

> In times of old, Judah fell to Babylon. Its people were taken captive and carried away to Babylon, and its religion suppressed; even national life itself was made over. . . . Today Japan may be likened to Babylon, Korea to Judah: Japanese names are forced on Koreans and Christians are forced to worship at the shrine.[74]

With this religious conviction they chose to go to prison or into exile rather than to pay homage to the Shinto shrines. The so-called Anti–Shinto-Shrine Worship Campaign could have contributed to refreshing the church's patriotic image.

However, their sacrifice meant little, because the church leadership, which now tended to avoid controversial issues, acquiesced to the demands of the colonial government. The resolution adopted in 1938 by the Twenty-seventh General Assembly of the Presbyterian Church in Korea stated:

> Whereas we understand that the Shinto shrine is no religion and will therefore not run counter to Christian doctrine; whereas we realize that paying homage to the shrine is a state ritual showing patriotism; we hereby resolve that we will pay homage to the shrine of our own accord and that we will participate in the national program of total spiritual mobilization as required of us as loyal subjects of the Emperor on the home front.[75]

The Anti-Shinto Shrine Worship Campaign, which was initiated by a small band of fundamentalist clergymen, could have mobilized the whole

Protestant church, because it carried a strong religious and patriotic appeal. Yet the church leadership actually went against the majority opinion of members. Opposition to the Japanese dictate was left to those individuals who regarded the shrine worship as idolatry and were willing to die for their faith. Thus, some schools under the fundamentalists' influence, including the P'yŏngyang Theological Seminary and Sungsil College, closed in protest.[76]

The Japanese colonial government arrested some 2,000 clerical and lay leaders who failed to respond clearly to the following three questions: (1) Was Shinto-shrine worship a national rite or a religious rite? (2) Which was higher, Amaterasu Omikami(Japan's highest god) or Christ? and (3) Which was more important, state or religion?[77] But the Korean Protestant community could not take a unified stand. It was divided into denominations, its leaders engaged in factional politics, and its members lost confidence in the leadership. Most of all, most church leaders did not want to risk being in opposition to the colonial government on this issue.

CONCLUSION

In the last two decades of Japanese colonial rule in Korea, the Protestant church community did not show any interest in nationalist politics and social reform. Instead, many prominent Christians, including Yun Ch'iho, Yu Hyŏnggi, Kim Hwallan, Yang Chusam, Chŏng In'gwa, Chu Yohan, and others became active collaborators with the Japanese.[78] It seems that some were forced to collaborate with the colonial government after their imprisonment and severe torture; others collaborated so that they could continue to operate their churches and schools; and still others to protect their wealth and position.[79]

In 1938, the Japanese colonial government launched the so-called Assimilation Campaign Between Japanese and Korean Churches to make the Korean Church a Japanese religious institution. Especially once the United States joined the Allies in World War II, the Protestant church suffered from Japanese oppression, since it had been introduced mostly by American missionaries and had maintained a close relationship with American Protestant Christianity. Finally in 1942, churches of all Protestant denominations were brought into one Christian group, Kyodan, which was completely under government control.[80]

The church's retreat from the front line of nationalist activities in the second half of Japanese rule occurred for a number of reasons. The religious community became institutionalized, and the position of church leaders in society changed. As a consequence, the church became a religion led by socially and economically established individuals with no desire to improve conditions for those who suffered indignity or even oppression under foreign domination. A series of conflicts developed over influence in the religious community itself. These factors combined to create a situation in which church leaders, whether or not they were politically oriented, could not mobilize the church for politics and were hardly interested in political activity at all. The Korean Protestant church was no longer a dynamic institution.

6 / The Protestant Church under Foreign Occupation, 1945–1948

In August 1945, to great national jubilation, Japanese rule in Korea came to an end as a result of the Allies' victory over the Axis powers. The end of Japanese rule, however, did not lead to an era of freedom for the nation. A line had been drawn across the peninsula at the 38th parallel dividing it into two zones. What was intended as a temporary line of demarcation came to show increasing signs of becoming a permanent boundary.[1]

The typical scholarly approach to the situation in Korea immediately after Liberation is to concentrate on the external circumstances behind the division, somehow overlooking Korean reactions to the event.[2] But after all, if history is about how and why humans respond to their circumstances, the historian should study how Koreans themselves reacted to the subsequent policies toward Korea that the United States and the Soviet Union pursued on behalf of their respective interests.

The overriding importance of the end of Japanese administration of Korea is that the event was not the product of the Koreans' own struggle for independence; it was a "gift." Kim Ku, then head of the provisional government in Shanghai, China, was seriously concerned with the sudden cessation of hostilities. He had a contingent of Korean guerrillas set to infiltrate the peninsula, but there was never any opportunity to deploy them. He was upset to realize that nonparticipation in the war effort would deprive Koreans of any say in postwar decisions about their country.[3] Kim's reaction is sufficient to draw our attention to the error of looking upon Korea's division exclusively in terms of the Allies' policies toward Korea. As Kim foresaw, due to the absence, or failure, of Korean participation in the effort to defeat Japan, the foreign powers entered Korea as "liberators." In other words, Koreans were responsible by their very inaction for a situation in which the foreign powers could do whatever they wished in the peninsula.

One also has to look into what Koreans, particularly political leaders, did during the occupation period from 1945 to 1948. Political leaders at home and those who returned following the departure of Japanese troops were engaged full-time in advancing their respective partisan interests, and no one thought seriously about the division at the 38th parallel, or for that matter which way the nation was to go. If the two superpowers set the stage for the confrontation in Korea, Korean political leaders themselves, divided in two ideological camps since the end of the March First Movement, worked deliberately or inadvertently to strengthen and perpetuate the division between north and south. Since political endeavors at home had the effect of helping the superpowers' policies rather than reversing them, Koreans were indeed responsible for the division of the country. The tragedy of Korea's division was not the Koreans' own doing, but Korean leaders who gained power under foreign influence must share the responsibility.

Nevertheless, some Koreans did attempt to start a new nation based on a coalition of leftist and rightist factions. As signs of Japan's defeat became clear, the Japanese authorities, faced with the prospect of having to abandon Korea, began to sound out certain Korean political leaders to allow them to form political organizations. What they had in mind was to prevent a power vacuum following their defeat in order to assure safe passage for the Japanese residents. Yŏ Unhyŏng, Cho Mansik, and other Korean leaders were contacted. Self-Governing Committees (Chach'ihoe), People's Committees (Inmin wiwŏnhoe), and others were organized throughout the peninsula. They were placed under an umbrella organization, the Committee for the Preparation of Korean Independence (Chosŏn kŏn'guk chunbi wiwŏnhoe) (CPKI hereinafter). The CPKI, a genuine native effort at government rising above partisan differences, showed brief success in building a new nation.[4]

In 1945, troops of the United States and the Soviet Union arrived in Korea as "liberators" for the purpose of disarming and repatriating Japanese troops. The "temporary" division at the 38th parallel was the beginning of hostile relations between north and south. Confronting each other as they were on the peninsula, the United States and the Soviet Union did not look with favor on the emergence of native political groups or political philosophies that were sympathetic to the opposite camp. The CPKI, a left-right coalition, was unwelcome to both foreign powers. In the south the American command found the CPKI far too left-wing for its taste; in the north the Soviet command could not accept Cho Mansik, whose politics were too far to the right.

Another reason for the failure of the CPKI was the political maneuvering of exiles who had just returned to the peninsula. These returnees had nothing to offer but reputations untainted by cooperation with the Japanese. They had some political advantage on this score, because the leaders who had stayed in Korea had shown at least minimal cooperation with the Japanese authorities. But the returnees did not have a political base immediately available for their maneuvering. They found upon their return that Yŏ Unhyŏng in the south and Cho Mansik in the north had already consolidated various political forces under the CPKI. The returned leaders were far behind Cho and Yŏ in terms of political initiative and organization. In the south, some of them influenced the Americans to disapprove of the CPKI, which led to the early demise of that organization. Syngman Rhee and other pro-American political leaders soon emerged in the south. In the north, CPKI vice-chairman Hyŏn Chunhyŏk was assassinated in late 1945, and Cho Mansik, the founder and chairman of the CPKI in the north, was placed under house arrest. Kim Il-sung and other pro-Soviet returnees took over the CPKI leadership. In short, two foreign powers were each anxious to develop domestic political forces favoring their ideology and interests. And those returnees without a political base at home wanted the backing of the occupation forces. There soon developed a political coalescence between the foreign forces and the returning exiles. This development doomed the CPKI.[5]

A great deal of research has been done on political developments following the liberation of Korea; new data have been uncovered and new methods have been applied from different perspectives. As is widely known, a great majority of the personages on the political scene during the early post-Liberation period were Protestant church members. In addition to moderate to left-wing leaders such as Kim Ch'angjun, Yŏ Unhyŏng, Kang Yang'uk, Hong Kiju, and Ch'oe Yonggŏn, major personalities of the right such as Syngman Rhee, Kim Ku, Yi Yunyŏng, and O Yunsŏn were also church leaders or Christians. For some reason the Christian background of these individuals is not mentioned at all, or only tangentially, in the literature.[6]

To gain a full understanding of the politics of the period, one cannot leave out the role of the Christian community—with its vast network of churches, the sheer number of its adherents, and its educated clergy.[7] More specifically, the fact that the leadership positions of the CPKI were assumed by Christian leaders with Christian education warrants particular attention. For example, Yŏ Unhyŏng had studied in mission schools and the P'yŏngyang seminary, and had once been an assistant minister in Seoul. Cho Mansik was one of the most influential church elders in P'yŏngyang. Yun Hayŏng and Han Kyŏngjik, church pastors, and Ham Sŏkhŏn, a famous social critic, led the CPKI and related political organizations in North P'yŏng'an Province. In the south, Kim Ch'angjun, Ch'oe Munsik, and Yi Chaebok, all of whom were church pastors, were also actively involved in the CPKI.[8] How did the Christian community in southern Korea react to the coming of forces from the United States, whose missionaries had introduced Protestantism some six decades earlier? And how did the church in the north—which was stronger than elsewhere in Korea—interact with the Soviet occupation forces and Kim Il-sung? Again, the CPKI's relations with the church remains one of the least explored subjects of the politics of the period.

The Protestant church played a different role in the two zones. In the north, the church, much larger and more united than in the south, took the political initiative, only to soon enter into an adversarial relationship with government. In the south, the church developed amicable relations with government and came to support it vigorously.[9]

Many historians and theologians view this phenomenon in terms of an inevitable division between Christianity and communism.[10] It was not, however, philosophical differences that caused conflict between Kim Il-sung and Protestant Christians, but rather differences on a purely political, nonreligious level. Initially, Kim's regime was not opposed to Christianity as such, and his regime included prominent Christian ministers and lay leaders, such as Kang Yang'uk, Hong Kiju, and Ch'oe Yonggŏn.[11] Kim himself had been brought up in a Christian family, and had been a church member.[12] Despite the antireligious inclination of most communists, it seems that the Kim regime did not oppose the church from the start, but was driven into an antichurch position only when the church set itself against the regime. Further evidence of this may be seen in the fact that a considerable number of Christians active in the CPKI in the south were socialists.[13] Rhetoric equating Christianity with anticommunism or communism with anti-Christianity is an oversimplification.

THE CHURCH IN THE NORTH

As mentioned, before the arrival of the troops of the two superpowers, Koreans were getting ready to start a new nation on the basis of a left-right coalition. Although this movement was a nationwide phenomenon, the political activity in the north, including that of the CPKI, was sponsored by church leaders or enjoyed their active participation. Gradually, in South P'yŏng'an Province, different groups such as the Self-Governing Committees and the People's Committees began rallying around the CPKI branch, led by Cho Mansik. Cho's group, along with Hyŏn Chunhyŏk's leftist group, then formed the People's Political Committee of the Five Provinces in the North (Ibuk odo inmin chŏngch'i wiwŏnhoe) (PPCFPN hereinafter), a coalition that established its leadership in the five northern provinces. Indeed, the coalition had such influence that the Soviet command found it necessary to consult with it in administering the northern half of the peninsula.[14]

From the Soviet point of view, however, Cho Mansik, with his Christian outlook and the Christian background of his organization, was not welcome. Furthermore, the Soviets, wishing to establish a Korean regime friendly toward Moscow, took a dim view of the Christian church as a whole because of its sympathy for the United States. The Soviets viewed the United States as the country that had introduced Protestantism to late Chosŏn Korea and promoted it until the outbreak of the Pacific War in 1941. Presumably, what made them even more uncomfortable was the growing influence of such Christians as Syngman Rhee, Kim Kyusik, and Yŏ Unhyŏng in the south. In this situation, the Soviets could not ignore the Christian element that dominated Cho's coalition in terms of leadership and organization.

Christians such as Cho Mansik, Yi Yunyŏng, O Yunsŏn, and Yun Hayŏng had already assumed political leadership when the Russians arrived in the northern part of the country. At the time of Liberation, both Pak Hŏnyŏng, foremost among Korean communists on the peninsula, and the left-leaning Yŏ Unhyŏng were active in the south. Kim Il-sung and other Korean communists returning from Yenan, China, and Siberia did not enjoy sufficient stature or popular support.[15] The Soviets were none too happy with Hyŏn Chunhyŏk, the leading communist figure in the north and an ally of Cho Mansik.[16] Furthermore, the leftist leaders were divided into a variety of small factions at the time. In its capacity as a "liberator" of Korea, the Soviet Union could not afford to use naked force to turn the political situation to its advantage. Instead, it adopted the policy of supporting the left-right coalition, the PPCFPN, led by Cho and Hyŏn.

Kim Il-sung, just thirty-three years old and well known as a guerrilla leader against Japan, began to take over the PPCFPN with Russian support. He was actively featured in public rallies, where Cho Mansik would present him as a former guerrilla leader and a returned hero.[17] Having no strong political base at home, Kim had difficulty advancing himself despite the Soviet support and the nationalist reputation he had earned as a guerrilla leader. After the assassination of Hyŏn and the house arrest of Cho, Kim Il-sung gained control of the PPCFPN in 1946. Kim then moved to deal with the Protestant church, which was not only the largest organized community in the north, but also the main base for Cho and his political organization.[18]

Soon after Liberation, Christians began their own political activities in earnest. By September 1945, Yun Hayŏng and Han Kyŏngjik, Christian ministers who had studied in America and had led regional People's Committees, and Yi Yup'il, a prominent church elder in North P'yŏng'an Province, formed the Christian Social Democratic Party (Kidokkyo sahoe minjudang), the first political party to appear following the Liberation. Other church leaders, including Yi Kihyŏk, Yi Kibaek, and Kang Man'u, actively participated in this party. In 1947, the Christian Liberal Party (Kidokkyo chayudang), under ministers Kim Hwasik, Song Chŏnggŭn, and Sin Sŏg'u, became active. In November 1945, Cho Mansik, just ousted from the PPCFPN, launched the Korean Democratic Party (Chosŏn minjudang) together with Yi Yunyŏng, a Christian minister, and O Yunyŏng, a prominent church elder.[19]

During the three-month period after its founding, the Korean Democratic Party's membership increased dramatically to some 500,000 by early 1946. At the time, there were only 4,530 members of various communist parties in the north. Cho Mansik's Korean Democratic Party also published three newspapers: *P'yŏngbuk minbo* [People's news in North P'yŏng'an Province], *Hwanghae minbo* [People's news in Hwanghae Province], and *Kangwŏn minbo* [People's news in Kangwŏn Province]. Communists such as Ch'oe Yonggŏn and Kim Ch'aek also joined this party as vice-president and secretary-general, respectively.[20] Like the Christian Social Democratic Party and the Christian Liberal Party, the Korean Democratic Party made use of existing church organizations and members to promote its cause.

At the same time, church leaders in the north cautiously activated church organizations and members. In October 1945, on the initiative of representatives of the six presbyteries in North P'yŏng'an Province, church leaders formed the Joint Presbytery of Five Provinces in the North (Ibuk odo yŏnhaphoe) to coordinate collective action for church affairs as well as political action in opposition to the Soviet authorities and Kim Il-sung. Church leaders held a series of revival meetings in order to activate and strengthen Christian spirituality and cohesiveness vis-à-vis secular authorities. The slogan of the revival was "Great Evangelical Meetings Celebrating Independence" (Tongnip kinyŏm chŏndo taehoe). Organized and spiritually unified, Christians began to stand against the Soviet occupation force and the Kim Il-sung group.[21]

As the USSR and Kim Il-sung took over the PPCFPN, political conflict emerged between Kim's group and the Protestant community. Although Kim enjoyed full Soviet backing and assistance, he could not gain political supremacy in the north immediately after he returned to the peninsula from Siberia because he had to deal with Cho Mansik, the best-known nationalist leader in the north, and the Protestant community, which supported Cho and other Christian leaders. Even after Cho was put under house arrest and Hyŏn was assassinated, the Protestant church community did not yield. Many Koreans who had longed for an independent country free from Soviet influence participated in the church's opposition to Kim Il-sung. The political battle between Kim's group and the Protestant community was waged on equal terms at least during the early stages.[22]

Early in 1946, the Joint Presbytery of Five Provinces in the North planned a mass rally to mark the anniversary of the March First Movement and to demonstrate its political influence. Kim Il-sung reacted by ordering Christian leaders arrested. The rally was held as planned, but not without incident. Communist forces stormed the rally and attacked the participants. Kim also held a separate rally of his own in the square in front of the P'yŏngyang railway station; this meeting was interrupted by an explosion.[23] Following these events, the Kim group and the Protestant community opposed each other on every issue. The Joint Presbytery of Five Provinces in the North boycotted the 1946 election. In November 1946, the above-mentioned Christian Socialist Party held a mass meeting marking the opening of its Yong'amp'o chapter. The meeting was interrupted when communist youths stormed it and beat up party leaders, most of them Christian. Soon thereafter, anticommunist demonstrations were held in Sinŭiju.[24] Clashes between procommunist and anticommunist forces occurred in the major cities and towns throughout the northern part of the peninsula. Christians led most of the anticommunist activities at the time.[25]

Presumably, Kim Il-sung decided that he could not gain popular support by force and that cooperation with Christian groups, which had the largest organization in the north and had long enjoyed social and political influence, was out of the question. The only choice left to him was a divide-and-rule approach. In 1946, his political advisers, Kang Yang'uk and Hong Kiju, themselves Christian ministers, prevailed upon influential ministers such as Kim Ŭngsun, Pak Sangsun, and Kim Iktu to form the pro–Kim Il-sung

Christian League of Korea (Chosŏn Kidokkyo yŏnmaeng). Kim Il-sung thereby divided successfully the Joint Presbytery of Five Provinces in the North, which had formerly stood firmly against him. Furthermore, he allowed only member churches to continue functioning; those outside the Christian League were ordered closed. Only member clergymen were allowed to work as ministers.[26] Church property was nationalized, and two theological seminaries with some 600 students were merged into one in 1950, with enrollment reduced to 120.[27] This policy resulted in a dramatic reduction in the size of the clergy and church.

At the same time, Kim Il-sung put ordinary church members under surveillance and suppression because they also stood against his policy and rule. According to secret documents prepared by the communist authorities, Kim's sensitivity to the activities of Christians throughout the northern part of the country was due to the Christians using their churches as bases for their anti-Soviet and anti-Kim activities. For example, in Sŏnch'ŏn County a secret communist agent reported at least "once a week" to his superior from 1946 to 1948 about the activities of Christians.[28] Christians were indeed the major targets of communist surveillance and suppression, and some ministers, church functionaries, and ordinary Christians thus began to move to southern Korea, an exodus that reached its height during the Korean War from 1950 to 1953.[29]

The clash between the Protestant church and the Kim Il-sung group in northern Korea has been explained exclusively in terms of the philosophical or ideological conflict between the two—that Christian idealism and Marxist materialism were irreconcilable.[30] This view is somewhat facile. It would be closer to the truth to say that the ideological dichotomy was a result of social and political conflict. In the early days, at least, Christian ministers and lay leaders such as Kang Yanguk, Hong Kiju, and Ch'oe Yonggŏn supported Kim Il-sung. Furthermore, Kim himself was born into a devoted Christian family and was raised in strong Christian surroundings. He attended church services and led church activities before the liberation of 1945.[31] In fact, church leaders in P'yŏngyang invited Kim Il-sung, Ch'oe Yonggŏn, and the Soviet command to a religious ceremony at the home of church elder Kim Hyŏnsŏk to welcome Kim Il-sung in late September 1945.[32] At this time, the relationship between church leaders and Kim Il-sung was friendly. In addition, Kim formed the Christian League of Korea together with prominent church leaders in 1946. Of course, Kim did so in order to advance his own political position, but one should recognize that he was not ideologically anti-Christian, at least in the early post-Liberation period. The church-government clash in the north should be understood in terms of the political and not ideological conflict between the two forces.

The political strength of the Protestant church in the north was tremendous by the time of the Liberation. The religious community in the north consisted of some 300,000 adherents and some 2,000 churches in addition to a well-educated and politically experienced leadership. When this community assumed political leadership after Liberation, it indeed became the major obstacle to the political maneuvering of the Kim Il-sung group, which had just returned to the peninsula and lacked a concrete political base at home except for Soviet support and a patriotic image. As we have seen, in terms of political initiative and organization, the returned leaders lagged far behind Cho Mansik and other political leaders backed by the religious community. In taking over the political organization of Cho Mansik and Hyŏn Chunhyŏk, for example, Kim Il-sung had to use force against Cho and his Christian followers.

The church-government clash in the north should be understood also in the context of the divided occupation of the peninsula by the Soviet Union and the United States. The Soviets, who wished to establish a Korean regime which would be ideologically and politically pro-Soviet, could not ignore the Protestant church, Korea's largest organized community. To the Russians and Kim Il-sung, the religious community was not welcome because it had been introduced and promoted mainly by missionaries from the country now occupying the south. The Soviets and Kim found that most Christians in the north were pro-American and pro–Syngman Rhee, and, in fact, that they "secretly" contacted political leaders in the south. The communists thus took over the Christians' political organization and suppressed Christian political activities. In the process, political conflict between the Kim group and the Protestant church community developed because each group insisted on its own course of action. The harsher Kim's repressive policy toward the religious community was, the more Christians moved south.

The church-government clash in the north and later the Korean War produced a huge migration of Christians to the south and contributed to the explosive growth of Protestantism there. The conflict in the north was also one of the major causes of the emergence of an anticommunist Christianity and church-government collusion in the south. The migrant Christians and the refugees who became Christians not only became anticommunist themselves, but also made anticommunists of their fellow Christians in the south by revealing their painful experience under the Kim Il-sung regime. To combat communism, these Christians cooperated with the anticommunist regimes of Syngman Rhee, Park Chung-hee, Chun Doo Hwan, and Roh Tae-woo.

THE CHURCH IN THE SOUTH

By the time American troops arrived in southern Korea, the organizational network of the Committee for the Preparation of Korean Independence, led by Yŏ Unhyŏng, covered the entire territory. But Yŏ's CPKI in the south was a less influential organization than Cho Mansik's CPKI in the north because in the south opinions were much more divided and interests much more varied.

However, like its counterpart organization in the north, the CPKI in the south also had a strong connection with the Protestant church community due to the region's vast network of churches and sheer number of adherents. Yŏ Unhyŏng, it will be recalled, was himself once assistant pastor of the Sŭngdong Church in Seoul after having studied in mission schools and the P'yŏngyang Presbyterian Theological Seminary.[33] His original CPKI included some well-known Christian ministers and lay leaders—Kim Ch'angjun, one of the thirty-three signatories of the Declaration of Independence in 1919; Yi Kyugap, a famous Methodist minister; Yi Man'gyu, also a minister; Yi Tonghwa, a Christian intellectual; and Kim Yonggi, a well-known church elder.

Among its local organizers and leaders in Kyŏnggi and Kangwŏn Provinces were the Reverend Hwang Hoesu, chairman of P'yŏngch'ang County; the Reverend Paek Kŭmsan, chairman of Hongsŏng County; the Reverend Yi Hayŏng, chairman of the city of Suwŏn; and the Reverend Kim Kwangno, chairman of Kap'yŏng County. In addition, the Reverends Ch'oe Munsik and Yi Chaebok, who later led the so-called Taegu disturbance in 1945, were also leaders in North Kyŏngsang Province.[34] Reverend Cho Hyangnok recalled that during his speaking tour through South Kyŏngsang Province during the early years after the Liberation he did not see a single county without a branch of the CPKI. He reported that most chairmen were either local church ministers or lay leaders.[35] In short, church ministers and lay leaders, who had led a variety of local community activities during the colonial period, also participated actively in the umbrella CPKI in the south.

Unlike its counterpart in the north, however, Protestants in the south were not united in their support for the CPKI, primarily because the religious community in the south was not as cohesive as its northern counterpart. Denominational leaders, regional leaders, and pro- and anti-Japanese church leaders had all been in Seoul. The religious community in the south, therefore, could not speak with one voice.[36] Christian participation in the CPKI was the main political trend in the church community during the early years after the Liberation, but it was based on individual involvement.

The presence of the United States army in the south and growing animosity toward the Soviet Union and its policies were primary factors in the collapse of the CPKI.[37] As the largest political organization, covering the entire southern zone, it was not welcomed by the U.S. military government.[38] U.S. officials, concerned only with the U.S.-Soviet confrontation on the peninsula, considered the CPKI to be a leftist political organization. According to Bruce Cumings, they simply did not like the existence of the CPKI itself. Instead, the U.S. military government began to work with elements tainted by collaboration with the Japanese. This generally well-to-do group naturally feared the loss of their vested interests in the new era.[39]

Like the CPKI in the north, the CPKI in the south collapsed because of political maneuvering by returned nationalist leaders. Untainted by cooperation with the Japanese, these political leaders returned to Korea as national heroes. Each leader had his own faction, and these factions were far behind the CPKI of Yŏ Unhyŏng in terms of political initiative, timing, and organization.[40] They also did not have their own political base at home upon their return from exile. They had to make up for their lack of a home base, and they found that the Korean Democratic Party (Han'guk minjudang) (hereinafter KDP), composed of many pro-Japanese and well-to-do right-wing Koreans, was immediately available to them. The KDP for its part, needed the returnees' nationalist reputation to offset its political weakness—its lack of resistance to the Japanese during the colonial period. A political alliance developed between the right-wing, formerly pro-Japanese elements and the returned political leaders, especially Syngman Rhee.[41] This alliance emerged as the leading force in the political scene of the south after the assassinations of Yŏ Unhyŏng, Kim Ku, and other prominent political leaders.

From 1945 to 1948, during this period of political chaos, the Protestant church community underwent a great change. As we have seen, although Protestants in the south were divided into various elements and thus could not speak politically with one voice, many church leaders and lay Christians actively participated in the CPKI organization before and after the Liberation. The U.S. occupation and the return of exiles, however, altered this political atmosphere in the religious community. Because most of the prominent political returnees, including Syngman Rhee, Kim Ku, and Kim Kyusik, were Christians, the church community, whose main political expression had been in CPKI activity, began to be divided into those supporting the CPKI (the pro–Yŏ Unhyŏng group) and those favoring Christian politicians returned from exile (the pro–Syngman Rhee faction, the pro–Kim Kyusik element, and the pro–Kim Ku Christians).[42] But the conflict within the church community actually boiled down to two groups: the CPKI and the anti-CPKI element led by Syngman Rhee.

The conflict between these two groups developed favorably for Syngman Rhee, primarily because the U.S. military government backed his anticommunist policy and a great number of Christians who fled from the north actively participated in the political maneuvering to eliminate leftist elements in the church. In 1946, for example, church leaders of the left and the middle of the road, such as the Reverend Kim Ch'angje and the Reverend Pak Sŏngsa of the CPKI, the Reverend Kal Honggi, and the Reverend Sin Hŭng'u of the YMCA formed the Democratic League of Christians (Kidokkyo minju yŏnmaeng) at the YMCA building in Seoul. A public meeting announcing its formation was disrupted when some 300 men from the Northwest Youth Corps (Sŏbuk ch'ŏngnyŏndan)—composed of anticommunist youth who had fled religious and political suppression under Kim Il-sung's rule—stormed in. Political rivalry in church circles deepened as it spread outward from Seoul, and violent clashes between leftists and rightists took place frequently in cities, towns, and villages—wherever there were churches and CPKI branches.[43] As Syngman Rhee emerged in 1948 as the first president of the Republic of Korea with the backing of the U.S. military government and the anticommunist Christians, most of them from the north, leftist elements in the church were purged.

The American occupation was the decisive factor in the waning of CPKI influence in the south. To Korean Christians, the United States was the Christian nation that had introduced Protestantism. The Christians on the whole had been the most pro-American element in Korea since the late nineteenth century. In addition, many church leaders obtained modern education in mission schools or in the United States with the support of American missionaries.[44] In 1945, the U.S. military government made Christmas a national holiday, the first time in the history of Korea. Additionally, the military government appointed many Christians to prominent positions. For example, it established the Advisory Council on October 5, 1945, and named eleven Koreans, of whom six were Christians, as members.[45] The

Americans also appointed many Protestants to other positions of responsibility. The circumstances were sufficiently ripe for a political rapprochement between the U.S. military government and the Protestant church community. CPKI followers in the religious community thereupon lost ground amid the left-right conflict.

The emergence of Syngman Rhee changed the political atmosphere in the church. Following his return from a lengthy exile during the period of Japanese rule, Rhee's political stock rapidly rose with his nationalist reputation, but he still lacked an organizational base of political activity.[46] To make up for this lack, Rhee managed to gain support among Christians. His job was made easier because most of his close advisers, including Hŏ Chŏng, Im Yŏngsin, Im Pyŏngjik, Cho Pyŏng'ok, Yi Kibung, and Hwang Sŏngsu, were Christians. Soon he had organized a solid following, which visibly increased especially with the passing of Yŏ Unhyŏng and Kim Ku from the scene. A parallel development in the consolidation of Rhee's position in the church community was a regrouping of Christian leaders who were under attack for their collaboration with the Japanese and who thus were groping for survival in the new era. They came forward in support of Syngman Rhee in the name of Christian unity and early independence. Such church leaders as the Reverend Kim Kwansik and the Reverend Chŏng In'gwa, who still held leadership positions, boosted Rhee and his anticommunist policy among church circles.[47]

Lastly, the Christians who migrated from the north accelerated the decline of CPKI influence in the church community and bolstered the strength of Syngman Rhee. The Christian migrants shifted church opinion, which was then being contested by rightists and leftists, toward an anticommunist position by revealing their experiences in the north. They also led Rhee's anticommunist campaign. These factors combined to eliminate leftist elements such as the CPKI and to strengthen Rhee's right-wing camp in the Protestant church community.[48]

7 / Protestant Christians and South Korean Politics, 1948–1980s

In the late 1940s, Protestant Christians found themselves supporting the formation of a pro-Christian government in the south and began enjoying its protection and sponsorship. The position of the Christian church in the south was now one of conformity with the government, and it continued into the era of Park Chung-hee. This attitude toward the government was a far cry from the defiance exhibited by Christians toward the Confucian establishment and the early Japanese colonial regime.

As mentioned, certain liberal scholars prefer to attribute the complicated religious-political association of the Protestant church simply to the pietist, fundamentalist, otherworldly theology to which most Korean Christians adhered. Theology is the main target of these scholars because they regard church-government cooperation as the product of an apolitical attitude basically caused by an apolitical theology—that is, a pietist, otherworldly theology.[1] This view seems to be in error on two counts. First, fundamentalist Christians did not take an apolitical position at all; they obviously favored the existing secular authority by arguing for church-state separation. Perhaps the liberal scholars are describing instead the conservative Christians' indifference to their own liberal political views. These observers also fail to see that the earlier Christians actively participated in political movements against the Confucian government and foreign rulers, even though their theological orientation was pietist, fundamentalist, and otherworldly. The liberal view's second error is its implication that action is motivated exclusively by ideas. The fundamentalist Christians who had opposed the secular power before Liberation now supported the government. This last development alone would be sufficient grounds for refuting the liberal argument. For a better understanding of the change in the political position of Protestant Christians, one would do better to examine systematically the changes in their social position and concomitant political acts, and then to speculate on the relationship between these changes and the fundamentalist, otherworldly, and pietist theology.[2]

From the late 1950s onward, voices of criticism against the government were heard from within the Protestant community. Christians such as Chang Chunha, editor of *Sasanggye* [The world of thought], an influential intellectual monthly, Ham Sŏkhŏn, Quaker preacher of national and international renown, Kim Sangdon, a leading opposition politician who later became mayor of Seoul, and Chŏng Ilhyŏng, an ordained minister and opposition politician, dared to raise their voices against their fellow Christian Syngman Rhee. These critics called for support of human rights, democracy, and social justice. Later in the 1960s, the speakers were mostly clergymen of the Christ Presbyterian Assembly in the Republic of Korea (Han'guk Kidokkyo changnohoe), a splinter group embracing a liberal theology.[3] It is the view of many observers that these Christian critics acted upon their liberal theology:[4] an argument that is only partially accurate. They were no more active in politics than were the fundamentalists under Japanese colonial rule. Moreover, along with the fundamentalists of their own times, they had remained silent under Syngman Rhee. Why then the sudden outburst of criticism beginning in the late 1960s? To what extent did Christian theology influence their political actions?

This splinter group, which had come into being in 1954 when its members were ousted from the parent denomination, followed an independent path and developed relations with world church organizations. Its pattern of action was similar to the way disillusioned young Confucians in the nineteenth century converted to Protestantism hoping to find and promote a new way of life. And just as their nineteenth-century predecessors had turned to a new religion, the members of this liberal minority, now outside the pale of the conservative church establishment, turned to new trends in theology. A few of these liberals began to criticize the parent church and in turn the government, which the conservative majority had supported, at times actively and at times passively.

Nevertheless, theirs remained voices in the wilderness which elicited little or no echo not only in the Protestant community under conservative control, but even in the liberal denomination to which they belonged. Why didn't all the pastors who belonged to the same liberal denomination and shared the same theology support the political programs of the liberal activists?

This question takes us beyond theological differences to some structural aspects of the Korean Protestant church. In the first place, because of the deep hostility and sense of rivalry between the parent denomination and the splinter group, the liberal minority could receive nothing but criticism in mainstream circles. Additionally, pastors of the liberal denomination were reluctant to involve themselves in controversial issues, much less antigovernment critiques, simply because their congregations were filled with established members of the community—as were the conservative churches. In other words, since pastors of the liberal denomination who sympathized with the Christian activists and shared their liberal theology were also under the restraint of lay leaders, they could not actively participate in the Christian political campaign for democracy, human rights, and social justice. For this reason, the political criticism emanating from the Protestant church in the 1970s remained the lonely action of liberal intellectuals.[5]

The ouster of the liberals from the parent church sharpened their sense of purpose and direction, setting them free to go their own way and hastening their acceptance of a new theology and Christian social activism. Their separation from the conservative church allowed the liberals to criticize the parent church and the authoritarian government. Interestingly, the very separation from the parent denomination that helped enable the liberals to criticize the government without any pressure from within also made their critical voice a lonely one. For its part, the government used the structural aspects of the Korean Protestant church, such as hostile denominationalism and the tension and conflict between clergymen and lay leaders, to minimize and stultify the influence of the critical voices. The government saw the possibility of deepening the rift between the conservatives and the liberals by coaxing the former into bringing pressure and criticism to bear on the liberals outside the main denomination.[6] The government also used lay leaders to persuade or pressure pastors not to involve themselves in controversial non-church-related politics.[7] The political activism that set itself against dictatorial trends in government had a shaky base within the inner structure of the church and had to heed the church's vulnerability as well as the government's arbitrariness.

THE SYNGMAN RHEE REGIME AND THE CHURCH, 1948–1960

Syngman Rhee ruled South Korea from 1948 to 1960. At his inauguration as the first president of the Republic of Korea on August 15, 1948, Rhee took an oath of office with his hand on the Bible, a gesture unprecedented in Korean history.[8] At the opening ceremony of the National Assembly, over which he presided as speaker before the inauguration, Rhee told the audience to rise and had Assemblyman Yi Yunyŏng, a Christian minister, lead a prayer of thanks. This was also unprecedented, and not even part of the printed program.[9] The first National Assembly and the first presidential inauguration in a land steeped in Confucianism, Buddhism, and folk cults were begun with Christian ceremonies.

As mentioned, Christian ministers and lay members assumed influential positions in politics and society in the Rhee era. Rhee himself was a church elder, and Vice-President Ham T'aeyŏng was a minister, as was Yi Yunyŏng, acting prime minister during the early years of the republic. The National Assembly included church ministers and lay leaders such as Kim Sangdon, Hwang Sŏngsu, Pak Yŏngch'ul, Kim Toyŏn, and Chŏng Ilhyŏng. Christian ministers and lay leaders accounted for 25 percent of the first Assembly, according to one survey.[10] According to Kim Yŏngmo, Christians occupied some 40 percent of political leadership positions, even though they constituted less than 10 percent of the South Korean population.[11] As expected, Christian ceremonies were widely adopted in public functions. All signs at the beginning of the Rhee regime indicated the opening of a "Christian era."[12]

Syngman Rhee "viewed himself as a national leader" and "transcended the demeaning competition of political parties and factions" that should and would be allowed in a democratic society. In James Palais's words, he "preferred to use agencies of coercion—the police and the army—to ensure his power rather than persuade political opponents."[13] What Rhee did to South Korea was to deprive its people of an opportunity to build a democratic system. What he did in the first chapter of the republican history of the country was to subjugate the legislative and judicial branches to the executive, place local government under centralized power, and suppress a free and responsible press with the police and the army.[14] He set a precedent for those who would follow.

The relationship between the Protestant community and this authoritarian regime was an amicable one that has generally been ignored by scholars.[15] Several intriguing questions remain unanswered: Why did the Protestant church consistently support the regime? What specific form did this support take, and what in particular did the church support? What bearing did the church's approval have on the continuation of Rhee's rule? Did the church undergo any change, politically or historically, by supporting his regime? These questions will be addressed by considering what brought the Protestant church into a leadership position in South Korean politics and society.

The Development of a Symbiotic Relationship

Some scholars have argued that the presence of the United States called forth a friendly response from Korean Christians and enabled cooperation between the occupation forces and the Protestant church. The *Han'guk hyŏndaesa* [History of contemporary Korea], prepared by the National History Compilation Committee, a government agency, pointed out that the stationing of American troops facilitated the advance of Christians to positions of responsibility.[16] In fact, the U.S. military government appointed many Christians to work in its offices. But one should not overemphasize this factor, for the American command did not particularly favor Christian elements over other political forces. According to Bruce Cumings, when the Americans arrived in Korea on September 9, 1945, they first sought support from collaborators with the Japanese, moderate nationalists, and generally well-to-do Koreans who later coalesced into the Korean Democratic Party (KDP) more than they looked for support from the CPKI of Yŏ Unhyŏng, which contained more Christians. For example, whereas five of twenty-six members of the cabinet proposed by the KDP were Christian, six out of ten members of the CPKI-proposed cabinet were Christian. The American command named eleven Koreans, of whom four were Christian, to the Advisory Council it established on October 9, 1945. However, among these four Christian leaders, Yŏ Unhyŏng soon resigned and Cho Mansik was still in North Korea. In effect, the American command had appointed only two Christians to the eleven-member council. Most of the appointed council members from the KDP were landlords, businessmen, and intellectuals.[17]

Scholars also have pointed out that the Christian community responded amicably to the emergence of Syngman Rhee as the first president of Korea, and cooperation between the two forces soon reached the point where a coalition between the secular and the spiritual was achieved. Rhee, Christians maintained, facilitated the advance of church leaders to high government positions.[18]

It is true that Rhee tried to obtain the church's support in order to make up for his lack of a home base upon his return from a long exile (1910–45). His maneuvering for Christian support worked well; not only was he the best-known Korean Christian leader, but his close advisers were also Christians.[19] But we should not overlook the important fact that church leaders had already assumed leadership positions in Korea by the time of his return. It would be superficial, therefore, to say that Christian leaders were appointed to higher government posts simply on the ground of religion. Such circumstances as the U.S. occupation and the emergence of Syngman Rhee helped Christians merely to consolidate their leadership position in society.

Christians had already become a dominant political force in Korea by the time of liberation from Japan. In 1944, there were 5,497 churches on the peninsula with congregations totaling 450,000.[20] There was simply no other group comparable in organization and number to the Christian church immediately after the Liberation. All other groups which would subsequently play a more significant role in politics, such as those for businessmen, bureaucrats, policemen, soldiers, and even politicians, were disorganized or at best in the process of regrouping. These groups were under attack for their collaboration with the Japanese during the colonial period.[21] Church leaders, moreover, had better education, more experience in politics and administration, and nationwide organizational networks at the time.[22] All these assets gave the Christians a formidable potential for political activity, especially during the early years after Liberation.

Many church leaders had played a leadership role not only in religious matters but also in secular affairs—that is, in matters of education, community, and even nationalist politics since the late nineteenth century. The late Reverend Kang Sinmyŏng, who lived through those years, recalled in 1983 that

> the early Korean church enlightened the country because the pastors played a major role as community leaders. The pastors were highly respected, and people consulted them about all community problems. Pastors were respected as leaders in the community. . . . Even people outside [the church] . . . began to respect the pastors.[23]

Both Christian and non-Christian Koreans respected church officials as religious leaders, teachers, and opinion-makers in their communities. It is no surprise, therefore, that most of the political leaders in the post-Liberation era were Christians, whether they were leftists or rightists, and that in 1952, 25 percent of the National Assemblymen elected by popular vote in South Korea were also Christians.[24]

The formation of two separate regimes in 1948 and the Korean War in 1950 strengthened the church in the south and caused it to develop a symbiotic relationship with the Syngman Rhee regime. The persecution of Christians in the north redounded to the Rhee regime's advantage, creating in the south an atmosphere in which anticommunism was upheld as a patriotic ideology befitting a loyal citizen of the Republic of Korea.[25] This atmosphere was strengthened by the numerous refugees from the north. (Most of them were Christians, and many of the others were converted after settling down in the south.)[26] As we have seen in chapter five, these North Korean Christian refugees helped Rhee eliminate leftist elements in the Protestant church community.

The Protestant church therefore supported Rhee's effort to establish an anticommunist ideology. In 1948, Rhee delivered an address before a conference of Presbyterian churches in the United States. He began by thanking the churches in America for bringing Christianity to Korea, and he noted great work in education, reform, and medicine that Protestantism had achieved for Korea. Therefore, he pledged that his government would do its best to further Christian doctrine in Korea. However, "the most urgent of all the problems" that his government and Christianity in Korea faced, Rhee continued, was "the Soviet-trained Red Army," which aspired "to communize the South" and "to wipe out Christianity." He warned American church leaders that the Red Army would "destroy both spiritual and intellectual enlightenment" that Americans had achieved in Korea. He then appealed for churches' active support of his government and of Korean Christians who were working together to combat communism. His speech was well received, and funds were immediately raised for the cause of anticommunism in Korea.[27] This was a time when anticommunist hysteria was sweeping the United States, and Senator McCarthy's witch-hunt to ferret out hidden agents and "fellow travelers" was creating widespread fear.[28]

The anticommunist hysteria in the United States was immediately reflected in South Korea, which was almost totally under American influence at the time. The Korean Protestant church, because of its long connection with the United States and the tremendous amount of relief money and goods obtained therefrom, performed a valuable service for Rhee by enhancing the cause of anticommunism to the point of equating it with the Christian mission. By appointing many Christians from North Korea—for example, as mentioned, Christian minister Yi Yunyŏng was Rhee's first prime minister—Rhee not only obtained the church's support but used it to consolidate his anticommunist policy.[29]

The so-called Incident of the Christianity and Procommunist Policy Pamphlet (Kidokkyo wa yonggong chŏngch'aek p'ampŭretŭ sakŏn) of 1951 would be the best example of church-government association in the anticommunist campaign.[30] This incident was initiated by Syngman Rhee himself in 1951 when he addressed a group of Christian National Assemblymen who had been invited to his temporary residence in Pusan. Rhee expressed indignation toward the Korean National Council of Churches (KNCC) and exasperation at the failure of the church to disassociate itself from the World Council of Churches, which in his view was too procommunist. On hand were fundamentalist pastor Song Sangsŏk, minister Yi Kyugap, and lay leader Hwang Sŏngsu. (The latter two were members of the National Assembly.) Rhee handed out an article in English that pointed out the WCC's "procommunist policies." Song, Yi, and Hwang translated this article and printed it as a pamphlet that was later circulated with the signatures of the twenty-two National Assemblymen.[31]

The pamphlet pointed out that the World Council of Churches was sympathetic toward communism because it kept in touch with church members in Eastern Europe as well as in the Soviet Union and called for the recognition of the People's Republic of China. Furthermore, the pamphlet claimed that the KNCC was affiliated with this "procommunist" world church body.[32] Under the circumstances of the Korean War and the Chinese participation in it, the pamphlet raised a great scandal in political and church circles. Church leaders in the KNCC had to respond defensively that no one was more anticommunist than they.[33] The Korean church, together with Rhee, had finally established a political formula: communism is anti-Christian and hence Christianity is anticommunist. Thus Christianity and the anticommunist political position were practically fused into one.

Mobilization of Church Resources for Elections

Church-government cooperation was not limited only to the development of an anticommunist ideology. During the twelve-year rule of Syngman Rhee, the Protestant community also mobilized its resources for his regime, particularly during elections. In the presidential election of 1952, the Korean Protestant church—all denominations and affiliated organizations—formed the Korean Church Committee for Election (Han'guk Kidokkyo sŏn'gŏ taech'aek wiwŏnhoe), which campaigned for Rhee and his followers. The committee said that the church should elect Rhee because, on a petition from the churches, he had abolished the idolatrous greeting of the national flag, he had installed chaplains in the military and the prisons (despite the numerical superiority of Buddhists at the time), and he had ordered all official ceremonies and events "Christianized."[34]

The church's election campaigning for Syngman Rhee was not limited to issuing statements. The religious community conducted its campaign systematically through the network of the Korean Church Committee for Election, which was based in some 3,500 churches with 700,000 adherents.[35] The churches' support had a significant meaning at a time when other political groupings were not grassroots movements. Contrary to such political parties, the religious community, which had been the center of social, educational, religious, cultural, and even political activities, was able to bring tremendous political strength to bear in its support for Rhee and his followers. Although some Christian politicians belonged to opposition parties, the whole church campaigned for Rhee without serious criticism from Christians in the opposition.

In addition to its organizational support, the Protestant community also used its newspapers and religious gatherings to campaign for Rhee. In every election, church newspapers containing extensive profiles of Rhee and his followers were sent free to all Christians.[36] They likened Rhee to Moses, and Yi Kibung, Rhee's running mate, to Joshua.[37] Defining the election as a religious battle of "Christians versus anti-Christians," church leaders led all Christians not only to vote for Rhee but also to campaign actively for him as if it were a religious mission God had given them.[38] On August 3, 1952, just two days before the election, some 3,500 churches across the country simultaneously held special prayer meetings for the election in order to put the finishing touches on the campaign.[39] To Christians, the election was political as well as religious, and the Protestant community gave its full support to Rhee.

During the years of church-government cooperation, the religious community gained many new converts and affiliates, particularly among the upper strata of society—the well-to-do professionals, businessmen, and politicians. Many of these people joined from secular rather than religious considerations.[40] Accordingly, the social composition of the religious community underwent a drastic change after 1945. Many clergymen had already become social and political leaders and therefore part of the upper stratum of society. There was also a dramatic change in the social status of the congregation when the upper strata of Koreans joined the church. Increasingly, elite Koreans were selected as lay leaders, who controlled matters of church administration and finance. Where the pastor used to be superior in terms of education, social prestige, and living standard to elders and deacons, now lay leaders attained high position and amassed wealth outside the church. Professional positions such as lawyers, medical doctors, and professors now eclipsed the position of the pastor.[41] In addition, the pastor was subjected to pressure and restraint from congregations led by rich lay leaders.[42] The church and its upper class tended to prefer social and political stability and thus to accommodate or support the government.

The authoritarian Rhee regime therefore was assisted not only by the police and the military, but also by church groups. The Protestant church systematically lent its undivided support to Rhee by justifying his government and its stand on communism. The church in turn was rewarded with particular favors and benefits.

THE STUDENT REVOLUTION, THE SECOND REPUBLIC, THE PARK CHUNG-HEE REGIME, AND THE CHURCH, 1960–1979

The Second Republic: Lack of Protestant Enthusiasm for Reform

The political vacuum left by Syngman Rhee's departure—forced by the Student Revolution of April 19, 1960—was a rare opportunity for South Korea to live up to the democracy it had professed since 1945.[43] The Second Republic, led by Yun Posŏn and Chang Myŏn, was not based on a grassroots political party but rather was led by the Korean Democratic Party, which was a factional alliance of elites. Existing from 1960 to 1961, the Second Republic offered the best opportunity until the 1990s to establish a democratic system in South Korea. However, the situation was not ripe for a system of open political competition and struggle that would be the first step toward democratic stability and consensus.[44]

The Student Revolution brought about an occasion for soul-searching not only for politicians but also for Christians. Some Christian youths and students called for a serious review of what the church had done in Rhee's time, and they demanded the removal of certain church leaders from their positions.[45] In the words of Kim Chaejun, a leading Christian theologian of the time:

> The day of April 19 was a blinding flash of lightning that pierced the darkness. It was a lofty action of ethics that threw the popular conscience into relief. The beam of light ignited a sudden stirring in the church, too. There appeared individual members who protested in agony that the church must be held responsible for the evil deeds of the old regime. And indeed several church organizations issued statements publicly admitting their own errors.[46]

Kim also noted that the church began to enter a time of self-criticism and reflection.

Contrary to Kim Chaejun's observation, no general change of attitude ensued within the Protestant community because it was by now an inextricable part of the social and political establishment. If Christians were temporarily reeling from the unexpected fall of Syngman Rhee, they felt no need for review or reform: to go back to the good old days of church-government cooperation under Rhee was all that occupied their minds. Since almost all Christian leaders had supported the Rhee regime, there were no church leaders who could seriously call for others to step down.

While Yun Posŏn, a Protestant, and Chang Myŏn, a Catholic, were competing to be president and premier of the Second Republic, church leaders were indirectly turning opinion within the Protestant community against Chang.[47] Yun was elected president of the Second Republic. For the post of premier, where real power resided under the new constitution, Yun nominated Kim Toyŏn, also a Protestant, as well as a leading member of Yun's faction, the *kup'a* (old group), in the Korean Democratic Party. But the National Assembly rejected Kim by one vote. Later, Yun nominated the Catholic Chang, who was the leading member of the opposing faction, the *sinp'a* (new group), and the National Assembly approved him. The squabble that arose between Kim, who was supported by the Protestant community, and Chang was regarded in political circles as a conflict between the new and old groups in the party; Christians viewed it as a Protestant-Catholic confrontation.[48] Even after Chang became premier, Protestants kept calling on him to step down, saying he lacked the ability and courage to cope with the difficult political situation of the time.[49] This episode reveals that the Protestant church did not change its political attitude as a result of the Student Revolution.

Chang Ha'gu, a Christian minister, commented on the church after the Student Revolution:

> There was a time when the church spearheaded a spirit of reform, running as it did ahead of the nation, but as it grew old like the span of human life, the church too lost its vigor. . . . Day was breaking and suddenly there were loud cries outside. But the church had no idea what the noise was about. Someone came up to the doorway and cried that it was morning, and only then did the church open its eyes, reluctantly. Eyes were open but not quite awake, as if rudely awakened from a sound sleep.[50]

In other words, the Protestant church was not awakened by the Student Revolution. As some Christians today argue, the Protestant community undertook no reflection or self-criticism about its cooperation with the Rhee regime, as Christian youths had demanded.[51] A statement prepared by Christian youths and students complained that "the church's calendar was still stuck on April 18," implying that the Protestant church was still in the pre-Revolution period.[52]

Protestant Support for Park Chung-hee

The short-lived Second Republic was overthrown in a military coup staged by Park Chung-hee, at that time a major general, who cleverly exploited the Korean psychology and the political situation.[53] A military dictatorship followed for eighteen years, from May 16, 1961, through October 26, 1979, when Park was shot by the director of the Korean Central Intelligence Agency, Kim Chaegyu.

Although some commentators credit Park with achieving sustained economic growth averaging 10 percent a year, he was an outright military dictator who nipped Korea's best opportunity for democracy, stifled the press, and curbed basic human rights.[54] His rule was indeed "the zenith of authoritarian government in the history of South Korea, in structure as well as content."[55] Park brought the military into government and politics. Suppressing all competing political organizations and activities, he established a police state. Moreover, during his rule serious socioeconomic problems developed. These included enormous foreign debts, miserable living conditions for labor forces, rapid urbanization, and unbalanced development between urban and rural areas. Economic growth was built on political, social, and human sacrifice.

During Park's eighteen-year rule, students, some politicians, some church leaders, and workers held widespread demonstrations against his repressive politics and economic policies. Koreans protested the resumption of diplomatic relations with Japan in 1964 and 1965; they resisted the constitutional revision that allowed for Park's third term; they called for the repeal of the "Restoration Constitution" (Yusin) established in 1971; and workers who had suffered from Park's economic policies joined the antigovernment movement in the Tongil Textile Company Incident, the Y. H. Trade Company Incident, and the Pusan-Masan Uprising of 1979. All of this resistance brought about conflict within Park's regime, culminating in his assassination by none other than one of his lieutenants, the director of the CIA of South Korea.[56]

Under Park Chung-hee, some Christian leaders dared to raise their voices against the government. Kim Chaejun, Mun Ikhwan, Pak Hyŏnggyu, Mun Tonghwan, and An Pyŏngmu, all Christian theologians or ministers, risked imprisonment when they called for social justice, respect for human rights, and democracy, but the majority of Christians went the easy way of supporting the regime. The political attitude of the absolute majority of church members was identical to that of their fellow Christians during the Syngman Rhee period. If there was any change, it was that the Christian influence on South Korean politics was reduced. Contrary to the political circumstances of the First Republic, the influence of the bureaucracy, military, police, political parties, and economic interests, as well as that of the students, grew larger and the political influence of the Protestant church dwindled proportionately in the 1970s. The church was transformed from a core political community in the First Republic to a secondary organization in Park's Korea.

Nevertheless, regarding opposition to Park, the church's position in South Korean politics was still significant. As has been pointed out, there was a group of Christians who continually dared to raise their voices against the Park regime. As Table 7.1 shows, only 542 pastors and 831 churches out of 11,582 clergy and 17,793 churches in the Protestant community were involved in this activism against the regime. The protesters were mostly from the Christ Presbyterian Assembly in the Republic of Korea (or Kijangp'a). Yet this protest was a significant change in the role of the Protestant church, which had supported secular powers since 1945. In addition, criticism of government repression raised by Korean Christians connected with the world Christian community reached the United States, where the press and church circles took up the cause. Even Washington brought pressure, albeit limited, to bear on the regime—a development that was very inconvenient and annoying to Seoul. Lastly, the South Korean government, which could control other political organizations and activities, could not stifle religious organizations and activities because of their strong ties with the Western world, especially the United States. Antigovernment students, politicians, and intellectuals who needed an organizational base therefore gathered in the liberal church, whence they continued to criticize the government.

Despite these activities, the political stance of the majority of church members was one of inaction during Park's rule. Claiming that the church should concern itself only with saving souls, most Protestant leaders tried to draw attention away from political realities, including, of course, the government's action. The church also stressed the apostle Paul's teaching that all political powers are ordained of God and that one should obey civil

TABLE 7.1
Numerical Comparison between the Kijangp'a and the Whole Protestant Church

	Kijangp'a	*Whole Protestant Church*
Churches	831	17,793
Pastors	542	11,582
Lay Members	214,347	4,867,658

SOURCE: Based on Han'guk Kidokkyo sahoe munje yŏn'guwŏn, *Han'guk kyohoe paengnyŏn chonghap chosa yŏn'gu: pogosŏ* [A comprehensive study of the Korean church during the last century: A report], (Seoul: Han'guk kidokkyo sahoe munje yŏn'guwŏn, 1982), p. 165.

authorities. The church also continued to make a case for anticommunism. The communists were the real enemy of Christ, and so to uphold a government that combated communism was to do the will of God.[57] The political inaction of the majority of Korean Christians was actually a political position that, actively or passively, supported the regime that a tiny group of their fellow Christians were criticizing.

The Annual National Prayer Breakfast Committee (Yŏllye kukka choch'an kidohoe), made up of conservative Christians during the 1970s when liberal Christians were increasing their criticism of Park Chung-hee, was one case of political activity on behalf of the regime. The committee sponsored prayer breakfasts, begun in the spring of 1966 by some national assemblymen of the government party. These events were attended not only by church leaders but also by dignitaries from business, government, and political circles. In 1968, President Park Chung-hee himself put in an appearance; in 1976, the prayer breakfast was elevated to the status of a regular ritual and given full press coverage.[58]

The Prayer Breakfast Committee's aim, according to a short history published under its auspices, was to gather leaders from business, government, academia, and political circles to pray to God for national unity, unification, and world peace. In actuality, prayer breakfasts were usually held to support the government and its policies. All participants prayed for the president to be a greater political leader as well as a spiritual leader of the nation, a shepherd of the souls in the land. They pledged in their prayer that they would all press on with his national goals.[59] For example, the Reverend Kim Chun'gon, president of the Campus Crusade for Christ (Taehak sŏn'gyohoe), preached the necessity of the Restoration Constitution at a prayer breakfast for President Park held in May 1973, and in 1974 the

Reverend Yi Sangno preached that "when church and government are harmonious through assistance and cooperation, the church will be holy and the state will prosper."[60] In other words, conservative Christians tried to improve the authoritarian government's reputation at home and abroad by showing that a good relationship existed between the secular and the spiritual.

Conservative Christian leaders also held frequent mass rallies in support of the government, including the World Pentecostal Campaign of 1973 and "Explosion '74" in the following year. Occasionally, well-known evangelists such as Billy Graham and Bill Bright were brought from overseas to conduct mass revivals. Millions of Christians were mobilized to Seoul Stadium or Yŏŭido Square for several days and nights. Such rallies enjoyed the felicitations of high government officials such as the prime minister, the speaker of the National Assembly, the mayor of Seoul, or others of commensurate rank.[61] These occasions were used to show that there was no suppression of religious activity under the Park regime.

Religious rallies were often held after the government's reputation had suffered a particular setback because of its repressive domestic policies or when liberal church leaders were arrested and their gatherings were disrupted by the government (see Table 7.2). Whether intended or not, the timing of these international revival rallies certainly helped the authoritarian government to improve its damaged reputation on each occasion. Conservative church leaders organized these mass rallies with a tremendous amount of money and cooperation from the government.

One quasi-religious body of the period should be mentioned—the Korean Christian Business Men's Committee (Han'guk Kidokkyo sirŏbinhoe). This organization came into being during the Korean War when Colonel Cecil R. Hill suggested the foundation of an organization on the model of the Christian Business Men's Committee International (CBMCI). Originally, the Korean committee was not politically oriented but rather was concerned with works of charity.[62] In 1967, however, Hwang Sŏngsu, a former national assemblyman and prominent lay leader, enlarged the organization by enlisting many Christian business magnates such as church elders Kim Indŭk, head of the Pyŏksan Group, and Chŏng T'aesŏng, head of the Sŏngch'ang Group. In 1968, the committee became affiliated with the CBMCI.[63] Its members were Christian businessmen, professors, doctors, and lawyers who were usually elders or deacons in their churches.

Since the Korean CMBCI members belonged to the upper strata of society, they naturally preferred stability to change. Furthermore, since they

TABLE 7.2
Timing of Revival Rallies in the Early 1970s

Year	*Month*	*Political Event*	*Revival*
1972	October	October Restoration Constitution	
	December	Reverend Ŭn Myŏnggi incident	
1973	April	Easter Sunrise Service incident	
	May	Theological Declaration incident	Billy Graham Crusade
	August	Kim Daejung kidnapping from Tokyo	
1974	April	National Federation of Youths and Students for Democracy case	Explosion '74

SOURCE: Based on ibid. and Han'guk Kidokkyo sahoe munje yŏn'guwŏn, *Ch'ŏn'gubaek ch'ilsimnyŏndae minjuhwa undong gwa Kidokkyo* [The democratization movement and Christianity in the 1970s], (Seoul: Han'guk Kidokkyo sahoe munje yŏn'guwŏn, 1983), "Purok: Ch'ŏn'gubaek ch'ilsimnyŏndae minjuhwa undong ilchi" (Appendix: A diary of the democratization movement in the 1970s).

had to cooperate with the government because of their business interests, they had to meet any request from the government (voluntarily or not). The CBMCI helped to finance religious mass rallies during the 1970s and even participated in the so-called Clean Up the Three Evil Elements Campaign (Samch'ŏng undong) in 1980.[64] The committee also provided a forum for government officials to defend their position and attack the liberal antigovernment Christian activists. At the national conference of the Christian Business Men's Committee of Korea on November 9, 1974, for example, Prime Minister Kim Chongp'il cited Romans 13 and 25 to argue that "the church must obey the government," because "God approved the government." He condemned the liberal Christians as "non-biblical and non-Christian."[65]

One additional example of religious-political cooperation in the 1970s and 1980s was the activities of the Korean Council of Christian Churches (Taehan Kidokkyo yŏnhaphoe) (KCCC) and the Korean Christian Association for Anticommunism (Taehan Kidokkyo pan'gong yŏnhaphoe) (KCAAC). Ministers Kim Yunch'an and Kim Chonggŭn formed these organizations to counter-balance the Korean National Council of Churches

(KNCC), an affiliate of the World Council of Churches (WCC), both of which were regarded by conservative Christians as overly liberal theologically and procommunist politically.[66] If the political activity of the Annual National Prayer Breakfast Committee, the mass revival rallies, and the Christian Business Men's Committee constituted indirect Christian support for the regime, that of the KCCC and KCAAC provided direct support for the anti-communist regime.

Whenever the KNCC criticized the government, the KCCC defended the regime and denounced liberal Christian activists. Whenever the regime's reputation suffered at home or abroad, the KCCC supported the government and its policies. Denouncing the liberal Christians who dared to raise their voices against the regime, the KCCC claimed that "the Bible teaches Christians to pray for the secular powers and to obey them," that "the antigovernment propaganda and demonstrations of Christians are not Christian acts based on biblical teachings," and that "in South Korea there is religious freedom, contrary to the claim of the liberal Christians."[67]

In November 1974, after the National Federation of Youths and Students for Democracy case (Minjuhwa ch'ŏngnyŏn haksaeng yŏnhap sakŏn), in which members of the organization were tried for violating the Anti-communist Law and the National Security Law, the KCCC invited Carl MacIntyre of the International Council of Christian Churches, a militant anticommunist, fundamentalist body, to Korea. MacIntyre denounced the activities of the WCC and the KNCC in a variety of public meetings, lectures, religious gatherings, press conferences, and KCCC meetings, all of which were given full press coverage. He was, of course, invited to the Blue House, the presidential residence, for a meeting with Park Chung-hee. He claimed repeatedly in these public appearances that the churches affiliated with the KNCC and the WCC were not only secularized but also used by, or aligned with, communism. He cited a variety of instances: churches in the Soviet Union and other communist countries participated in the WCC, and the WCC offered political and financial support to leftist guerrillas in Africa and Latin America. He then appealed to Koreans, particularly Christians, to join the anticommunist crusade.[68] The KCCC and MacIntyre raised a Christian defense for anticommunist authoritarianism, arguing that South Korea needed a strong leader and government to confront communism in the north. The KCCC and the government asserted that South Korea had no choice but to sacrifice some freedom and rights in combating communist North Korea.[69]

Therefore, the majority of Protestant Christians turned their backs on liberal Christian activists and supported the authoritarian regime for a variety of doctrinal, political, social, and denominational reasons. First, as we have seen, South Korean Protestants became strongly anticommunist because of the persecution of Christians in the north immediately after the liberation of 1945, and particularly during the Korean War of 1950–1953. They were willing to sacrifice some freedom and rights in order to combat communism. To them, liberal Christian criticism of the anticommunist government was a dangerous activity that disturbed social and political stability. The conservative majority in the Korean Protestant community took especially seriously the liberal church's connection to the WCC, which it considered procommunist.

Second, hostile relations among churches and church leaders led conservative Christian leaders to ignore or criticize liberal Christian activism. Having fought, sometimes physically, for personal and regional interests since the 1930s, Protestant leaders did not wish to override their factional, denominational, and doctrinal differences, even though they professed Christian reconciliation in public. In this situation, the conservative majority was not likely to follow the liberal Christian initiative, but rather to ignore or refute it.

Most important, the social meaning of the Korean Protestant church had undergone a great change since the liberation from Japan. With the development of a social and political atmosphere favorable to the church, leaders who were equipped with better education, more experience in administrative affairs, and nationwide organization came to assume leadership positions in politics and society. Because the Protestant community had gained many new converts and affiliates, particularly from the upper strata of society,[70] and because church leaders generally came from the upper classes as well, the church tended to protect the "pro-Christian" social and political reality under Syngman Rhee, avoid controversial issues, and seek social and political stability under Park Chung-hee and other military dictators.[71]

LIBERAL CHRISTIAN ACTIVISM AGAINST DICTATORSHIP, 1960S–1980S

We have seen how Protestant groups entered into a symbiotic modus vivendi with the powers that be in the south, how this relationship tended to give rise to an apolitical atmosphere in the church, and how it affected politics in the south overall. Even in this era of religious-political association, however, there were Christians who took a stand against the government of Syngman Rhee and the authoritarian regimes of three military generals: Park Chung-hee, Chun Doo Hwan, and Roh Tae-woo.

Christian opposition to the Rhee and Park regimes consisted of individual action in the early years, but in the 1970s Christian activists began acting in groups and in the name of the church. As we have mentioned, this was a significant change in the post-Liberation history of the Protestant church and in the relationship between the church and the government. Furthermore, these Christian activists of the 1970s and 1980s not only dared to criticize the government but also assumed leadership in the antigovernment movement, which absorbed students, some intellectuals, workers, and farmers. The Christian movement now became one of the political forces to be reckoned with in South Korea. It is important, therefore, to ask who these antigovernment Christian activists were and what made them speak out. How did these Christians absorb a variety of antigovernment forces outside the religious community, and what brought the Christians to leadership positions in the antigovernment movement? What were their goals, strategies, strengths, and limitations?[72]

Most of the Christian activists of the 1970s and 1980s belonged to the liberal-leaning Christ Presbyterian Assembly in the Republic of Korea, the group that split in 1954 from the mainstream Presbyterian church, which was the largest denomination in South Korea. Their church was affiliated with the KNCC and the WCC. The ostensible reason for the separation was that Kim Chaejun, Song Ch'anggŭn, and other faculty at the Chosŏn Theological Seminary, the only Presbyterian seminary at the time, were teaching "new theology" (*sin sinhak*), which challenged the fundamentalism of the Korean Presbyterian Church. Yet, as we have seen earlier, underneath the theological dispute was a political conflict among regional factions, particularly between the northwesterners, who had assumed hegemony in church politics in the early twentieth century, and the non-northwesterners led by the Hamgyŏng-Kando group, who had been isolated from church politics and administration. The latter group had been critical of northwestern hegemony as well as pietist, fundamentalist theology.[73]

The political conflict between the two groups resumed shortly after Liberation, when the northwesterners who had been imprisoned, exiled, or semi-retired, sought to regain their hegemony over the church. Since control of the Chosŏn seminary was especially important because it produced clergymen, the northwestern group began to criticize Kim Chaejun and other faculty in an attempt to take over the seminary or to oust the liberal group from the denomination. The liberals were too weak at the time: even with the followers they had produced from their own seminary, they could not overcome the northwesterners' numerical superiority. Kim Chaejun and his colleagues were ostracized by the fundamentalist northwesterners in 1953 for subverting fundamentalist orthodoxy, and thereupon they started their own denomination.[74]

Church leaders who led the new denomination had been extremely cautious in their speech and action while under the control of the fundamentalist Christians, but could now, for example, freely denounce fundamentalist theology. Rejecting "pharisaism in all forms" and the "narrow isolationism" of the parent church, they launched a "new church" movement that aimed for "freedom of evangelism and theological education" in addition to "an open-door policy in their relations with the world Christian community."[75] They criticized the Korean church establishment for being totally isolated not only from Korean society but also from the world Christian community. They attempted to establish their position intellectually and politically in the Korean church community, calling for reform of the parent church and introducing new trends that had developed in the world Christian community since the end of World War II. They spoke out against the Park regime in the mid-1960s and assumed leadership in the antigovernment movement in the 1970s and 1980s.

After the liberal Christians founded their denomination in 1954, they declared that they "desired to march in order to witness Christ in every dimension of human life." But although one liberal church historian has argued that the new denomination began to participate in social and political affairs at this time,[76] liberal Christian activism against the government did not appear in the 1950s or the early 1960s. Whether the liberals were still cowed by the fundamentalists or too weak to speak out, as a group they behaved no differently from the majority of Christians under Syngman Rhee.[77]

According to An Pyŏngmu, a liberal theologian and Christian activist, he and other liberal Christians began their political involvement when Park Chung-hee attempted to revise the constitution to allow for his third term in 1969."[78] However, Christian political activism had appeared several years earlier. In 1965, Christians protested the government's subservient posture in seeking to reopen relations with Japan. In 1967, they denounced election irregularities, and in 1968, YMCA youth formed the Social Development Corps of Christian Students (Haksaeng sahoe kaebaltan) to work on behalf of factory workers, homeless people in cities, refugees from urban areas, and other socially disadvantaged groups. Christians therefore began to resist the regime of Park Chung-hee in the mid-1960s.[79]

Yet it was in the early 1950s that liberal Christians had come into contact with new theological trends and the new outlook on society and politics represented by the WCC. Why, then, did they wait a decade before openly expressing their views? It may be that they had to rally and regroup after their expulsion from the mother church. Two other reasons are more likely, however. One is that liberal Christians came to be concerned about political developments only after the Student Revolution of 1960 and Park Chung-hee's coup d'etat of 1961. The other is that the WCC, the source of inspiration for Christian liberals in Korea, did not turn toward political action until the 1960s and 1970s. In other words, growing theological radicalism in the world church community at the time influenced Korean liberal Christians.[80]

In the 1960s, Christian liberals in the world church community became increasingly concerned with a series of social and political problems arising out of industrialization, urbanization, and the Cold War. They appealed to the secular powers to take a more humane approach to these problems. As we have seen in chapter two, by the mid-1960s, liberal Christians had come to believe that the ideas they promoted had to be carried out by direct action. They argued that Christians themselves had to launch social and political movements to eliminate evil from society. Harvey Cox's *The Secular City* (1965), Moltmann's *The Theology of Hope* (1964), and Shaull's *The Theology of Revolution* (1966) were published in this period. According to these theologians, discussion of God was at the same time a political discussion. Refusing to set religion and politics apart, they argued that the church is not a place to debate "exodus" (human liberation) abstractly and idealistically, but a community that actually takes part in bringing this exodus about, "an institution exercising critical liberty vis-à-vis society." This radical transformation of world church theology in the mid-1960s directly influenced Korean Christian liberals to act on behalf of social justice, human rights, and democratization.[81]

We find a series of parallels between domestic liberals and liberal theologians abroad during the period. As mentioned, the Christ Presbyterian Assembly in the Republic of Korea set up the Committee on Church and Society (Kyohoe wa sahoe wiwŏnhoe) in 1967 to work out social programs,[82] one year after the WCC had held a conference on "Church and Society" attended by representatives of the Korean liberal denomination.[83] As a matter of fact, Korean Christian activists in the 1970s and 1980s openly declared that they were influenced by Bonhoeffer, Moltmann, Cox, and like-minded theologians as they launched their campaigns for human rights, social justice, and democratization.[84] Also, the statements, sermons, and prayers of the liberals at that time show the same tenets, symbols, and language that were used in the publications of the WCC. They declared, for example, that Christians should be concerned not with the rich but with the poor, not with world powers but with minor nations, and that the Bible should be read not in the abstract but in terms of the here and now.[85]

Even though Korean Christian liberals began their political activism against Park Chung-hee in the mid-1960s, it was not until the 1970s that they came to assume leadership in the antidictatorship movement and absorbed a variety of antigovernment groups outside the church. In October 1972, Park Chung-hee, alarmed by the outcome of the presidential election of 1971, launched what he called a restoration program (Yusin) under an amended constitution (Yusin). He tightened restrictions across the board, eliminated all democratic elements, and established a police state.[86] In the face of harsher controls, most of the opposition politicians, journalists, professors, and students who had frequently played a critical role in South Korean politics were finally silenced. Those who still dared to protest against the government were removed from their jobs. This meant that they lost not only their means of living but also their forum for criticism.

It was immediately apparent that some Christian liberals who had opposed Park Chung-hee since the mid-1960s had churches and affiliated institutions that the government could not control—at least not as much as it controlled political parties, the press, and universities. Even though the church was not primarily a political institution, the antigovernment forces outside the church had friends in the church community and began to rally around the Christian liberals. The liberals had buildings where outside groups could meet and organizations through which they could spread their arguments. In this sense, some churches played a role similar to the role they had performed for Korean nationalists early in the colonial period.[87] This was one of the main reasons liberal Christians became leaders in the antigovernment movement and the liberal church came to function as a political center for this movement.

But it was not just the church organization that brought Christian liberals to leadership positions in the antigovernment movement of the 1970s. Most important, it was the recognition that Christian liberals were the first to break the silence of the dark age of the Yusin system and that they continued to resist Park Chung-hee more strongly than other groups. For example, in December 1972, the Reverend Ŭn Myŏnggi, a liberal pastor in Chŏnju, North Chŏlla Province, criticized the Yusin system in an all-night prayer meeting at his church and became the first clergyman arrested by the government during the Yusin period (1972–79).[88] In February 1973, two clergymen of the Yŏngdŭngp'o branch of the Urban Industrial Mission (Tosi sanŏp sŏn'gyohoe) (UIM) were arrested for criticizing the Yusin system and its labor policy.[89] At an Easter sunrise service held atop Namsan (South Mountain) on April 23, 1973, the Reverend Pak Hyŏnggyu and members of the Korean Student Christian Federation (Han'guk Kidok haksaenghoe) (KSCF) passed out leaflets demanding the repeal of the Yusin Constitution and restoration of the democratic process.[90] When these individuals were arrested on sedition charges, the activist Christians, the KNCC, the KSCF, the Korean Coalition of Christian Women (Han'guk kyohoe yŏsŏng yŏnhaphoe), and other church-affiliated agencies petitioned government authorities to release Christians in custody and restore democracy. Many church groups at home followed suit by holding prayer meetings and making public statements in support of imprisoned church leaders and Christian students.[91] In short, whereas groups outside the church were silent at the beginning of the Yusin period, liberal Christians began to protest. Their actions induced other groups to rally around the demand for democratic reform. It is clear that these liberal Christians had the faith to protest because of their sense of religious mission and their willingness to suffer martyrdom. Their religious faith gave them courage and justification for their political action.

During the Yusin period, the Christian activists' churches were the major forum for antigovernment protest. With most criticism by journalists, intellectuals, and students banned, and critics of the government expelled from their jobs, church services and prayer meetings provided channels of communication that kept activists posted on developments in the political arena at a time when the press was no longer free to report political events. For example, the publicizing of the National Federation of Youths and Students for Democracy case in 1974 would not have been possible if not for the KSCF and the YMCA. Christian student activists used the offices and programs of these Christian agencies to keep other youth and student activists informed.[92] The Christian Building (Kidokkyo hoegwan) and the YMCA were also used for discussions that led to the formation of the National Council for the Restoration of Democracy (Minju hoebok kungmin yŏnhap) headed by Yun Posŏn, Ham Sŏkhŏn, and Kim Daejung. (Kim Daejung was elected president in late 1997 and took office in 1998.) In fact, the

Christian Building and the YMCA were the headquarters, as it were, of antigovernment activity in the 1970s and 1980s.[93] Liberal churches such as the Saemunan Church, the Cheil Church of Seoul, the Kyŏngdong Church, and the Hanbit Church were gathering points for those who were willing to act for human rights, social justice, and democracy.

During the Yusin period, liberal churches disseminated social and political news not only to church members but, through them, to the general public. (College campuses across the country also functioned as a major news medium.) When a pastor, church staff member, or student was arrested, for example, the church and church-related agencies lost no time making a written protest and communicating particulars of the case to church members through its network of organizations.[94] The nature of the Yusin program was revealed to the public, and suppression of antigovernment activities was made known. When in 1974 members of the National Federation of Youths and Students for Democracy were arrested for violating the Anticommunist Law and the National Security Law, KNCC members met to discuss possible responses. The church and related agencies declared that, contrary to the government charges, the detainees were not communists but only opposed certain government policies. The KNCC organized services and prayer meetings.[95]

The liberal churches were also instrumental in transmitting news of political developments in South Korea to interested churches overseas, particularly those in the United States, despite government attempts to prevent adverse publicity from reaching the American government and public. Working largely through the WCC, the liberal churches in South Korea managed to keep Japan, Canada, and West Germany as well as the United States informed of developments. Christian activists found international church conferences and seminars and visits of foreign church leaders to Korea to be convenient occasions to air their political grievances. In this way they gained a favorable response from abroad—not only moral support but also financial assistance.[96] In Washington, D.C., the North American Coalition for Human Rights in Korea, established by the WCC and churches in the United States and Canada, began publishing *Korea/Update* and *Korean Weekly Report*; in New York, the International Christian Network for Democracy in Korea, with its periodical *Korean Scope*, was formed; and in Japan, the Emergency Christian Conference on Korean Problems (Kakoku mondal Kirisutosha kenkyukai) came into being and began issuing a periodical called *Korean Communiqué*. These organizations and periodicals were established to publicize repression in Korea and to exert pressure on South

Korean authorities.[97] In sum, Korean Christian activists played an important role in the antigovernment movement by transmitting news of South Korea to the United States and other Western democracies and by bringing foreign pressure to bear on the Korean government.

It was only natural that antigovernment forces outside the church rallied to the liberal Christians with their organizational network and outside resources. In addition, the liberal Christian church embraced a variety of programs that could absorb activist groups, including those for students, journalists, workers, farmers, and women. The Urban Industrial Mission, the Christian Farmers Federation of Korea, the KSCF, the YMCA, the YWCA, and the Korean Coalition of Christian Women—all controlled by liberal Christian intellectuals—attracted different social segments and groups. The monthly *Kidokkyo sasang* [Christian thought] and the Christian Broadcasting Station were also available to these various groups.[98] The Christian liberals who led these organizations and programs assumed leadership in the movement against the dictatorship, and their churches and affiliated agencies became centers of the movement. It was no surprise that when the United Mass Movement for Democracy and Unification (Minju t'ong'il minjung undong yŏnhap) was established in the early 1980s as a joint endeavor of twenty-four different groups—including Catholics, Buddhists, and a whole array of democratic organizations—to promote human rights, social justice, and democracy, the Reverend Mun Ikhwan emerged as its chairman.

The political activity of liberal Christians was sustained by their political theology and religious convictions; they pressed on in the face of difficulty and persecution. The "Theological Declaration of Korean Christians," issued on May 20, 1973, read in part: "God is the ultimate vindicator of the oppressed, the weak, and the poor," and "His Messianic kingdom will be the haven of the dispossessed, the rejected, and the downtrodden." As Jesus once stood before Pontius Pilate, who represented the might of the Roman Empire, Korean Christians now faced, the declaration concluded, an inquest by the authorities of "our oppressed and poor people standing against political oppression and participating in the transformation of history."[99] Without a doubt, their religious faith was their strongest weapon. This trend continued during and after the 1980 Kwangju Uprising against the military leaders who took over the government after the assassination of Park Chung-hee.

But liberal Christians had other weapons that the government could not control completely and that other antigovernment groups lacked. As we have seen, the church had an organization at home and abroad. Partly because of the liberal churches' special relations with the United States and other Western democracies, the South Korean authorities had to approach them with a caution they did not feel obliged to exercise when dealing with other civilian organizations. More immediately, whenever harsh means were applied to church representatives, the government had to face the swift reaction of churches and their affiliates, which was not always easy to parry. Liberal Christians could divulge news of government repression of their religious activities through the church network. News of their protests was transmitted overseas, raising even more problems for the government. Churches in the United States and other Western democracies immediately requested their governments to pressure the South Korean authorities.

Nevertheless, with all their religious dedication and their indomitable spirit, liberal Christians have been unable to go very far toward realizing a democratic system, faced as they have been with the intransigence characterizing the repressive policies of the regimes in South Korea. Some scholars and commentators concerned with South Korean politics have argued that this "failure" has been due mainly to the repressive government and its foreign supporters.[100] What these people have failed to consider, however, is what organizational base the liberal Christians had, how effectively they mobilized it for their cause, and how church members in particular and the public in general reacted to the liberals' movement.

Liberal Christians did not mobilize their organizational base and network effectively because the Korean Protestant church community had been divided (1) organizationally into some one hundred denominations and sects; (2) theologically into conservative and liberal groups; and (3) politically into progovernment and antigovernment churches. As we have seen in earlier chapters, there has been deep hostility among different church groups, and liberal Christians have remained a small minority, accounting for only one-fifteenth of the total Christian population (as of 1979).[101] Instead of support or sympathy, they have received criticism from their conservative fellow Christians. Liberal Christians have been attacked by the Christian majority as a heretic group whose acts are un-Christian. Their liberal theological orientation was one of the driving forces for continuing political action against the dictatorial regime, but it was also paradoxically their main weakness.

The liberal Christians have never achieved strong cohesion or a clear unity of action toward the government. Their central organ, the KNCC, is a loosely organized council of six denominations representing the Christ Presbyterian Assembly in the Republic of Korea, the Jesus Presbyterian Church of Korea, the Salvation Army in Korea, the Methodist Church, the Anglican Church, and the Christ Evangelical Church of Korea (a small evangelical group), among some one hundred denominations and sects. Unlike organizations such as the Catholic Church, these six denominations do not necessarily act in concert under one centralized policy or directive.[102] Usually, a political statement issued by the KNCC is supported morally or nominally, but not actively or organizationally, by the six affiliated denominations.

Christian liberals in the 1970s and 1980s dared to raise their voices against the government, but they did so against the general current of Protestant opinion. This is one of the reasons that it was not liberal pastors, but rather liberal Christian intellectuals (the so-called *kigwan moksa*) working in church-related agencies such as seminaries, schools, the YMCA, and radio stations, who became the leading Christian activists. Such individuals were free from direct control and pressure by a congregation. For example, Christian activists Kim Chaejun, Mun Ikhwan, Mun Tonghwan, and An Pyŏngmu were faculty members at the Han'guk Theological Seminary; Pak Hyŏnggyu, later a pastor, was the chief editor of the monthly *Kidokkyo sasang*; and Kim Kwansŏk was general secretary of the KNCC.[103] The liberal Christian elite in Seoul used the names of their denominations in protesting dictatorial rule, but they could not mobilize their churches and congregations for their cause; they could not even receive much moral support from their fellow Christians. The liberal Christian movement of the 1970s and 1980s remained a weak elitist activity and an urban or "Seoul" phenomenon.

As we have seen earlier, the weakness of liberal Christian activism can be seen clearly in the very nature of church organization as a social institution. Lay leaders with higher social status and greater financial means tend to avoid controversial political issues and to accept the existing political reality. Against such an orientation by congregational leaders, it was difficult for liberal ministers to participate in political action alongside other liberal theologians and clergymen. It seems that most Korean clergymen, sensitive to the attitudes of their congregations, became more concerned with church management and job security than with social and political affairs.

The two cases of the Reverends Pak Hyŏnggyu and Kang Wŏnyong demonstrate how congregations resisted clerical activism. These two pastors of churches in Seoul belonged to the Christ Presbyterian Assembly in the Republic of Korea, which was the denomination most active against the government. They participated in the antidictatorial movement of the 1970s. As the 1980s set in, however, they went different ways politically.

While Pak continued to criticize the new military dictatorship after the Kwangju Uprising, Kang cooperated with the regime.

Pak's congregation at the Cheil Church of Seoul demanded that he discontinue his involvement in controversial secular affairs and concentrate on his congregation. Pak ignored this demand, and his congregation divided into pro- and anti-Pak groups. Every Sunday the two groups engaged in verbal and physical combat. The anti-Pak group even physically attacked their pastor.[104] On the other hand, Kang of the Kyŏngdong Church in Seoul changed his political position under pressure from a powerful elder whose influence increased rapidly in the congregation in 1980. According to a church source, this elder was a four-star general who helped lead the 1980 military coup with Chun Doo-hwan. Ignoring his denomination's political position and critics within his congregation, Kang followed this powerful lay leader.[105] Although these two ministers acted differently, it is clear that their political activism was influenced by their congregations, which kept them under constant pressure financially and politically.

Liberal Christian activism looked like a movement of the whole Korean Protestant church, or at least a movement of the six denominations under the KNCC, because it was carried out in the name of the KNCC and its affiliated denominations. However, its effect and scope were limited. It could mobilize neither the church members who made up some 25 percent of the total population nor all Christians in liberal denominations. One could blame their "failure" on the repressive government, of course, but the fact remains that liberal Christian activists did not develop an effective strategy to overcome the hostile relations within and among denominations, theological divisions, and their congregations' general attitude of nonparticipation in politics.[106]

Liberal Christian activism, however, has not faded altogether before the counter-measures the government has taken, for the activists have had strong religious faith. Christian political activism, it seems, will continue as long as repressive rule continues, because the church is the major institution available for the antigovernment movement as a forum, organizational base, and communication network at home and abroad. Recently, there are signs—if feeble—that the movement is prodding for reform within the church, and liberal Christians are joining hands with students, workers, farmers, intellectuals, and women through the Urban Industrial Mission, the Christian Farmers Federation, the KSCF, the YMCA, the YWCA, and like-minded organizations. Through these programs and activities, liberal Christian activism might develop into a grassroots movement. Furthermore, government critics in these organizations may join and promote reform in churches across the country. However, the liberal Christian movement is not likely to overcome factional and denominational hostility and doctrinal differences to form a unified front against the authoritarian government. Liberal activists pressured by congregations are not likely to be able to persuade conservative Christians in particular and the public in general to their way of thinking. It seems that they will continue to represent a lone religious voice in the near future.

Conclusion

Following its arrival in Korea in the late nineteenth century, Protestantism grew rapidly to be a formidable social force, with membership in Protestant denominations consisting of one quarter of the total population of South Korea just one century later. Underlying the remarkable growth of the new religion from the West was a new spirit of reform amidst feelings of frustration with the encroachment of Japan and, later, a desire to regain independence from Japanese colonial rule. After the liberation from Japan in 1945, church growth accelerated. This was achieved in a pro-Western, pro-Christian atmosphere created by secular political forces. Following the Korean War, along with the social and political unrest accompanying rapid economic growth and urbanization in the 1960s, 1970s, and 1980s, the congregations continued to grow. In short, the growth of Protestantism in Korea has been a historical phenomenon resulting from the church's involvement, positively or negatively, in a series of changes and developments in society and politics. As a matter of fact, religion cannot be isolated from social and political trends in society. The Protestant church is also a living, breathing organism made up of individuals who experience events in history.[1]

The relationship between the Protestant church community and Korean politics, however, has commonly been studied almost exclusively in terms of the former's theological and doctrinal orientation. This is because those who have taken this approach have thought of religion too narrowly as a creed based on a system of beliefs around which its adherents rally. Furthermore, such an ideological approach implies that differences in theology and doctrine alone produce different positions in social and political affairs.

While it is partly true that theology has influenced the Korean church's political behavior, this study has shown that theology has functioned rather to justify and reinforce Protestant Christians' political positions and activities, which have been oriented primarily by their social status and the historical circumstances under which they have had to live. In other words, the church's outlook on society and politics has undergone changes depending on its social composition and historical circumstances. This study has therefore tried to explain the church's political positions and actions in close relation to its growth.

The church's growth meant a numerical expansion of its followers as well as enlargement of its influence in Korea. Expansion also meant a numerical increase in professionals such as clergymen, journalists, teachers, and staff to direct the Protestant denominations' various religious, educational, social, and cultural organizations and institutions. These include churches, colleges, high schools, hospitals, the YMCA, newspapers, periodicals, and other outreach agencies. In other words, the Protestant church became institutionalized in the process of growth, and a church hierarchy came into being and a leadership was formed. This religious leadership came to exercise a vast influence beyond the walls of the Protestant church. Protestantism thus progressed from being an unaccepted religious sect one century ago to being an accepted, and even prominent, religion.

As the Protestant denominations became institutionalized and church leadership positions carried a tremendous social and political influence, there appeared factions and groupings within the religious community, which were enveloped by division, conflict, and rivalry. As church members, particularly clerical and lay leaders, secured their positions socially and economically, the church's social and political attitude was transformed from defiance toward established society and power to conformity to the authorities and the status quo. Protestant Christianity went through a very interesting metamorphosis, from a revolutionary religion—trying to supplant Confucianism and opposing early Japanese colonial rule—to an established religion, conservative in tenor and in league with the status quo in late colonial Korea and obviously later in South Korea.

The first converts to the new religion from the West were the poor and the downtrodden, who were the subjects of social discrimination by the Confucian society, and some young *yangban* elites who were politically alienated in court politics. At the beginning, therefore, the outlook of this small group of Christians was one of defiance toward the Confucian establishment. The early Protestant church was indeed the leading force for social and political reform. During the early Japanese colonial period, the religion grew rapidly to be the largest organized community for colonized

Koreans, as many frustrated Koreans joined to seek spiritual solace and an organizational base for nationalist activity. During this period the church came to serve as a social and political community of Koreans, and the Japanese colonial government considered the religious community to be a "hotbed" of anti-Japanese activities. In short, the more the colonial government suppressed the Protestant church, the more Koreans joined it, and the more influence it had on Koreans. Church leaders thus emerged as community, regional, and national leaders.

The position and role of the Protestant church changed during the late colonial period as a result of certain historical developments. Especially after the failed March First Movement in 1919, the Protestant church no longer was the center of nationalist activity. Its role in nationalist politics was diminished partially because Japan's somewhat more relaxed policy of "cultural rule" (*bunka seiji*) led to an upsurge in political and social organizations outside the religious community. It is partially true that since the socialists and communists, who denounced religion as an opiate for the people, began to lead the Korean nationalist struggle during the late colonial period, the Protestant church became aloof from and critical of such radical ideas and activities. Considering these facts, however, this book has attempted to explain why the Protestant church community came to denounce even moderate educational and cultural activities, and why some prominent Protestant church leaders came to collaborate with the Japanese government in late colonial Korea.

With the retreat of Japan and the arrival of United States troops, liberation in 1945 brought a great change to Protestantism in South Korea. Protestant Christianity now assumed an entirely new character: a religion approved of and shared by the United States and the government of Syngman Rhee. Rhee, the first president of South Korea, was himself a Christian. The religious community now provided a majority of highly placed officials, national assemblymen, intellectuals, and professionals. The religion from the West had come to play a tremendous role in society and politics, and church leaders found themselves members of the social, economic, and political establishment. There soon developed an amicable relationship between Protestantism and secular authority: a relationship that continued in the 1970s and 1980s between conservative Christians and the authoritarian regimes of Park Chung-hee, Chun Doo Hwan, and Roh Tae-woo.

Christian activism for human rights, democratization, and social justice, which began in the mid-1960s and became significant in the 1970s and 1980s, should also be understood in the context of change in the church's social composition and its institutionalization. Although liberal Christian activism did not achieve its goal in the short term, its development was a significant change in a religious community that was otherwise preponderantly progovernment or apolitical. Liberal church leaders raised a voice of conscience against the government for the first time since Liberation. They began to gain strength within the church as young Christians joined them, and consolidated their position by absorbing political forces outside the church that were critical of the authoritarian regimes. University students, intellectuals, laborers, and farmers who needed a leadership and organizational base began to rally around liberal Christian leaders and organizations. By entering or affiliating with the church, these activists could gain some protection and continue their political activity against the government by using the church's organizations. As a result, Christian political activism emerged as one of the core antigovernment forces by the 1970s.

The Protestant community had numerous followers and organizational bases. In addition to a well-educated leadership, it maintained influential educational, social, and cultural institutions such as universities, high schools, the YMCA, the YWCA, newspapers, periodicals, and broadcasting stations. One might be tempted to judge Christian political activism on behalf of human rights, social justice, and democracy in the 1970s and 1980s as a product of this entire religious community. This activism, however, did not enjoy the support of the whole Korean Protestant church community. Far from it. Because church members, especially clerical and lay leaders, were well established in society, they did not like liberal political activism against the government, which they saw as having the potential to destroy social and political stability. In short, political activism by church members did not receive a positive reaction from the majority of Korean Christians.

In addition, the growth of Protestantism and resultant internal structural change influenced the church's political behavior. In the process of its numerical expansion and institutionalization, there appeared factions and groupings within the church, and the religious community was soon enveloped in division, conflict, and rivalry among more than one hundred denominations and groupings. The Korean Protestant church could not produce unified social and political action. Thus, liberal political activists in the 1970s and 1980s could not receive unified support from the religious community, but faced a negative reaction from rival denominations and the conservative Christian majority.

Theology performed a critical role during the church's growth from a tiny group to a large community and from an outcast and alienated group to a community of socially and economically established individuals. Pietist fundamentalist theology functioned politically and positively for the Korean reform movement in the late nineteenth century, for it was adopted by those Koreans who wished to change the existing Confucian system. As we have seen, a small number of commoners and reform-minded young *yangban* who had been alienated sociopolitically from the Confucian establishment joined the early Protestant church. Theology that taught complete separation from a "heathen" system such as Confucianism made the early converts more radical in reforming their country. The same fundamentalist theology, which became more apocalyptic and eschatological during the early colonial period, functioned as a political theology that preached an exodus from alien rule and the coming of the Messiah to build a paradise. This theology inspired those Korean Christians who wished to throw off the Japanese colonial yoke.

During the late colonial period, however, church leaders tried to make the religious community aloof from even moderate social and political movements. Particularly those church leaders who believed that their socioeconomic interests were dependent on the church's noncontroversial position in politics and society wished to avoid a militant stand against foreign rule. During this period, they attempted to justify their apolitical stance by emphasizing the so-called pure faith (*sunsu sinang*). After Liberation, Christians ceased to criticize social and political injustice at the hands of South Korean governments. They came to justify even the authoritarian regimes of Syngman Rhee, Park Chung-hee, and other military leaders. Since Christianity is a matter of the soul and politics a matter of this world, fundamentalist church leaders said, Christians should devote themselves exclusively to the work of saving souls. They first called for the separation of the church from the state, but later they argued that Christians should obey the secular powers, saying that all authorities were ordained by God. In particular, Christians who had migrated from the north tended to justify the anticommunist regimes in the south as religious missions, arguing that communism oppresses Christianity and hence that fighting communism is Christian. The Korean Protestant church thus became an anticommunist church (*pan'gongjok kyohoe*). The apolitical "pure faith movement" in late colonial Korea and later in South Korea, I have thus argued here, was not a purely religious movement based on an evangelical theological and doctrinal orientation, but a religious justification for the transformed social position and accompanying class interest of certain Protestants.

The transformation of the Korean Protestant church into a religious community of the establishment, many scholars have argued, happened during the American occupation and the twelve-year rule of Syngman Rhee. They have pointed out that the presence of the United States and the emergence of Syngman Rhee called forth a friendly response from Korean Protestant Christians; and that cooperation among the three forces (Americans, Syngman Rhee, and Protestantism) began and facilitated the advance of Christians to positions of responsibility in society and government.[2] While it is true that the U.S. military government and Syngman Rhee appointed many Christians to important positions, one should not overemphasize this point, for Christians had already assumed leadership positions in politics and society by the time of Liberation in 1945. It would be superficial, therefore, to say that Christian leaders were appointed to higher government posts simply based on their religion. Such circumstantial factors as the U.S. occupation and the emergence of Syngman Rhee helped Christians merely to consolidate their leadership position in society.

Nevertheless, as church leaders increased their status in society, the attitude of the religious community underwent change in political matters. Protestants soon developed a symbiosis with the Syngman Rhee regime and a theological justification for it. During the years of church-government cooperation, the religious community welcomed many new converts and new affiliates, particularly among the upper strata of society. Accordingly, the social composition of the Protestant church, especially clerical and lay leaders' socioeconomic status, once again underwent a drastic change. Naturally, the Protestant church tended to prefer social and political stability and accommodated the government.

A Korean social theorist, Yong-shin Park, describes these religious and intellectual professionals in the Protestant church as "those who climbed up the social ladder" by joining the ever-growing church, receiving modern education and new political training offered by the church, and participating in social and political activity. He also points out that once Protestants climbed to the top, they formed "a group of authoritarian and hierarchical leaders." The Protestant church, according to him, used to be a community of "eccentric Christians" (*pyŏllan Yesu chaeng'i*), who desired to reform Confucian society and work for independence from Japanese colonial rule. Under the leadership of these economically and socially well-established religious and intellectual professionals, it became a community of "ordinary people" (*p'yŏngbŏmhan saramdŭl*) who lost energy for social and political change.[3] The Protestant church was no longer a dynamic social and political force.

Such a metamorphosis did not happen suddenly under the rule of the U.S. military force and Syngman Rhee after 1945. The Protestant church, I have argued here, by the 1930s was already becoming a "pure faith" community operated by socially and economically well-established individuals. Clerical and lay leaders, whose salaries and positions depended on a stable and uncontroversial church, tried to avoid any confrontation with the Japanese colonial government after the 1919 mass demonstration.

It is difficult to predict how the Korean Protestant church will function in South Korean politics and society in the future. It seems clear, however, that the answer depends primarily on whether the church will overcome hostile denominationalism, the apolitical or progovernment orientation of church members, and a general atmosphere of longing for stability and harmony. It is likely that the social and political expression of the conscience of some liberal Christians will not be silenced as long as there are issues. The church's role in politics and society, however, is not likely to be as influential as the number of its followers and the size of its organizations indicate. It seems that the Protestant church, which is operated by well-established clerical and lay leaders, will not show a dramatic change in the near future. Therefore, a more accurate perception of the Korean Protestant church's social and political roles may lie with those who take a less sanguine view of the course of history.

NOTES

INTRODUCTION

1. On the celebration of the centennial of Protestant evangelism in 1984 and 1985, see "Kaesin'gyo paengnyŏn kinyŏm haengsa ilchŏng" (Schedule of the celebration of the centennial of Protestantism), *Han'guk ilbo* [The Korean times], August 16, 1984. Also see *Kŭrisŭch'an* [Voices of Christians], August 25, 1984, and September 1, 1984; *Kidok sinbo* [The Christian times], April 13, 1985; and Han'guk Kidokkyo paekchunyŏn kinyŏmsaŏp hyŏbŭihoe, *Han'guk Kidokkyo paengnyŏn: Kinyŏmsaŏp yoram* [Hundred years of the Korean Protestant church: An outline of commemorative events], (Seoul: Han'guk kidokkyo paekchunyŏn kinyŏmsaŏp hyŏbŭihoe, 1984).

2. The following data are provided by the Korea Overseas Information Service, a government agency:

Year	*Number of Adherents*
1978	5,293,884
1979	5,986,609
1980	7,180,627
1981	7,637,010

According to the statistics, the number of Protestant Christians increased by a yearly average of some seven hundred thousand from 1979 to 1981. One can reasonably assume that Christians numbered around one-fourth of the total population in South Korea in 1984. See *Statistical Data on Korea* (Seoul: Korean Overseas Information Service, 1982), Section 50. Also see Kim Chunggi, "Han'guk kyohoe ŭi sŏngjang kwajŏng" (The process of church growth in Korea), *Hyŏndae sahoe*, vol. 1, no. 1 (Spring 1983), pp. 101–26, especially p. 104.

According to more recent data, Protestant Christians numbered 11,888,374 in 1990. See Han'guk chonggyo sahoe yŏn'guso, ed., *Han'guk chonggyo yŏn'gam*

[The yearbook of Korean religions], (Seoul: Han'guk chonggyo sahoe yŏn'guso/Hallimwŏn, 1993), p. 83.

3. Samuel H. Moffett, "Korea," in *The Church in Asia*, ed. Donald E. Hoke (Chicago: Moody Press, 1975), pp. 369–83, especially p. 369.

4. For a brief description of Christianity in South Korea today, see Donald N. Clark, *Christianity in Modern Korea* (Lanham, Md., New York, and London: University Press of America/The Asia Society, 1986), p. 1. According to *Chung'ang ilbo* [Central daily news], Chicago version, February 25, 1994, p. 4, five of the ten largest Protestant churches in the world are in Korea. They are Yŏŭido Full Gospel Church (the largest), Nambu Full Gospel Church in Anyang (second), Kŭmnan Methodist Church in Seoul (seventh), Sungŭi Methodist Church in Seoul (ninth), and Chuan Presbyterian Church in Seoul (tenth). This report is based on *Almanac of the Christian World, 1993–1994*.

5. Martin E. Marty, "Foreword," to Everett N. Hunt, *Protestant Pioneers in Korea* (Maryknoll, N.Y.: Orbis Books, 1980), pp. ix–xi, especially p. x.

6. See my article "Protestantism in Late Confucian Korea: Its Growth and Historical Meaning," *The Journal of Korean Studies*, vol. 8 (1992), pp. 139–64, especially pp. 142–44. For Christian evangelism in other Asian countries, see Richard H. Drummond, *A History of Christianity in Japan* (Grand Rapids, Mich.: William B. Eerdmans Publishing Co., 1971); Irwin Scheiner, *Christian Converts and Social Protest in Meiji Japan* (Berkeley: University of California Press, 1970); Yamaji Aizan, *Essays in the Modern Japanese Church: Christianity in Meiji Japan* (Ann Arbor: Center for Japanese Studies, University of Michigan, 1999); Ka-che Yip, *Religion, Nationalism, and Chinese Students: The Anti-Christian Movement of 1922–1927* (Bellingham: Western Washington University, 1980); Daniel H. Bays, ed., *Christianity in China: From the Eighteenth Century to the Present* (Stanford: Stanford University Press, 1996); and George Thomas, *Christian Indians and Indian Nationalism, 1885–1950* (Frankfurt am Main, West Germany: Verlag Peter D. Lang, 1979).

7. For details, see the works cited in note 6.

8. A leading Korean historian, Han Woo-keun (Han Ugŭn), has said that "the progressive, democratic spirit of American Protestantism made the institutions founded by missionaries the natural breeding places for leaders of the resistance. With practically all public institutions controlled by Japan, large numbers of young people turned to the Protestant churches and the mission schools." See his survey, *The History of Korea* (Honolulu: University of Hawaii Press, 1971), trans. Kyung-shik Lee, p. 458. However, most scholars have ignored the subject of relations between the Protestant church and Korean progressive

and nationalist movements. Recently, Kenneth M. Wells has discussed the issue in his *New God, New Nation: Protestants and Self-Reconstruction Nationalism in Korea, 1896–1937* (Honolulu: University Hawaii Press, 1990).

9. See chapter 4.

10. See chapter 5.

11. Christian ministers and lay leaders accounted for 25 percent of the first National Assembly. See *Kidok sinmun*, June 25, 1952. Also see Allen D. Clark, *A History of the Church in Korea* (Seoul: The Christian Literature Society, 1971), p. 305. For more scholarly works, see Dong Suh Bark, "The American-Educated Elite in Korean Society," in *Korea and the United States: A Century of Cooperation*, ed. Young-nok Koo and Dae-sook Suh (Honolulu: University of Hawaii Press, 1984), pp. 263–80, especially pp. 271–75; and Bae-ho Hahn and Kyu-t'ae Kim, "Korean Political Leaders (1952–1962): Their Social Origins and Skills," *Asian Survey*, vol. 2, no. 7 (July 1963), pp. 305–23, especially Table "Religious Backgrounds of Leaders (1962)."

12. Kim Yŏngmo, *Han'guk chibaech'ŭng yŏn'gu* [A study of the ruling class in Korea], (Seoul: Ilchogak, 1982), pp. 191–93.

13. For details, see Pak Hŭisŭng, "Han'guk sahoe ŭi pyŏnhwa wa Pulgyo" (Social change and Buddhism in Korea), *Hyŏngsanggwa insik*, vol. 18, no. 4 (Winter 1994), pp. 39–60, especially pp. 47–48.

14. Ibid., p. 48; and Yi Manyŏl, *Han'guk Kidokkyo wa yŏksa ŭisik* [Korean Christianity and historical consciousness], (Seoul: Chisik sanŏpsa, 1981), pp. 118–21.

15. See, for example, Kuksa p'yŏnch'an wiwŏnhoe, *Han'guk hyŏndaesa* [A history of contemporary Korea], (Seoul: T'amgudang, 1982), pp. 130–31; and Pak Hŭisŭng, "Han'guk sahoe ŭi pyŏnhwa wa Pulgyo," pp. 44–48.

16. See, for example, the works of the following scholars: Everett N. Hunter, Kenneth B. Wells, L.G. George Paik, Kim Yangsŏn, Yi Yŏnghŏn, Kim Kwangsu, and Min Kyŏngbae.

17. For example, see Stephen Neil, *Colonialism and Christian Mission* (New York: McGraw-Hill Book Co., 1966); and Pak Sun'gyŏng, "Han'guk minjok kwa Kidokkyo ŭi munje" (A question before the Korean church and nation), in *Pundan sidae wa Han'guk sahoe* [Korean society in divided Korea], ed. Pyŏn Hyŏng'yun (Seoul: Kkach'i, 1985), pp. 345–70, and Kang Ton'gu, "Han'guk Kidokkyo nŭn minjokchuŭijŏgiŏnna" (The Korean church: Was it nationalistic?), *Yŏksa pip'yŏng*, no. 27 (Winter 1994), pp. 317–27.

18. See my article "Protestantism in Late Confucian Korea: Its Growth and Historical Meaning," pp. 148–53.

19. See the section on Karl Marx and Friedrich Engels in L.S. Feuer, ed.,

Basic Writings on Politics and Philosophy (Garden City, N.Y.: Doubleday Press, 1959), p. 399.

1 / THE GROWTH OF PROTESTANTISM

1. According to government data, in 1990 there were 11,888,374 Protestants and 2,632,990 Catholics in South Korea. That same year, the total population was 43,520,119. See Korean Overseas Information Service, *Statistical Data on Korea* (Seoul: Overseas Information Service, 1982), column 50; Kyŏngje kihoegwŏn chosa t'onggyeguk, *Han'guk t'onggye yŏn'gam* [Korea statistical yearbook], (Seoul: Kyŏngje kihoegwŏn, 1987), p. 36; and Han'guk chonggyo sahoe yŏn'guso, *Han'guk chonggyo yŏn'gam* [The yearbook of Korean religions], (Seoul: Han'guk chonggyo sahoe yŏn'guso/Hallimwŏn, 1993), p. 208.

In North Korea, where Protestantism was an influential religion until 1945, there were 10,000 Protestants and 4,000 Catholics by the mid-1980s. But the religion has been growing slowly since the North Korean regime declared a "new policy" on religion which recognized religious activity. According to one source, there are two Protestant churches (the Pongsu Church, founded in October 1988, and the Ch'ilgok Church, established in 1992) and some 500 home churches (*kajŏng kyohoe*). For details, see Han'guk Kidokkyo yŏksa yŏn'guso, *Pukhan kyohoesa* [History of Christianity in North Korea], (Seoul: Han'guk Kidokkyo yŏksa yŏn'guso, 1996), pp. 439–84, especially pp. 474–84. Also see Barbara Slavin, "N. Korea opens doors to U.S. Christians," *USA Today*, February 26, 1997.

2. Ro Bong-Rin and Marlin L. Nelson, eds., "Preface," *Korean Church Growth: Explosion* (Taichung, Taiwan: Asian Theological Association/World of Life Press, 1983), p. 1.

3. See note 4 in the introduction to this book.

4. Han'guk kidokkyo paekchunyŏn kinyŏmsaŏp hyŏbŭihoe, *Han'guk Kidokkyo paengnyŏn: Kinyŏmsaŏp yoram* [Hundred years of the Korean Protestant church: An outline of commemorative events], (Seoul: Han'guk Kidokkyo paekchunyŏn kinyŏmsaŏp hyŏbŭihoe, 1984), pp. 49–50.

5. Martin Marty's "Foreword" to Everett N. Hunt, Jr., *Protestant Pioneers in Korea* (Maryknoll, N.Y.: Orbis Books, 1980), p. x.

6. See, for example, Stephen Neil, *Colonialism and Christian Mission* (New York: McGraw-Hill, 1966); Richard H. Drummond, *A History of Christianity in Japan* (Grand Rapids, Mich.: William B. Eerdmans, 1971); Otis Cary, *A History of Christianity in Japan*, vol. 2 (Rutland, Vt., and Tokyo: Charles E. Tuttle Co., 1976); Ka-che Yip, *Religion, Nationalism, and Chinese Students:*

The Anti-Christian Movement of 1922–1927 (Bellingham, Wash.: Western Washington University, 1980); and George Thomas, *Christian Indians and Indian Nationalism, 1885–1950: An Interpretation in Historical and Theological Perspectives* (Frankfurt am Main, West Germany: Verlag Peter D. Lang, 1978).

7. For the anti-Western, anti-Christian atmosphere, see the following works: James B. Palais, *Politics and Policy in Traditional Korea* (Cambridge, Mass.: Harvard University Press, 1975), especially pp. 19–55 and 176–280; Martina Deuchler, *Confucian Gentlemen and Barbarian Envoys: The Opening of Korea, 1976–1885* (Seattle: University of Washington Press, 1977); Kim Key-Hiuk, *The Last Phase of the East Asian World Order: Korea, Japan, and the Chinese Empire, 1860–1882* (Berkeley and Los Angeles: University of California Press, 1980), especially pp. 31–76; Ching Young Choe, *The Rule of the T'aewon'gun, 1864–1873: Restoration in Korea* (Cambridge, Mass.: Harvard Yenching Institute, 1972); Donald L. Baker, "Confucians Confront Catholicism in Eighteenth-Century Korea" (Ph.D. diss., University of Washington, 1983); and Yi Nŭnghwa, *Chosŏn Kidokkyo kŭp oegyosa* [History of Christianity and foreign relations of Korea], (Seoul: Hangmun'gak, 1968; original edition, 1928).

8. See David Chung, "Religious Syncretism in Korean Society" (Ph.D. diss., Yale University, 1959); Spencer J. Palmer, *Korea and Christianity* (Seoul: Hollym Corporation, 1967), pp. 3–18; Yun Sŏngbŏm, *Kidokkyo wa Han'guk sasang* [Christianity and Korean thought], (Seoul: Taehan Kidokkyo sŏhoe, 1964), chap. 1 and p. 249; and "Hwanin, Hwanung, Hwan'gŏm ŭn got Hananim ida" (Hwanin, Hwanung, and Hwan'gŏm: Truly God), *Sasanggye* [World of thought], vol. 2, no. 5 (May 1963), pp. 258–71.

9. See my articles "Protestantism in Late Confucian Korea," *Journal of Korean Studies*, vol. 8 (1992), pp. 139–64, particularly pp. 141–42, and "Han'guk Kaesin'gyo sŏngjang e taehan yŏksahakjŏk sŏlmyŏng sido" (The growth of Protestantism in Korea: A historical explanation), *Kidokkyo sasang*, vol. 33, no. 4 (April 1989), pp. 102–120.

10. See, for example, Han'guk Kidokkyo sahoe munje yŏn'guwŏn, *Han'guk kyohoe paengnyŏn chonghap chosa yŏn'gu-pogosŏ* [A comprehensive study of the Korean church during the last century: A report], (Seoul: Han'guk Kidokkyo sahoe munje yŏn'guwŏn, 1982), pp. 129–42, especially pp. 129–30 and 140.

11. See my article, "Han'guk Kaesin'gyo sŏngjang e taehan yŏksahakjŏk sŏlmyŏng sido," pp. 102–120.

12. Korean Christians who think that they joined the church because of its social and political activism are just 0.6 percent. See Hyŏndae sahoe yŏn'guso,

Han'guk kyohoe sŏngjang gwa sinang yangt'ae e kwahan chosa yŏn'gu [A survey on the growth of Christianity and form of faith in Korea], (Seoul: Hyŏndae sahoe yŏn'guso, 1981), Table II-122, p. 160. See also p. 46.

13. For the so-called Nevius Methods, see Charles A. Clark, *The Korean Church and the Nevius Methods* (New York: Fleming H. Revell Co., 1930). For a general description on indirect missionary strategy, see Allen D. Clark, *A History of the Church in Korea* (Seoul: The Christian Literature Society, 1971); and George L. Paik, *The History of Protestant Missions in Korea, 1832–1910* (P'yongyang: Union Christian College, 1929).

14. See my article, "Protestantism in Late Confucian Korea," pp. 142–43.

15. W. F. Mallalieu, "Mission in Korea," *The Korean Repository*, vol. 1, no. 9 (September 1892), pp. 286–87. Also see Irwin Scheiner, *Christian Converts and Social Protest in Meiji Japan* (Berkeley: University of California Press, 1970), pp. 7–9.

In his *New God, New Nation: Protestants and Self-Reconstruction Nationalism in Korea, 1896–1937* (Honolulu: University of Hawaii Press, 1990), Kenneth M. Wells does not agree with my view, claiming that the Nevius method was not applied "to all non-Western mission fields. . . , not even applied in China, to the chagrin of Dr. Nevius, who had designed it for that country. Its use in Korea was actually unique." See his book, note 73 on p. 183.

George L. Paik, a pioneer in studying church history in Korea, states very clearly that "As Korea was one of the youngest Protestant foreign mission fields, missionaries had naturally used the methods that had previously evolved elsewhere. Among others, that known as the Nevius method, was studied and tried with success." See Paik's *The History of Protestant Missions in Korea*, pp. 159–60.

According to Min Kyŏngbae, a leading church historian in Korea, the principles of the Nevius method were not new to missionaries at the time. A British missionary, Henry Venn, had already suggested—and missionaries practiced—the so-called self-supporting church or self-governing church strategies in Asia and Africa already in the 1860s. The Nevius method and similar missionary strategies were widely practiced in almost all mission fields. See Min's *Han'guk ŭi Kidokkyohoesa* [A church history of Korea], (Seoul: Taehan Kidokkyo sŏhoe, 1968), pp. 70–71.

16. See Gordon H. Chapman, "Japan: A Brief Christian History," in *The Church in Asia*, ed. Hoke, pp. 302–27. For more details, see Otis Cary, *A History of Christianity in Japan*, vol. 2, chaps. 6 and 7; and Irwin Scheiner, *Christian Converts and Social Protest in Meiji Japan*, pp. 10–18.

17. For example, Kim Kyusik, Kim Ku, Yŏ Unhyŏng, Syngman Rhee, Hŏ

Chŏng, Cho Mansik, Chŏng Han'gyŏng, and other prominent political leaders were Christians.

18. Before 1884, some Koreans had already been in contact with Protestantism during travel in Manchuria and China. For details, see Paik, *History of Protestant Missions in Korea*, pp. 28–90. For a biographical work on an early convert, see Yi Tŏkchu, *Nara ŭi tongnip kyohoe ŭi tongnip* [The nation's independence and the church's independence], (Seoul: Kidokkyomunsa, 1988), especially pp. 23–50.

19. See Fred Harvey Harrington, *God, Mammon, and the Japanese: Dr. Horace N. Allen and Korean-American Relations, 1884–1905* (Madison: University of Wisconsin Press, 1944), pp. 11–12. Also see Yi Tŏkchu, *Nara ŭi tongnip kyohoe ŭi tongnip*, pp. 40–50; and Min Kyŏngbae, *Han'guk ŭi Kidokkyohoesa*, pp. 55–57.

20. For the following historical information before and after the opening of Korea in 1876, I heavily rely on the works of James B. Palais, Martina Deuchler, Kim Key-Hiuk, Donald L. Baker, and Yi Nŭnghwa. See note 7.

21. Much earlier than this, Gregorio de Cespedes, a Jesuit missionary, visited Korea along with Konishi Yukinaga, a Christian daimyo, during Toyotomi Hideyoshi's invasion in 1594. For details, see Paik, *The History of Protestant Missions in Korea*, pp. 28–29; and James Huntley Grayson, *Korea: A Religious History* (Oxford: Clarendon Press, 1989), pp. 176–77.

22. For a brief history of persecution, see Paik, *The History of Protestant Missions in Korea*, pp. 30–43; and Grayson, *Korea: A Religious History*, pp. 178–84. For a more analytical discussion of this subject, see Donald L. Baker, "Confucians Confront Catholicism," and his "The Martyrdom of Paul Yun: Western Religion and Eastern Ritual in 18th Century Korea," *Transactions of the Royal Asiatic Society*, vol. 54 (Korea Branch, 1979), pp. 33–58.

23. See Baker, "Confucians Confront Catholicism," and "The Martyrdom of Paul Yun."

24. Kim Hongjip, an influential court official, brought this small pamphlet into Korea on his return from Japan in 1880. It was widely circulated among court officials and *kaehwa* (enlightenment) elite. For the whole text, see Cho Ilmun's translation published by Kon'guk taehakkyo ch'ulp'anbu in 1977. For this quotation, see pp. 24–35.

25. For details, see Chŏng Okcha, "Sinsa yuramdan ko" (A study of the gentlemen's excursion group), *Yŏksa hakpo*, vol. 27 (1965), pp. 105–42.

26. For example, Yun Ch'iho stayed in Japan for further observation of the country's modernization. See *Yun Ch'iho ilgi* [Yun Ch'iho's diary], January 1–16, 1883.

27. Paik, *The History of Protestant Missions in Korea*, pp. 81–82.

28. Ibid., pp. 82–106; and Harrington, *God, Mammon, and the Japanese*, pp. 12–13.

29. Paik, *The History of Protestant Missions in Korea*, pp. 43–60.

30. For details, see Harold H. Cook, *Korea's 1884 Incident: Its Background and Kim Ok-kyun's Elusive Dream* (Seoul: Royal Asiatic Society, Korea Branch, 1972).

31. Harrington, *God, Mammon, and the Japanese*, pp. 90–91.

32. For details, see ibid., chap. 3.

33. See *The Foreign Missionary*, vol. 44, no. 5 (July 1885), p. 76. Also see Harrington, *God, Mammon, and the Japanese*, chap. 4, especially p. 55.

34. For example, since poor Koreans "were not charged" at all in the missionary hospitals, Allen and other missionaries earned "an ever-greater admiration" from Koreans. See ibid., pp. 65–67.

35. Ibid. Also see W. F. Mallalieu, "Mission in Korea," pp. 286–87.

36. See the report to the eighth annual meeting of the Methodist Episcopal Mission, (August 1892), p. 266.

37. For details, see C. I. Kim and Han-kyo Kim, *Korea and the Politics of Imperialism, 1876–1910* (Berkeley and Los Angeles: University of California Press, 1967), chap. 5; and Hilary Conroy, *The Japanese Seizure of Korea, 1868–1910: A Study of Realism and Idealism in International Relations* (Philadelphia: University of Pennsylvania Press, 1960), chaps. 5 and 6.

38. *Yun Ch'iho ilgi* [Yun Ch'iho's Diary], March 7, 1890.

39. Ibid., April 8, 1893.

40. See Vipan Chandra, *Imperialism, Resistance, and Reform in Late Nineteenth Century Korea: Enlightenment and Independence Club* (Berkeley: University of California, Institute of East Asian Studies, 1988); and Sin Yongha, *Tongnip hyŏphoe yŏn'gu* [A study of the Independence Club], (Seoul: Ilchogak, 1976).

41. Chŏngdong was the name of the block where the U.S. legation was located. This group's name itself strongly indicates its pro-Western, pro-American political orientation.

42. Harrington, *God, Mammon, and the Japanese*, pp. 44–47 and 211–66. King Kojong and *kaehwa* elite such as Sŏ Chaep'il and Yun Ch'iho came to seek American help for Korea.

43. Lillias H. Underwood, *Fifteen Years among the Top-knots or Life in Korea* (Boston, New York, and Chicago: American Tract Society, 1904), p. 28.

44. Yu Yŏng'ik (Lew, Young Ick), "Kaehwagi taemi insik" (Korean view on America during the period of "enlightenment"), in Yu Yŏng'ik et al.,

Han'gugin ŭi taemi insik: yŏksajŏgŭrobon hyŏngsŏng kwajŏng [Korean view on America: A historical study on its formation], (Seoul: Minŭmsa, 1994), pp. 55–141.

45. Ibid., p. 81.

46. Harrington, *God, Mammon, and the Japanese*, chaps. 11–13.

47. See chapter 3 in this book.

48. Song Ch'anggŭn, "Chosŏn Kidokkyo ŭi wigi" (Crisis of Korean Christianity), *Sinhak chinam*, no. 3 (May 1934). This article and his other essays are carried in Chu T'aeik's *Manu Song Ch'anggŭn* [A biography of Song Ch'anggŭn], (Seoul: Manu Song Ch'anggŭn sŏnsaeng kinyŏm saŏphoe, 1978), pp. 143–52. The quotation is from p. 145.

49. See my article, "Protestantism in Late Confucian Korea," p. 151.

50. For a systematic discussion on the social composition of the early Protestant church, see Yong-shin Park, "Protestant Christianity and Social Change in Korea" (Ph.D. diss., University of California-Berkeley, 1975), pp. 70–92.

51. For a systematic discussion of the slave society issue in Korea, see James B. Palais, "A Search for Korean Uniqueness," *Harvard Journal of Asiatic Studies*, vol. 55, no. 2 (December 1995), pp. 409–25, particularly pp. 414–18, and *Confucian Statecraft and Korean Institutions: Yu Hyŏngwŏn and the Late Chosŏn Dynasty* (London and Seattle: University of Washington Press, 1996), especially chap. 6.

52. In order to understand how the Protestant church grew in the northwest, see Roy E. Shearer, *Wildfire: Church Growth in Korea*, chaps. 4 and 5; Yi Kwangnin, "Kaehwagi kwansŏ chibang gwa Kaesin'gyo" (Protestantism in the northwest at the turn of the century), in his *Han'guk kaehwa sasang yŏn'gu* [Studies on the Korean enlightenment thought], (Seoul: Ilchogak, 1979), pp. 226–50; and Min Kyŏngbae, "Han'guk kŭndae munhwa wa Kidokkyo ŭi hyŏngt'ae mit kŭ yŏnghyang pŏmwi" (Christianity in modern Korea: Its distribution pattern and the scope of influence on culture), *Han'guk sahak*, no. 1 (June 1982), pp. 226–50.

53. For discussion of discrimination toward northwesterners during the Chosŏn period, see Edward W. Wagner, "The Ladder of Success in Yi Dynasty Korea," *Occasional Papers on Korea*, no. 1 (April 1974), University of Washington, pp. 1–8, and "The Civil Examination Process as Social Leaven: The Case of the Northern Provinces in the Yi Dynasty," *Korea Journal*, vol. 17, no. 1 (January 1977), pp. 22–27; Yi Ihwa, *Han'guk ŭi p'abŏl* [Korean factionalism], (Seoul: Ŏmun'gak, 1983), pp. 120–30; and Yi Kwangnin, "Kaehwagi kwansŏ chibang gwa Kaesin'gyo."

54. William M. Baird, "Notes on a Trip into Northern Korea," *The Independent*, May 20, 1897.

55. Paik, *The History of Protestant Missions in Korea*, pp. 203–4, especially p. 204.

56. The conversion of the upper *yangban* class was more difficult than that of the non-*yangban* population, but some progressive *yangban* elite, who were excluded from conservative-controlled court politics, joined Protestant churches. It is interesting to note that earlier in the eighteenth century some *namin* (southern faction) *yangban* elite, who were also excluded from meaningful careers in the Confucian bureaucracy, converted to Catholic Christianity. See Donald N. Baker, "Confucians Confront Catholicism in Eighteenth-Century Korea."

57. As early as 1884, Yun Ch'iho believed that any reform must be effected at the grassroots level rather than through revolution from above. See *Yun Ch'iho ilgi*, December 6, 1884; and Pak Chŏngsin (Park, Chung-shin), "Yun Ch'iho yŏn'gu" (A study of Yun Ch'iho), *Paeksan hakpo*, no. 23 (1977), pp. 341–88, especially pp. 350–62.

58. See my "Yun Ch'iho yŏn'gu"; and Kim Yŏnghwi, *Chaong Yun Ch'iho sŏnsaeng yakchŏn* [A brief biography of Yun Ch'iho], (Seoul: Kidokkyo Chosŏn kamnihoe, 1934), p. 54. After 1884, Yun went so far as to say that for Korea to reform was to Christianize the nation and that the salvation of Korea consisted only in accepting Christianity. See *Yun Ch'iho ilgi*, February 19 and March 8, 1893, and March 30, 1889. On Sŏ Chaep'il, see Channing Liem, *America's Finest Gift to Korea: The Life of Philip Jaisohn* (New York: The William-Frederick Press, 1952), pp. 29–56.

59. For details, see Paik, *The History of Protestant Missions in Korea*, pp. 356–58; and Yi Manyŏl, *Han'guk Kidokkyo wa minjok ŭisik* [Korean Christianity and national consciousness], (Seoul: Chisik sanŏpsa, 1991), pp. 260–61.

60. James Gale, *Korea in Transition* (New York: Eaton and Mains, 1909), p. 195.

61. Harrington, *God, Mammon, and the Japanese*, pp. 44–47 and 221–66.

62. Ibid., chap. 12.

63. Ibid.; and C. I. Kim and Han-kyo Kim, *Korea and the Politics of Imperialism*, pp. 125–26.

64. See Yu Yŏng'ik (Lew, Young-Ick), "Kaehwagi taemi insik," p. 81.

65. Harrington, *God, Mammon, and the Japanese*, pp. 100–101.

66. On Japanese policy toward Christianity in the early colonial period, see Aoyagi Kōtarō, *Chōsen tōchiron* [Rule of Korea], (Keijo: Chōsen kenkyūkai, 1932), pp. 417–27; and Chōsen sōtokufu, *Shisei nijugogenshi* [A history of

twenty-five years of administration], (Keijo: Chōsen sōtokufu, 1935), pp. 187–88 and pp. 493–96.

67. See "Kyohoe wa chŏngbu sai e kyojehal myŏt chokŏn" (Terms regulating church and state), *Kŭrisŭdoin hoebo*, October 3, 1901. Also see Arthur J. Brown, *The Mastery of the Far East* (New York: Charles Scribner's Sons, 1919), pp. 543–44 and chap. 34.

68. Kuksa p'yŏnch'an wiwŏnhoe, *Han'guk tongnip undongsa* [History of the Korean independence movement], vol. 1 (Seoul: Kuksa p'yŏnch'an wiwŏnhoe, 1965), p. 452; Chu Yohan, *An Tosan chŏnjip* [Complete works of An Ch'angho], (Seoul: Samjungdang, 1971), p. 28; and Paik, *The History of Protestant Missions in Korea*, pp. 349–53.

69. As for the revival movement, see Paik, *The History of Protestant Missions in Korea*, pp. 359–78; and Clark, *A History of the Church in Korea*, pp. 157–71. Also see a recent study on this subject, Sŏ Chŏngmin, "Ch'ogi Han'guk kyohoe taebuhŭng undong ihae: minjok undong gwaŭi kwallyŏn ŭl chungsimŭro" (Understanding of the revival movement in the early Korean church: With its relations with nationalist movement as the central subject), in Yi Manyŏl, et al., *Kidokkyo wa minjok undong* [Christianity and the nationalist movement], (Seoul: Posŏng, 1986), pp. 233–82.

70. For the missionaries' attitude in the early colonial period, see Frank Baldwin, "Missionaries and the March First Movement: Can Moral Men Be Neutral?" in *Korea Under Japanese Colonial Rule*, ed. Andrew C. Nahm (Kalamazoo, Mich.: Western Michigan State University, The Center for Korean Studies, 1973), pp. 193–219; and Paik, *The History of Protestant Missions in Korea*, pp. 349–54 and 413–17.

71. *Taehan maeil sinbo*, March 13, 1910.

72. *Taehan maeil sinbo*, March 15, 1910.

73. The revival movement was a collective religious experience. Christians stayed together for several days and nights, sang hymns, prayed loudly, and studied the Bible. Through such an emotional gathering they gained a sense of togetherness.

74. Yi Kwangnin, *Han'guksa kangjwa*, pp. 495–96; and Paik, *The History of Protestant Missions in Korea*, p. 353.

75. About Ch'ŏndogyo leaders' pro-Japanese activities, see Yi Kwangnin, *Han'guksa kangjwa*, pp. 486 and 493. A young political activist of the period, Ch'oe Myŏngsik, recalled that "as late as 1905, when the protectorate treaty was signed, . . . Christian churches were in fact the only places where Koreans could come into contact with Western culture . . . and could readily assemble for meetings." See Ch'oe Myŏngsik, *Anak sakŏn kwa samil undong gwa na*

[The Anak Incident, the March First Movement and I], (Seoul: Kŭkhŏ chŏn'gi p'yŏnch'an wiwŏnhoe, 1970), p. 14.

76. Kim Yangsŏn, *Han'guk Kidokkyosa yŏn'gu* [A historical study of Korean Christianity], (Seoul: Kidokkyomunsa, 1971), p. 107.

77. See the statistics in Han'guk Kidokkyo sahoemunje yŏn'guwŏn, *Han'guk kyohoe paengnyŏn chonghap chosa yŏn'gu: pogosŏ*, pp. 146–60.

78. Chōsen Sōtokufu, *Kyō kankoku kanpō* [The official gazette of old Korea], vol. 22 (August 13, 1910), pp. 997–98. Also see Son Insu, *Han'guk kŭndae kyoyuksa* [A history of modern education in Korea], (Seoul: Yŏnse taehakkyo ch'ulp'anbu, 1971), pp. 29–159, especially p. 29. At the time, there were 823 schools related to Christianity and other religions. See Tawara Sonnichi, *Kankoku kyōiku no genjō* [The present state of education in Korea], (Keijō: Chōsen sōtokufu gakufu, 1910), pp. 49–50.

79. See Tawara Sonnichi, *Kankoku kyōiku no genjō*, pp. 55–56. The number could be larger, because the statistics only reveal the student population of Presbyterian and Methodist schools.

80. In the 1910s, the Korean Protestant church published several newspapers and periodicals, among them *Yesugyo hoebo* [The Christian news], *Kŭrisŭdoin hoebo* [The Christian advocate], *Kidok sinbo* [The Christian messenger], *Sinhak segye* [World of theology], *Sŏnmin* [The chosen people], and so on.

81. For the establishment of the independent Presbyterian Church of Korea, see Paik, *The History of Protestant Missions in Korea*, pp. 387–91; and Clark, *A History of the Church in Korea*, pp. 172–77. There were eight presbyteries representing North P'yŏng'an, South P'yŏng'an, Hwanghae, Kyŏnggi, Ch'ungch'ŏng, Chŏlla, Kyŏngsang, and Hamgyŏng.

82. See Kwak Allyŏn, *Kyohoe sajŏn huijip* [Digest of the Presbyterian Church of Korea], (Keijō: Chōsen yashogyo shōkai, 1918), pp. 47–50.

83. *Taehan maeil sinbo*, August 21, 1907.

84. On relations between the Protestant churches and the colonial government, see the following memoirs and secondary works: Sŏnu Hun, *Minjok ŭi sunan: Paegoin sakŏn* [Suffering nation: The 105 Men Case], (Seoul: Tongnip chŏngsin pogŭbhoe, 1955); Pak Ŭnsik, *Han'guk t'ongsa* [The tragic history of Korea], (Seoul: Pagyŏngsa, 1974), especially the section "Paegisibin chi tangok" (Imprisonment of 120 men); Brown, *The Mastery of the Far East*, pp. 571–80; Kang Wijo, *Ilche t'ongch'iha Han'guk ŭi chonggyo wa chŏngch'i* [Religion and politics under Japanese imperialist rule], (Seoul: Taehan kidokkyo sŏhoe, 1977); Chŏn T'aekpu, *Han'guk Kidokkyo ch'ŏngnyŏnhoe undongsa* [A history of the Korean 'YMCA' movement], (Seoul: Chŏng'ŭmsa,

1978), pp. 97–252; and Yi Ŭnsuk, *Minjok undongga anae ŭi sugi: Sŏkando sichonggi* [Notes by the wife of an activist for independence] (Seoul: Chŏng'ŭmsa, 1975).

85. Yi Kwangsu, "Sin saenghwallon" (On new life), *Taehan maeil sinbo*, September 6–October 19, 1918. Also see this article and others in *Yi Kwangsu chŏnjip* [Complete works of Yi Kwangsu], vol. 17 (Seoul: Samjungdang, 1962), pp. 515–54. See particularly pp. 544–45.

86. On relations between the Protestant church and the March First Movement, see Kim Yangsŏn, "Samil undong gwa Kidokkyo" (The March First Movement and Christianity), in *Samil undong osipchunyŏn kinyŏm nonjip* [Selected essays to mark the fiftieth anniversary of the March First Movement], ed. Ko Chaeuk (Seoul: Tonga ilbosa, 1969), pp. 235–70; Pak Yŏngsin (Park, Yong-shin), "Sahoe undong ŭrosŏ ŭi samil undong ŭi kujo wa kwajŏng" (The March First Movement: Its structure and process as a social movement), *Hyŏnsanggwa insik*, vol. 3, no. 1 (Spring 1978), pp. 5–23; and Yi Manyŏl, "Kidokkyo wa samil undong" (Christianity and the March First Movement), ibid., pp. 51–84.

87. See chapter 4 in this book.

88. For a fine study of nationalist activism in the 1920s, see Michael E. Robinson, *Cultural Nationalism in Colonial Korea, 1920–1925* (Seattle: University of Washington Press, 1988).

89. Ibid., pp. 49–50. See also Chōsen Sōtokufu Keimukyoku, *Chōsen chian jōkyō* [Conditions of public order in Korea], (Keijō: Chōsen sōtokufu, 1922), p. 91.

90. See my article, "Ch'ŏn'gubaek isimnyŏndae Kaesin'gyo chidoch'ŭng gwa minjokchuŭi undong" (The relationship between Protestant leaders and the nationalist movement in early colonial Korea: A social history), *Yŏksa hakpo*, no. 134–135 (September 1992), pp. 142–63.

91. See Victor W. Peter, "What Korean Young People Are Thinking," *The Korean Mission Field*, vol. 28, no. 5 (May 1932), pp. 92–95, and no. 6 (June 1932), pp. 129–32.

92. See chapter 4 in this book.

93. According to data compiled by a Westerner, in 1924 there were 254,534 church members and 4,000 clergymen and other church workers. See T. Stanley Soltau, *Korea: The Hermit Nation and Its Response to Christianity* (London: World Dominion Press, 1932), p. 114. According to a Japanese source, already in 1910 there were 1,116 teachers in over 800 church-related schools. See Tawara Sonnichi, *Kankoku kyōiku no genjō*, pp. 49–50. A Korean source tells us that by 1919 there were 1,517 teachers in church-related schools, but

this number grew to 2,789 in 1925. See Yi Nŭnghwa, *Chosŏn Kidokkyo kŭp oegyosa*, pp. 220 and 223.

94. See my article, "Ch'ŏn'gubaek isimnyŏndae kaesin'gyo chidoch'ŭng gwa minjokchuŭi undong," pp. 160–63.

95. As for the "annexation" of the Korean Protestant church into the Japanese church by the colonial government, see Kim Yangsŏn, *Han'guk Kidokkyosa yŏn'gu*, pp. 202–4.

96. On Japanese domestic policy during the war, see Richard H. Mitchell, *Thought Control in Prewar Japan* (Ithaca, N.Y.: Cornell University Press, 1976). Also see Masao Maruyama, *Thought and Behavior in Modern Japanese Politics* (London: Oxford University Press, 1969); and Han'guk Kidokkyo yŏksa yŏn'-guso, *Pukhan kyohoesa*, pp. 234–35.

97. On Japanese policy on Korea during the war, see Kang Chaeŏn, *Ilcheha sasimnyŏnsa* [Forty-year history under Japan's imperialist rule], (Seoul: P'ulbit, 1984), pp. 100–125; and Kang Man'gil, *Han'guk hyŏndaesa* [A history of contemporary Korea], (Seoul: Ch'angjakkwa pip'yŏngsa, 1984), pp. 32–38. As for the policy toward the church, see Clark, *A History of the Church in Korea*, pp. 221–31; and Yi Yŏnghŏn, *Han'guk kidokkyosa* [The history of the Korean church], (Seoul: Concordia ch'ulp'ansa, 1978), chap. 13.

98. Yi Yŏnghŏn, *Han'guk Kidokkyosa*; and Han'guk Kidokkyosa yŏn'guso, *Han'guk Kidokkyo wa sinsa ch'ambae munje* [The Korean Christian church and the shrine worship issue], (Seoul: Han'guk Kidokkyosa yŏn'guso, 1991), and Kim Yangsŏn, *Han'guk kidokkyosa yŏn'gu*, pp. 172–97.

99. The Presbyterian Church, the largest denomination, formally decided in 1938 to have its members pay homage to the Shinto shrine. See Clark, *A History of the Church in Korea*, pp. 221–31; and Kim Yangsŏn, *Han'guk Kidokkyosa yŏn'gu*, pp. 186–90.

100. According to Min Kyŏngbae, since Catholics and Methodists considered Shinto-shrine worship as a national rite from the beginning, they did not have any serious internal debate. See his *Han'guk ŭi Kidokkyohoesa*, p. 102.

101. See Han'guk Kidokkyo yŏksa yŏn'guso, *Pukhan kyohoesa*, p. 235.

102. See Min Kyŏngbae, *Han'guk ŭi Kidokkyohoesa*, pp. 102–5; Kim Yangsŏn, *Han'guk Kidokkyosa yŏn'gu*, pp. 202–4; and Han'guk Kidokkyo yŏsa yŏn'guso, *Pukhan kyohoesa*, pp. 234–35.

103. For details, see chapter 4 in this book.

104. Such prominent church leaders as Pak Hŭido, Chu Yo-han, Yun Ch'iho, Chŏng In'gwa, Kim Hwallan, Ch'ae P'ilgŭn, Yu Hyŏnggi, and others actively participated in the Japanese war-mobilization campaign.

105. Allen D. Clark, however, says that the reduction of the Christian pop-

ulation during this period was due mainly to the fact that Christians went underground. See his *A History of the Church in Korea*, p. 231.

106. For a recent work on the history of Christianity in North Korea, see Han'guk Kidokkyo yŏksa yŏn'guso, *Pukhan kyohoesa*.

107. There is no systematic study on the growth of Protestantism in contemporary South Korea, but some that point out factors for it. The best work thus far is Shearer, *Wildfire: Church Growth in Korea*. Also see Ro Bong-Rin, "Non-Spiritual Factors in Church Growth," and Harold S. Hong, in *Korean Church Growth: Explosion*, ed. Ro Bong-Rin and Marlin L. Nelson, pp. 159–70; and Harold S. Hong, "Social, Political, and Psychological Aspects of Church Growth," in ibid., pp. 171–81.

108. Yi Manyŏl, "Han'guk Kidokkyo wa yŏksa ŭisik" (Korean Christianity and historical consciousness), *Kidokkyo sasang* (August 1980), pp. 62–74, especially pp. 65–69; and Samuel H. Moffett, "Korea," p. 379. Sundays and Christmas, for example, were officially designated national holidays during the U.S. military rule, and military chaplains were instituted by Syngman Rhee in 1951.

109. For details, see Han'guk Kidokkyo yŏsa yŏn'guso, *Pukhan kyohoesa*, pp. 343–438.

110. We do not know exactly how many Christians there were in the north by the time of Liberation. According to a recent study, in 1940 there were 2,097 Protestant churches and 228,339 adherents. See ibid., p.343.

111. As for the political conflict between the Protestant church community and the Kim Il-sung regime, see Kim Yangsŏn, *Han'guk Kidokkyo haebang simnyŏnsa* [The ten-year history of the Korean church since the Liberation], (Seoul: Taehan Yesugyo changnohoe ch'onghoe, chonggyo kyoyukpu, 1956), pp. 45–48 and 62–75; Clark, *A History of the Church in Korea*, pp. 234–36 and 239–45; Chang Pyŏng'uk, *Yugio kongsan namch'im kwa kyohoe* [The communist invasion to the south and Christianity], (Seoul: Han'guk kyoyuk kongsa, 1983), pp. 20–116; and Han'guk kidokkyo yŏksa yŏn'guso, *Pukhan kyohoesa*, pp. 343–425.

112. Donald N. Clark, *Christianity in Modern Korea* (Lanham, Md., New York, and London: The Asia Society/University Press of America, 1986), p. 16. For this religious migration, see also Han'guk Kidokkyo yŏsa yŏn'guso, *Pukhan kyohoesa*, pp. 418–22.

113. Bruce Cumings, *The Origins of the Korean War: Liberation and the Emergence of Separate Regimes, 1945–1947* (Princeton, N.J.: Princeton University Press, 1981), pp. 424–26.

114. For example, most of the larger churches in the south, including

Yŏngnak Church, Ch'unghyŏn Church, Kyŏngdong Church, and Sŏngnam Church, were founded by immigrant clergymen as "refugees' churches." See, for example, Yŏngnak kyohoe hongbo ch'ulp'anbu, *Yŏngnak kyohoe samsibonyŏnsa* [Thirty-five-year history of Yŏngnak Church], (Seoul: Yŏngnak kyohoe, 1983), pp. 41–47 and 62–159; and Ch'unghyŏn isibonyŏnsa p'yŏnch'an wiwŏnhoe, *Ch'unghyŏn isibonyŏnsa* [Twenty-five-year history of Ch'unghyŏn Church], (Seoul: Ch'unghyŏn kyohoe, 1979), pp. 45–67. Also see Kangsŏ kunji p'yŏnsuhoe, *Kangsŏ kunji* [Records of Kangsŏ County], (Seoul: Kangsŏ kunji p'yŏnsuhoe, 1967), pp. 350–52.

For a brief scholarly discussion on Yŏngnak Church, see Donald N. Clark, *Christianity in Korea*, pp. 23–24.

115. For example, Syngman Rhee appointed many Christians, including Yi Yunyŏng, a migrated clergyman, to his cabinet. See Yi Yunyŏng, *Paeksa Yi Yunyŏng hoekorok* [Memoirs of Yi Yunyŏng], (Seoul: Sach'o, 1984). Also see Pak Hŭisŭng, "Han'guk sahoe ŭi pyonhwa wa Pulgyo" (Social change and Buddhism in Korea), *Hyŏnsanggwa insik*, vol. 18, no. 4 (Winter 1994), pp. 39–60, especially pp. 44–48.

116. Han'guk Kidokkyo sahoe munje yŏn'guwŏn, *Han'guk kyohoe paengnyŏn chonghap chosa yŏngu*, pp. 139–40.

117. Ibid.

118. Han Wansang, "Han'guk kyohoe ŭi yangjŏk sŏngjang gwa kyoindŭl ŭi kach'igwan" (The quantitative growth of the Korean church and Christians' values), in Han'guk Kidokkyo munhwa yŏn'guso, *Han'guk kŭndaehwa wa Kidokkyo* [Korean modernization and Christianity], (Seoul: Sungjŏn taehakkyo, 1983), pp. 121–56, especially pp. 126–30.

119. *Kamni hoebo* [Methodist bulletin], January 1, 1952, p. 4.

120. Ibid., January 1, 1953, p. 16.

121. Chang, *Yugio kongsan namch'im kwa kyohoe*, pp. 326–32; and Yi Chupong, "Han'guk sahoe wa kyohoe sŏngjang" (The church growth in Korean society), *Kidokkyo sasang*, vol. 25, no. 9 (September 1981), pp. 27–35, especially pp. 28–32.

122. On the dictatorial rule of Syngman Rhee and Park Chung-hee, see James B. Palais, "Human Rights in the Republic of Korea" (Asia Watch Report), *Human Rights in Korea* (New York and Washington, D.C.: Asia Watch, 1986), pp. 1–339.

123. Han'guk Kidokkyo sahoe munje yŏn'guwŏn, *Han'guk kyohoe paengnyŏn chonghap chosa yŏn'gu*, p. 140.

124. Hyŏndae sahoe yŏn'guso, *Han'guk kyohoe sŏngjang gwa sinang yangt'ae e kwanhan chosa yŏn'gu*, p. 29, Table I-4. Also see pp. 30–31.

125. Han'guk Kidokkyo sahoe munje yŏn'guwŏn, *Han'guk kyohoe paengnyŏn chonghap chosa yŏn'gu*, p. 110, Table I-136.

126. Hyŏndae sahoe yŏn'guso, *Han'guk kyohoe sŏngjang gwa sinang yangt'ae e kwahan chosa yŏn'gu*, Table I-20, p. 63.

127. Ibid., Table II-22, p. 66.

128. See various articles in Han'guk kŭrisŭch'an akademi, *Han'guk kyohoe sŏngnyŏng undong ŭi hyŏnsang gwa kujo* [The spiritual movement in the Korean church: Its phenomenon and structure], (Seoul: Han'guk kŭrisŭch'an akademi, 1981).

129. For a short scholarly observation of Yŏŭido sunbogŭm kyohoe, see Donald N. Clark, *Christianity in Modern Korea*, pp. 24–26.

130. Jai Poong Ryu, "From Chosen to Taehan: Social Change in Twentieth Century Korea" (Ph.D. diss., University of Minnesota, 1972), p. 147.

2 / THE THEOLOGICAL ORIENTATION OF THE PROTESTANT CHURCH

1. For a general understanding of theology in Korea, see Yu Tongsik, *Han'guk sinhak ŭi kwangmaek: Han'guk sinhaksa sŏsŏl* [Patterns of theology in Korea: A history of theology in Korea: An introduction], (Seoul: Chŏnmangsa, 1982); Ryu Tongshik (Yu Tongsik), "Rough Road to Theological Maturity," in *Asian Voices in Christian Theology*, ed. Gerald H. Anderson (Maryknoll, N.Y.: Orbis Books, 1976), pp. 161–77; G. C. Oothuizen, *Theological Battleground in Asia and Africa* (London: C. Hurst Co., 1972), pp. 225–41; Harvie N. Conn, "Korean Theology: Where Has It Been? Where Is It Going?" *Sinhak chinam*, vol. 39, no. 2 (Summer 1972), pp. 52–81; and Pak Yonggyu, *Han'guk changnogyo sasangsa* [A history of Presbyterian theological thought in Korea], (Seoul: Ch'ongsin taehak ch'ulp'anbu, 1992).

2. Han Wansang, *Chŏ najŭn kossŭl hyanghayŏ* [Toward the lower depths], (Seoul: Chŏnmangsa, 1978), pp. 22, 141–42, and 246.

3. For the history of theological transformation in the West in general and in America in particular, see Franklin L. Baumer, *Modern European Thought: Continuity and Change in Ideas, 1900–1950* (New York and London: Macmillan Publishing Co., 1977), especially chap. 5, sec. 2; Donald W. Treadgold, *A History of Christianity* (Belmont, Mass.: Norland Publishing Co., 1979), chap. 15; Arthur C. McGiffert, *The Rise of Modern Religious Ideas* (New York: Macmillan Publishing Co., 1921); Darril Hudson, *The Ecumenical Movement in World Affairs* (Washington, D.C.: The National Press, 1969); Lefferts A. Loetscher, *The Broadening Church: A Study of Theological Issues in the Presbyterian Church since 1868* (Philadelphia: University of Pennsylvania

Press, 1954); Hubert Cunliffe-Jones, *Christian Theology Since 1900* (London: Gerald Duckworth and Co., 1970); William B. Gatewood, Jr., ed., *Controversy in the Twenties: Fundamentalism, Modernism, and Evolution* (Nashville, Tenn.: Vanderbilt University Press, 1969); C. Allyn Russell, *Voices of American Fundamentalism: Seven Biographical Studies* (Philadelphia: The Westminster Press, 1976); George M. Marsden, *Fundamentalism and American Culture: The Shaping of Twentieth-Century Evangelicalism, 1870–1925* (New York and Oxford: Oxford University Press, 1980); Ronald C. White, Jr., and C. Howard Hopkins, *The Social Gospel: Religion in Changing America* (Philadelphia: Temple University Press, 1976); James Ward Smith and A. Leland Jamison, eds., *The Shaping of American Religion*, vol. 1 of *Religion in American Life*, and *Religious Perspectives in American Culture*, vol. 2 of *Religion in American Life* (Princeton, N.J.: Princeton University Press, 1961); and Winthrop S. Hudson, *American Protestantism* (Chicago: University of Chicago Press, 1961).

4. For Pak Hyŏngnyong's critique of liberal theologies, see his *Pak Hyŏngnyong paksa chŏjak chŏnjip* [Complete works of Dr. Pak Hyŏngnyong], vols. 8 and 9 (Seoul: Han'guk Kidokkyo kyoyuk yŏn'guwŏn, 1981). It is interesting to note that Pak Hyŏngnyong was a student activist against Japanese rule during the colonial period. See Sungjŏn taehakkyo p'alsimnyŏnsa p'yŏnch'an wiwŏnhoe, *Sungjŏn taehakkyo p'alsimnyŏnsa* [Eighty-year history of Sungjŏn University], (Seoul: Sungjŏn taehakkyo, 1979), pp. 333–40.

5. See my article, "Kuhanmal ilche ch'ogi Kidokkyo sinhak kwa chŏngch'i: Chinbojŏk sahoe undonggwa minjokchuŭi undong ŭl chungsimŭro" (Christian theology and politics in late Confucian and early colonial Korea: A discussion on the church's progressive social activism and nationalist movement), *Hyŏnsanggwa insik*, vol. 17, no. 1 (Spring 1993), pp. 103–25, especially pp. 123–25.

6. Yu, *Han'guk sinhak ŭi kwangmaek*, pp. 28–30; and Min Kyŏngbae, *Kŭrisŭch'an akademi simnyŏnsa* [The ten-year history of the Christian Academy], (Seoul: Kŭrisŭch'an akademi, 1975), pp. 19–30. Min, for example, divides Korean Protestant Christians into two camps—"social participation" and "nonparticipation." He places even Kil Sŏnju, one of the earlier "political ministers," in the latter group because he was a fundamentalist and otherworldly church leader.

7. See my article, "Kuhanmal ilche ch'ogi ŭi Kidokkyo sinhak kwa chŏngch'i," pp. 107–14, and my Ph.D. dissertation, "Protestant Christians and Politics in Korea, 1884–1980s," University of Washington, 1987, pp. 120–30.

8. Yu, *Han'guk sinhak ŭi kwangmaek*, p. 56; Min, *Kurisuch'an akademi*

simnyonsa, pp. 20–21, and Arthur J. Brown, *The Mastery of the Far East* (New York: Charles Scribner's Sons, 1919), p. 541.

9. See my article, "Kuhanmal ilche ch'ogi ŭi Kidokkyo sinhak kwa chŏngch'i," pp. 114–23, and my Ph.D. dissertation, "Protestant Christians and Politics in Korea," pp. 130–46. One may find a millenarian tradition in Korea in the *Chonggamnok* [Book of prognostication] prophecy and the Tonghak religious teaching.

10. Unlike the earlier revival movement, the revival meetings in late colonial Korea were otherworldly and shamanistic. See Yun Sŏngbŏm, *Kidokkyo wa Han'guk sasang* [Christianity and Korean thought], (Seoul: Taehan Kidokkyo sŏhoe, 1964), pp. 185–98, especially, pp. 194–98.

11. For details, see Kim Yongbok, "Haebanghu kyohoe wa kukka" (Church and state since the Liberation), in Han'guk Kidokkyo sahoe munje yŏn'guwŏn, ed., *Kukka kwŏlyŏk kwa Kidokkyo* [State power and Christian church], (Seoul: Minjungsa, 1982), pp. 191–252, especially see pp. 201–204.

12. From 1945 to 1961, many Christians, including Ham Sŏkhŏn, Chang Chunha, Chŏng Ilhyŏng, and Kim Sangdon criticized Rhee's authoritarian rule, but they were without any moral or organizational backing from the churches.

13. Brown, *The Mastery of the Far East*, p. 540.

14. See the works cited in note 4 in this chapter.

15. Since the original passage is not available, an excerpt by Kim Yangsŏn is used. Kim, *Han'guk Kidokkyo haebang simnyŏnsa* [The ten-year history of the Korean church since the Liberation], (Seoul: Taehan Yesugyo changnohoe ch'onghoe chonggyo kyoyukpu, 1955), pp. 173–74. P'yŏngyang Presbyterian Theological Seminary was opened in 1901 as the only educational institution that trained pastors for the Korean Presbyterian Church.

16. For Christian critiques of Confucian values and practices in the early missionary period, see Yong-shin Park, "Protestant Christianity and Social Change in Korea" (Ph.D. diss., University of California-Berkeley, 1975) pp. 94–104. For the case of eighteenth-century Korean Catholics on ancestor worship, see George L. Paik, *The History of Protestant Missions in Korea, 1832–1910* (P'yŏngyang: Union Chosŏn Christian College, 1929; reprint, Yonsei University Press, 1970), pp. 33–35.

17. "Obstacles Encountered By Korean Christians," *The Korean Repository*, vol. 1, no. 4 (April 1895), pp. 145–51, quoted from p. 148.

18. George H. Jones, "Open Korea and Its Methodist Mission," *The Gospel in All Lands*, September 1898, pp. 391–96.

19. See *Kuseron* [On the salvation of the world], pp. 15–17. Since the orig-

inal is not available, I quoted and translated from Yi Manyŏl, *Han'guk Kidokkyo wa minjok ŭisik* [Korean Christianity and nationalist consciousness], (Seoul: Chisik sanŏpsa, 1991), p. 223.

20. George H. Jones, "Open Korea and Its Methodist Mission," p. 392.

21. Ibid., p. 394.

22. See the articles in *Kŭrisŭdoin hoebo* [The Christian advocate], June 23, 1896, and the article, "Should Polygamists Be Admitted to the Christian Church?" in three parts in *The Korean Repository*, vol. 3, no. 6 (June 1896), pp. 288–92, no. 7 (July 1896), pp. 323–33, and no. 8 (August 1896), pp. 350–60. Also see Yong-shin Park, "Protestant Christianity and Social Change in Korea," pp. 164–76.

23. See *Tongnip sinmun* [The independent], April 21, April 22, June 16, and September 5 of 1896, January 4, February 12, and March 12 of 1898, and *Kŭrisŭch'an sinmun* [The Christian news], January 3 and June 20, 1901.

24. *The Church at Home and Abroad*, vol. 16, no. 8 (August 1894), p. 120.

25. Brown, *The Mastery of the Far East*, p. 541; Yu, *Han'guk sinhak ŭi kwangmaek*, pp. 55–59; and Min, *Kŭrisŭch'an akademi simnyŏnsa*, pp. 19–30.

26. See Yun Ch'iho, *Yun Ch'iho ilgi* [Yun Ch'iho's diary], April 18, 1893 (English), May 18, 1890 (English), April 30, 1891 (English), and March 30, 1889 (Korean). For work on Yun Ch'iho, see Donald N. Clark, "Yun Ch'i-ho (1864–1945): Portrait of a Korean Intellectual in an Era of Transition," *Occasional Papers on Korea*, no. 4 (September 1975), University of Washington, pp. 36–76; and Pak Chŏngsin (Chung-shin Park), "Yun Ch'iho yŏn'gu" (A study of Yun Ch'iho), *Paeksan hakpo*, no. 23 (1977), pp. 341–88. Also see the numerous articles that appeared in *Chosŏn Kŭrisŭdoin hoebo*, *Kŭrisŭdo sinmun*, *Tongnip sinmun*, and *Taehan maeil sinbo*.

27. Yun, *Yun Ch'iho ilgi*, March 30, 1889.

28. For more details, see C. C. Vinton, "Presbyterian Mission Work in Korea," *The Missionary Review of the World*, vol. 6, no. 9 (September 1893). Also see Pak Yŏngsin (Park, Yong-shin), "Kidokkyo wa Han'gŭl undong" (Christianity and Hangŭl movement), in Yu Tongsik et al., *Kidokkyo wa Hang'uk yŏksa* [Christianity and Korean history], (Seoul: Yŏnse taehakkyo ch'ulp'anbu, 1996), pp. 39–69, and Paik, *The History of Protestant Missions in Korea*, p. 202. For a systematic study of early missionary strategies, see Pak Yŏngsin, "Ch'ogi Kaesin'gyo sŏn'gyosa úi sŏn'gyo undong chŏlyak" (Early Protestant missionaries' strategies for evangelism), *Tongbanghak chi*, no. 46/47/48 (June 1985), pp. 529–53. Also see chapters 3 and 4 in this book.

29. See my Ph.D. dissertation, "Protestant Christians and Politics in Korea," pp. 377–430.

30. Brown, *The Mastery of the Far East*, p. 541.

31. Kil Sŏnju, "Malsehak" (Eschatology), *Yŏnggye Kil Sŏnju moksa chŏjakjip* [Works of the Reverend Kil Sŏnju], (Seoul: Taehan Kidokkyo sŏhoe, 1968), pp. 21–141, quoted from p. 28. This "Malsehak" was originally published in 1930.

32. Brown, *The Mastery of the Far East*, pp. 540–41; Yu, *Han'guk sinhak ŭi kwangmaek*, pp. 28–30; and Min, *Kŭrisŭch'an akademi simnyŏnsa*, pp. 20–21.

33. For a critique of the conventional view, see my article, "Kuhanmal ilche ch'ogi ŭi Kidokkyo sinhak kwa chŏngch'i," pp. 114–23.

34. Kil Sŏnju, "Malsehak," p. 139.

35. On Kil Sŏnju's life, see Kil Chin'gyŏng, *Yŏnggye Kil Sŏnju* [Kil Sŏnju: A biography], (Seoul: Chongno sŏjŏk, 1980); Kim Yangsŏn, "Aeguk ŭi sin'gyo puhŭng: Kil Sŏnju" (Kil Sŏnju and revival as patriotic activity), in *Kidokkyo chŏndoja yugin* [Six Christian evangelists], ed. Sin'gumunhwasa (Seoul: Sin'gumunhwasa, 1976), pp. 101–11; Kim Kwangsu, *Han'guk Kidokkyo inmulsa* [History of Korea's Christian personalities], (Seoul: Kidokkyomunsa, 1974), pp. 137–46; Yu, *Han'guk sinhak ŭi kwangmaek*, pp. 55–60; and Kim Insŏ, "Yŏnggye sŏnsaeng sojŏn" (A short biography of teacher Kil Sŏnju), *Sinang saenghwal* [Christian life], vol. 1, no. 12 (December 1932), pp. 26–31, vol. 2, no. 1 (January 1933), pp. 24–28, vol. 2, no. 2 (February 1933), pp. 26–30, and vol. 2, no. 3 (March 1933), pp. 25–30.

36. Kil Chin'gyŏng, *Yŏnggye Kil Sŏnju*, chap. 4.

37. Ibid., pp. 240–42.

38. Ibid., chap. 4, especially pp. 269–73.

39. *Taehan maeil sinbo*, March 10, 1908.

40. W. L. Swallen, *Sunday School Lesson on the Book of Exodus*, "Preface," p. 4. Quoted from Kim Yong-bock, ed., *Minjung Theology: People as the Subjects of History* (Singapore: The Christian Conference of Asia, 1981), p. 104. Swallen's book was translated into Korean in 1909.

41. Brown, *The Mastery of the Far East*, pp. 543–46, and Yi Yŏnghŏn, *Han'guk kidokkyosa* [A history of the Korean church], (Seoul: Concordia ch'ulp'ansa, 1978), pp. 112–23.

42. Yi Kwangsu, "Sinsaenghwallon" (On new life), in *Yi Kwangsu chŏnjip* [Complete works of Yi Kwangsu], no. 17, (Seoul: Samjungdang, 1969), pp. 515–54.

43. Brown, *The Mastery of the Far East*, pp. 568–70.

44. Nym Wales and Kim San, *Song of Ariran* (San Francisco: Rampart Press, 1941), p. 75.

45. See two local church leaders' reasons to convert to Christianity and to participate in the March First Movement in Tongnip undongsa p'yŏnch'an wiwŏnhoe, ed., *Tongnip undongsa charyojip* [Documents on history of the inde-

pendence movement], vol. 6 (Seoul: Tongnip yukongja kigŭm unyong wiwŏnhoe, 1973), p. 604.

46. Some scholars, who have studied this issue only in terms of textual analysis with a liberal bias, argue that the so-called apoliticization of the Protestant church was mainly due to the otherworldly theology and had occurred by the annexation of 1910. However, having considered the issue historically in terms of contextual analysis, I do not agree with those arguments. The so-called apoliticization actually occurred after the March First Movement of 1919. The role of otherworldly theology in the early colonial period was different from that in the second half of the colonial period. For the argument based primarily on textual analysis, see Min, *Kŭrisŭch'an akademi simnyŏnsa*, pp. 19–20.

47. Yi Kwangsu, "Chaesaeng" (Rebirth), *Yi Kwangsu chŏnjip*, no. 3 (Seoul: Samjungdang, 1969), pp. 129–78, particularly pp. 146–63. This novel originally appeared in *Tong'a ilbo* in 1924–25. And O Sangsun, "Sidaego wa kŭ hŭisaeng" (The agony of times and its victims), *P'yehŏ* [Ruins], vol. 1, no. 3 (March 1932), pp. 31–34.

48. Kim Insŏ, "P'yŏngyang kyohoe ch'oegŭn ŭi samdae chiphoe" (Three recent revival meetings in P'yŏngyang church community), *Sinang saenghwal*, vol. 1, no. 3 (March 1932), pp. 31–34.

49. See my article, "Ch'ŏn'gubaek isimnyŏndae kaesin'gyo chido, *Sinang saenghwal*, vol. 1, no. 7 (July 1932), pp. 7–10, particularly p. 9.

50. According to my reading of various biographies of Kil Sŏnju, he was devoted solely to the revival movement after the March First Movement. See Kil Chin'gyŏng, *Yŏnggye Kil Sŏnju,* chap. 4.

51. Kim Insŏ, "Nŏhŭido ttohan kagojŏ hanŭnya?" (Do you want to go their way, too?), *Sinang saenghwal,* vol. 1, no. 7 (July 1932), pp. 7–10, esp. p. 9.

52. On the Anti–Shrine Worship Campaign, see Lee Kun Sam, *The Christian Confrontation with Shinto Nationalism* (Philadelphia: The Presbyterian and Reformed Publishing Co., 1966); and Han'guk Kidokkyo yŏksa yŏn'guso, ed., *Han'guk Kidokkyo wa sinsa ch'ambae munje* [Korean Christian church and shrine worship issue], (Seoul: Han'guk Kidokkyo yŏksa yŏn'guso, 1991).

53. Quote from Kim Yangsŏn, *Han'guk Kidokkyo haebang simnyŏnsa*, p. 293.

54. Pak Hyŏngnyong, *Kyoŭi sinhak sŏsŏl* [Dogmatic theology: An introduction], (Seoul: K'albin ch'ulp'ansa, 1964), preface.

55. "Chosŏn sinhaksaeng chinjŏngsŏ" (The students' petition of the Chosŏn Theological Seminary), in Kim Yangsŏn, *Han'guk Kidokkyo haebang simnyŏnsa*, pp. 216–17.

56. See William B. Gatewood, Jr., ed., *Controversy in the Twenties:*

Fundamentalism, Modernism, and Evolution, pp. 3–46; and C. Allyn Russell, *Voices of American Fundamentalism: Seven Biographical Studies*, pp. 13–16 and pp. 213–14.

57. Kim Yangsŏn, *Han'guk Kidokkyo haebang simnyŏnsa*, pp. 173–79.

58. On the establishment of the Chosŏn Theological Seminary, see Kim Chaejun, *Pŏmyonggi* [Autobiography of Kim Chaejun], vol. 1 (Toronto: Ch'ilsŏng kwanggosa, 1981), pp. 219–29.

59. For details on this controversy, see Kim Yangsŏn, *Han'guk Kidokkyo haebang simnyŏnsa*, pp. 214–27.

60. See ibid., pp. 245–64.

61. For the rivalry between Pak and Kim Chaejun, see ibid., pp. 227–45.

62. On Pak Hyŏngnyong's life, see Pak Yonggyu, *Han'guk kyohoe inmulsa*, vol. 3, pp. 107–140, and Yu Tongsik, *Han'guk sinhak ŭi kwangmaek*, pp. 186–99.

63. For Pak's political activity, see Sungjŏn taehakkyo p'alsimnyŏnsa p'yŏnch'an wiwŏnhoe, *Sungjŏn taehakkyo p'alsimnyŏnsa*, pp. 333–40.

64. See Kim Yangsŏn, *Han'guk Kidokkyo haebang simnyŏnsa*, p. 293; and Pak Hyŏngnyong, *Kyoŭi sinhak*, preface.

65. Pak, *Chŏnjip*, vol. 8, pp. 21–33. This article was first published in 1935.

66. For Pak's attack on liberal theology, see ibid. The twenty volumes of Pak's complete works were reprinted by his students in 1981. Therefore, the complete works were not reprinted in the original chronology.

67. For a brief discussion on Renan, Strauss, and Schleiermacher, see Frank L. Baumer, *Modern European Thought*, pp. 367–473; and Donald W. Treadgold, *A History of Christianity*, pp. 199–206. For Pak's critique of them, see Pak, *Chŏnjip*, vol. 8, pp. 56–58 and pp. 140–56.

68. For Pak's critique of liberal theologies, see Pak, *Chŏnjip*, vols. 8 and 9.

69. *The Secular City* (London: SCM Press, 1965). For Pak's critique, see Pak, *Chŏnjip*, vol. 8, pp. 296–303.

70. *Honest to God* (Philadelphia: Westminster Press, 1963). For Pak's critique, see ibid., pp. 296–303.

71. Pak, *Chŏnjip*, vol. 8, pp. 302–303.

72. Song Sangsŏk, *Munje ŭi Kidokkyo wa yonggong chŏngch'aek p'amp'uretŭ wa yoch'ŏngsŏ chŏnmal* [A report on the controversy regarding "The Church and the Procommunist Policy"], (Pusan, 1951), p. 160. Also see Kim Yangsŏn, *Han'guk Kidokkyo haebang simnyŏnsa*, pp. 160–61.

73. For Pak's theory of the relationship between liberal Christians and communism, see his *Chŏnjip*, vol. 9, chaps. 12 and 13. Quoted from pp. 88–90.

74. Pak, *Chŏnjip*, vol. 9, pp. 107 and 117.

75. Ch'ae Kiŭn, *Han'guk kyohoesa* [A history of the Korean church],

(Seoul: Yesugyo munsŏ sŏn'gyohoe, 1977), p. 225. For more fundamentalist arguments on the connection between liberal Christians and communism, see Kim Ùihwan, *Tojŏn pannŭn posu sinhak* [Conservative theology under attack], (Seoul: Sŏgwang muhwasa, 1970), chap. 4; Pak, *Chŏnjip*, vol. 9, chaps. 12 and 13; and Han Ch'ŏlha, Na Hakchin, and An Pongho, "Kyohoe wa kukka" (Conversation on church and state), in *Haebang sinhak kwa Tosi sanŏp sŏn'gyo* [Theology of liberation and the Urban Industrial Mission], ed. Kyŏnghyang sinmunsa (Seoul: Kyŏnghyang sinmunsa, 1982), pp. 11–22.

76. Kim Ùihwan, "Han'guk kyohoe ŭi chŏngch'i ch'amyŏ munje" (On political participation of the Korean church), *Sinhak chinam* [Presbyterian Theological Review], vol. 30, no. 1 (January–March 1973), pp. 25–32 and 50. Quoted from p. 25 and p. 50.

77. Ibid., pp. 26–27. Also see Hwang Sŏngsu, *Kyohoe wa kukka* [Church and state], (Seoul: Sinmang'aesa, 1972), pp. 308–309.

78. Kim Ùihwan, "Han'guk kyohoe ŭi chŏngch'i ch'amyŏ munje," pp. 26–28.

79. Ibid., pp. 28–32.

80. For details, see chap. 6 of this book.

81. *Sŏnggyŏng haesŏk munje yŏn'gu wiwŏn pogosŏ* [Report by the committee to study controversial points in reading the Bible]. Quoted from Kim Yangsŏn, *Han'guk Kidokkyo haebang simnyŏnsa*, p. 181.

82. Ibid., pp. 178–79.

83. Ibid., p. 185.

84. In 1935, the General Assembly required that participants in the translation project issue a public apology. See ibid., pp. 176–85, and Conn, "Korean Theology: Where Has It Been? Where Is It Going?" p. 55.

85. Kim Taehŏn, an elder in Seoul, donated sufficient funds to open the seminary in 1940. For the background of the opening of this seminary, see Kim Chaejun, *Pŏmyonggi*, vol. 1, pp. 219–35.

86. "Sinhak kyoyuk inyŏm" (Guidelines for theological education), in Kim Yangsŏn, *Han'guk Kidokkyo haebang simnyŏnsa*, pp. 193–94.

87. "Chosŏn sinhak haksaeng chinjŏngsŏ," in ibid., pp. 216–22.

88. Kim Yangsŏn, *Han'guk Kidokkyo haebang simnyŏnsa*, pp. 268–86.

89. "Kim Chaejun kyosu ŭi chinsulsŏ" (Statement of Professor Kim Chaejun), in ibid., pp. 222–25. Quoted from pp. 223–24.

90. "Pŏpt'ong samsipp'al ch'onghoe ŭi sŏnŏnsŏ" (Statement of the lawful thirty-eighth general assembly), in ibid., pp. 281–84. Quoted from p. 283.

91. On Kim Chaejun's life, see his autobiography, *Pŏmyonggi*, 2 vols. Also see Chŏn Kyŏng'yŏn, "Kim Chaejun non" (On Kim Chaejun), *Sasanggye*, vol. 14, no. 4 (April 1966), pp. 204–15, and Pak Hyŏnggyu, "No moksa ŭi pisang-

han hyŏnsil ch'amyŏ" (Extraordinary political participation of an aging minister), *Wŏlgan chung'ang*, no. 45 (December 1971), pp. 103–5.

92. On the separation of this liberal group from the parent church, see Kim Yangsŏn, *Han'guk Kidokkyo haebang simnyŏnsa*, pp. 214–67.

93. For a short biography of Mun Ikhwan, the most prominent Christian activist during the 1970s and 1980s, see Ko Ŭn, "Mun Ikhwan ŭl malhanda" (On Mun Ikhwan), *Miju tong'a ilbo* [The Tonga daily news, L.A. edition], June 24, 25, and 26, 1986.

Mun Ikhwan was born in Manchuria in 1918 to Mun Chaerin, a Christian minister. He graduated from the Chosŏn Theological Seminary in 1947 and Princeton Theological Seminary in 1955. He was on the faculty of the Han'guk (formerly Chosŏn) Theological Seminary and pastor of the Hanbit Church, founded by a group of Christian activists. He leaped to fame in 1976 when he completed a translation of the Old Testament in cooperation with a Catholic theologian. Since the so-called Statement for democratization case (*minju kukuk sŏnŏn sakŏn*) of 1976, in which he participated, he served time in jail or was placed under house arrest from time to time. Mun was the chairman of the United Mass Movement for Democracy and Unification founded in 1984. Although he earned fame principally as a theologian and political activist for democracy and unification, he was also a well-known poet. He shocked the world in 1992 with his secretly planned visit to Kim Il-sung in P'yŏngyang for discussion on unification. He passed away in 1994. Tens of thousands of Koreans participated in his funeral.

94. Kim Chaejun's conversation with Yi Yŏngho in a YMCA citizens' forum, *Simin nondan* [Citizens' forum], (Seoul: YMCA, 1977), p. 91.

95. Yi Kyejun's conversation with Cho Hyangnok at a YMCA citizens' forum, ibid., p. 143.

96. Kim Chaejun, *In'gan igie* [Because I am a human being], (Seoul: Hyangninsa, 1971), p. 153.

97. "Han'guk kidokcha sinang sŏnŏn" (Theological declaration of Korean Christians) issued on May 20, 1973. This has been regarded as the founding declaration of the Christian movement for democracy during the 1970s and 1980s in South Korea. For an English translation, see Emergency Christian Conference on Korean Problems, ed., *Documents on the Struggle for Democracy in Korea* (Tokyo: Shinkyo shuppansha, 1975), pp. 37–43. Also see "Our View of Current Situation of Nation" (statement), issued on May 29, 1986, by the Christ Presbyterian Church in the Republic of Korea, p. 2.

98. During the 1960s and 1970s, liberal and radical theological works in the West, such as John Robinson's *Honest to God*, Harvey Cox's *The Secular*

City, Jurgen Moltmann's *Theology of Hope,* and so forth influenced liberal Korean Protestant leaders. For the influence of radical theology on Korean liberals, see Young-suk Yi, "Liberal Protestant Leaders Working for Social Change: South Korea, 1957–1984" (Ph.D. diss., University of Oregon, 1990), especially chaps. 4 and 5.

99. On radical theologies, see Paul Lehman, *The Transfiguration of Politics* (New York: Harper and Row, 1975); J. Deotis Roberts, *A Black Theology* (Philadelphia: The Westminster Press, 1974); Thomas H. McFadden, ed., *Liberation, Revolution, and Freedom* (New York: The Seabury Press, 1975); David Johnson, ed., *Uppsala to Nairobi* (Geneva and New York: World Council of Churches, 1975); J. G. Davies, *Christians, Politics and Violent Revolution* (New York: Orbis Books, 1976); and James H. Cone, *A Black Theology of Liberation* (Philadelphia and New York: J. B. Lippincott Co., 1970).

100. Quoted from Joseph M. Shaw, R.W. Franklin, Harris Kaasa, and Charles W. Buzicky, eds., *Readings in Christian Humanism* (Minneapolis: Augsburg Publishing House, 1982), p. 586. Bonhoeffer wrote the letter on July 18, 1944.

101. Jurgen Moltmann, *Theology of Hope: On the Ground and the Implications of a Christian Eschatology* (New York: Harper and Row, 1967, first U.S. edition), pp. 327–28.

102. Cone, *A Black Theology of Liberation*, pp. 17–49 and 228–49.

103. For details, see Alfred Fierro, *The Militant Gospel* (New York: Orbis Books, 1977).

104. For details, see Young-suk Yi, "Liberal Protestant Leaders Working for Social Change," chaps. 4 and 5.

105. Yi Changsik, "Pogŭm ŭi chayu, Hananim ŭi sŏn'gyo chujang" (Advocacy for freedom of faith and Missio Dei), *Kidokkyo sasang*, no. 277 (July 1981), pp. 97–107, particularly pp. 102–3.

106. See "Sasŏl" (Editorial), *Tong'a ilbo*, July 6, 1965.

107. *Theological Declaration of Korean Christians* (*Han'guk kidokcha sinang sŏnŏn*), in *Documents on the Struggle for Democracy in Korea*, ed. The Emergency Christian Conference on Korean Problems, pp. 38–39. I rely on the translation in this valuable collection of Korean Protestant activism.

108. Kim Yŏng'il, "Han'guk Kidokkyo ŭi sahoe ch'amyŏ" (Social participation of the Korean church), *Sindong'a*, no. 126 (February 1975), pp. 164–97, particularly pp. 186–87.

109. On the close relations of the fundamentalist Christian group with the government, see Kim Yongbok, "Haebanghu kyohoe wa kukka," pp. 233–35.

110. Liberal Christian leaders had to write articles or publish pamphlets in order to explain defensively the WCC, its stand, and their own activity. See, for

example, Cho Sŭnghyŏk, *Tosi sanŏp sŏn'gyo ŭi insik* [Understanding of the Urban Industrial Mission], (Seoul: Minjungsa, 1981); and Han'guk Kidokkyo sahoe munje yŏn'guwŏn, *Segye kyohoe hyŏbŭihoeran muŏsin'ga* [What is the World Council of Churches?], (Seoul: Han'guk Kidokkyo sahoe munje yŏn'guwŏn, 1984), especially Cho Sŭnghyŏk's "Preface."

111. Kim Kyŏngnae and Hong Chiyŏng, *Ch'onghwa wa yusin* [General harmony and the restoration], (Seoul: Kŭmnan ch'ulp'ansa, 1975). Kim Kyŏngnae was a famous journalist and a fundamentalist church elder. Hong Ch'iyŏng consistently criticized liberal activism during the 1970s. Although his official title was president of the Society for Religious Studies in Korea (Han'guk chonggyo yŏn'guhoe), an obscure organization, many church leaders regarded him as a mysterious person.

112. Hong Chiyŏng, *Sanŏp sŏn'gyo nŭn muŏsŭl norinŭn'ga* [What is the Urban Industrial Mission after?], (Seoul: Kŭmnan ch'ulp'ansa, 1979).

113. *Haebang sinhak kwa Tosi sanŏp sŏn'gyo* [Liberation theology and the Urban Industrial Mission] was published in 1982 as a book, but the articles in this volume appeared previously in the *Kyŏnghyang sinmun.*

114. *Taehak kwa sasang* [College and thought] by *Kyŏnghang sinmunsa* [Kyŏnghyang daily news] was published in 1982 as a book, but the articles in this volume also appeared previously in the *Kyŏnghyang sinmun.*

115. Kyŏnghyang sinmunsa, ed., *Haebang sinhak kwa Tosi sanŏp sŏn'gyo*, pp. 168 and 172.

3 / THE KOREAN PROTESTANT CHURCH AS A SOCIAL INSTITUTION

1. For example, see the introduction to Emergency Christian Conference on Korean Problems, ed., *Documents on the Struggle for Democracy in Korea* (Tokyo: Shinkyo shuppansha, 1975), pp. 1–28. The writer errs in describing the anti–Park Chung-hee movement centered in the KNCC in the 1970s as a campaign of the Christian churches as a whole, even including Catholics, because he ignores the structure of the Korean Protestant church.

2. The number of sects and denominations varies from 70 to 100. Only six denominations were affiliated with the KNCC. According to a 1979 statistic, congregations affiliated with the KNCC accounted for only two million members out of a total of six million Protestants. The six denominations were the Jesus Presbyterian Church in Korea (T'onghapp'a), the Christ Presbyterian Assembly in the Republic of Korea (Kijangp'a), the Methodist Church, the Salvation Army, the Anglican Church, and the Evangelical Church (Pogŭm

Kyohoe). See Han'guk Kidokkyo sahoe munje yŏn'gowŏn, *Han'guk kyohoe paengnyŏn chonghap chosa yŏn'gu: pogosŏ* [A comprehensive study of the Korean church during the last century: A report], (Seoul: Han'guk Kidokkyo sahoe munje yŏn'guwŏn, 1982), pp. 163 and 165.

3. For my critical discussion on this subject, see chapter two in this book. Also see Yu Tongsik, *Han'guk sinhak ŭi kwangmaek: Han'guk sinhaksa sŏsŏl* [Patterns of theology in Korea: A history of theology in Korea: An introduction], (Seoul: Chŏnmangsa, 1982); Min Kyŏngbae, *Kŭrisŭch'an akademi simnyŏnsa* [The ten-year history of the Christian Academy], (Seoul: Han'guk kŭrisŭch'an akademi, 1975); and Harold Hakwon Sunoo, *Repressive State and Resisting Church: The Politics of CIA in South Korea* (Fayette, Missouri: Korean American Cultural Association, 1976).

4. According to one source, there were 121 Protestant denominations and sects in 1993. See Han'guk chonggyo sahoe yŏn'guso, *Han'guk chonggyo yŏn'gam* [The yearbook of Korean religions], (Seoul: Han'guk chonggyo sahoe yŏn'guso/Hallimwŏn, 1993), pp. 528–29.

5. Presbyterians account for some 60 percent of all Protestant Christians in South Korea. Han'guk Kidokkyo sahoe munje yŏn'guwŏn, *Han'guk kyohoe paengnyŏn chonghap chosa yŏn'gu: pogosŏ*, pp. 162–63.

6. This information was obtained in interviews with Korean church leaders such as Kang Sinmyŏng, former moderator of the Jesus Presbyterian Church (T'onghapp'a) and former president of Sungsil University, and Pak Myŏngsu, former moderator of the Jesus Presbyterian Church (Hapdongp'a) and board member for various Christian agencies. Also see Kim Chaejun, *Pŏmyonggi* [Autobiography of Kim Chaejun], (Toronto: Ch'ilsŏng kwanggosa, 1981), vol. 1, pp. 144–47.

7. Yi Kwangsu, "Kŭmil Chosŏn ŭi Yasogyohoe ŭi hŏmjŏm" (Some defects in the Korean church today), *Ch'ŏngch'un*, no. 11 (1917), pp. 76–83, especially pp. 76–77.

8. Various denominations began missionary activities in Korea in the following years:

1884	The Northern Presbyterian Church
1885	The Northern Methodist Church
1889	The Presbyterian Church of Victoria (Australia)
1890	The Church of England
1892	The Southern Presbyterian Church
1893	The Canadian Presbyterian Church
1896	The Southern Methodist Church

1903 The Seventh-Day Adventist Church
1907 The Oriental Missionary Society
1908 The Salvation Army

9. Min Kyongbae, *Han'guk minjok kyohoe hyŏngsŏng saron* [A historical study on the formation of a nationalist church in Korea], (Seoul: Yŏnse taehakkyo ch'ulp'anbu, 1974), pp. 55–56.

10. For internal conflict and related activities in the Korean Protestant church community, see Kim Chaejun, *Pŏmyonggi*, vol. 2, p. 131; An Sŏngjin, "Ŏrini wa uri" (Children and we), *Kŭrisŭch'an*, July 9, 1960; and Pak Myŏngsu, *Munpakke sori issŏ* [Voices outside the gate], (Seoul: Yesugyo munsŏ sŏn'gyohoe, 1976), p. 208. The writers discuss the content of interchurch bickering and its adverse repercussions for children and society on the basis of events in which adult church members engaged in physical fights—hurling rocks and punching each other. One can readily imagine that the relationships would be extremely strained between the separate groups after such fights.

11. See the map in T. Stanley Soltau, *Korea: The Hermit Nation and Its Response to Christianity* (London: World Dominion Press, 1932), p. 21. For more details, see George L. Paik, *The History of Protestant Missions in Korea, 1832–1910* (P'yŏngyang: Union Christian College, 1929; reprint, Yonsei University, 1970), pp. 198–201 and 382–84; and Allen D. Clark, *A History of the Church in Korea* (Seoul: The Christian Literature Society, 1971), pp. 111–12.

12. For the rift in the Korean Protestant church, see Kim Yangsŏn, *Han'guk Kidokkyo haebang simnyŏnsa* [The ten-year history of the Korean church since the Liberation], (Seoul: Taehan Yesugyo changnohoe ch'onghoe chonggyo kyoyukpu, 1955), pp. 146–286.

13. Kim Chaejun, *Pŏmyonggi*, vol. 1, p. 226. Also see Kim Insŏ, "Sŏnmin nambuk punyŏl ŭi hwa" (North-south split of a chosen people), *Sinang saenghwal*, vol. 5, no. 10 (October 1936), pp. 18–23. In this article, Kim Insŏ, a prominent church journalist, pointed out that confrontation between northwesterners and southerners in church politics occurred as early as the 1930s.

14. In 1926, out of 299,543 Christians, 86,474 were found in the northwestern region. See Yi Nŭnghwa, *Chosŏn Kidokkyo kŭp oegyosa* [History of Christianity and foreign relations in Korea], (Seoul: Hangmun'gak, 1969: original edition, 1928), pp. 212–13. In 1910, 457 out of 823 church-related schools were located in the three northwestern provinces. See Tawara Sonnichi, *Kankoku kyōiku no genjō* [The present state of education in Korea], (Keijō: Chōsen sōtokufu gakufu, 1910), pp. 49–50. From 1912 to 1936, the General Assembly of the Korean Presbyterian Church was held in this region fourteen out of twenty-five times. See "P'yŏngyang chi p'yŏnŏn" (Report from P'yŏng-

yang), *Sinang saenghwal*, vol. 5, no. 9 (September 1936), p. 36. According to this source, while four missionaries and six others from non-northwestern regions became moderators for the General Assembly, fifteen northwesterners were elected to that position. One estimate has been made that two-thirds of the Korean Presbyterian Christians were located in this region. See Kim Chaejun, *Pŏmyonggi*, vol. 1, p. 226, and vol. 2, p. 31.

15. At a time when few had training in theological seminaries abroad, Song Ch'anggŭn and Kim Chaejun were not fully accepted in the P'yŏngyang Presbyterian Theological Seminary—despite their excellent educational background—simply because they hailed from the Hamgyŏng-Kando region. See Chu T'aeik, *Man'u Song Ch'anggŭn* [A biography of Song Ch'anggŭn], (Seoul: Man'u Song Ch'anggŭn sŏnsaeng kinyŏm saŏphoe, 1978), pp. 45–47; Kim Chaejun, *Pŏmyonggi*, vol. 1, pp. 171–81; and Kim Yangsŏn, *Han'guk Kidokkyo haebang simnyonsa*, p. 190.

16. Kim, *Pŏmyonggi*, vol. 1, pp. 183, 192, and 220–33.

17. On the campaign against Shinto-shrine worship, see Kun Sam Lee, *The Christian Confrontation with Shinto Nationalism* (Philadelphia: The Presbyterian and Reformed Publishing Co., 1966); and Kim Yangsŏn, *Han'guk Kidokkyosa yŏn'gu* [A historical study of Korean Christianity], (Seoul: Kidokkyomunsa, 1971), pp. 172–99.

18. For circumstances surrounding the founding of the Chosŏn Theological Seminary, see Kim Chaejun, *Pŏmyonggi*, vol. 1, pp. 219–33; Chu T'aeik, *Man'u Song Ch'anggŭn*, pp. 59–63; and Kim Yangsŏn, *Han'guk Kidokkyo haebang simnyŏnsa*, pp. 185–94.

19. Concerning demands that church leaders who bent to pressure to worship at Shinto shrines should retire from leadership positions, see Kim Yangsŏn, *Han'guk Kidokkyo haebang simnyŏnsa*, pp. 43–45; Clark, *A History of the Church in Korea*, pp. 228 and 234–36; and Shim Koon Sik, *Till the End of the Age: The Life of Reverend Sang Dong Han* (Pusan, South Korea: Kosin College Press, 1984), pp. 98–100 and 218–23.

20. The campaign began with a petition submitted by fifty-one students at the Chosŏn Theological Seminary for the creation of a fundamentalist theological seminary. These students were either from the northwest region or former students of the leading fundamentalist theologian, Pak Hyŏngnyong. They accused some faculty members of the Chosŏn Theological Seminary, including Kim Chaejun, the founder, of being excessively liberal. For details, see "Chosŏn sinhak haksaeng chinjŏngsŏ" (The students' petition of the Chosŏn Theological Seminary), in Kim Yangsŏn, *Han'guk Kidokkyo haebang simnyŏnsa*, pp. 216–17.

21. On the separation of the Christ Presbyterian Assembly in the Republic of Korea (Han'guk Kidokkyo changnohoe) from the parent Presbyterian church, Jesus Presbyterian Assembly of Korea (Taehan Yesugyo changnohoe), see Kim Yangsŏn, *Han'guk Kidokkyo haebang simnyŏnsa*, pp. 185–286, and Kim Chaejun, *Pŏmyonggi*, vol. 2, pp. 114–19 and 130–47. This issue is discussed in greater detail in chapter 2 of this book.

22. In reference to the split into two large Presbyterian groups, the Hapdongp'a and T'onghapp'a, see Yi Yŏnghŏn, *Han'guk Kidokkyosa* [A history of the Korean church], (Seoul: Concordia ch'ulp'ansa, 1978), pp. 318–55.

23. Min Kyŏngbae, *Kurisuch'an akademi simnyonsa*, p. 30. Also see his article "Han'guk kŭndae munhwa wa Kidokkyo ŭi hyŏngt'ae mit kŭ yŏnghyang pŏmwi" (Christianity in modern Korea: Its distribution pattern and the scope of influence on culture), *Han'guk sahak*, no. 1 (June 1982), pp. 226–50.

24. This information was obtained in interviews with prominent Korean church leaders such as Kang Sinmyŏng, Pak Myŏngsu, and Kim Yunsik and with Korean Christian ministers in the Seattle area where I studied and in Seoul where I conducted my research in 1989, 1993, and 1996. Also see Kim Chaejun, *Pŏmyonggi*, vol. 2, pp. 131–32 and 144–47.

25. Ibid., p. 131.

26. See, for example, various articles by Kim Insŏ in *Sinang saenghwal*, vols. 1 and 2 (December 1932 through March 1933).

27. See Han'guk chonggyo sahoe yŏn'guso, *Han'guk chonggyo yŏn'gam*, pp. 528–29.

28. Since most Christians in the northwest were Presbyterians under the administration of the Northern Presbyterian Mission, Presbyterians outnumbered all other Protestants there from the very beginning of Protestant evangelism in Korea. In 1979, for example, out of 4,867,657 Protestant Christians, 2,798,191 were Presbyterians, and among 17,793 Protestant churches there were 9,923 Presbyterian churches. See Han'guk Kidokkyo sahoe munje yŏn'guwŏn, *Han'guk kyohoe paengnyŏn chonghap chosa yŏn'gu*, p. 163.

29. On the more rapid growth of the Presbyterian church, see Roy E. Shearer, *Wildfire: Church Growth in Korea*, (Grand Rapids, Mich.: William E. Eerdmans Publishing Co., 1966), chap. 3.

30. In order to understand how the Protestant church grew in the northwest, see ibid., chaps. 4 and 5; Yi Kwangnin, "Kaehwagi kwansŏ chibang gwa Kaesin'gyo" (Protestantism in the northwest at the turn of the century), in his *Han'guk kaehwa sasang yŏn'gu* [Studies on Korean enlightenment thought], (Seoul: Ilchogak, 1979), pp. 226–50; Min Kyŏngbae, "Han'guk kŭndae munhwa wa Kidokkyo ŭi hyŏngt'ae mit kŭ yŏnghyang pŏmwi" (Christianity

in modern Korea: Its distribution pattern and the scope of influence on culture), *Han'guk sahak*, no. 1 (June 1982), pp. 226–50; and his *Han'guk minjok kyohoe hyŏngsŏng saron*, pp. 193–95.

31. For the discussion of the discrimination toward northwesterners during the Chosŏn period, see Edward W. Wagner, "The Ladder of Success in Yi Dynasty Korea," *Occasional Paper on Korea*, no. 1 (April 1974), University of Washington, pp. 1–8, and "The Civil Examination Process as Social Leaven: The Case of the Northern Provinces in the Yi Dynasty," *Korea Journal*, vol. 17, no. 1 (January 1977), pp. 22–27. Also see Yi Ihwa, *Han'guk ŭi p'abŏl* [Korean factionalism], (Seoul: Ŏmun'gak, 1983), pp. 120–30; and Yi Kwangnin, "Kaehwagi kwansŏ chibang gwa kaesin'gyo."

32. One of the earlier missionaries who made a trip to the region was impressed by "the independent, manly spirit" of the northwesterners. See William M. Baird, "Notes on a Trip into Northern Korea," *The Independent*, May 20, 1897.

33. Tawara, *Kankoku kyōiku no genjō*, pp. 49–50.

34. Paik, *The History of Protestant Missions in Korea*, pp. 382–84.

35. Commoners and young members of the elite alienated from the Confucian establishment who joined the new religious community became the first Koreans to receive modern education and modern political training in the church's political machinery and in agencies that encouraged lay participation. Not surprisingly, they came to be leading figures in reform activities and nationalist politics. They include Yun Ch'iho, Yi Sangjae, Kim Kyusik, Sin Hŭng'u, An Ch'angho, Yi Sŭnghun, Cho Mansik, Yi Sŭngman, and Namgung Ŏk.

36. This information was obtained from interviews with Korean church leaders such as Kang Sinmyŏng, Pak Myŏngsu, and Kim Yunsik. Some scholars argue that the stationing of American troops facilitated the advance of Christians such as Syngman Rhee in politics, and Rhee also promoted church leaders to political positions of leadership. See Pak Hŭisŭng, "Han'guk sahoe ŭi pyŏnhwa wa Pulgyo" (Change in Korean society and Buddhism), *Hyŏnsanggwa insik*, vol. 18, no. 4 (Winter 1994), pp. 39–60, especially pp. 44–48; and Kang Inch'ŏl, "Haebanghu Han'guk Kaesin'gyohoe wa kukka simin sahoe" (The Korean Protestant church, state and civil society after the Liberation), in Han'guk sahoesa yŏn'guhoe, ed., *Hyŏndae Han'guk ŭi chonggyo wa sahoe* [Religion and society in contemporary Korea], (Seoul: Munhakkwa chisŏngsa, 1992), pp. 98–141, especially pp. 104–6 and 131–40.

Nevertheless, one should not overlook the important fact that church leaders had already assumed leadership positions in Korea by the time of Liberation. Therefore, it would be superficial to argue that Christian leaders were appointed to higher government posts simply on religious grounds. Such circumstantial factors as the U.S. occupation and the emergence of Syngman Rhee helped Christians merely to consolidate their leadership position in society. See my dissertation, "Protestant Christians and Politics in Korea" (University of Washington, 1987), chaps. 5 and 6. Also see my chapter in *Cambridge History of Korea*, vol. 4 (Cambridge and New York: Cambridge University Press, forthcoming).

37. For cases of the tension and conflict between pastors and elders that began to appear in the 1930s, see Kim Insŏ, "P'yŏngyang tongsin" and "Chosŏn kyohoe ŭi nanmaek" (The Korean church in chaos), *Sinang saenghwal*, vol. 2, no. 5 (May 1933), pp. 4–6; "Isipsam nohoe ŭi tŭngjŏng munje" (Agenda of the 23rd session of the presbytery), ibid., vol. 2, no. 11–12 (December 1933), pp. 4–7; "Ko isipsa ch'onghoe" (Recommendations for discussion at the 24th general assembly), ibid., vol. 4, no. 8 (August–September 1935), pp. 7–10, and others in *Sinang saenghwal.*

38. For example, Christians prayed, consoled, and supported the church leaders and fellow Christians who were imprisoned after the March First Movement. See Han'guk kyohoe sahakhoe, comp., *Chosŏn Yesugyo changnohoe sagi* [Historical records of the Korean Presbyterian church], vol. 2 (Seoul: Yŏnse taehakkyo ch'ulp'anbu, 1977), pp. 27, 65, 152, and 213.

39. See James B. Palais, "Human Rights in the Republic of Korea," in *Human Rights in Korea: An Asia Watch Report* (1986), pp. 1–339, especially pp. 302–15. Also see *Tong'a ilbo*, September 24 and 29, 1984; *Chugan Han'guk*, April 28, 1984, pp. 30–31; *Korea Communique* (Tokyo), no. 50 (January 1984); and *Kankoku tsushin* by Kankoku mondai kirisutosha kinkyu kai (Tokyo), no. 103 (September 1984). For Pak's letter to his foreign and domestic friends and the protest issued by the KNCC, see *Sinhan minbo* [The new Korea], Los Angeles, November 1, 1984. There is also an important publication distributed by the North American Coalition for Human Rights in Korea, *Now! The Current Situation of Seoul Jaeil (Cheil) Church, 1983–1985*, prepared by the Reverend Pak Hyŏnggyu and his followers. This document contains photographs, Pak's sermons, a brief explanation of the situation, and an appeal to Christians at home and abroad.

40. Park Yong-shin, "Protestant Christianity and Social Change in Korea" (Ph.D. diss., University of California-Berkeley, 1975), pp. 70–93.

41. Paik, *The History of Protestant Missions in Korea*, pp. 130, 164–65.

42. Ibid., p. 261.

43. Yi Kwangnin, *Han'guk kaehwa sasang yŏn'gu*, pp. 239–54.

44. See No Ch'ijun, "Ilcheha Han'guk changno kyohoe ch'onghoe t'onggye e taehan yŏn'gu" (A study on the statistics of the Korean Presbyterian Church

under Japanese colonial rule), Han'guk sahoesa yŏn'guhoe, *Hyŏndae Han'guk ŭi chonggyo wa sahoe*, pp. 66–97, especially p. 93. Also see No Ch'ijun, *Ilcheha Han'guk Kidokkyo minjok undong yŏn'gu* [Korean Christian nationalist movement under Japanese colonial rule], (Seoul: Han'guk Kidokkyo yŏksa yŏn'guso, 1993), pp. 107–13.

45. These individuals, who had religious, educational and cultural occupations, were emerging in society as a "new class." For the numerical growth of this group, see Soltau, *Korea: The Hermit Nation and Its Response to Christianity*, p. 114; and Yi Nŭnghwa, *Chosŏn Kidokkyo kŭp oegyosa*, pp. 220 and 223.

46. Soltau, *Korea: The Hermit Nation and Its Response to Christianity*, p. 114.

47. Yi Nŭnghwa, *Chosŏn Kidokkyo kŭp oegyosa*, pp. 220 and 223.

48. Kim Chaejun's dialogue with Kim Sŏngsik, "Sahoe e ch'aegimjinŭn kyohoe, che kinŭng tahanŭn chisig'in" (The church which is responsible for society and the intellectuals who play their given role in society), *Wŏlgan Chosŏn* (December 1983), pp. 58–68, particularly pp. 63–64.

49. See the list of elders in Huam kyohoe samsibonyŏnsa p'yŏnch'an wiwŏnhoe, *Huam kyohoe samsibonyŏnsa* [The thirty-five-year history of Huam Church], (Seoul: Huam kyohoe, 1981). No page number is available.

50. See Kim Chongsŏ, "Sŏngsŭrŏum ŭi p'ap'yŏnhwa in'ga" (Is it that the sacred became fragmented?), *Hyŏnsanggwa insik*, vol. 18, no. 4 (Winter 1994), pp. 11–38, particularly p. 16.

51. See Han'guk kidokkyo paekchunyŏn kinyŏmsaŏp hyŏbŭihoe, *Han'guk Kidokkyo paengnyŏn: Kinyŏm saŏp yoram* [One hundred years of the Korean Protestant church: An outline of commemorative events], (Seoul: Han'guk Kidokkyo paekchunyŏn kinyŏm saŏp hyŏbŭihoe, 1984), p. 48.

4 / THE PROTESTANT CHURCH AND EARLY NATIONALIST POLITICS, 1880–1919

1. In 1907, the protectorate government enforced the Peace Preservation Law, which banned social and political organizations and the right of assembly except for religious communities.

2. For my research critique of Sin Yongha, see "Han'guk hyŏndaesa e issŏsŏ Kaesin'gyo ŭi chari: Tongniphyŏphoe undong ŭl pogiro sama" (The place of the Protestant church in the history of modern Korea: Taking the Independence Club Movement as an example), *Ssial ŭi sori*, no. 99 (March 1989), pp. 181–89. In this critique I have pointed out that Sin's monumental work on the

Independence Club Movement, *Tongnip hyŏphoe yŏn'gu* [A study of the Independence Club], (Seoul: Ilchogak, 1976), does not clearly connect the movement to the Protestant church community and thus fails to see its social and organizational base. Ten years later, however, Sin Yongha came to realize the importance of the Protestant church for understanding the nationalist movement. See his "Han'guk Kidokkyo wa minjok undong" (The Korean Protestant church and the nationalist movement), in *Han'guk Kidokkyo sahoe undong* [Social movement of the Korean Protestant church], ed. Chŏn Taeryŏn and No Chongho (Seoul: Noch'ulp'an, 1986), pp. 34–44.

3. See, for example, George H. Jones, "Open Korea and Its Methodist Mission," *The Gospel in All Lands*, September 1898, pp. 391–96; and S.F. Moore, "An Incident in the Streets of Seoul," *The Church at Home and Abroad*, August 1894, pp. 119–20. Also see Kim Yŏnghwi, *Chwaong Yun Ch'iho sŏnsaeng yakchŏn* [A brief biography of Yun Ch'iho], (Seoul: Kidokkyo Chosŏn kamnihoe, 1934), p. 55.

4. Earlier, Korean Catholics also stood firmly against ancestor worship, but at that time the Confucian establishment was strong enough to persecute these anti-Confucian religious and social elements. In 1866 alone, nine Catholic missionaries and some 8,000 Korean Catholics were executed. See Nyung Kim, "The Politics of Religion in South Korea, 1974–89: The Catholic Church's Political Opposition to the Authoritarian State" (Ph.D. diss., University of Washington, 1993), pp. 210–11. Also see Ching Young Choe, *The Rule of the Taewŏn'gun, 1864–1873: Restoration in Yi Korea* (Cambridge, Mass.: East Asian Research Center, Harvard University, 1977), chap. 10.

When Protestant converts criticized Confucian teachings, including ancestor worship, during the late nineteenth century, the Confucian government, which was shaken by internal and external challenges, was moving toward collapse and could not persecute them.

5. Jones, "Open Korea and Its Methodist Mission," p. 394.

6. Ibid., p. 392.

7. On developments in the early church community in the Confucian society, see the following works: Annie L. A. Baird, *Daybreak in Korea: A Tale of Transformation in the Far East* (New York: Fleming H. Revell Co., 1909); Lillias H. Underwood, *Fifteen Years Among the Top-knots or Life in Korea* (Boston, New York, and Chicago: American Tract Society, 1904); George W. Gilmore, *Korea From Its Capital* (Philadelphia: Presbyterian Board of Publication and Sunday-School Work, 1892); and James S. Gale, *Korea in Transition* (New York: The Young People's Missionary Movement of the United States and Canada, 1909).

8. Baird, *Daybreak in Korea*, p. 108; and Kil Sŏnju, "Malsehak" (Eschatology), in *Yŏnggye Kil Sŏnju moksa chŏjakchip* [Works of the Reverend Kil Sŏnju], (Seoul: Taehan Kidokkyo sŏhoe, 1968), pp. 21–141, especially p. 28. This article was originally published in 1930. This mode of address is still in use among churchgoers.

9. See Moore, "An Incident in the Streets of Seoul."

10. Daniel L. Gifford, "The Influence of Missionary Work Upon the Life of the Korean," *The Student Missionary Appeal* (addresses at the Third International Convention of Student Volunteer Movement for Foreign Mission, Cleveland, February 23–27, 1898) (New York: Student Volunteer Movement, 1989), pp. 361–64; W. L. Swallen, "Polygamy and the Church," *The Korean Repository*, vol. 2, no. 8 (August 1895), pp. 289–94; and *Chosŏn kŭrisŭdoin hoebo* [The Christian advocate], June 23, 1897.

11. Baird, *Daybreak in Korea*, pp. 62–85; Jones, "Open Korea and Its Methodist Mission," p. 392; and Yun Ch'iho, "A Synopsis of What I Was and What I Am," *The Gospel in All Lands*, June 1887, pp. 274–75.

12. Kim, *Chwaong Yun Ch'iho sŏnsaeng yakchŏn*, p. 55; and Yun, "A Synopsis of What I Was and What I Am."

13. Baird, *Daybreak in Korea*, pp. 107–23; and Yun, "A Synopsis of What I Was and What I Am," pp. 274–75.

14. Korean Christians' identification of reform activity with Christianization is clearly revealed in Yun Ch'iho's thought. For example, Yun said that "Christianity is the only salvation to Coreans (Koreans)," *Yun Ch'iho ilgi* [Yun Chi'ho's diary], April 8, 1893; and "Christianity is the salvation and hope of Corea [Korea]," ibid., February 19, 1893). Also see Ibid., March 30, 1889.

15. Ch'oe Myŏngsik, *Anak sakŏn kwa samil undong gwa na* [The Anak Incident, the March First Movement, and I], (Seoul: Kŭkhŏ chŏn'gi p'yŏnch'an wiwŏnhoe, 1970), p. 14.

16. Chōsen Sōtokufu, *Kyō kankoku kanpō* [The official gazette of old Korea], vol. 22 (August 13, 1910), pp. 997–98.

17. Son Insu, *Han'guk kŭndae kyoyuksa* [A history of modern education in Korea], (Seoul: Yŏnse taehakkyo ch'ulp'anbu, 1971), pp. 29–159, especially p. 29.

18. Yi Kwangnin, *Han'guksa kangjwa* [Roundtable discussion of Korean history], (Seoul: Ilchogak, 1983), no. 5, p. 541. Yi's table is based on Ch'a Chaemyŏng, comp., *Chosŏn Yesugyo changnohoe sagi*, vol. 1 (Seoul: Taehan Yesugyo changnohoe, 1928). However, it is interesting to note that in 1911, just one year later, the Presbyterian denomination had 1,448 churches, according to Kim Yangsŏn, the leading authority on church history in Korea. See Kim's

Han'guk Kidokkyosa yŏn'gu [A historical study of Korean Christianity], (Seoul: Kidokkyomunsa, 1971), p. 107.

19. See Yung-Chung Kim, *Women of Korea: A History from Ancient Times to 1945* (Seoul: Ewha Womans University Press, 1976), pp. 210–12.

20. For example, see Kyŏngsin chung kodŭng hakkyo, *Kyŏngsin p'alsimnyŏnsa* [Eighty-year history of the Kyŏngsin School], (Seoul: Kyŏngsin chung kodŭng hakkyo, 1966), pp. 34–35.

21. See George L. Paik, *The History of Protestant Missions in Korea* (P'yŏngyang: Union Christian College, 1929; reprint, Yonsei University Press, 1970), p. 230.

22. Sunday school, Christian Endeavors, the Evangelical Society of Women, the Debating Society, and the Speech Meeting were programs common in the early churches in Korea, but the last two were particularly popular among Korean Christians.

23. Sin, *Tongnip hyŏphoe yŏn'gu*, pp. 112–17; and Paejae chung kodŭng hakkyo, *Paejaesa* [A History of the Paejae School], (Seoul: Paejae chung Kodŭng hakkyo, 1955), pp. 61, 84–89, and 110–11.

24. *Hyŏpsŏng hoebo* [Newsletter of Hyŏpsŏnghoe], "Nonsŏl" (Editorial), February 19, 1898.

25. For the list of topics, see Paejae chung kodŭng hakkyo, *Paejaesa*, pp. 86–88. For a recent study on the "slave" issue in Korea, see James B. Palais, "A Search for Korean Uniqueness," *Harvard Journal of Asiatic Studies*, vol. 55, no. 2 (December 1995), pp. 409–25, particularly pp. 414–18; and *Confucian Statecraft and Korean Institutions: Yu Hyŏngwŏn and the Late Chosŏn Dynasty* (London and Seattle: University of Washington Press, 1996), chap. 6.

26. For example, the first local debating society was established in Sorae (Songch'ŏn), Hwanghae Province, where the first Protestant church was founded. See *Hyŏpsŏng hoebo*, January 8, 1898.

27. Saemunan kyohoe ch'ilsimnyŏnsa kanhaeng wiwŏnhoe, *Saemunan kyohoe ch'ilsimnyŏnsa* [Seventy-year history of the Saemunan Church], (Seoul: Saemunan kyohoe, 1958), pp. 27–32, especially p. 28.

28. Yun Ch'iho translated Robert's *Rules of Order* under the title *Ŭihoe t'ongsang kyuch'ik*. It was greatly favored among Korean Christians, reflecting enthusiasm for acquiring modern procedures of public debate and parliamentary deliberation. See *The Korean Repository*, vol. 5 (April 1898), p. 157; and *Yun Ch'iho ilgi*, March 18, 1898.

29. *The Independent*, "Editorial," December 3, 1896.

30. On the Independence Club, see the following works: Sin, *Tongnip hyŏphoe yŏn'gu*; two articles of Pak Yŏngsin (Park Yong-shin), "Tongnip

hyŏphoe chido seryŏk ŭi sangjing gwa ŭisik kujo" (The Independence Club leaders: Structure of their symbol and consciousness), *Tongbanghak chi*, no. 20 (December 1978), pp. 147–70, and "Wirobut'ŏ ŭi kaehyŏk esŏ araerobut'ŏ ŭi kaehyŏk ŭro: Sŏ Chaep'il ŭi undong chŏlyak" (From reform from above to reform from below: Strategic change of Sŏ Chaep'il), *Hyŏnsanggwa insik*, vol. 20, no. 1 (Spring 1996), pp. 41–65. Also see Vipan Chandra, *Imperialism, Resistance, and Reform in Late Nineteenth-Century Korea: Enlightenment and the Independence Club* (Berkeley: University of California, Institute of East Asian Studies, 1988).

31. Sŏ Chaep'il completed his medical studies at George Washington University. For his life and activity see Kim Tot'ae, *Sŏ Chaep'il paksa chasŏjŏn* [Biography of Dr. Sŏ Chaep'il], (Seoul: Susŏnsa, 1948); Channing Liem, *America's Finest Gift to Korea: The Life of Philip Jaisohn* (New York: The William-Frederick Press, 1952); and Se Eung Oh, *Dr. Philip Jaisohn's Reform Movement, 1896–1898: A Critical Appraisal of the Independence Club* (Lanham, Md.: University Press of America, 1995).

32. Yun Ch'iho studied a wide range of subjects, including divinity, at Emory and Vanderbilt Universities. On Yun Ch'iho's life and activity, see Kim Yŏnghwi, *Chwaong Yun Ch'iho sŏnsaeng yakchŏn*; Kim Hyung-chan, *Yun Ch'i-ho, 1865–1945. Letters in Exile: The Life and Times of Yun Ch'i-ho* (Covington, Ga.: Rhoades Printing Co., 1980); Pak Chŏngsin (Park Chung-shin), "Yun Ch'iho yŏn'gu" (A study of Yun Ch'i-ho), *Paeksan hakpo*, no. 23 (1977), pp. 341–88; and Yu Yŏngyŏl, *Kaehwagi ŭi Yun Ch'iho yŏn'gu* [A study of Yun Ch'iho during the time of enlightenment], (Seoul: Han'gilsa, 1985).

33. See Sin, *Tongnip hyŏphoe yŏn'gu*, pp. 81–112 and 123–33.

34. Ibid., pp. 93–95.

35. Ibid., pp. 95–106.

36. Ibid., pp. 88 and 93–95.

37. See my "Han'guk hyŏndaesa e issŏsŏ Kaesin'gyo ŭi chari."

38. Ch'oe, *Anak sakŏn kwa samil undong gwa na*, pp. 5–85.

39. Ibid., pp. 17–76.

40. Ibid., pp. 74–76.

41. Ibid., pp. 15–22. Also see, Anak kunchi p'yŏnch'an wiwŏnhoe, *Anak kunchi* [Annals of Anak County], (Seoul: Anak kunchi p'yŏnch'an wiwŏnhoe, 1976), pp. 97–124.

42. Ch'oe, *Anak sakŏn kwa samil undong gwa na*, pp. 74–95.

43. *Hyŏpsŏng hoebo*, January 8, 1898.

44. See Paejae chung kodŭng hakkyo, *Paejaesa*, pp. 81–89 and 109–14; and Sin, *Tongnip hyŏphoe yŏn'gu*, pp. 94–106.

45. Kyŏngsin chung kodŭng hakkyo, *Kyŏngsin p'alsimnyŏnsa yaksa*, pp. 30 and 36–37; and Sin, *Tongnip hyŏphoe yŏn'gu*, pp. 94–106.

46. *Tongnip sinmun* [The Independent], October 12, 1898.

47. Sin, *Tongnip hyŏphoe yŏn'gu*, pp. 106–107.

48. *Tongnip sinmun*, February 19, 1897.

49. Kim Insŏ, "Yŏnggye sŏnsaeng sojŏn" (A short biography of the Reverend Kil Sŏnju), *Sinang saenghwal*, vol. 1, no. 12 (January 1933), pp. 24–28, especially p. 27. On Kil Sŏnju's life and activity, see Kil Chin'gyŏng, *Yŏnggye Kil Sŏnju* [Kil Sŏnju: A biography], (Seoul: Chongno sŏjŏk, 1980), chap. 4.

50. Evangelistic endeavors were also particularly successful in Sŏnch'ŏn, Ŭiju, Pukch'ŏng, Kanggye, and Taegu from the early period of the Christian mission. See Roy E. Shearer, *Wildfire: Church Growth in Korea* (Grand Rapids, Mich.: William E. Eerdmans Publishing Co., 1966), chaps. 4 and 5.

51. *Hwangsŏng sinmun*, December 9 and 11, 1898. Also see Sin, *Tongnip hyŏphoe yŏn'gu*, pp. 479–80.

52. See No Ch'ijun, *Ilcheha Han'guk Kidokkyo minjok undong yŏn'gu* [Korean Christian nationalist movement under Japanese colonial rule], (Seoul: Han'guk kidokkyo yŏksa yŏn'guso, 1993), pp. 42–46.

53. The official activity of the Independence Club ended on December 25, 1898.

54. F. A. McKenzie, *Korea's Fight for Freedom* (New York: Fleming H. Revell Co., 1920), p. 192.

55. Ibid., p. 182.

56. James E. Fisher, *Democracy and Mission Education in Korea* (New York: Teachers' College, Columbia University, 1928), p. 159.

57. This has been a unique tradition in the Korean Protestant church since its beginning.

58. T. Stanley Soltau, *Korea: The Hermit Nation and Its Response to Christianity* (London: World Dominion Press, 1932), p. 114.

59. Tawara Sonnichi, *Kankoku kyōiku no genjō* [The present state of education in Korea], (Keijō: Chōsen sōtokufu gakufu, 1910), pp. 49–50.

60. In the second decade of the twentieth century, the Korean Protestant church published many newspapers and periodicals, among them *Yesugyo hoebo* [The Christian news], *Kŭrisŭdoin hoebo* [Korean Christian advocate], *Kidok sinbo* [The Christian messenger], *Sikhak segye* [World of theology], *Kongdo* [Public justice], *Sŏnmin* [The chosen people], *Ch'ŏngnyŏn* [Youth], and *Kidok ch'ŏngnyŏn* [Christian youth].

61. For the establishment of this independent presbytery, see Paik, *The History of Protestant Missions in Korea*, pp. 387–91; and Allen D. Clark, *A History*

of the Church in Korea (Seoul: The Christian Literature Society, 1971), pp. 172–77.

62. Ch'oe, *Anak sakŏn kwa samil undong gwa na*, pp. 14–17.

63. For details, see Han Kyumu, "Kuhanmal Sangdong ch'ŏngnyŏnhoe ŭi sŏllip kwa hwaltong" (The foundation and activity of Sangdong Young Men's Academy in the last period of the Chosŏn Dynasty), (M.A. thesis, Sŏgang taehakkyo, 1988).

64. On the Sinminhoe, see Yi Chaesun, "Sinminhoe wa sanae ch'ongdok amsal ŭmmo sakŏn" (The Sinminhoe and the alleged attempt on the life of Governor-General Terauchi), *Hyŏnsanggwa insik*, vol. 5, no. 3 (Autumn 1978), pp. 143–72; and Yun Kyŏngno's works, including "Paegoin sakŏn ŭl t'onghaebon sinminhoe yŏn'gu" (A study of the Sinminhoe through examining the case of the 105 Men), (Doctoral thesis, Koryŏ taehakkyo, 1988).

65. See Han, "Kuhanmal Sangdong ch'ŏngnyŏnhoe ŭi sŏllip kwa hwaltong," p. 11.

66. Ibid., pp. 8–11.

67. See Yun Kyŏngno, *Han'guk kŭndaesa ŭi Kidokkyosajŏk ihae* [Modern Korean history from the perspective of the history of Christianity], (Seoul: Yŏngminsa, 1992), pp. 31–38.

68. For details, see chapter two.

69. Paek Nakchun, "Han'guk kyohoe ŭi p'ippak-sanae ch'ongdok mosal misu ŭmmo ŭi ŭmmo e taehayŏ" (Persecution of the Korean church with particular reference to the alleged attempt on the life of Governor-General Terauchi), *Sinhak nondan*, no. 7 (1962), pp. 14–29, particularly see p. 17.

70. Arthur J. Brown, *The Mastery of the Far East*, (New York: Charles Scribner's Sons, 1919), p. 569.

71. Yu Tongsik, *Han'guk sinhak ŭi kwangmaek: Han'guk sinhaksa sŏsŏl* [Patterns of theology in Korea: A history of theology in Korea: An introduction], (Seoul: Chŏnmangsa, 1982), chap. 1, particularly pp. 28–30; and Min Kyŏngbae, *Kŭrisŭch'an akademi simnyŏnsa* [The ten-year history of the Christian Academy], (Seoul: Kŭrisŭch'an akademi, 1975), pp. 19–30.

72. *Taehan maeil sinmun* [Korea daily news], March 12, 1908.

73. Ibid., December 1, 1905.

74. Ch'oe, *Anak sakŏn kwa samil undong gwa na*, pp. 14–17.

75. Nym Wales and San Kim, *Song of Ariran* (San Francisco: Rampart Press, 1941), p. 75.

76. Quoted from Tongnip undongsa p'yŏnch'an wiwŏnhoe, ed., *Tongnip undongsa charyojip* [Documents on the history of the independence movement], (Seoul: Tongnip undongsa p'yŏnch'an wiwŏnhoe, 1973), p. 604. The passage

is the inflammatory harangue of Kang Wŏnbae, a local Christian evangelist in Kyŏngsang Province.

77. Ibid. This is Ch'oe Hyanghyŏn's street speech. Ch'oe was a local church leader.

78. For example, the Reverend Kil Sŏnju symbolically applied the concept of "the day" and "the millennium" to promises of the day of independence and well-being that was to follow. See the second section of chap. two.

79. Tawara Sonnichi, *Kankoku kyōiku no genjō*, pp. 57–58.

80. Brown, *The Mastery of the Far East*, pp. 568–70.

81. Uchida Ryohei, "Ryuki kaigenji" (Secret events in the years of the protectorate), in *Chōsen tōchi shiryo* [Historical documents on Japanese rule of Korea], vol. 4, ed. Kim Chŏngju (Tokyo: Kankoku shiryo kenkyuzō, 1970), pp. 13–205, especially p. 120.

82. On the Japanese colonial policy toward Christianity in Korea, see Wi Jo Kang, *Religion and Politics in Korea under the Japanese* (New York: Edwin Mellon Press, 1987); Kang Chaeŏn, *Ilcheha sasimnyŏnsa* [Forty-year history under Japan's imperialist rule], (Seoul: P'ulbit, 1984), pp. 23–125; Tawara Sonnichi, *Kankoku kyōiku no genjō*, pp. 44–70; and Aoyagi Kōtarō, *Chōsen tōchiron* [An essay on the rule of Korea], (Keijō: Chōsen kenkyūkai, 1932), pp. 417–27.

83. Chŏng Kyo, *Taehan kyenyŏnsa* [A history of the last years of the Yi Dynasty], (Seoul: Kuksa p'yŏnch'an wiwŏnhoe, 1957), pp. 343–46 and 386–410. This was originally written during the period 1864–1910. Also see Yi Manyŏl, "Kaesin'gyo ŭi sŏn'gyo hwaltong gwa minjok ŭisik" (Protestant mission and national consciousness), *Sahak yŏn'gu*, no. 36 (April 1983), pp. 191–219, particularly pp. 214–16.

84. Ch'oe, *Anak sakŏn kwa samil undong gwa na*, p. 246.

85. Brown, *The Mastery of the Far East*, pp. 568–70.

86. For details, see chapter one.

87. For a contemporary Western observation, see Brown, *The Mastery of the Far East*, pp. 570–80. Also see Kim Yangsŏn, *Han'guk Kidokkyosa yŏn'gu*, pp. 104–5; and Yun Kyŏngno, *Han'guk kŭndaesa ŭi Kidokkyosajŏk ihae*, pp. 173–202.

88. Yun Kyŏngno, ibid., p. 182. Also see Paek, "Han'guk kyohoe ŭi p'ipak," p. 22.

89. On the March First Movement, see Frank Baldwin, "The March First Movement: Korean Challenge, Japanese Response" (Ph.D. diss., Columbia University, 1969); and Ko Chaeuk, ed., *Samil undong osipchunyŏn kinyŏm nonjip* [Selected essays to mark the fiftieth anniversary of the March First Movement], (Seoul: Tong'a ilbosa, 1989).

90. See Kuksa p'yŏnch'an wiwŏnhoe, ed., *Ilche ch'imyakha Han'guk samsibyungnyŏnsa* [The thirty-six-year history of Korea under Japanese imperial rule], vol. 4 (Seoul: T'amgudang, 1969), pp. 905–8; and Kim, "Samil undong gwa Kidokkyo," p. 264.

91. For example, see the following works written by Koreans: Kang Hŭngsu, *Chosŏn tongnip hyŏlt'usa* [A history of Koreans' bloody struggle for independence], (Seoul: Koryŏ munhwasa, 1946); Kim Sŏngjin, *Ilche ŭi haksal manhaeng ŭl kobal handa* [We accuse Japanese imperialism of atrocities], (Seoul: Mirae munhwasa, 1983); and Yi Chong'yul, *Samil undong gwa minjok ŭi hamsŏng* [The cries of the people in the March First Movement], (Seoul: Inmundang, 1984).

92. For the influence of Woodrow Wilson's principles of national self-determination on the March First Movement, see Baldwin, "The March First Movement: Korean Challenge, Japanese Response"; "Wilsŭn, minjok chagyŏlchuŭi, samil undong" (Wilson, national self-determination, and the March First Movement), in *Samil undong osipchunyŏn kinyŏm nonjip*, ed. Ko Chaeuk, pp. 515–32; and Yi Pohyŏng, "Samil undong e issŏsŏ ŭi minjok chakyŏlchuŭi toip kwa ihae" (How principles of self-determination were introduced into the March First Movement and how they were perceived), in ibid., pp. 175–87.

93. On the Sinhan ch'ŏngnyŏndang, see Kim Yangsŏn, "Samil undong gwa Kidokkyo" (The March First Movement and Christianity), in *Samil undong osipchunyŏn kinyŏm nonjip*, ed. Ko Chaeuk, pp. 240–41; and Sin Yongha, "Samil undong palbal kyŏngwi" (The situation of the outbreak of the March First Movement), in *Han'guk kŭndae saron* [Essays on modern Korean history], vol. 2, ed. Yun Pyŏngsŏk, Sin Yongha, and An Pyŏngjik (Seoul: Chisik sanŏpsa, 1977), pp. 38–112, particularly pp. 48–54. Also see his article "Sinhan ch'ŏngnyŏndang ŭi tongnip undong" (The independence movement of the New Korean Young Men's Society), *Han'guk hakpo*, vol. 12, no. 3 (Autumn 1986), pp. 94–142.

94. See Kim Yangsŏn, "Samil undong gwa Kidokkyo," pp. 240–41; Pak Hansŏl, "Samil undong chudoch'e hyŏngsŏng e taehan koch'al" (A study of the formation of main groups for the March First Movement), in *Samil undong osipchunyŏn kinyŏm nonjip*, ed. Ko, pp. 189–201, particularly p. 193; and Sin, "Samil undong palbal kyŏngwi," pp. 48–54. According to Sin Yongha's 1986 study, other party members—Kim Sunae and Paek Namgyu—were sent to Kyŏngsang and Chŏlla Provinces. See his "Sinhan ch'ŏngnyŏndang ŭi tongnip undong," pp. 113–16.

95. Kil Chin'gyŏng, *Yŏnggye Kil Sŏnju*, pp. 269–73.

96. Sŏnu Hyŏk directly contacted the following significant participants in

the March First Movement: Yi Sŭnghun, Kil Sŏnju, Yang Chŏnbaek, Pyŏn Insŏ, Kim Sŏndu, Kang Kyuch'an, To In'gwŏn, Kang Sŏngt'aek, Yi Tŏk-hwan, Yun Wŏnsam, Kim Tong'wŏn, and Yun Sŭng'ŭn. See Kim Yangsŏn, "Samil undong gwa Kidokkyo," pp. 240–41.

97. On Yi Sŭnghun's life, see Kim Kisŏk, *Namgang Yi Sŭnghun* [A biography of Yi Sŭnghun], (Seoul: Hyŏndae kyoyuk ch'ongsŏ ch'ulp'ansa, 1964); Kim Tot'ae, *Namgang Yi Sŭnghun jŏn* [A biography of Yi Sŭnghun], (Seoul: Mun'gyosa, 1950); and Yun Kyŏngno, "Kidokkyo minjok kyŏngje undonggwa Yi Sŭnghun" (The Christian movement for a national economy and Yi Sŭnghun), in his *Han'guk kŭndaesa ŭi Kidokkyosajŏk ihae*, pp. 339–83.

98. Yi Sŭnghun directly contacted the following significant participants in the March First Movement:

1. Christian Leaders
   Seoul: Ham T'aeyŏng, Yi Kapsŏng, Chŏng Ch'unsu, O Hwayŏng, O Kisŏn, Hyŏn Sun, Yu Myŏnggŭn, Kim Sehwan, Kim P'ilsu, O Sanggŭn
   Northwestern Region: Yang Chŏnbaek, Kil Sŏnju, Kim Pyŏngjo, Yun Yŏdae, Yi Myŏngnyong, Paek Sich'an, Hong Sŏng'ik, Son Chŏngdo, An Sehang

2. Ch'ŏndogyo Leaders
   Song Chin'u, Ch'oe Namsŏn, Ch'oe Rin, Hyŏn Sangyun

3. Youth Leader
   Pak Hŭido (Christian)

For details, see Kim Yangsŏn, "Samil undong gwa Kidokkyo," pp. 242–51; and Chōsen sōtokufu, *Chōsen dokuritsu sojo jiken* [The March First disturbance for Korean independence], Tongnip undong p'yŏnch'an wiwŏnhoe, ed., *Tongnip undongsa charyojip*, no. 1, pp. 851–1182, particularly pp. 864–70.

99. Pak Hŭido had studied at Sungsil School in P'yŏngyang and at the Hyŏpsŏng Theological Seminary. He was a section director for youth at the YMCA in 1919. After the March First Movement, he published *Sinsanghwal*, one of the earlier socialist journals. See Michael Robinson, "*Sinsaenghwal* and early Korean Marxism," paper presented at Korea Seminar, University of Washington, May 17, 1985.

100. The student groups under Pak Hŭido were as follows (listed by school):
Yŏnhŭi: Kim Wŏnbyŏk, Yun Hayŏng, Yi Pyŏngju
Posŏng: Kang Kidŏk, Chu Ik
Kyŏngsŏng Med.: Han Wigŏn, Kim Hyŏnggi

Kyŏngsŏng Chŏnsu: Yun Chayŏng, Yi Konghu
Kyŏngsŏng Tech.: Chu Chong'ik, Song Chŏng'u
Severance Med.: Yi Yongsŏl Kim Sŏnggu Pae Tongsŏ

Under the college student groups were high school student groups. See Chōsen sōtokufu, *Chōsen dokuritsu sojo jiken*, pp. 867–70; Kim Yangsŏn, "Samil undong gwa Kidokkyo," pp. 242–45; Kim Taesang, "Samil undong gwa haksaengch'ŭng" (The March First Movement and students), in *Samil undong osipchunyŏn kinyŏm nonjip*, ed. Ko, pp. 301–11, particularly pp. 302–4.

101. Kim Yangsŏn, "Samil undong gwa Kidokkyo," pp. 240–58; Kim T'aesang, "Samil undong gwa haksaengch'ŭng," p. 303; Sin, "Samil undong palbal ŭi kyŏngwi," pp. 70–84; and Kil, *Yŏnggye Kil Sŏnju*, pp. 269–73.

102. The secret meeting places where students leaders gathered for the March First Movement included:

February 20: Sŭngdong Church
February 25: Chŏngdong Church
February 26: Chŏngdong Church
(at Reverend Yi P'ilju's residence)
February 28: Chŏngdong Church
Sŭngdong Church

See Kim Yangsŏn, "Samil undong gwa Kidokkyo," pp. 303–4.

103. Wales and Kim, *Song of Ariran*, pp. 74–88.

104. Christian church leaders in Seoul sent secret delegates to churches across the country to instigate local church leaders for the planned demonstration. *Number of dispatched delegates:* P'yŏngyang, 5; Ch'ŏngjin, 2; Ulsan, 2; Sŏnch'ŏn, 3; Ch'unch'ŏn, 2; Kwangju, 6; Anju, 2; Chŏngju, 3; Chŏnju, 3; Ch'ŏlwŏn, 5; Wŏnju, 2; Mokp'o, 3; Kanggye, 3; Pusan, 5; Kunsan, 3; Wŏnsan, 5; Kyŏngju, 2; Namwŏn, 2; Taegu, 5; Hamhŭng, 5; Ch'ŏngju, 3; Sŏngjin, 3; Masan, 3; Kimhae, 2; Miryang, 2; *total, 81*. See Kim Yangsŏn, "Samil undong gwa Kidokkyo," p. 251.

5 / PROTESTANT CHRISTIANS AND THE LATE NATIONALIST MOVEMENT, 1919–1945

1. O Sangsun, "Sidaego wa kŭ hŭisaeng" (The agony of the times and its victims), *P'yehŏ* [Ruins], vol. 1, no. 1 (July 1920), pp. 21–24, particularly see pp. 21–22.

2. Yi Kwangsu, "Chaesang" (Rebirth), *Yi Kwangsu chŏnjip* [Complete works of Yi Kwangsu], no. 3 (Seoul: Samjungdang, 1969), pp. 129–98, particularly pp. 146–49. This novel appeared originally in *Tong'a ilbo* in 1924–1925.

3. Tong'in (Associates), "Sang'yŏ" (Afterthoughts), *P'yehŏ*, vol. 1, no. 1 (July 1920), pp. 121–29, particularly pp. 122–23.

4. For the policy shift and the Korean response, see Kang Chaeŏn, *Ilcheha sasimnyŏnsa* [Forty-year history under Japan's imperialist rule], (Seoul: P'ulbit, 1984), pp. 66–69; Michael E. Robinson, *Cultural Nationalism in Colonial Korea, 1920–1925* (Seattle: University of Washington Press, 1988), pp. 44–47; and Frank Baldwin, Jr., "The March First Movement: Korean Challenge and Japanese Response," (Ph.D. diss., Columbia University, 1967), pp. 214–24.

5. For details, see Robinson, *Cultural Nationalism in Colonial Korea*, chap. 2.

6. Kim Chunyŏp and Kim Ch'angsun, *Han'guk kongsanjuŭi undongsa* [The history of the Korean Communist movement], vol. 2, (Seoul: Ch'ŏnggye yŏn'guso, 1986), p. 101.

7. Robinson, *Cultural Nationalism in Colonial Korea*, p. 48.

8. On the communist movement in Korea, see Kim and Kim, *Han'guk kongsanjuŭi undongsa*, 5 vols; Robert A. Scalapino and Chong-sik Lee, *Communism in Korea, Part I: Movement* (Berkeley: University of California, Center for Japanese and Korean Studies, 1972); and Dae-sook Suh, *Documents of Korean Communism, 1918–1948* (Princeton, N.J.: Princeton University Press, 1967).

9. On the Sin'ganhoe, see Scalapino and Lee, *Communism in Korea: The Movement*, pp. 101–5 and 112–19; Chong-sik Lee, *Korean Workers' Party: A Short History* (Stanford, Calif.: Hoover Institute Press, 1978), pp. 25–32; and Kim Chunyŏp and Kim Ch'angsun, *Han'guk kongsanjuŭi undongsa*, vol. 3, pp. 34–72.

10. The Japanese colonial authorities estimated that there were only 260 branches with 37,000 members. See Scalapino and Lee, *Communism in Korea: The Movement*, p. 112.

11. See No Ch'ijun, *Ilcheha Han'guk Kidokkyo minjok undong* [Korean Christian nationalist movement under Japanese colonial rule], (Seoul: Han'guk Kidokkyosa yŏn'guso, 1993), pp. 225–27. See also Robinson, *Cultural Nationalism in Colonial Korea*, pp. 144–56; Cho Chihun, *Han'guk minjok undongsa* [A history of the Korean nationalist movement], (Seoul: Nanam, 1993), pp. 252–64; Sim Chiyŏn, *Hŏ Hŏn yŏn'gu* [A study of Hŏ Hŏn], (Seoul: Yŏksa pip'yŏngsa, 1994), pp. 62–82; and Kim Chunyŏp and Kim Ch'angsun, *Han'guk kongsanjuŭi undongsa*, vol. 3, pp. 34–72.

12. On the church's retreat from nationalist politics, see my article,

"Ch'ŏn'gubaek isimnyŏndae kaesin'gyo chidoch'ŭng gwa minjokchuŭi undong" (The relationship between Protestant leaders and the nationalist movement during the 1920s: A social history), *Yŏksa hakpo*, no. 134–135 (September 1992), pp. 143–63, particularly pp. 154–61.

13. Victor W. Peter, "What Korean Young People Are Thinking," *The Korean Mission Field* (two parts), vol. 28, no. 5 (May 1932), pp. 92–95, and no. 6 (June 1932), pp. 129–32, especially p. 93 in part one.

14. Ibid., p. 93.

15. Ibid. Also see Yi Taewi, "Sahoejuŭi wa Kidokkyo ŭi kŭ ich'akchŏmi ŏttŏhan'ga" (Where do socialism and Christianity meet?), (two parts), *Ch'ŏngnyŏn*, vol. 3, no. 8 (August 1923), pp. 8–11, and no. 9 (September 1923), pp. 8–12, especially p. 8 in part one.

16. See Chong-sik Lee, *Korean Workers' Party*, pp. 1–32; Kim and Kim, *Han'guk kongsanjuŭi undongsa*, vol. 2; and Scalapino and Lee, *Communism in Korea*, vol. 1, chap. 1. According to the memoir of Sin Suk, a nationalist, Yŏ Unhyŏng was the first Korean to translate "The Communist Manifesto" into Korean. He also translated into Korean other socialist and communist material received from the British Labor Party and the Koryŏ Communist Party, and distributed them among Koreans in Manchuria. See Sin Suk, "Pansegi ŭi chŭng'ŏn" (Witness of the last half-century), no. 8, *Tong'a ilbo*, April 19, 1964.

17. See Suh Dae Sook, *The Korean Communist Movement, 1918–1948* (Princeton, N.J.: Princeton University Press, 1967), p. 18. Also see Scalapino and Lee, *Communism in Korea*, pp. 37–46.

18. Sim Chiyŏn, *Hŏ Hŏn yŏn'gu*, pp. 34–47.

19. See Yun Ch'unbyŏng, *Han'guk Kidokkyo sinmun chapchi paengnyŏnsa, 1885–1985* [Christian newspapers and periodicals, 1885–1985: A history], (Seoul: Taehan Kidokkyo ch'ulp'ansa, 1984), pp. 56–57 and 69. Also see "Chojik" (Organization) in the first issue of *Sinsaenghwal*, pp. 69–70.

20. See Kim and Kim, *Han'guk kongsanjuŭi undongsa*, vol. 2, pp. 36–37.

21. Recently, young Korean historians began to see the significance of Yi Taewi for understanding early Korean socialism or Christian socialism. See Ch'ae Hyŏnsŏk, "Yi Taewi ŭi saeng'ae wa hwaltong" (Yi Taewi: His life and activity), in *Ilcheha Han'guk Kidokkyo wa sahoejuŭi* [Christianity and socialism in Korea under Japanese rule], ed. Kim Hŭngsu (Seoul: Han'guk Kidokkyo yŏksa yŏn'guso, 1992), pp. 253–65. However, no one has explained how and where he adopted socialism.

According to Ch'ae's biography, Yi Taewi (1896–1982) was born in North P'yŏng'an Province, became a Christian, and received modern education in Sinsŏng hakkyo, a mission school. In 1913, he went to China to receive a high school education, and then in 1916, he began to study political science at Peking National University, and graduated in 1920. In 1921, he returned to Korea and became a YMCA director for student affairs. It seems probable that he began to study socialism while he was at Peking National University, where early Chinese socialists such as Ch'en Tu-hsiu, Li Ta-chao, and Mao Tse-tung worked. It should also be mentioned that he and other Christian socialists were influenced by a Japanese Christian socialist, Kagawa Toyohiko, whose works were translated into Korean during the 1920s. See Kang Myŏngsuk, "Ch'ŏn'gubaek isimnyŏndae Chosŏn Kidokkyo ŭi sahoejuŭi insik e kwanhan yŏn'gu" (A study on Christian understanding of socialism during the 1920s), (M.A. thesis, Ihwa yŏja taehakkyo, 1991), pp. 21–48.

22. For a recent study on this subject, see Kim Hŭngsu, ed., *Ilcheha Han'guk Kidokkyo wa sahoejuŭi.*

23. Yi Taewi, "Sahoejuŭi wa Kidokkyo ŭi kuich'akchŏmi ŏttŏhan'ga," p. 9 in part one.

24. Yi Taewi, "Sahoe hyŏngmyŏng ŭi Yesu" (Jesus for social revolution), *Ch'ŏngnyŏn*, vol. 8, no. 5 (June 1928), pp. 17–19.

25. Yu Kyŏngsang, "Sahoejuŭija Yesu" (Jesus: A socialist), *Ch'ŏngnyŏn*, vol. 3, no. 7 (July-August 1923), pp. 32–37. Note Yu's title.

26. Yi Taewi, "Sahoejuŭi wa Kidokkyo sasang" (Socialism and Christian thought), *Ch'ŏngnyŏn*, vol. 3, no. 5 (May 1923), pp. 9–15, especially p. 9.

27. Ibid., p. 11.

28. Yi Taewi, "Sahoejuŭi wa Kidokkyo ŭi kuich'akchŏmi ŏttŏhan'ga," p. 8 in part one.

29. Ibid., p. 12 in part two.

30. See Kang Wŏndon, "Ilcheha sahoejuŭi undong gwa Han'guk Kidokkyo" (Socialist movement and Korean Christianity under Japanese colonial rule), in *Ilcheha Han'guk Kidokkyo wa sahoejuŭi*, ed. Kim Hŭngsu, pp. 25–57, especially pp. 42–56.

31. Ibid., p. 48.

32. Kim Ch'angje, "Minjung ŭi chonggyo" (A religion of the people), *Ch'ŏngnyŏn*, vol. 6, no. 2 (February 1926), pp. 12–14.

33. Kim Ch'angje, "Sahoejuŭi hwalsallon" (A thesis on the life and death of socialism), *Samyŏng* [Mission], no. 5 (1927), pp. 22–24, especially p. 23.

34. For the anti-Christian movement of leftist groups, see Min Kyŏngbae, *Han'guk Kidokkyo sahoe undongsa* [A history of the social movement of the Korean Christian church], (Seoul: Taehan Kidokkyo ch'ulp'ansa, 1988), pp. 210–14. Also see Kim Kwŏnjŏng, "Ilcheha sahoejuŭijadŭl ŭi pan Kidokkyo undong" (Anti-Christian movement of socialists under Japanese imperial rule), (M.A.

thesis, Sŭngsil taehakkyo, 1995); and Chang Ch'angjin, "Ilcheha Minjok munje nonjaenggwa panjonggyo undong" (Debate on national problems and anti-religion movement under Japanese colonial rule), (M.A. thesis, Sŏul taehakkyo, 1994).

35. See Kim Kyŏngsik, "Sahoejuŭi esŏ Kidokkyoro sasang ŭl torik'igi kkaji" (Conversion of my thought from socialism to Christianity), *Kidok sinbo*, April 6 and 20, 1927.

36. For the life and thought of Kagawa Toyohiko, see George B. Bikle, Jr., *The New Jerusalem: Aspects of Utopianism in the Thought of Kagawa Toyohiko* (Tucson: University of Arizona Press for the Association for Asian Studies, 1976).

On the Christian involvement in the early Japanese socialist movement, see Peter Duus and Irwin Scheiner, "Socialism, Liberalism, and Marxism, 1901–1931," in *Modern Japanese Thought*, ed. Bob Tadashi Wakabayashi (Cambridge: Cambridge University Press, 1998), pp. 147–206, especially pp. 152–59.

37. *Kidok sinbo*, a leading Christian newspaper, carried the translation of Kagawa Toyohiko seven times in a series titled "Kidokkyo sahoejuŭiron" (Thesis on Christian socialism). For details, see Kang Myŏngsuk, "Ch'ŏn'gubaek isimnyŏndae Chosŏn Kidokkyo ŭi sahoejuŭi insik e kwanhan yŏn'gu," particularly pp. 21–48. According to Kang's fine study, it is clear that Korean Christian socialists were greatly influenced by Kagawa Toyohiko, a fellow Christian socialist in Japan.

38. See Min, *Han'guk kidokkyo sahoeundongsa*, pp. 234–70.

39. Song Ch'anggŭn, "Onŭl Chosŏn kyohoe ŭi samyŏng" (The task before the church of Korea today), in *Man'u Song Ch'anggŭn* [A biography of Song Ch'anggun], (Seoul: Man'u Song Ch'anggŭn sŏnsaeng kinyŏm saŏphoe, 1978), pp. 153–60, especially p. 153. This originally appeared in *Sinhak chinam* in 1933.

40. Kim Insŏ, "Chosŏn kyohoe ŭi sae tonghyang" (New trends in the Korean church), *Sinang saenghwal*, vol. 2, no. 3 (March 1933), pp. 4–6, especially p. 4.

41. Kim Insŏ, "Nŏhŭido ttohan kagojŏ hanŭnya" (Do you want to go their way, too?), *Sinang saenghwal*, vol. 1, no. 7 (July 1932), pp. 7–10, particularly p. 9.

42. Ch'ae Chŏngmin, "Kyonong undong ŭi pulga" (The Church's movement to improve rural society is not right), *Sinang saenghwal*, vol. 5, no. 7 (July 1936), pp. 6–10, especially, pp. 7–8.

43. Luke 4: 1–13.

44. Ch'ae, "Kyonong undong ŭi pulga," p. 6.

45. This table was taken from Chōsen sōtokufu keimukyoku, *Chōsen chian jōkyō* [Conditions of public order in Korea], (Keijō: Chōsen sōtokufu, 1922), p. 76.

46. Nym Wales and Kim San, *Song of Ariran* (San Francisco: Rampart Press, 1941), pp. 83–88.

47. Ibid., pp. 74–79.

48. Ibid., p. 83.

49. Ibid., pp. 83–88.

50. Ibid., p. 83.

51. Sin Ch'aeho, "Isipsegi sin kungmin" (A new nation in the twentieth century), in *Sin Ch'aeho chŏnjip* [Complete works of Sin Ch'aeho], special volume (Seoul: Tanje Sin Ch'aeho sŏnsaeng kinyŏm saŏphoe, 1977), pp. 219–29.

52. Sin Ch'aeho, "Yong gwa yong ŭi tae kyŏljŏn" (Two dragons locked in a fight to the finish), in ibid., pp. 282–83.

53. For details, see Chang Ch'angjin, "Ilcheha minjok munje nonjaenggwa panjonggyo undong—ch'ŏn'gubaek isimnyŏndae sahoejuŭijadŭl ŭi pan kidokkyo undong ŭl chungsimŭro," and Kim Kwŏnjŏng, "Ilcheha sahoejuŭijadŭl ŭi pan kidokkyo undong." These studies, however, only see the conflict between the two camps from an ideological perspective: that is, a "theism-atheism" incompatibility. It seems that they have not paid sufficient attention to the Christian socialist activity, its relations to non-Christian socialists, and its relations to the church community.

On this issue, see Sin Chuhyŏn, "Ch'ŏn'gubaek isimnyŏndae Han'guk Kidokkyoindŭl ŭi minjok undong e kwanhan ilkoch'al: Sahoe kyŏngje undong ŭl chungsimŭro" (A study on nationalist activities of Korean Christians during the 1920s: Their socioeconomic activities), (M.A. thesis, Sungmyŏng yŏja taehakkyo, 1986); and Kang Myŏngsuk, "Ch'ŏn'gubaek isimnyŏndae Chosŏn Kidokkyo ŭi sahoejuŭi insik e kwanhan yŏn'gu."

54. *Tong'a ilbo*, "Sasŏl" (Editorial), January 7, 1922. Also see "Sasŏl," October 26, 1923, and "Sasŏl," December 27, 1928.

55. Yi Kwangsu, "Kŭmil Chosŏn ŭi Yasogyohoe ŭi hŏmjŏm" (Some defects in the Korean church today), *Ch'ŏngch'un*, January, 1917, pp. 77–81, especially p. 77.

56. See Kim Insŏ, "P'yŏngyang nohoe ŭi sang'ŭihan hŏnbŏp sujŏng'an e taehaya" (On the constitutional amendment introduced to the P'yŏngyang Presbytery), *Sinang saenghwal*, vol. 2, no. 8 (August 1932), pp. 4–6, especially p. 5.

57. Kim Ch'angje, "Hyŏnha Kidokkyo undong ŭi panghyang ŭn ŏdiro" (What is the direction of today's Christian movement?), *Kidok sinbo*, January 20, 1932.

58. Kim Wŏnbyŏk, "Hyŏndae sasang gwa Kidokkyo" (Modern thoughts

and Christianity), *Ch'ŏngnyŏn*, vol. 3, no. 7 (July-August 1932), pp. 22–24, especially p. 23.

59. T. Stanley Soltau, *Korea: The Hermit Nation and Its Response to Christianity* (London: World Dominion Press, 1932), p. 114.

60. Yi Nŭnghwa, *Chosŏn Kidokkyo kŭp oegyosa* [History of Christianity and foreign relations in Korea], (Seoul: Hangmun'gak, 1968; original edition, 1928), pp. 220 and 223.

61. Kim Insŏ, "Chŏng isipi ch'onghoe" (Recommendations to the 22nd general assembly), *Sinang saenghwal*, vol. 2, no. 9 (September 1933), pp. 4–7, especially p. 5.

62. *Tonga ilbo*, "Sasŏl," January 7, 1922. Also see *Tonga ilbo*, "Sasŏl," July 1929.

63. See No Ch'ijun, "Ilcheha Han'guk changnokyohoe ch'onghoe t'onggye e taehan yŏn'gu" (A study on the statistics of the Korean Presbyterian Church under Japanese colonial rule), in Han'guk sahoesa yŏn'guhoe, *Hyŏndae Han'guk ŭi chonggyo wa sahoe* [Religion and society in contemporary Korea], (Seoul: Munhakkwa chisŏngsa, 1992), pp. 66–97, especially p. 93.

64. For a sociological discussion on institutionalization of religions, see Thomas F. O'Dea, *The Sociology of Religion* (Englewood Cliffs, N.J.: Prentice-Hall, Inc., 1966), pp. 47–51, and his *Sociology and the Study of Religion* (New York and London: Basic Books, 1970), chap. 13.

65. On the status and role of elders in a Presbyterian form of church, see "Hŏnbŏp" (Constitution), in comp. Kwak Alyŏn, *Kyohoe sajŏn huijip* [Digest of the Presbyterian Church of Korea], (Keijo: Chosen yashogyo shokai, 1918), pp. 74–120, particularly pp. 88 and 90.

66. For example, see Kim Insŏ, "Isipsam nohoe ŭi tungjŏng munje" (Agenda of the 23rd session of the Presbytery), *Sinang saenghwal*, vol. 2, no. 11–12 (December 1933), pp. 4–7; "Ko isipsa ch'onghoe" (Recommendations for discussion at the 24th general assembly), ibid., vol. 4, no. 8 (August-September 1935), pp. 7–10; "Sŏnmin nambuk punyŏl ŭi hwa" (North-south split of a chosen people), ibid., vol. 5, no. 10 (October 1936), pp. 18–23; and "Ch'onghoe pullip munje e taehaya" (On the rift in the general assembly), ibid., vol. 5, no. 10 (October 1936), pp. 24–26.

67. For discussion on the church as a social institution and some dilemmas of institutionalization, see Purnell Hardy Benson, *Religion in Contemporary Culture: A Study of Religion Through Social Science* (New York: Harper and Brothers, 1960); and O'Dea, *Sociology and the Study of Religion*, chap. 13, and *The Sociology of Religion*, pp. 90–97.

68. Kim Insŏ, "P'yŏngyang t'ongsin," pp. 31–32. Also see Kim Insŏ, "P'yŏngyang nohoe ŭi sang'ŭihan hŏnbŏp sujŏng'an e taehaya," pp. 4–6.

69. Kim Insŏ, "Kyŏngnam nohoe ŭi kyori munje" (Doctrinal problem in the Kyŏngnam Presbytery), *Sinang saenghwal*, vol. 1, no. 3 (March 1932), pp. 4–7, particularly p. 7.

70. Kim Insŏ, "P'yŏngyang nohoe ŭi sang'ŭihan hŏnbŏp sujŏng'an e taehaya," p. 5. Also see his articles "Chosŏn kyohoe ŭi ch'aegimjanŭn kŭ nuguin'ga," pp. 2–5, and "Chosŏn kyohoe ŭi nanmaek," pp. 4–6.

71. For example, church ministers played *hwat'u*, a traditional card game, during a religious cultivation conference, and they were interrogated by the police because it was regarded as gambling at the time. See Kim Insŏ, "Yuhaeng suyanghoe ŭi t'arak ŭl kyeham" (Corruption at fashionably held cultivation conference: A warning), *Sinang saenghwal*, vol. 2, no. 10 (October 1933), pp. 4–6.

72. See, for example, Kim Insŏ, "Sŏnmin nambuk punyŏl ŭi hwa" and "Ch'onghoe pullip munje e taehaya."

73. On Chu Kich'ŏl's life, see Kim Ch'ungnam, *Sun'gyoja Chu Kich'ŏl moksa ŭi saeng'ae: Chindalle p'ilttae kabŏrin saram* [The life of a martyr: The Reverend Chu Kich'ŏl who did not wait to see spring flowers], (Seoul: Paekhap ch'ulp'ansa, 1974); and Yi Yŏnghŏn, *Han'guk Kidokkyosa* [A history of the Korean church], (Seoul: Concordia ch'ulp'ansa, 1978), pp. 210–18.

74. Since the original passage is not available, a quotation by Yi Manyŏl is used. Yi Manyŏl, "Kaesin'gyo úi chŏllae wa ilcheha kyohoe wa kukka" (The introduction of Protestantism, and church and state under Japanese colonial rule), in ed. Han'guk Kidokkyo sahoemunje yŏn'guwŏn, *Kukka kwŏllyŏk kwa Kidokkyo* [The state power and Christian Church], (Seoul: Han'guk Kidokkyo sahoemunje yŏn'guwŏn, 1982), pp. 35–190, quoted from p. 188.

75. See *The Records of the 27th General Assembly*, the Korean Presbyterian Church, p. 9. This can be found easily in Min Kyŏngbae, *Han'guk ŭi Kidokkyohoesa* [A church history of Korea], (Seoul: Taehan Kidokkyo sŏhoe, 1968), a popular historical survey of the Korean church, p. 103.

76. For the Korean church's Anti-Shrine Worship Campaign, see Han'guk Kidokkyo yŏksa yŏn'guso, *Han'guk Kidokkyo wa sinsa ch'ambae munje* [The Korean Christian church and the shrine worship issue], (Seoul: Han'guk Kidokkyo yŏksa yŏn'guso, 1991); and Kim Yangsŏn, *Han'guk Kidokkyosa yŏn'gu* [A historical study of Korean Christianity], (Seoul: Kidokkyomunsa, 1971), pp. 177–204. The Anti-Shrine Worship Campaign has been regarded by Korean Christians as one of their proudest activities against Japanese colo-

nial rule. Some scholars have described it as a campaign by the whole Korean Protestant church, and claimed that most Christians participated in the campaign. See Jai Poong Ryu, "From Chosen to Daehan: Social Change in 20th Century Korea," (Ph.D. diss., University of Minnesota, 1972), especially p. 145. However, it was an activity of a handful of clergymen and lay members.

77. Kim Yangsŏn, *Han'guk Kidokkyosa yŏn'gu*, p. 201.

78. For details, see Min Kyŏngbae, *Han'guk ŭi Kidokkyohoesa*, pp. 103–5, and Kim Taesang, *Ilcheha kangje illyŏk sut'alsa* [A history of the exploitation of manpower under Japanese colonial rule], (Seoul: Chŏng'ŭmsa, 1975), pp. 144–46.

79. See Im Chongguk, *Ch'in'il munhangnon* [Pro-Japanese literature], (Seoul: Pyŏnghwa ch'ulp'ansa, 1966), pp. 23 and 90; and Pak Chŏngsin, "Yun Chi'ho yŏn'gu" (A study of Yun Chi'ho), *Paeksan hakpo*, pp. 341–92, especially pp. 383–86.

80. Kim Yangsŏn, *Han'guk Kidokkyosa yŏn'gu*, pp. 202–4.

6 / THE PROTESTANT CHURCH UNDER FOREIGN OCCUPATION, 1945–1948

1. For a general understanding of the division of Korea, see Bruce Cumings, *The Origins of the Korean War: Liberation and the Emergence of Separate Regimes, 1945–1947*, vol. 1 (Princeton, N.J.: Princeton University Press, 1981), and *The Origins of the Korean War: The Roaring of the Cataract, 1947–1950*, vol. 2 (1990); Bruce Cumings, "American Policy and Korean Liberation," in *Without Parallel: American-Korean Relationship Since 1945*, ed. Frank Baldwin (New York: Pantheon Books, 1973), pp. 39–103; Dae-Suk Suh, *The Korean Communist Movement, 1918–1948* (Princeton, N.J.: Princeton University Press, 1967), chap. 10; and Glen D. Paige, *The Korean People's Republic* (Stanford, Calif.: Stanford University Press, 1966), chaps. 1 and 2.

2. This is a common argument of "nationalist" Korean scholars. For example, see Pak Sun'gyŏng, "Han'guk minjok kwa Kidokkyo ŭi munje: Minjok pundanŭl nŏmŏsŏnŭn kil" (A question before the Korean church and nation: How to transcend national division), in *Pundan sidae wa Han'guk sahoe* [Korean society in divided Korea], ed. Pyŏn Hyŏngyun (Seoul: Kkach'i, 1985), pp. 345–70. In English, see Andrew C. Nahm, "The Emergence of the 'Democratic' People's Republic of Korea," in *The Politics of North Korea*, ed. Jae Kyu Park and Jung Gun Kim (Seoul: Kyŏngnam University Press, 1979), pp. 37–59.

3. Kim Ku, *Paekpŏm ilchi* [Kim Ku's diary], (Seoul: Tongmyŏngsa, 1947), pp. 350–53.

4. For details, see Bruce Cumings, *The Origins of the Korean War*, vol. 1, pp. 68–91.

5. Ibid., pp. 91–100; and Nahm, "The Emergence of the 'Democratic' People's Republic of Korea," pp. 41–48.

6. Scholars such as Cumings, Nahm, Paige, Suh, and Chong-sik Lee have mentioned that these Korean leaders were "Christian," but have spent just one sentence or one paragraph on their Christian background. Often they are misinformed about these leaders' social and religious background. Scalapino and Lee, for example, treat Yŏ Unhyŏng as a graduate of Chinglung University in Nanking, China, but according to Yŏ's brother, he never graduated. See Robert A. Scalapino and Chong-sik Lee, *Communism in Korea: The Movement*, part 1, (Berkeley: University of California Press, 1972), p. 223; and Yŏ Unhong, *Mongyang Yŏ Unhyŏng* [A biography of Yŏ Unhyŏng], (Seoul: Ch'ŏnghaksa, 1967), pp. 10–20. Recently, however, some scholars have begun to see the importance of this subject. See, for example, Yong-ho Choe, "Christian Background in the Early Life of Kim Il-sŏng," *Asian Survey*, vol. 26, no. 10 (October 1986), pp. 1082–91.

7. For the organizational strength of the Protestant church by the time of the Liberation, see the statistics in *Chōsen nenkan* [Korean annals], (Keijō: Keijō nipponsha, 1945), pp. 210–11. For the educational level of Christians, see Bark Dong Suh, "American-Educated Elite in Korean Society," in *Korea and the United States: A Century of Cooperation*, ed. Young-nok Koo and Dae-suk Suh (Honolulu: University of Hawaii Press, 1984), pp. 263–80, especially pp. 271–75.

8. The existing studies have not mentioned at all the relationship between the CPKI and the Protestant community. Cho Hyangnok, a clergyman who visited South Kyŏngsang Province immediately after the Liberation, found that almost everywhere he went the People's Committees were organized and led by either local church ministers or lay leaders. See Chang Pyŏng'uk, *Yugio kongsan namch'im kwa kyohoe* [The communist invasion to the south and Christianity], (Seoul: Han'guk kyoyuk kongsa, 1983), p. 155.

9. For a general understanding of the Protestant church after the Liberation, see ibid., pp. 12–76, 118–40. Also see Kim Yangsŏn, *Han'guk Kidokkyo haebang simnyŏnsa* [The ten-year history of the Korean church since the Liberation], (Seoul: Taehan Yesugyo changnohoe ch'onghoe kyoyukpu, 1955), pp. 223–306.

10. Ibid., pp. 62–70; Chang Pyŏng'uk, *Yugio kongsan namch'im kwa kyohoe*, 105–9; and Kim Yongbok, "Minjok pundan sogŭi Han'guk Kidokkyo" (Korean Christianity in the era of national division), in ed. Han'guk Kidokkyo munhwa

yŏn'guso, *Han'guk sahoe wa Kidokkyo* [Korean society and Christianity], (Seoul: Sungjŏn taehakkyo, 1984), pp. 257–99, especially pp. 263–64.

11. Kim Yangsŏn, *Han'guk Kidokkyo haebang simnyŏnsa*, p. 69.

12. See Choe, "Christian Background in the Early Life of Kim Il-sŏng."

13. Christian ministers such as Kim Ch'angjun, Yi Chaebok, and Ch'oe Munsik actively joined the CPKI. For details, see my following discussion in this chapter.

14. Cumings, *The Origins of the Korean War*, vol. 1, pp. 391–92; and Chong-sik Lee, "Politics in North Korea: Pre–Korean War Stage," *China Quarterly*, no. 14 (April-June 1963), pp. 3–16, particularly p. 4.

15. Cumings, *The Origins of the Korean War*, vol. 1, pp. 397–403; and Chong-sik Lee, "Politics in North Korea," p. 4.

16. Hyŏn Chunhyŏk was assassinated in broad daylight in P'yŏngyang on September 28, 1945. For more on Hyŏn, see Nahm, "The Emergence of the 'Democratic' People's Republic of Korea," p. 44; and Lee, "Politics in North Korea," p. 6.

17. The largest public rally at which Cho introduced Kim was held on October 14, 1945.

18. For details on the organizational strength of the Protestant church in the north before and after Liberation, see Han'guk Kidokkyo yŏksa yŏn'guso, *Pukhan kyohoesa* [History of Christianity in North Korea], (Seoul: Han'guk Kidokkyo yŏksa yŏn'guso, 1996), pp. 343–75.

19. For details, see Kim Yangsŏn, *Han'guk Kidokkyo haebang simnyŏnsa*, pp. 62–65; Kim Yongbok, "Minjok pundan sogŭi Han'guk Kidokkyo," pp. 258–63; Chang Pyŏng'uk, *Yugio kongsan manch'im kwa kyohoe*, pp. 24–34; and Han'guk Kidokkyo yŏksa yŏn'guso, *Pukhan kyohoesa*, pp. 383–401.

20. Han'guk Kidokkyo yŏksa yŏn'guso, *Pukhan kyohoesa*, p. 385.

21. Kim Yangsŏn, *Han'guk Kidokkyo haebang simnyŏnsa*, pp. 45–48. Kim Yangsŏn was a prominent archaeologist and historian who died in 1971. He was also an ordained clergyman who graduated from Sungsil College and P'yŏngyang Theological Seminary. Since he had participated in the activity of the church or had observed it closely, his book contains a tremendous amount of valuable historical documents on the Korean church as well as his own experiences. One may regard this book as a primary source. Also see Han'guk kidokkyo yŏksa yŏn'guso, *Pukhan kyohoesa*, pp. 395–401.

22. Kim Yangsŏn, *Han'guk Kidokkyo haebang simnyŏnsa*, pp. 62–75.

23. Ibid., pp. 65–68; and Chang Pyŏng'uk, *Yugio kongsan namch'im kwa kyohoe*, pp. 47–49.

24. Kim, *Han'guk Kidokkyo haebang simnyŏnsa*, p. 68; and Chang, *Yugio kongsan namch'im kwa kyohoe*, pp. 40–45.

25. For example, see Amerasian Data Research Service, Inc. (comp.), *Sŏnch'ŏn chi* [Records of Sŏnch'ŏn County, North P'yŏng'an Province, 1946–1947], (Washington, D.C.: 1985). This contains valuable documents such as secret reports on Christians and other residents in the county and analyses of their political leanings. Most of these documents were prepared by the communist authorities and secret intelligence agents.

26. Kim Yangsŏn, *Han'guk Kidokkyo haebang simnyŏnsa*, pp. 69–75; and Chang Pyŏng'uk, *Yugio kongsan namch'im kwa kyohoe*, pp. 57–69.

27. Chang, *Yugio kongsan namch'im kwa kyohoe*, pp. 93–96.

28. See the "Chŏngbo pogo" (Intelligence report) by Pak Chŏngbae, a communist intelligence agent, of December 25, 1946. Also see the report by the Sŏnch'ŏn haksaeng minch'ŏng chŏngbo pogoban (Intelligence Team of the Democratic Youth League of Students in Sŏnch'ŏn County), a communist student group, of November 12, 1946. The two reports were compiled in *Sŏnch'ŏn chi*. No page numbers are available.

29. See the "Sŏnch'ŏn chunghakkyo namjosŏn tochu haksaeng chosap'yo" (List of Sŏnch'ŏn Middle School students who fled to the south) and the "Sŏnch'ŏn sang'ŏp hakkyo namjosŏn toju haksaeng chosap'yo" (List of Sŏnch'ŏn Commercial School students who fled to the south) in *Sŏnch'ŏn chi*.

30. See, for example, Ch'ae Kiŭn, *Han'guk kyohoesa* [A history of the Korean church], (Seoul: Yesugyo munsŏ sŏn'gyohoe, 1977), p. 212.

31. Yong-ho Choe, "Christian Background in the Early Life of Kim Il-sŏng." Christian minister Hong Kiju was Kim's vice-premier, and another minister, Kang Yang'uk, who was Kim's uncle, was Kim's secretary-general.

32. See Han'guk Kidokkyo yŏksa yŏn'guso, *Pukhan kyohoesa*, p. 393. Also see Kim Kihyŏk, *Kim Hyŏnsŏk changno chŏn'gi* [A biography of elder Kim Hyŏnsŏk], (Seoul: Macmillan, 1981), pp. 273–78.

33. See Yŏ Unhong, *Mongyang Yŏ Unhyŏng*, and Cumings, *The Origins of the Korean War*, vol. 1, pp. 474–75.

34. Chang Pyŏng'uk, *Yugio kongsan namch'im kwa kyohoe*, pp. 154–55. Chang is a Methodist minister in South Korea, and his book is heavily tainted with right-wing political views. Nevertheless, it contains a tremendous amount of valuable material, including his interviews with a variety of church leaders.

35. See Chang's interview with the Reverend Cho Hyangnok in ibid., p. 155.

36. On the disunity of the Protestant church community in the south, see ibid., pp. 118–22 and 152–60. Also see Kim Yangsŏn, *Han'guk Kidokkyo haebang simnyŏnsa*, pp. 49–59 and 146–288.

37. Cumings, *The Origins of the Korean War*, vol. 1, pp. 122–87.

38. Ibid., pp. 123–39.

39. Ibid., pp. 91–213. Also see Sim Chiyŏn, *Han'guk minjudang yŏn'gu* [A study of the Korean Democratic Party], vol. 1 (Seoul: P'ulbit, 1982), especially part 1.

40. Cumings, *The Origins of the Korean War*, vol. 1, part 2; and Yi In-soo, "Competing Korean Elite Politics in South Korea After World War II, 1945–1948," (Ph.D. diss., New York University, 1981), pp. 94–232.

41. See Sim Chiyŏn, *Han'guk minjudang yŏn'gu*, vol. 1, part 1.

42. Chang Pyŏng'uk, *Yugio kongsan namch'im kwa kyohoe*, pp. 118–25.

43. For details, see ibid., pp. 121–25. For the Northwest Corps' terrorist activity, see Bruce Cumings, *The Origins of the Korean War*, vol. 2, pp. 198–203 and 244–59.

44. Bark, "The American-Educated Elite in Korean Society," pp. 271–75.

45. Cumings, *The Origins of the Korean War*, vol. 1, p. 147.

46. Rhee left Korea in 1910 for exile in the United States and returned to the country in 1945. On his life, see Yu Yŏng'ik (Young Ick Lew), *Yi Sŭngman ŭi sam kwa kkum—Taet'ongryŏng i toegi kkaji* [The life and dream of Syngman Rhee—Prior to his assumption of the presidency in 1948], (Seoul: Chung'ang ilbosa, 1996). For details on this issue, see pp. 206–8.

47. See Ko Wŏnsŏp, *Panminja choesanggi* [Criminal records on collaborators], (Seoul: Paengyŏng munhwasa, 1949), pp. 131–37; and Minjok chŏnggyŏng munhwa yŏn'guso, *Ch'in'ilp'a kunsang* [The collaborators], (Seoul: Minjok chŏnggyŏng munhwa yŏn'guso, 1948), reprinted as an appendix in Kil Chinhyŏn, *Yŏksa e tasi munnŭnda* [Let history reply], (Seoul: Samminsa, 1984), pp. 49–50. Prominent Christians such as Chŏng Ch'unsu, Yang Chusam, Chŏn P'ilsun, Sin Hŭng'u, Yun Ch'iho, and Ch'a Chaemyŏng were among the Christian collaborators.

48. Chang Pyŏng'uk, *Yugio kongsan namch'im kwa kyohoe*, pp. 122–25 and 303–4.

7 / PROTESTANT CHRISTIANS AND SOUTH KOREAN POLITICS, 1948–1980S

1. Yu Tongsik, *Han'guk sinhak úi kwangmaek: Han'guk sinhaksa sŏsŏl* [Patterns of theology in Korea: A history of theology in Korea], (Seoul: Chŏnmangsa, 1982), pp. 28–30; Han Wansang, *Chŏ najŭn kosŭl hyanghayŏ* [Toward the lower depths], (Seoul: Chŏnmangsa, 1978), pp. 22, 141–42, and 246; and Keun-soo Hong, "The Political Implications of Jesus in Reference to the Current Korean Political Situation" (unpublished thesis for Doctorate of Ministry, Eden Theological Seminary, 1976).

2. For a general discussion on the relationship of ideas and actions in history, see Gordon S. Wood, "Intellectual History and the Social Sciences," in *New Directions in American Intellectual History*, ed. John Higham and Paul K. Conkin (Baltimore and London: The Johns Hopkins University Press, 1979), pp. 27–41.

3. For more on the Christ Presbyterian Assembly in the Republic of Korea, see chapter 2.

4. See note 1.

5. Although liberal Christian activists received moral support from their fellow liberal clergymen who issued statements, they could not draw on their active participation or organizational support because these clergymen were established religious professionals and because their churches, like the more conservative churches, were under the influence of socioeconomically and politically established lay leaders. However, liberal Christian activism had begun to draw the active participation of Christian youths and students.

6. See James B. Palais, "Human Rights in the Republic of Korea," Asia Watch Committee, *Human Rights in Korea* (Washington, D.C.: Asia Watch, 1986), pp. 1–339, especially see pp. 303–15.

7. For example, Reverend Pak Hyŏnggyu, a liberal Christian activist and pastor of the Cheil Church of Seoul, had been under pressure from his congregation not to participate in political activity against the regime. And Reverend Kang Wŏnyong of the Kyŏngdong Church became a leading Christian collaborator with the Chun Doo-hwan regime in 1980. (These two cases will be discussed later in the chapter.) All ministers, liberals and conservatives, feel pressure from their congregation one way or another.

8. *Kidok sinmun*, August 15, 1948.

9. "Chehŏn kukhoe kaehoe kidomun" (Prayer offered at the opening of the first National Assembly), in Yi Yunyŏng, *Paeksa Yi Yunyŏng hoegorok* [Memoirs of Yi Yunyŏng], (Seoul: Sach'o, 1984), part 3, "Materials," pp. 267–68.

10. For example, 50 out of 210 National Assemblymen in 1952 were Christians. See *Kidok sinmun*, June 25, 1952. Also see Allen D. Clark, *A History of the Church in Korea* (Seoul: The Christian Literature Society, 1971), p. 305; and Samuel H. Moffett, "Korea," in *The Church in Asia*, ed. Donald E. Hoke (Chicago: Moody Press, 1975), pp. 369–83, particularly p. 380. According to Moffett, most of Rhee's first cabinet members were also Christians. Also see Dong Suh Bark, "The American-Educated Elite in Korean Society," in *Korea and the United States: A Century of Cooperation*, ed. Young-nok Koo and Dae-sook Suh (Honolulu: University of Hawaii Press, 1984), pp. 263–80, especially

pp. 271–75; and Bae-ho Han and Kyu-t'ae Kim, "Korean Political Leaders (1952–1963): Their Social Origins and Skills," *Asian Survey*, vol. 3, no. 7 (July 1963), pp. 305–23, and Table IX, "Religious Backgrounds of Leaders (1962)."

11. Kim Yŏngmo, *Han'guk chibaech'ŭng yŏn'gu* [A study of the ruling class in Korea], (Seoul: Ilchogak, 1982), pp. 191–93.

12. Yi Manyŏl, *Han'guk Kidokkyo wa yŏksa ŭisik* [Korean Christianity and historical consciousness], (Seoul: Chisik sanŏpsa, 1981), pp. 118–21.

13. James B. Palais, "Democracy in South Korea, 1948–1972," in *Without Parallel,* ed. Frank Baldwin (New York: Pantheon Books, 1973), pp. 318–57, especially p. 322.

14. Ibid., pp. 321–28.

15. Recently, some Korean scholars have begun to study this issue, but their works are not interpretative. See, for example, Kim Yongbok, "Haebanghu kyohoe wa kukka" (Church and state since the Liberation), in ed. Han'guk Kidokkyo sahoe munje yŏn'guwŏn, *Kuksa kwŏllyŏk kwa Kidokkyo* [State power and Christian church], (Seoul: Minjungsa, 1982), pp. 191–252; and Ch'oe Chonggo, "Cheil konghwaguk kwa Han'guk Kaesin'gyohoe" (The first republic and the Korean Protestant church), *Tongbanghak chi*, nos. 46–48 (1985), pp. 601–24.

16. Kunsa p'yŏnch'an wiwŏnhoe, *Han'guk hyŏndaesa* [History of contemporary Korea], (Seoul: T'amgudang, 1982), pp. 130–31.

17. Bruce Cumings, *The Origins of the Korean War*, vol. 1 (Princeton, N.J.: Princeton University Press, 1981), pp. 87 and 96.

18. See Ch'oe Chonggo, "Cheil konghwaguk kwa Han'guk Kaesin'gyohoe"; Kim Yongbok, "Haebanghu kyohoe wa kukka"; and Kunsa p'yŏnch'an wiwŏnhoe, *Han'guk hyŏndaesa.*

19. For example, his early political advisors, such as Yi Kibung, Im Yŏngsin, Hŏ Chŏng, Kim Yong'u, and Yun Ch'iyŏng, were Christians.

20. *Chōsen nenkan* (1945), pp. 210–11.

21. Gregory Henderson, *Korea: The Politics of the Vortex* (Cambridge, Mass.: Harvard University Press, 1968), p. 275.

22. See notes 10 and 20.

23. See the Reverend Kang Sinmyŏng's article (actually a short memoir), "The Dignity of Korean Pastors," in *Korean Church Growth: Explosion*, ed. Ro Bong-Rin and Martin L. Nelson (Taichung, Taiwan: Word of Life Press/Asia Theological Association, 1983), pp. 301–8, particularly pp. 304–6. Also see Clark, *A History of the Church in Korea*, p. 305.

24. *Kidok sinmun*, June 25, 1952.

25. Kim Yangsŏn, *Han'guk Kidokkyo haebang simnyŏnsa* [The ten-year history of the Korean church since the Liberation], (Seoul: Taehan Yesugyo changnohoe ch'onghoe chonggyo kyoyukpu, 1955), pp. 130–32.

26. For details, see chapter five.

27. Syngman Rhee delivered this speech at the fifty-fifth conference of officers and members of the Foreign Missionary Board and Committees in the United States and Canada, held January 4–7, 1948, in Columbus, Ohio. See Rhee's speech in *Conference Report* (New York: E.O. Jenkin's Printing House, 1949), p. 61.

28. On McCarthyism, see Michael P. Rogin, *The Intellectuals and McCarthy: The Radical Specter* (Cambridge, Mass., and London: M.I.T. Press, 1967); and Thomas C. Reeves, *The Life and Times of Joe McCarthy: A Biography* (New York: Stein and Day, 1982).

29. Yi Yunyŏng, *Paeksa Yi Yunyŏng hoegorok*, pp. 128–30.

30. See Song Sangsŏk, *Munje ŭi Kidokkyo wa yonggong chŏngch'aek p'amp'ŭret'ŭ wa yoch'ŏngsŏ chŏnmal* [A report on the controversy regarding the church and the procommunist policy], (Pusan, printed materials, 1951).

31. "Chinsang pogo" (A report on the real facts of the case), in ibid., sections 6–7.

32. See "Chinsang pogo," ibid., sections 1–5 and 9–10.

33. "Han'guk Kidokkyo yŏnhaphoe sŏngmyŏngsŏ" (A statement by the Korean National Council of Churches), Kim Yangsŏn, *Han'guk Kidokkyo haebang simnyŏnsa*, pp. 160–61.

34. *Kidok kongbo* [The Christian news], August 4, 1952. Also see *Kidok sinmun*, August 4, 1952.

35. These data are based on a report on the committee published in *Kidok sinmun* on August 4, 1952.

36. Ibid. Also see Ch'oe, "Cheil konghwaguk kwa Han'guk kaesin'gyohoe," p. 612.

37. *Kidok kongbo*, May 28, 1956.

38. See "Chŏn'guk Kidokkyodo yege koham" (We call upon all Korean Christians), *Kidok kongbo*, August 4, 1952.

39. See the report on the Committee in *Kidok kongbo*, August 4, 1952.

40. See Kim Chaejun's dialogue with Kim Sŏngsik, "Sahoe e ch'aegimjinŭn kyohoe, che kinŭng tahanŭn chisigin" (The church which is responsible for and the intellectuals who play their role in society), *Wŏlgan Chosŏn* (December 1983), pp. 58–68, particularly pp. 63–64.

41. Ibid., p. 63.

42. Ibid., pp. 62–65. Also see Kim Chaejun's dialogue with Ch'oe Ilnam, "Kwŏlyŏgŭn pŏbŭl chibaehalsu ŏpda" (Power cannot control law), *Sindong'a*, (December 1983), pp. 264–77, particularly pp. 270–71.

43. On the Second Republic, see Palais, "Democracy in South Korea, 1948–1972," pp. 328–31. Also see Sungjoo Han, *The Failure of Democracy in Korea* (Berkeley, Los Angeles, and London: University of California Press, 1974).

44. Palais, "Democracy in South Korea," pp. 328–31.

45. Kim Tongsu, "Han'guk Kidokkyonŭn saerowŏjŏya handa" (The Korean church should be renewed), *Kŭrisŭch'an* [The Christian voices], July 9, 1960; Saemunan kyohoe ch'ŏngnyŏn iltong (A group of youths of Saemunan Church), "Kyohoe chŏnghwarŭl wihan sŏngmyŏngsŏ" (Statement for purification of the Korean Protestant church), *Kŭrisŭch'an*, December 10, 1960. Also see the demand issued by a conference of young clergymen of Seoul under the title "Pup'aenŭn chegŏ toeŏya handa, kyohoenŭn t'ong'il toeŏya handa" (Down with corruption, up with church unity), *Kŭrisŭch'an*, July 9, 1960.

46. Kim Chaejun, "Sailgu ihu ŭi Han'guk kyohoe" (The Korean church after the student revolution of 1960), *Kidokkyo sasang*, vol. 5, no. 4 (April 1961), pp. 34–41, particularly p. 36.

47. Pak Ch'angmuk, "Che I konghwakuk kwa Han'guk kyohoe" (The Second Republic and the Korean Protestant church), *Kŭrisŭch'an*, August 9, 1960.

48. Han, *The Failure of Democracy in Korea*, pp. 107–23.

49. See "Kwŏnduŏn" (Foreword), *Kidokkyo sasang*, vol. 4, no. 9 (October 1960), pp. 7–9, particularly p. 9. Also see Pak Ch'angmuk, "Che I konghwakuk kwa Han'guk kyohoe."

50. Chang Ha'gu, "Hyŏngmyŏng gwa kyohoe ŭi pansŏng" (The student revolution of 1960 and the church's reflection), *Kidokkyo sasang*, vol. 8, no. 6 (June 1960), pp. 219–24, particularly p. 219.

51. See note 45.

52. See Saemunan kyohoe ch'ŏngnyŏn ildong, "Kyohoe Chŏnghwarŭl wihan sŏngmyŏngsŏ."

53. See Palais, "Democracy in South Korea," pp. 331–37.

54. Han Sŭngjo, "Pak chŏnggwŏn sipp'alyŏn" (The eighteen years under the Park Chung-hee regime), *Han'gul ilbo* [The Korean times], October 26, 1984.

55. Palais, "Democracy in South Korea," pp. 331–34.

56. For a short description of the Yusin period, see Palais, "Human Rights in the Republic of Korea," pp. 17–25; and Harold Hakwon Sunoo, *Repressive State and Resisting Church: The Politics of CIA in South Korea* (Fayette, Missouri: Korean American Cultural Association, 1976).

57. See Ch'ae Kiŭn, "Han'guk kyohoe sŏnŏnmun pip'an" (A critique of a

liberal Christian's statement against the government) in his *Han'guk kyohoesa* [A history of the Korean church], (Seoul: Yesugyo munsŏ sŏn'gyohoe, 1977), Appendix, pp. 221–25. This article was originally written for *Kidok sinbo*, the conservative church newspaper. Also see Kim Ùihwan, *Tojŏ pannŭn posu sinhak* [Conservative theology under attack], (Seoul: Sŏgwang munhwasa, 1970), and his article, "Han'guk kyohoe ŭi chŏngch'i ch'amyŏ munje" (On political participation of the Korean church), *Sinhak chinam*, vol. XL, no. 1 (January-March 1973), pp. 25–32 and 50.

58. See Yŏllye kukka choch'an kidohoe chunbi wiwŏnhoe (Annual National Prayer Breakfast Committee), *Kukka choch'an kidohoe yŏnhyŏk* [A short history of the national prayer breakfast committee], (Seoul: Yŏllye kukka choch'an kidohoe chunbi wiwŏnhoe, 1979), section 1.

59. No Hongsŏp, "Kŭrisŭdogyo yebae ŭi chŏngsin: choch'an kidohoenŭn chungji toeŏyaman handa" (The meaning of Christian services: Put a stop to the prayer breakfast), *Sasanggye*, vol. 14, no. 4 (April 1966), pp. 76–80, particularly p. 78.

60. See Kim Yongbok, "Haebanghu kyohoe wa kukka," particularly pp. 233–34.

61. Kim Joon-gon (Kim Chun'gon), "Korea's Total Evangelization Movement," in *Korean Church Growth: Explosion*, ed. Ro and Nelson, pp. 17–50.

62. Han'guk Kidokkyo sirŏbinhoe, *Han'guk Kidokkyo sirŏbinhoe yaksa* [A short history of the Christian Business Men's Committee of Korea], (Seoul: Han'guk Kidokkyo sirŏbinhoe, 1983), n.p.

63. See section "Han'guk ssibiemssi ch'angnip" (The founding of CBMC of Korea), in ibid.

64. See section "Sarang ŭi kyŏlyŏn undong chŏn'gae" (Beginning of "Establishment of Love Relationship" Campaign), in ibid.

65. See *Tong'a yŏn'gam* [Tong'a yearbook], (Seoul: Tong'a ilbosa, 1975), p. 527.

66. For details, see Ch'ae Kiŭn, "Han'guk kyohoe sŏnŏnmun pip'an," pp. 221–25.

67. Ibid. Also see Kaehŏn munje wa yangsim chayu sŏnŏn ŭl wihan Kidokkyo sŏngjikcha iltong (A group of Christian clergymen for a declaration on constitutional amendment and freedom of conscience), "Kaehŏn munje wa yangsim chayu sŏnŏn" (A declaration of constitutional amendment and freedom of conscience), *Chosŏn ilbo*, September 4, 1969; and Taehan Kidokkyo yŏnhaphoe (KCCC), "Kaehŏn e taehan uri ŭi sosin" (Our view on the constitutional amendment), ibid., September 5, 1969.

68. Kim Yŏng'il, "Han'guk Kidokkyo ŭi sahoe ch'amyŏ" (Social participa-

tion of the Korean church), *Sindong'a*, no. 126 (February 1975), pp. 164–97, particularly pp. 188 and 194; and Kim Yongbok, "Haebanghu kyohoe wa kukka," pp. 218–20 and 233–35.

69. See Park Chung-hee's presidential announcement, statements, and order in *Han'guk yŏn'gam* [Korean yearbook], (Seoul: Han'guk yŏn'gamsa, 1972), pp. 165–69.

70. See chapter one in this book.

71. Han'guk Kidokkyo sahoe munje yŏn'guwŏn, *Han'guk kyohoe paengnyŏn chonghap chosa yŏ'gu: pogosŏ*, pp. 109–117, particularly Table I-136 on p. 110.

72. The following materials on this Christian activism are available: The Emergency Christian Conference on Korean Problems, ed., *Documents on the Struggle for Democracy in Korea* (Tokyo: Shinkyo Shuppansha, 1975); Christian Institute for the Study of Justice and Development, *Presence of Christ Among Minjung* (Seoul: CISJD, 1981); Palais, "Human Rights in the Republic of Korea"; Han'guk Kidokkyo sahoe munje yŏn'guwŏn, *Ch'ŏn'gubaek ch'ilsimnyŏndae minjuhwa undonggwa Kidokkyo*; Yi Suŏn, "Ch'ilsimnyŏndae panch'eje moksadŭl" ("Anti-regime" clergymen in the 1970s), *Sindong'a*, vol. 27, no. 9 (September 1984), pp. 168–93; and Kim Yŏng'il, "Han'guk kyohoe ŭi sahoe ch'amyŏ." Also see the following periodicals: *Korea/Update*, *Korea Communique*, *Korea Weekly Report*, *Korea Scope*, and *Asian Rights Advocate*.

73. For details, see chapter two in this book.

74. Unlike in the 1930s, when the liberals individually challenged the fundamentalist orthodoxy but submitted to it because they were neither many nor united, the liberals in the early 1950s did not bow to the fundamentalist attack because they were now united as a group around the Chosŏn Theological Seminary.

75. See "Pŏpt'ong samsipp'al ch'onghoe ŭi sŏnŏnsŏ" (Statement of the lawful thirty-eighth general assembly) issued by the splinter group. This document is in *Han'guk Kidokkyo haebang simnyŏnsa*, comp. Kim Yangsŏn, pp. 281–84, particularly p. 283.

76. Yi Changsik, "Pogŭm ŭi chayu, Hananim sŏn'gyo chujang" (Advocacy for freedom of faith and *Mission Dei*), *Kidokkyo sasang*, no. 277 (July 1981), pp. 97–107, particularly see pp. 100–107.

77. Christian activists themselves confessed that they were no different from the majority of Christians under Syngman Rhee, but had begun to raise their voices against Park Chung-hee by the mid-1960s. See Han'guk Kidokkyo sahoe munje yŏn'guwŏn, *Ch'ŏn'gubaek ch'ilsimnyŏndae minjuhwa undong gwa Kidokkyo*, pp. 42–43.

78. See Kim Yŏng'il, "Han'guk Kidokkyo ŭi sahoe ch'amyŏ," p. 178.

79. Han'guk Kidokkyo sahoe munje yŏn'guwŏn, *Ch'ŏn'gubaek ch'ilsimnyŏndae minjuhwa undong gwa Kidokkyo*, pp. 41–54.

80. Ibid., pp. 61–66.

81. For details, see Alfred Fierro, *The Militant Gospel* (New York: Orbis Books, 1977).

82. Yi Changsik, "Pogŭm ŭi chayu, Hamnanim ŭi sŏn'gyo chujang," p. 102.

83. Since the liberal denomination joined the WCC in 1960, its leaders had participated actively in every conference sponsored by the world Christian body.

84. Han'guk Kidokkyo sahoe munje yŏn'guwŏn, *Ch'ŏn'gubaek ch'ilsimnyŏndae minjuhwa undong gwa Kidokkyo*, pp. 65–68; and Kim Yŏng'il, "Han'guk Kidokkyo ŭi sahoe ch'amyŏ," pp. 186–89.

85. See, for example, "Han'guk Kidokkyo sinang sŏnŏn" (Theological declaration of Korean Christians), May 20, 1973, and "Sŏnŏnmun" (Declaration) issued by the Christ Presbyterian Assembly in the Republic of Korea on September 28, 1973. These two statements are translated into English and compiled in the Emergency Christian Conference on Korean Problems, ed., *Documents on the Struggle for Democracy in Korea*, pp. 37–46.

86. Palais, "Democracy in South Korea," pp. 349–50, and "Human Rights in the Republic of Korea," pp. 17–25.

87. Even the students who had been the most active force against the government were nearly in "a state of complete silence" after Park Chung-hee exercised a *wisuryŏng* (garrison decree) on October 15, 1971. See Han'guk Kidokkyo sahoe munje yŏn'guwŏn, *Ch'ŏn'gubaek ch'ilsimnyŏndae minjuhwa unding gwa Kidokkyo*, p. 130.

88. Ibid., pp. 159 and 225.

89. Ibid., p. 256.

90. Ibid., pp. 159–61.

91. Ibid., pp. 169–82 and 213–33.

92. Ibid., pp. 174–79.

93. Ibid., pp. 181–82; and Yi Suŏn, "Ch'ilsimnyŏndae panch'eje moksadŭl," pp. 172–73. Kim Daejung, a Catholic layman, worked very closely with Protestant activists for democracy and human rights.

94. Han'guk Kidokkyo sahoe munje yŏn'guwŏn, *Ch'ŏn'gubaek ch'ilsimnyŏndae minjuhwa unding gwa Kidokkyo*, pp. 174–77.

95. Immediately after the government announced its own version of the case on May 27, 1974, churches such as Saemunan Church and the Cheil Church of Seoul and church-affiliated institutions such as the KNCC, the KSCF, and the Mogyo kidohoe (Thursday prayer meeting) held a variety of religious gatherings and ceremonies not only to denounce the government version but also to

show their solidarity with detainees. See Han'guk Kidokkyo sahoe munje yŏn'gu-wŏn, *Ch'ŏn'gubaek ch'ilsimnyŏndae minjuhwa undong gwa Kidokkyo*, pp. 174–75. The favorite device that the South Korean government had relied on frequently for clamping down on opposition forces was to accuse them of being favorable to Communist North Korea or to communism in general. The government tried the case of the National Federation of Youths and Students for Democracy under the Anticommunist Law and the National Security Law. The Committee for Human Rights of the KNCC and other church institutions not only denounced the government's story, but also argued that the detainees were only critics of dictatorship.

96. See, for example, letters and statements issued by the world Christian community in the Emergency Christian Conference on Korean Problems, ed., *Documents on the Struggle for Democracy in Korea*, pp. 132–71.

97. During the 1980s, the North American Coalition for Human Rights in Korea was run by Peggy Billings, Chairman, and Pharis Harvey, Executive Director; the International Christian Network for Democracy in Korea by Mun Tonghwan, Chairman; and the Emergency Christian Conference on Korean Problems by John M. Nakajima, Chairman.

98. Newspapers and magazines were forced to end their publications or to bow to the government during the Yusin Constitution period, but the monthly magazine, *Kidokkyo sasang*, continued to be the active forum for those intellectuals and journalists who were expelled from the press and the campus. It also functioned as their partial means of support.

99. "Han'guk Kidokkyo sinang sŏnŏn," in *Documents on the Struggle for Democracy in Korea*, ed. Emergency Christian Conference on Korean Problems, pp. 27–34.

100. During the 1980s, most activists in the antigovernment movement in South Korea held this position.

101. See *Haptong yŏn'gam* [Haptong yearbook], (Seoul: Haptong t'ongsinsa, 1983), p. 299; and *Chosŏn ilbo*, January 18, 1982.

102. Kim Yŏng'il, "Han'guk Kidokkyo ŭi sahoe ch'amyŏ," pp. 185–86.

103. Yi Suŏn, "Ch'ilsimnyŏndae panch'eje moksadŭl," pp. 164–97.

104. For details, see Palais, "Human Rights in the Republic of Korea," pp. 302–315; *Tong'a ilbo*, September 24 and 29, 1984; *Chugan Han'guk* [The Korea times weekly], April 28, 1984, pp. 30–31; *Korea Communique* (Tokyo), no. 50 (January 1984); *Kankoku tsusin* [Korean report] by Kankoku modai kirisutosha kikyukai (Tokyo), no. 103 (September, 1984); and Sŏul cheil kyohoe (Cheil Church in Seoul), "Now! The Current Situation of Seoul Jaeil Church," a pamphlet, October 1983–June 1985.

105. Kang became a member of the Kunchŏng chamun wiwŏnhoe (Advisory Committee for the President on National Affairs). The information on Kang is based on my interviews with a variety of Korean church leaders who visited the United States and Canada in the early 1980s after the Kwangju Uprising.

106. The Christian activism in the 1970s and 1980s was one of "statement-arrest." In other words, the Christian activists issued a statement for democracy, social justice, and human rights, and were arrested immediately. During the 1980s and early 1990s, they did not adopt other devices to achieve their political goal.

CONCLUSION

1. See Thomas F. O'Dea, *The Sociology of Religion* (Englewood Cliffs, N.J.: Prentice-Hall, 1966), p. 1.

2. See, for example, Kuksa p'yŏnch'an wiwŏnhoe, *Han'guk hyŏndaesa* [A history of contemporary Korea], (Seoul: T'amgudang, 1982), pp. 130–31; and Pak Hŭisŭng, "Han'guk sahoe ŭi pyŏnhwa wa Pulgyo" (Social change and Buddhism in Korea), *Hyŏnsanggwa insik*, vol. 18, no. 4 (Winter 1994), pp. 39–60, especially pp. 44–48.

3. For details, see Pak Yŏngsin (Yong-shin Park), "Kidokkyo wa sahoe palchŏn" (Christianity and social progress), in his *Yŏksa wa sahoe pyŏndong* [Historical and social change], (Seoul: Minyŏngsa/Han'guk sahoehak yŏn'guso, 1987), chapter 10.

BIBLIOGRAPHY

OFFICIAL SOURCES

Asian Languages

American Data Research Service, compiled. *Sŏnch'ŏn chi, 1946, 1947* [Records of Sŏnch'ŏn County, North P'yŏng'an Province, 1946–1947]. Washington, D.C., 1985.

Anak kunji p'yŏnch'an wiwŏnhoe, ed. *Anak kunji* [Annals of Anak County]. Seoul: Anak kunchi p'yŏnch'an wiwŏnhoe, 1976.

Ch'a Chaemyŏng, comp. *Chosŏn Yesugyo changnohoe sagi* [A historical record of the Jesus Presbyterian Church in Korea]. Keijō: Chosŏn Yesugyo changnohoe, 1928.

Chōsen sōtokufu. *Kyō kankoku kanpō* [The official gazette of old Korea], vol. 22. Keijō: Chōsen sōtokufu, August 13, 1910.

———. *Shisei nijūgonenshi* [A history of twenty-five years of administration]. Keijō: Chōsen sōtokufu, 1935.

Chōsen sōtokufu keimukyoku. *Chōsen chian jōkyō* [Conditions of public order in Korea]. Keijō: Chōsen sōtokufu, 1922.

Ch'unghyŏn isibonyŏnsa p'yŏnch'an wiwŏnhoe. *Ch'unghyŏn isibonyŏnsa* [Twenty-five-year history of Ch'unghyŏn Church]. Seoul: Ch'unghyŏn kyohoe, 1978.

Han'guk chonggyo sahoe yŏn'guso. *Han'guk chonggyo yŏn'gam* [The yearbook of Korean religions]. Seoul: Han'guk chonggyo sahoe yŏn'guso/Hallimwŏn, 1993.

Han'guk Kidokkyo paekchunyŏn kinyŏmsaŏp hyŏbŭihoe. *Han'guk Kidokkyo paengnyŏn: Kinyŏmsaŏp yoram* [Hundred years of the Korean Protestant church: An outline of commemorative events]. Seoul: Han'guk Kidokkyo paekchunyŏn kinyŏmsaŏp hyŏbŭihoe, 1984.

Han'guk Kidokkyo sahoe munje yŏn'guwŏn. *Ch'ŏn'gubaek ch'ilsimnyŏndae min-*

juhwa undong gwa Kidokkyo [The democratization movement and Christianity in the 1970s]. Seoul: Han'guk Kidokkyo sahoe munje yŏn'guwŏn, 1983.

———. *Han'guk kyohoe paengnyŏn chonghap chosa yŏn'gu: Pogosŏ* [A comprehensive study of the Korean church during the last century: A report]. Seoul: Han'guk Kidokkyo sahoemunje yŏn'guwŏn, 1982.

———. *Segye kyohoe hyŏbŭihoeran muŏsin'ga* [What is the World Council of Churches?]. Seoul: Han'guk Kidokkyo sahoe munje yŏn'guwŏn, 1983.

Han'guk Kidokkyo sirŏbinhoe. *Han'guk Kidokkyo sirŏbinhoe yaksa* [A short history of the Christian Business Men's committee]. Seoul: Han'guk Kidokkyo sirŏbinhoe, 1983.

Han'guk kyohoe sahakhoe, comp. *Chosŏn Yesugyo changnohoe sagi* [A historical record of the Jesus Presbyterian Church of Korea], vol. 2. Seoul: Yŏnse taehakkyo ch'ulp'anbu, 1977.

Huam kyohoe samsibonyŏnsa p'yŏnch'an wiwŏnhoe. *Huam kyohoe samsibonyŏnsa* [The thirty-five-year history of Huam Church]. Seoul: Huam kyohoe, 1981.

Kangsŏ kunji p'yŏnsuhoe. *Kangsŏ kunji* [Records of Kangsŏ County]. Seoul: Kangsŏ kunchi p'yŏnsuhoe, 1967.

Kim Chŏngju, ed. *Chōsen tōchi shiryō* [Historical documents on the Japanese rule of Korea], vol. 4. Tokyo: Kankoku shiryō kenkyūjo, 1970.

Kwak Alyŏn (Allen D. Clark). *Kyohoe sajŏn hwijip* [Digest of the Presbyterian Church of Korea]. Keijō: Chōsen yashogyō shōkai, 1918.

———, comp. *Taehan Yesugyo changnohoe hŏnbŏp* [Constitution of the Jesus Presbyterian Church of Korea]. Seoul: Taehan Kidokkyo sŏhoe, 1957.

Kyŏngje kihoegwŏn chosa t'onggyeguk. *Han'guk t'onggye yŏn'gam* [Korea statistical yearbook]. Seoul: Kyŏngje kihoegwŏn, 1987.

Kyŏngsin chunggodŭng hakkyo. *Kyŏngsin p'alsimnyŏn yaksa* [A short history of eighty years of Kyŏngsin School]. Seoul: Kyŏngsin chunggodŭng hakkyo, 1966.

Paejae chunggodŭng hakkyo. *Paejaesa* [A history of Paejae School]. Seoul: Paejae chunggodŭng hakkyo, 1955.

Saemunan kyohoe ch'angnip paengnyŏn kinyŏm saŏphoe. *Saemunan kyohoe munhŏn saryojip* [Historical documents of Saemunan Church]. Seoul: Saemunan kyohoe, 1987.

Saemunan kyohoe ch'ilsimnyŏnsa kanhaeng wiwŏnhoe. *Saemunan kyohoe ch'ilsimnyŏnsa* [Seventy-year history of Saemunan Church]. Seoul: Saemunan kyohoe, 1958.

Sungjŏn taehakkyo p'alsimnyŏnsa p'yŏnch'an wiwŏnhoe. *Sungjŏn taehakkyo p'alsimnyŏnsa* [Eighty-year history of Sungjŏn University]. Seoul: Sungjŏn taehakkyo, 1979.

Tawara Sonnichi. *Kankoku kyōiku no genjō* [The present state of education in Korea]. Keijō: Chōsen sōtokufu gakufu, 1910.

———. *Kankoku kyōiku no kiō oyobi genzai* [Education in Korea, past and present]. Keijō: Chōsen sōtokufu gakufu, 1909.

———. *Kankoku kyōiku to keisatsu gyōsei* [Education in Korea and police administration]. Keijō: Chōsen sōtokufu, 1909.

Tongnip undongsa p'yŏnch'an wiwŏnhoe, ed. *Tongnip undongsa charyojip* [Documents on history of independence movement], vols. 1 and 6. Seoul: Tongnip undongsa p'yŏnch'an wiwŏnhoe, 1973.

Uchida Ryohei. *Ryuki Kaigen hiji* [Secret events in the years of protectorate]. In *Chōsen tōchi shiryō* [Historical documents on Japanese rule of Korea], vol.4, ed. Kim Chŏngju. Tokyo: Kankoku shiryō kenkyūjo, 1970, pp. 13–205.

Yŏllye kukka choch'an kidohoe chunbi wiwŏnhoe. *Kukka choch'an kidohoe yŏnhyŏk* [A short history of the national prayer breakfast committee]. Seoul: Yŏllye kukka choch'an kidohoe chunbi wiwŏnhoe, 1979.

Yŏngnak kyohoe hongbo ch'ulp'anbu. *Yŏngnak kyohoe samsibonyŏnsa* [Thirty-five-year history of Yŏngnak Church]. Seoul: Yŏngnak kyohoe, 1983.

English Language

Christ Presbyterian Church in the Republic of Korea. "Our View of Current Situation of Nation" (Statement), May 29, 1986.

Christian Institute for the Study of Justice and Development. *Presence of Christ Among Minjung*. Seoul: Christian Institute for the Study of Justice and Development, 1981.

Emergency Christian Conference on Korean Problems, ed. *Documents on the Struggle for Democracy in Korea*. Tokyo: Shinkyo shuppansha, 1975.

Jeil (Cheil) Church. *Now! The Current Situation of Seoul Jaeil Church, 1983–1985*. Seoul: Jeil Church, 1985.

Korean Overseas Information Service. *Statistical Data on Korea*. Seoul: Korean Overseas Information Service, 1982.

Pacific-Asia Resources Center. *Korea, May 1980: People's Uprising in Kwangju*. Tokyo: Pacific-Asia Resources Center, 1980.

DIARIES, AUTOBIOGRAPHIES, BIOGRAPHIES, AND MEMOIRS

Asian Languages

Ch'oe Myŏngsik. *Anak sakŏn kwa samil undong gwa na* [The Anak Incident, the March First Movement and I]. Seoul: Kŭkhŏ chŏn'gi p'ŏnch'an wiwŏnhoe, 1970.

Chŏn Kyŏng'yŏn. "Kim Chaejun non" (On Kim Chaejun). *Sasanggye,* vol. 14, no. 4 (April 1966), pp. 204–15.

Chu T'aeik. *Man'u Song Ch'anggŭn* [A biography of Song Ch'anggŭn]. Seoul: Man'u Song Ch'anggŭn sŏnsaeng kinyŏm saŏphoe, 1978.

Chu Yohan. *An Tosan chŏnjip* [Complete works of An Ch'angho]. Seoul: Samjungdang, 1971.

Kil Chin'gyŏng. *Yŏnggye Kil Sŏnju* [Kil Sŏnju: A biography]. Seoul: Chongno sŏjŏk, 1980.

Kim Chaejun. *Pŏmyonggi* [Autobiography of Kim Chaejun]. 2 vols. Toronto: Ch'ilsŏng kwanggosa, 1981 and 1982.

Kim Ch'ungnam. *Sun'gyoja Chu Kich'ŏl moksa ŭi saeng'ae: Chindalle p'ilttae kabŏrin saram* [The life of a martyr: The Reverend Chu Kich'ŏl who did not wait to see spring flowers]. Seoul: Paekhap ch'ulp'ansa, 1974.

Kim Insŏ. "Yŏnggye sŏnsaeng sojŏn" (A short biography of the teacher Kil Sŏnju). Four parts. *Sinang saenghwal* [Christian life], vol. 1, no. 12 (December 1932), pp. 26–31; vol. 2, no. 1 (January 1933), pp. 24–28; vol. 2, no. 2 (February 1933), pp. 26–30; and vol. 2, no. 3 (March 1933), pp. 25–30.

Kim Kihyŏk. *Kim Hyŏnsŏk changno chŏn'gi* [A biography of elder Kim Hyŏnsŏk]. Seoul: Maengmillan, 1981.

Kim Kisŏk. *Namgang Yi Sŭnghun* [A biography of Yi Sŭnghun]. Seoul: Hyŏndae kyoyuk ch'ongsŏ ch'ulp'ansa, 1964.

Kim Ku. *Paekpŏm ilchi* [Kim Ku's diary]. Seoul: Tongmyŏngsa, 1947.

Kim Tot'ae. *Namgang Yi Sŭnghunjŏn* [A biography of Yi Sŭnghun]. Seoul: Mun'gyosa, 1950.

Kim Tot'ae, ed. *Sŏ Chaep'il paksa chasŏjŏn* [Autobiography of Dr. Sŏ Chaep'il]. Seoul: Susŏnsa, 1948.

Kim Yangsŏn. "Aeguk ŭi sin'gyo puhŭng: Kil Sŏnju" (Kil Sonju and revival as patriotic activity). In *Kidokkyo chŏndoja yugin* [Six Christian evangelists], ed. Sin'gumunhwasa. Seoul: Sin'gumunhwasa, 1979, pp. 101–111.

Kim Yŏnghwi. *Chwaong Yun Ch'iho sŏnsaeng yakchŏn* [A brief biography of Yun Ch'iho]. Keijō: Kidokkyo Chosŏn kamnihoe, 1934.

Ko Ŭn. "Mun Ikhwan ŭl malhanda" (On Mun Ikhwan). *Miju tong'a ilbo* [The Tonga Daily News], Los Angeles edition, June 24, 25, and 26, 1986.

Pak Hyŏnggyu. "No moksa ŭi pisanghan hyŏnsil ch'amyŏ" (Extraordinary political participation of an aging minister). *Wŏlgan chung'ang,* no. 45 (December 1971), pp. 103–5.

Pak Myŏngsu. *Munpakke sori issŏ* [Voices outside the gate]. Seoul: Yesugyo munsŏ sŏn'gyohoe, 1976.

Sim Chiyŏn. *Hŏ Hŏn yŏn'gu* [A study of Hŏ Hŏn]. Seoul: Yŏksa pip'yŏngsa, 1994.

Sin Suk. "Pansegi ŭi chŭng'ŏn" (Witness of the last half-century), *Tong'a ilbo,* no. 8, April 19, 1964.

Sin'gumunhwasa, ed. *Kidokkyo chŏndoja yugin* [Six Christian evangelists]. Seoul: Sin'gumunhwasa, 1976.

Yi Tŏkchu. *Nara ŭi tongnip kyohoe ŭi tongnip* [The nation's independence and the church's independence]. Seoul: Kidokkyomunsa, 1988.

Yi Ŭnsuk. *Minjok undongga anae ŭi sugi—sŏgando sijonggi* [Notes by the wife of an activist for independence]. Seoul: Chŏng'ŭmsa, 1975.

Yi Yunyŏng. *Paeksa Yi Yunyŏng hoegorok* [Memoirs of Yi Yunyŏng]. Seoul: Sach'o, 1984.

Yŏ Unhong. *Mongyang Yŏ Unhyŏng* [A biography of Yŏ Unhyŏng]. Seoul: Ch'ŏnghaksa, 1967.

Yu Yŏng'ik (Lew, Young Ick). *Yi Sŭngman ŭi sam kwa kkum—Taet'ongnyŏng i toegi kkaji* [The life and dream of Syngman Rhee—Prior to his assumption of presidency in 1948]. Seoul: Chung'ang ilbo, 1996.

Yun Ch'iho. *Yun Ch'iho ilgi* [Yun Ch'iho's diary], vol. 1. Seoul: Kuksap'yŏnch'an wiwŏnhoe, 1973.

English Language

Ch'oe, Yong-ho. "Christian Background in the Early Life of Kim Il-sŏng." *Asian Survey,* vol. 26, no. 10 (October 1986), pp. 1082–99.

Kim, Hyung-ch'an. *Yun Ch'i-ho, 1865–1945. Letters in Exile: The Life and Times of Yun Ch'i-ho.* Covington, Ga.: Rhoades Printing Co., 1980.

Liem, Channing. *America's Finest Gift to Korea: The Life of Philip Jaisohn.* New York: Fleming H. Revell, 1908.

Reeves, Thomas C. *The Life and Times of Joe McCarthy: A Biography.* New York: Stein and Day, 1982.

Shim, Koon-sik. *Till the End of the Age: The Life of Reverend Sang Dong Han.* Trans. by Han T. Kitai. Pusan: Kosin College Press, 1984.

Underwood, Horace G. *The Call of Korea.* New York: Fleming H. Revell, 1908.

Underwood, Lillias H. *Fifteen Years among the Topknots or Life in Korea.* Boston, New York, and Chicago: American Tract Society, 1904.

Wales, Nym, and Kim San. *Song of Ariran.* San Francisco: Rampart Press, 1941.

Yun Ch'iho, *Yun Chiho ilgi* [Yun Ch'iho's Diary], vols. 1–8. Seoul: Kuksap'yŏnch'an wiwŏnhoe, 1973–1986.

BOOKS ARTICLES, AND DISSERTATIONS

Asian Languages

An Sŏngjin. "Orini wa uri" (Children and us). *Kŭrisŭch'an,* July 9, 1960.

Aoyagi Kōtaro. *Chōsen tōchiron* [An essay on the rule of Korea]. Keijō: Chōsen kenkyūkai, 1932.

Boldŭwin P'ŭrangkŭ (Baldwin, Frank). "Wilsŭn, minjok chagyŏlchuŭi, samil undong" (Wilson, national self-determination, and the March First Movement). In *Samil undong osipchunyŏn kinyŏm nonjip* [Selected essays to mark the fiftieth anniversary of the March First Movement], ed. Ko Chaeuk. Seoul: Tong'a ilbosa, 1969, pp. 515–32.

Ch'ae Chŏngmin. "Kyonong undong ŭi pulga" (The church's movement to improve rural society is not right). *Sinang saenghwal,* vol. 5, no. 7 (July 1936), pp. 6–10.

Ch'ae Hyŏnsŏk. "Yi Taewi ŭi saeng'ae wa hwaltong" (Yi Taewi: His life and activity). In *Ilcheha Han'guk Kidokkyo wa sahoejuŭi* [Christianity and socialism in Korea under Japanese rule], ed. Kim Hŭngsu. Seoul: Han'guk Kidokkyo yŏksa yon'guso, 1992, pp. 253–65.

Ch'ae Kiŭn. *Han'guk kyohoesa* [A history of the Korean church]. Seoul: Yesugyo munsŏ sŏn'gyohoe, 1977.

Chang Ch'angjin. "Ilcheha minjok munje nonjaeng gwa pan chonggyo undong" (Debate on national problems and antireligion movement under Japanese colonial rule). M.A. thesis, Sŏul taehakkyo, 1994.

Chang Ha'gu. "Hyŏngmyŏnggwa kyohoe ŭi pansŏng" (The student revolution of 1950 and the church's reflection). *Kidokkyo sasang,* vol. 8, no. 6 (June 1960), pp. 219–24.

Chang Pyŏng'uk. *Yugio kongsan namch'im kwa kyohoe* [The communist invasion to the south and Christianity]. Seoul: Han'guk kyoyuk kongsa, 1983.

Cho Chihun. *Han'guk minjok undongsa* [A history of Korean nationalist movement]. Seoul: Nanam, 1993.

Cho Ilmun, trans. *Chosŏn ch'aegyak* [Ch'ao-hsien ts'e-lueh, Strategy for Korea]. Written by Huang Chun-hsien. Seoul: Kŏn'guk taehakkyo ch'ulp'anbu, 1977.

Cho Sŭnghyŏk. *Tosi sanŏp sŏn'gyo ŭi insik* [Understanding of the Urban Industrial Mission]. Seoul: Minjungsa, 1981.

Ch'oe Chonggo. "Cheil konghwaguk kwa Han'guk kaesin'gyohoe" (The first republic and the Korean Protestant church). *Tongbang hakchi,* no. 46–48 (1985), pp. 601–24.

Chŏn T'aekpu. *Han'guk Kidokkyo ch'ŏngnyŏnhoe undongsa* [A history of the Korean 'YMCA' movement]. Seoul: Chŏng'ŭmsa, 1978.

Chŏn Taeryŏn and No Chongho, eds. *Han'guk Kidokkyo sahoe undong* [Social movement of the Korean Protestant church]. Seoul: Noch'ulp'ansa, 1986.

Chŏng Kyo. *Taehan kyenyŏnsa* [A history of the last years of the Yi Dynasty]. Seoul: Kuksa p'yŏnch'an wiwŏnhoe, 1957.

Chŏng Okcha. "Sinsa yuramdan ko" (A study on the gentlemen's excursion group). *Yŏksa hakpo,* vol. 27 (1965), pp. 105–42.

Han Ch'ŏlha, Na Hakchin, and An Pongho. "Kyohoe wa kukka" (Conversation on church and state). In *Haebang sinhak kwa Tosi sanŏp sŏn'gyo* [Theology of liberation and the Urban Industrial Mission], ed. Kyŏnghyang sinmunsa. Seoul: Kyŏnghyang sinmunsa, 1982, pp. 11–22.

Han Ch'ŏlhwi. "Chŏnsiha Chosŏn ŭi sinsa ch'ambae wa Kidokkyoin ŭi chŏhang" (Christians' resistance to worshiping at the Shinto shrine during the war years). In *Singminji sidae Han'guk ŭi sahoe wa chŏhang* [Resistance to colonial rule in Korean society], ed. Iinuma Jiro and Kang Chaeŏn. Seoul: Paeksan sŏdang, 1982, pp. 297–344.

Han Kyumu. "Kuhanmal Sangdong ch'ŏngnyŏnhoe ŭi sŏllip kwa hwaltong" (The foundation and activity of Sangdong Young Men's Academy in the last period of the Yi Dynasty). M.A. thesis, Sŏgang taehakkyo, 1988.

Han Sŏngjo. "Pak chŏnggwŏn sipp'alyŏn" (The eighteen years under the Park Chung-hee regime). *Han'guk ilbo,* October 26, 1984.

Han Wansang. *Chŏ najŭn kosŭl hyanghayŏ* [Toward the lower depths]. Seoul: Chŏnmangsa, 1978.

———. "Han'guk kyohoe ŭi yangjŏk sŏngjang gwa kyoindŭl ŭi kach'igwan" (The quantative growth of the Korean church and Christians' values). In Han'guk Kidokkyo munhwa yŏn'guso, *Han'guk kŭndaehwa wa Kidokkyo* [Korean modernization and Christianity]. Seoul: Sungjŏn taehakkyo, 1983, pp. 121–56.

Han'guk Kidokkyo munhwa yŏn'guso. *Han'guk kŏndaehwa wa Kidokkyo* [Korean modernization and Christianity]. Seoul: Sungjŏn taehakkyo, 1983.

———. *Han'guk sahoe wa Kidokkyo* [Korean society and Christianity]. Seoul: Sungjŏn taehakkyo, 1984.

Han'guk Kidokkyo sahoe munje yŏn'guwŏn, ed. *Kukka kwŏllyŏk kwa Kidokkyo* [State power and Christian church]. Seoul: Minjungsa, 1982.

Han'guk Kidokkyo yŏksa yŏn'guso. *Han'guk Kidokkyo wa sinsa ch'ambae munje* [The Korean Christian church and the shrine worship issue]. Seoul: Han'guk kidokkyo yŏksa yŏn'guso, 1991.

———. *Pukhan kyohoesa* [History of Christianity in North Korea]. Seoul: Han'guk Kidokkyo yŏksa yŏn'guso, 1996.

Han'guk kŭrisŭch'an akademi. *Han'guk kyohoe sŏngnyŏng undong ŭi hyŏn-*

sang gwa kujo [The spiritual movement in the Korean church: Its phenomenon and structure]. Seoul: Han'guk kŭrisŭch'an akademi, 1981.

Han'guk sahoesa yŏn'guhoe. *Hyŏndae Han'guk ŭi chonggyo wa sahoe* [Religion and society in contemporary Korea]. Seoul: Munhakkwa chisŏngsa, 1992.

Han'guk yŏn'gamsa. *Han'guk yŏn'gam* [Korean yearbook]. Seoul: Han'guk yŏn'gamsa, 1972.

Hapdong yŏn'gamsa. *Hapdong yŏn'gam* [Hapdong yearbook]. Seoul: Hapdong yŏn'gamsa, 1983.

Hong Chiyŏng. *Sanŏp sŏngyonŭn muŏsŭl norinŭn'ga* [What is the Urban Industrial Mission after?]. Seoul: Kŭmnan ch'ulp'ansa, 1979.

Huang Tsun-hsien. *Ch'ao-hsien ts'e-lüeh* [Strategy for Korea], trans. by Cho Ilmun into Korean. Seoul: Kŏn'guk taehakkyo ch'ulp'anbu, 1977.

Hwang Sŏngsu. *Kyohoe wa kukka* [Church and state]. Seoul: Sinmang'aesa, 1972.

Hyŏndae sahoe yŏn'guso. *Han'guk kyohoe sŏngjanggwa sinang yangt'ae e kwanhan chosa yŏn'gu* [A survey on the growth of Christianity and form of faith in Korea]. Seoul: Hyŏndae sahoe yŏn'guso, 1982.

Iinuma Jirō and Kang Chaeŏn, eds. *Singminji sidae Han'guk ŭi sahoe wa chŏhang* [Resistance to colonial rule in Korean society]. Seoul: Paeksan sŏdang, 1982.

Kang Chaeŏn. *Ilcheha sasimnyŏnsa* [Forty-year history under Japan's imperialist rule]. Seoul: P'ulbit, 1984.

Kang Hŭngsu. *Chosŏn tongnip hyŏlt'usa* [A history of Korea's bloody struggle for independence]. Seoul: Koryŏ munhwasa, 1946.

Kang Inchŏl. "Haebanghu Han'guk kaesin'gyohoe wa kukka simin sahoe" (The Korean Protestant church, state, and civil society after the Liberation). In Han'guk sahoesa yŏn'guhoe, *Hyŏndae Han'guk ŭi chonggyo wa sahoe* [Religion and society in contemporary Korea]. Seoul: Munhakkwa chisŏngsa, 1992, pp. 98–141.

Kang Man'gil. *Han'guk hyŏndaesa* [A history of contemporary Korea]. Seoul: Ch'angjakkwa pip'yŏngsa, 1984.

———. *Han'guk kŭndaesa* [A history of modern Korea]. Seoul: Ch'angjakkwa pip'yŏngsa, 1984.

———. "Minjok undongsa ch'ŭngmyŏn esŏbon ch'ŏn'gubaek isimnyŏndae Chosŏnsa" (A history of the twenties from the viewpoint of the nationalist movement). *Yŏksa pip'yŏng*, no. 1 (Summer 1985), pp. 119–29.

Kang Myŏngsuk. "Ch'ŏn'gubaek isimnyŏndae Chosŏn Kidokkyo ŭi sahoejuŭi insik e kwanhan yŏn'gu" (A study on Christian understanding of socialism during the 1920s). M.A. thesis, Ihwa yŏja taehakkyo, 1991.

Kang Ton'gu. "Han'guk Kidokkyo nŭn minjokchuŭijŏgiŏnna" (The Korean church: Was it nationalistic?). *Yŏksa pip'yŏng*, no. 27 (Winter 1994), pp. 317–27.

Kang Tongjin. *Ilche ŭi Han'guk ch'imnyak chŏngch'aeksa* [A history of Japanese imperialist policies of aggression toward Korea]. Seoul: Han'gilsa, 1980.

Kang Wijo. *Ilche t'ongch'iha Han'guk ŭi chonggyo wa chŏngch'i* [Religion and politics under Japanese imperialist rule]. Seoul: Taehan Kidokkyo sŏhoe, 1977.

Kang Wŏndon. "Ilcheha sahoejuŭi undong gwa Han'guk Kidokkyo" (Socialist movement and Korean Christianity under Japanese colonial rule). In *Ilcheha Han'guk Kidokkyo wa sahoejuŭi* [Christianity and socialism in Korea under Japanese rule], ed. Kim Hŭngsu. Seoul: Han'guk Kidokkyo yŏksa yŏn'guso, 1992.

Keijō nipponsha. *Chōsen nenkan* [Korean annual]. Keijō: Keijō nipponsha, 1945.

Kidok kyomunsa. *Han'guk Kidokkyo tae yŏn'gam* [The great yearbook of Korean Christianity]. Seoul: Kidokkyomunsa, 1993.

Kidokkyo sasang, ed. *Han'guk ŭi chŏngch'i sinhak* [Political theology in Korea]. Seoul: Taehan Kidokkyo sŏhoe, 1984.

Kil Chinhyŏn. *Yŏksa e tasi munnŭnda* [Let history reply]. Seoul: Samminsa, 1984.

Kil Sŏnju. *Yŏnggye Kil Sŏnju moksa chŏjakchip* [Works of the Reverend Kil Sŏnju]. Seoul: Taehan Kidokkyo sŏhoe, 1968.

Kim Chaejun. *In'gan igie* [Because I am a human being]. Seoul: Hyangninsa, 1971.

———. "Kwŏllyŏgŭn pŏbŭl chibaehalsu ŏpda" (Power cannot control law). Conversation with Ch'oe Illam, *Sindong'a*, December, 1983, pp. 264–77.

———. "Sailgu ihu ŭi Han'guk kyohoe" (The Korean church after the Student Revolution of 1960). *Kidokkyo sasang*, vol. 5, no. 4 (April 1961), pp. 34–41.

———and Kim Sŏngsik. "Sahoe e ch'aegimjinŭn kyohoe, che kinŭng tahanŭn chisigin: Taedam" (The church which is responsible for and the intellectuals who play their role in society: A dialogue), *Wŏlgan Chosŏn*, December 1983, pp. 58–68.

Kim Ch'angje. "Hyŏnha Kidokkyo undong ŭi panghyang ŭn ŏdiro" (In which direction is today's Christian movement going?), *Kidok sinbo*, January 20, 1932.

———. "Minjung ŭi chonggyo" (A religion of the people). *Ch'ŏngnyŏn*, vol. 6, no. 2 (February 1926), pp. 12–14.

———. "Sahoejuŭi hwalsallon" (A thesis on the life and death of socialism). *Samyŏng* [Mission], no. 5 (1927), pp. 22–24.

Kim Chongsŏ. "Sŏngsŭrŏum ŭi p'apyŏmhwa in'ga" (Is it that the sacred became fragmented?). *Hyŏnsanggwa insik*, vol. 18, no. 4 (Winter 1994), pp. 11–38.

Kim Chunggi. "Han'guk kyohoe ŭi sŏngjang kwajŏng" (The process of church growth in Korea). *Hyŏndae sahoe,* vol. 1, no. 1 (Spring 1983), pp. 101–26.

Kim Chunyŏp and Kim Ch'angsun. *Han'guk kongsanjuŭi undongsa* [A history of the communist movement in Korea]. 5 vols. Seoul: Ch'ŏngye yŏn'guso, 1986.

Kim Hŭngsu, ed. *Ilcheha Han'guk Kidokkyo wa sahoejuŭi* [Christianity and socialism in Korea under the Japanese rule]. Seoul: Han'guk Kidokkyo yŏksa yŏn'guso, 1992.

Kim Insŏ. "P'yŏngyang kyohoe ch'oegŭn ŭi samdae chiphoe" (Three recent revival meetings in P'yŏngyang church community). *Sinang saenghwal,* vol. 1, no. 3 (March 1932), pp. 7–10.

———. "Kyŏngnam nohoe ŭi kyori munje" (Doctrinal problem in the Kyŏngnam presbytery). *Sinang saenghwal,* vol. 1, no. 3 (March 1932), pp. 4–7.

———. "Chosŏn kyohoe ch'aegimjanŭn kŭ nuguin'ga" (Who is the person in charge of the Korean church?). *Sinang saenghwal,* vol. 1, no. 4 (April 1932), pp. 2–5.

———. "Nŏhŭido ttohan kagojŏ hanŏnya" (Do you want to go their way, too?). *Sinang saenghwal,* vol. 1, no. 7 (July 1932), pp. 7–10.

———. "Kŭn isibil ch'onghoe" (Exhortation for the twenty-first general assembly). *Sinang saenghwal,* vol. 1, no. 11 (November 1932), pp. 7–10.

———. "Chosŏn kyohoe ŭi sae tonghyang" (New trends in the Korean church). *Sinang saenghwal,* vol. 2, no. 3 (March 1933), pp. 4–6.

———. "Chosŏn kyohoe ŭi nanmaek" (The Korean church in chaos). *Sinang saenghwal,* vol. 2, no. 5 (May 1933), pp. 4–6.

———. "P'yŏngyang nohoe ŭi sang'ŭihan hŏnbŏp sujŏng'an e taehaya" (On the constitutional amendment introduced to the P'yŏngyang presbytery). *Sinang saenghwal,* vol. 2, no. 8 (August 1933), pp. 4–6.

———. "Chŏng isibi ch'onghoe" (Recommendations to the twenty-second general assembly). *Sinang saenghwal,* vol. 2, no. 9 (September 1933), pp. 4–7.

———. "Yuhaeng suyanghoe ŭi t'arak ŭl kyeham" (Corruption at fashionably held cultivation conference: A warning). *Sinang saenghwal,* vol. 2, no. 10 (October 1933), pp. 4–6.

———. "Moksa yegye tŭril kŏt" (What laymen should give their pastors). *Sinang saenghwal,* vol. 2, no. 11–12 (December 1933), pp. 4–6.

———. "Isipsam nohoe ŭi tŭngjŭng munje" (Agenda of the twenty-third session of the presbytery). *Sinang saenghwal,* vol. 2, no. 11–12 (December 1933), pp. 4–7.

———. "Changhyŏn kyohoe ch'uk punyŏlho" (Is the Changhyon Church divided finally?). *Sinang saenghwal,* vol. 3, no. 6 (June 1934), pp. 2–5.

———. "Ko isipsa ch'onghoe" (Recommendations for the discussion at the twenty-fourth general assembly). *Sinang saenghwal,* vol. 4, no. 8 (August–September 1935), pp. 7–10.

———. "Sŏnmin nambuk punyŏl ŭi hwa" (North-south split of a chosen people). *Sinang saenghwal,* vol. 5, no. 10 (October 1936), pp. 18–23.

———. "Ch'onghoe pullip munje e taehaya" (On the rift in the general assembly). *Sinang saenghwal,* vol. 5, no. 10 (October 1936), pp. 24–26.

———. "P'yŏngyang chi p'yŏnŏn" (Letter from P'yŏngyang). *Sinang saenghwal,* vol. 6, no. 9 (October 1936), pp. 36.

Kim Kwangsu. *Han'guk Kidokkyo inmulsa* [History of Korea's Christian personalities]. Seoul: Kidokkyomunsa, 1974.

Kim Kwŏnjŏng, "Ilcheha sahoejuŭijadŭl ŭi pan Kidokkyo undong" (Anti-Christianity movement of socialists under Japanese imperial rule). M.A. thesis, Sungsil taehakkyo, 1995.

Kim Kyŏngnae and Hong Chiyŏng. *Ch'onghwa wa yusin* [General harmony and the restoration]. Seoul: Kŭmnan ch'ulp'ansa, 1975.

Kim Kyŏngsik. "Sahoejuŭi esŭ Kidokkyoro sasang ŭl torik'igi kkaji" (Conversion of my thought from socialism to Christianity). *Kidok sinbo,* April 6 and 20, 1927.

Kim Pyŏngsŏ. "Han'guk kyohoe ŭi chonggyosŏnggwa kech'ŭngsŏng yŏn'gu" (On the religiosity and stratification of the Korean church). In *Han'guk sahoe wa Kidokkyo* [Christianity in Korean society], ed. Han'guk Kidokkyo munhwa yŏn'guso. Seoul: Sungjŏn taehakkyo, 1984, pp. 102–69.

Kim Sŏngjin. *Ilche ŭi haksal manhaeng ŭl kobalhanda* [We accuse Japanese imperialism of atrocities]. Seoul: Mire munhwasa, 1983.

Kim Taesang. *Ilcheha kangje illyŏk sut'alsa* [A history of exploitation of manpower under the Japanese colonial rule]. Seoul: Chŏng'ŭmsa, 1975.

———. "Samil undong gwa haksaengch'ŭng" (The March First Movement and students). In *Samil undong osipchunyŏn kinyŏm nonjip* [Selected essays to mark the fiftieth anniversary of the March First Movement], ed. Ko Chaeuk. Seoul: Tong'a ilbosa, 1969, pp. 301–11.

Kim Tongsu. "Han'guk Kidokkyonŭn saerowŏjŏya handa" (The Korean church should be renewed). *Kŭrisŭch'an,* July 9, 1960.

Kim Tŭkhwang. *Han'guk chonggyosa* [A history of Korean religions]. Seoul: Haemunsa, 1963.

Kim Ŭihwan. "Han'guk kyohoe ŭi chŏngch'i ch'amyŏ munje" (On political participation of the Korean church). *Sinhak chinam,* vol. 30, no. 1 (January–March 1973), pp. 25–32 and 50.

———. *Tojŏn pannŭn posu sinhak* [Conservative theology under attack]. Seoul: Sŏgwang muhwasa, 1970.

Kim Wŏnbyŏk. "Hyŏndae sasanggwa Kidokkyo" (Modern thoughts and Christianity). *Ch'ŏngnyŏn,* vol. 3, no. 7 (July–August 1932), pp. 22–24.

Kim Yangsŏn. *Han'guk Kidokkyo haebang simnyŏnsa* [The ten-year history of the Korean church since the liberation]. Seoul: Taehan Yesugyo changnohoe ch'onghoe chonggyo kyoyukpu, 1955.

———. *Han'guk Kidokkyosa yŏn'gu* [A historical study of Korean Christianity]. Seoul: Kidokkyomunsa, 1971.

———. "Samil undong gwa Kidokkyo" (The March First Movement and Christianity). In *Samil undong osipchunyŏn kinyŏm nonjip* [Selected essays to mark the fiftieth anniversary of the March First Movement], ed. Ko Chaeuk. Seoul: Tong'a ilbosa, 1969, pp. 235–70.

Kim Yongbok. "Haebanghu kyohoe wa kukka" (Church and state since the liberation). In *Kukka kwŏllyŏk kwa Kidokkyo* [State power and Christianity], ed. Han'guk Kidokkyo sahoe munje yŏn'guwŏn. Seoul: Minjungsa, 1982, pp. 191–252.

———. "Han'guk Kidokkyo paengnyŏn ŭi yŏksa wa hyŏnhwang" (The Korean church during its one-hundred-year history and its current status). Han'guk Kidokkyo sahoe munje yŏn'guwŏn, *Han'guk kyohoe paengnyŏn chonghap chosa yŏn'gu: Pogosŏ* [A comprehensive study of the Korean church during the last century: A report]. Seoul: Han'guk Kidokkyo sahoe munje yŏn'guwŏn, 1982. pp. 129–42.

———. "Minjok pundan sogŭi Han'guk Kidokkyo" (Korean Christianity in the era of national division). In *Han'guk sahoe wa Kidokkyo* [Korean society and Christianity], ed. Han'guk Kidokkyo munhwa yŏn'guso. Seoul: Sungjŏn taehakkyo, 1984, pp. 257–99.

Kim Yŏng'il. "Han'guk Kidokkyo ŭi sahoe ch'amyŏ" (Social participation of the Korean church). *Sindong'a,* no. 126 (February 1975), pp. 164–97.

Kim Yŏngmo. *Han'guk chibaech'ŭng yŏn'gu* [A study of the ruling class in Korea]. Seoul: Ilchogak, 1982.

Ko Chaeuk, ed. *Samil undong osipchunyŏn kinyŏm nonjip* [Selected essays to mark the fiftieth anniversary of the March First Movement]. Seoul: Tong'a ilbosa, 1969.

Ko Wŏnsŏp. *Panminja choesanggi* [Criminal records on collaborators]. Seoul: Paegyŏng munhwasa, 1949.

Kuksa p'yŏnch'an wiwŏnhoe. *Han'guk hyŏndaesa* [A history of contemporary Korea]. Seoul: T'amgudang, 1982.

———. *Han'guk tongnip undongsa* [History of the Korean independence movement], vol. 1. Seoul: Kuksa p'yŏnch'an wiwŏnhoe, 1965.

———. *Ilche ch'imyakha Han'guk samsip'yungnyŏnsa* [The thirty-six-year history of Korea under Japanese imperial rule], vol. 4. Seoul: Kuksa p'yŏnch'an wiwŏnhoe, 1969.

Kyŏnghyang sinmunsa. *Haebang sinhak kwa Tosi sanŏp sŏn'gyo* [Theology of liberation and the Urban Industrial Mission]. Seoul: Kyŏnghyang sinmunsa, 1982.

———. *Taehak kwa sasang* [College and thought]. Seoul: Kyŏnghyang sinmunsa, 1982.

Min Kyŏngbae. *Han'guk Kidokkyo sahoe undongsa* [A history of social movement of the Korean Christian church]. Seoul: Taehan Kidokkyo ch'ulp'ansa, 1988.

———. "Han'guk kŭndae munhwa wa Kidokkyo ŭi hyŏngt'ae mit kŭ yŏnghyang pŏmwi" (Christianity in modern Korea: Its distribution pattern and the scope of influence on culture). *Han'guk sahak,* no. 1 (June 1982), pp. 226–50.

———. *Han'guk minjok kyohoe hyŏngsŏng saron* [A historical study on the formation of a nationalist church]. Seoul: Yŏnse taehakkyo ch'ulp'anbu, 1974.

———. *Han'guk ŭi Kidokkyohoesa* [A church history of Korea]. Seoul: Taehan Kidokkyo sŏhoe, 1968.

———. *Kŭrisŭch'an akademi simnyŏnsa* [The ten-year history of the Christian Academy]. Seoul: Kŭrisŭch'an akademi, 1975.

Minjok chŏnggyŏng munhwa yŏn'guso. *Chin'ilp'a kunsang* [The collaborators]. Seoul: Minjok chŏnggyŏng munhwa yŏn'guso, 1948.

Mun Sojŏng. "Wijŏng ch'ŏksa undong e kwanhan sahoehakchŏk yŏn'gu" (A study of *wijŏng ch'ŏksa* movement from the viewpoint of sociology of knowledge). *Han'guk hakpo,* vol. 10, no. 3 (Autumn 1984), pp. 56–81, and vol. 10, no. 4 (Winter 1984), pp. 93–111.

No Ch'ijun. "Ilcheha Han'guk changnogyohoe ch'onghoe t'onggye e taehan yŏn'gu" (A study on the statistics of the Korean Presbyterian church under Japanese colonial rule). In Han'guk sahoesa yŏn'guhoe, *Hyŏndae Han'guk ŭi chonggyo wa sahoe* [Religion and society in contemporary Korea]. Seoul: Munhakkwa chisŏngsa, 1992. pp. 66–97.

———. *Ilcheha Han'guk Kidokkyo minjok undong yŏn'gu* [Korean Christian nationalist movement under Japanese colonial rule]. Seoul: Han'guk Kidokkyo yŏksa yŏn'guso, 1993.

No Hongsŏp. "Kŭrisŭdogyo yebae ŭi chŏngsin: Choch'an kidohoenŭn chungji toeŏyaman handa" (The meaning of Christian services: Put a stop to the prayer breakfast). *Sasanggye,* vol. 14, no. 4 (April 1966), pp. 76–80.

O Chiyŏng. *Tonghaksa* [A history of Tonghak]. Seoul: Munsŏn'gak, 1973; original edition, 1938.

O Sangsun. "Sidaego wa kŭ hŭisaeng" (The agony of the times and its victims). *P'yehŏ,* vol. 1, no. 1 (July 1920), pp. 21–24.

Paek Nakchun. "Han'guk kyohoe ŏi p'ippak—T'ŭkhi sanae ch'ongdok mosal misu ŭmmo ŭi ŭmmo e taehayŏ" (Persecution of the Korean church with particular reference to the alleged attempt on the life of Governor-General Terauchi). *Sinhak nondan,* no. 7 (1962), pp. 14–29.

Pak Ch'angmuk. "Chei konghwaguk kwa Han'guk kyohoe" (The second republic and the Korean Protestant church). *Kŭrisŭch'an,* August 9, 1960.

Pak Chŏngsin (Park, Chung-shin). "Ch'ŏn'gubaek isimnyŏndae Kaesin'gyo chidoch'ŭng gwa minjokchuŭi undong" (The relationship between Protestant leaders and the nationalist movement in early colonial Korea: A social history). *Yŏksa hakpo,* no. 134–135 (September 1992), pp. 142–63.

———. "Han'guk hyŏndaesa e issŏsŏ Kaesin'gyo ŭi chari: Tongnip hyŏphoe undong ŭl pogiro sama" (The place of the Protestant church in the history of modern Korea: Taking the Independence Club Movement as an example). *Ssial ŭi sori,* no. 99 (March 1989), pp. 181–89.

———. "Kuhanmal ilche ch'ogi Kidokkyo sinhak kwa chŏngch'i: Chinbojŏk sahoe undong gwa minjokchuŭi undong" (Christian theology and politics in late Confucian and early colonial Korea: A discussion on the church's progressive social activism and nationalist movement). *Hyŏnsanggwa insik,* vol. 17, no. 1 (Spring 1993), pp. 103–25.

———. *Kŭndae Han'guk kwa Kidokkyo* [Modern Korea and Christianity]. Seoul: Minyóngsa, 1997.

———. "Tokugawa sidae ŭi yugyo wa sanŏphwa" (Confucianism and industrialization in Tokugawa Japan). *Hyŏnsanggwa insik,* vol. 7, no. 3 (Autumn 1983), pp. 89–102.

———. "Yun Ch'iho yŏn'gu" (A study of Yun Ch'iho). *Paeksan hakpo,* no. 23 (1977), pp. 341–88.

Pak Hansŏl. "Samil undong chudoch'e hyŏngsŏng e taehan koch'al" (A study of the formation of main groups for the March First Movement). In *Samil undong osipchunyŏn kinyŏm nonjip* [Selected essays to mark the fiftieth anniversary of the March First Movement], ed. Ko Chaeuk. Seoul: Tong'a ilbosa, 1969, pp. 189–201.

Pak Hŭisŭng. "Han'guk sahoe ŭi pyọnhwa wa Pulgyo" (Social change and

Buddhism in Korea). *Hyŏnsanggwa insik,* vol. 18, no. 4 (Winter 1994), pp. 39–60.

Pak Hyŏngnyong. *Kyo ŭi sinhak sŏsŏl* [Dogmatic theology]. Seoul: Kalbin ch'ulp'ansa, 1963.

———. *Pak Hyŏngnyong paksa chŏjak chŏnjip* [Complete works of Dr. Pak Hyŏngnyong]. 12 vols. Seoul: Han'guk Kidokkyo kyoyuk yŏn'guwŏn, 1981.

Pak Sun'gyŏng. "Han'guk minjok kwa Kidokkyo ŭi munje" (A question before the Korean church and nation). In *Pundan sidae wa Han'guk sahoe* [Korean society in divided Korea], ed. P'yŏn Hyŏng'yun. Seoul: Kkach'i, 1985, pp. 345–70.

Pak Ŭnsik. *Han'guk tongnip undong chi hyŏlsa* [The bloody history of the Korean independence movement]. Seoul: Ŏmun'go, 1973; original edition, 1920.

———. *Han'guk t'ongsa* [A tragic history of Korea]. Seoul: Pagyŏngsa, 1974.

Pak Yonggyu. *Han'guk changnogyo sasangsa* [A history of Presbyterian theological thought in Korea]. Seoul: Ch'ongsin taehak ch'ulp'anbu, 1992.

———. *Han'guk kyohoe inmulsa* [Personalities in the Korean church]. 3 vols. Seoul: Pogŭm munsŏ sŏn'gyohoe, 1975.

Pak Yŏngsin (Park, Yong-shin). "Ch'ogi Kaesin'gyo sŏn'gyosa ui sŏn'gyo undong chŏllyak" (Early Protestant missionaries' strategies for evangelism). *Tongbanghak chi,* no. 46/47/48 (June 1985), pp. 529–53.

———. "Kidokkyo wa Han'gŭl undong" (Christianity and Han'gŭl movement). In Yu Tongsik et al., *Kidokkyo wa Han'guk yŏksa* [Christianity and Korean history]. Seoul: Yŏnse taehakkyo ch'ulp'anbu, 1996, pp. 39–69.

———. "Kidokkyo wa sahoe palchŏn" (Christianity and social progress). In Pak Yŏngsin, *Yŏksa wa sahoe pyŏndong* [Historical and social change]. Seoul: Minyŏngsa/Han'guk sahoehak yŏn'guso, 1987, chapter 10.

———. "Sahoe undong ŭrosŏ ŭi samil undong ŭi kujo wa kwajŏng" (The March First Movement: Its structure and process as a social movement). *Hyŏnsanggwa insik,* vol. 3, no. 1 (Spring 1978), pp. 5–23.

———. "Tongnip hyophoe chido seryŏk ŭi sangjing gwa ŭisik kujo" (The Independence Club Leaders: Structure of their symbol and consciousness). *Tongbanghak chi,* no. 20 (December 1978), pp. 147–70.

———. "Wirobutŏ ŭi kaehyŭk esŏ araerobutŏ ŭi kaehyŏk ŭro: Sŏ Chaep'il ŭi undong chŏlyak" (From reform from above to reform from below: Strategic change of Sŏ Chaep'il), *Hyŏnsanggwa insik,* vol. 20, no. 1 (Spring 1996), pp. 41–65.

Pyŏn Hyŏng'yun, ed. *Pundan sidae wa Han'guk sahoe* [Korean society in divided Korea]. Seoul: Kkach'i, 1985.

Sim Chiyŏn. *Han'guk minjudang yŏn'gu* [A study of the Korean Democratic Party], vol. 1. Seoul: P'ulbit, 1982.

Sin Ch'aeho. *Sin Ch'aeho chŏnjip* [Complete works of Sin Ch'aeho]. Special volume. Seoul: Tanje Sin Ch'aeho sŏnsaeng kinyŏm saŏphoe, 1977.

Sin Chuhyŏn. "Ch'ŏn'gubaek isimnyŏndae Han'guk Kidokkyoindŭl ŭi minjok undong e kwanhan ilgoch'al: sahoe kyŏngje undong ŭl chungsimŭro" (A study of nationalist activities of Korean Christians during the 1920s: Focusing on their socioeconomic activities). M.A. thesis, Sungmyŏng yŏja taehakkyo, 1986.

Sin Yongha. *Tongnip hyŏphoe yŏn'gu* [A study of the Independence Club]. Seoul: Ilchogak, 1976.

———. "Han'guk Kidokkyo wa minjok undong" (The Korean Protestant church and nationalist movement). In *Han'guk Kidokkyo sahoe undong* [Social movement of the Korean Protestant church], ed. Chŏn Taeryŏn and No Chongho. Seoul: Noch'ulp'ansa, 1986, pp. 34–44.

———. "Samil undong palbal kyŏngwi" (The situation of the outbreak of the March First Movement). In *Han'guk kŭndae saron* [Historical essays on modern Korea], ed. Yun Pyŏngsŏk, Sin Yongha, and An Pyŏngjik, vol. 2. Seoul: Chisik sanŏpsa, 1977, pp. 38–112.

———. "Sinhan ch'ŏngnyŏndang ŭi tongnip undong" (The independence movement of the New Korean Young Men's Society). *Han'guk hakpo,* vol. 12, no. 3 (Autumn 1986), pp. 94–142.

Sŏ Chŏngmin. "Ch'ogi Han'guk kyohoe taebuhŭng undong ihae—minjok undonggwaŭi kwallyŏn ŭl chungsimŭro" (Understanding of the revival movement in the early Korean church—With its relations with nationalist movement as the central subject). In Yi Manyŏl et al., *Kidokkyo wa minjok undong* [Christianity and the nationalist movement]. Seoul: Posŏng, 1986, pp. 233–82.

Son Insu. *Han'guk kŭndae kyoyuksa* [A history of modern education in Korea]. Seoul: Yŏnse taehakkyo ch'ulp'anbu, 1971.

Song Ch'anggŭn. "Onŭl Chosŭn kyohoe ŭi samyŏng" (The task before the church of Korea today). *Sinhak chinam* (1930). Also in Chu T'aeik, *Man'u Song Ch'anggŭn* [A biography of Song Ch'anggŭn]. Seoul: Man'u Song Ch'anggŭn sŏnsaeng kinyŏm saŏphoe, 1978, pp. 156–60.

Song Sangsŏk. *Munje ŭi Kidokkyo wa yonggong chŏngch'aek p'amp'ŭretŭ wa yoch'ŏngsŏ chŏnmal* [A report on the controversy regarding "The Church and the Procommunist Policy"]. Pusan, printed materials, 1951.

Sŏnu Hun. *Minjok ŭi sunan—paegoin sakŏn* [Suffering nation—The 105 Men Case]. Seoul: Tongnip chŏngsin pogŭphoe, 1955.

Tong'a ilbosa. *Tong'a yŏn'gam* [Tong'a yearbook]. Seoul: Tong'a ilbosa, 1975.

Tong'il sasang yŏn'guwŏn. *Haebang sinhak kwa kongsanjuŭi* [Theology of liberation and communism]. Seoul: P'yŏngbŏm sŏdang, 1984.

Tong'in (Associates). "Sang'yŏ" (Afterthoughts). *P'yehŏ,* vol. 1, no. 1 (July 1920), pp. 121–29.

Yi Chaesun. "Sinminhoe wa sanae ch'ongdok amsal ŭmmo sakŏn" (The Sinminhoe and the alleged attempt on the life of Governor-General Terauchi). *Hyŏnsanggwa insik,* vol. 5, no. 3 (Autumn 1978), pp. 143–72.

Yi Changsik. "Pogŭm ŭi chayu, Hananim ŭi sŏn'gyo chujang" (Advocacy for freedom of faith and *Missio Dei*). *Kidokkyo sasang,* no. 277 (July 1981), pp. 97–107.

Yi Chong'yul. *Samil undong gwa mijok ŭi hamsŏng* [People cried out in the March First Movement]. Seoul: Inmundang, 1984.

Yi Chupong. "Han'guk sahoe wa kyohoe sŏngjang" (The church growth in Korean society). *Kidokkyo sasang,* vol. 25, no. 9 (September 1981), pp. 27–35.

Yi Ihwa. *Han'guk ŭi p'abŏl* [Korean factionalism]. Seoul: Ŏmun'gak, 1983.

Yi Kwangnin. *Han'guk kaehwa sasang yŏn'gu* [A study on the Korean enlightenment thought]. Seoul: Ilchogak, 1979.

———. *Han'guk kaehwasa yŏn'gu* [A study on the history of enlightenment in Korea with reference to the 1880s]. Seoul: Ilchogak, 1969.

———. *Han'guksa kangjwa* [Roundtable discussions of Korean history], no. 5. Seoul: Ilchogak, 1983.

———. *Kaehwadang yŏn'gu* [A study of the Progressive Party]. Seoul: Ilchogak, 1973.

Yi Kwangsu. "Chaesaeng" (Rebirth). *Yi Kwangsu chŏnjip* [Complete works of Yi Kwangsu], no. 3. Seoul: Samjungdang, 1969, pp. 129–98.

———. "Kŭmil Chosŏn ŭi Yasogyohoe ŭi hŏmjŏm" (Some defects in the Korean church today). *Ch'ŏngch'un,* January, 1917, pp. 77–81.

———. "Sinsaenghwallon" (On new life). *Yi Kwangsu chŏnjip,* no. 17. Seoul: Samjungdang, 1969, pp. 515–554.

Yi Manyŏl. *Han'guk Kidokkyo wa minjok ŭisik* [Korean Christianity and nationalist consciousness]. Seoul: Chisik saŏpsa, 1991.

———. "Han'guk Kidokkyo wa yŏksa ŭisik" (Korean Christianity and historical consciousness). *Kidokkyo sasang,* August 1980, pp. 62–74.

———. *Han'guk Kidokkyo wa yŏksa ŭisik* [Korean Christianity and historical consciousness]. Seoul: Chisik sanŏpsa, 1981.

———. "Kaesin'gyo ŭi chŏllae wa ilcheha kyohoe wa kukka" (The introduction of Protestantism, and church and state under Japanese colonial rule). In *Kukka kwŏllyŏk kwa Kidokkyo* [The state power and Christian church], ed. Han'guk Kidokkyo sahoe munje yŏn'guwŏn. Seoul: Minjungsa, 1982, pp. 35–190.

———. "Kaesin'gyo ŭi sŏn'gyo hwaltong gwa minjok ŭisik" (Protestant mission and national consciousness). *Sahak yŏn'gu,* no. 36 (April 1983), pp. 191–219.

———. "Kidokkyo wa samil undong" (Christianity and the March First Movement). *Hyŏnsanggwa insik,* vol. 3, no. 1 (Spring 1978), pp. 51–84.

——— et al. *Kidokkyo wa minjok undong* [Christianity and nationalist movement]. Seoul: Posŏng, 1986.

Yi Nŭnghwa. *Chosŏn Kidokkyo kŭp oegyosa* [History of Christianity and Korea]. Seoul: Hangmun'gak, 1969; original edition, 1928.

Yi Pohyŏng. "Samil undong e issŏsŏ ŭi minjok chagyŏlchuŭi ŭi toip kwa ihae" (How principles of national self-determination were introduced into the March First Movement and how they were perceived). In *Samil undong osipchunyŏn kinyŏm nonjip,* ed. Ko Chaeuk. Seoul: Tong'a ilbosa, 1969, pp. 175–87.

Yi Suŏn. "Ch'ilsimnyŏndae pan cheje moksadŭl" (Anti-regime clergymen in the 1970s). *Sindong'a,* vol. 27, no. 9 (September 1984), pp. 168–93.

Yi Taewi. "Naŭi isang hanŭnba minjok kyohoe" (A nationalist church: What I idealize). *Ch'ŏngnyŏn,* vol. 3, no. 6 (June 1923), pp. 11–16.

———. "Sahoejuŭi wa Kidokkyo sasang" (Socialism and Christian thoughts). *Ch'ŏngnyŏn,* vol. 3, no. 5 (May 1923), pp. 9–15.

———. "Sahoejuŭi wa Kidokkyo ŭi kŭich'akchŏmi ŏttŏhan'ga" (Where do socialism and Christianity meet?). *Ch'ŏngnyŏn,* vol. 3, no. 8 (August 1923), pp. 8–11, and no. 9 (September 1923), pp. 8–12.

———. "Sahoe hyŏngmyŏng ŭi Yesu" (Jesus for social revolution). *Ch'ŏngnyŏn,* vol. 8, no. 5 (June 1928), pp. 17–19.

Yi Tonhwa. *Ch'ŏndogyo ch'anggŏnsa* [A history of the formation of Ch'ŏndogyo]. Seoul: Ch'ŏndogyo chung'ang ch'ongniwŏn, 1933.

Yi Wŏn'gyu. "Han'guk sinhaksaengdŭl ŭi ŭisik kujo" (Thinking structure of seminary students in Korea), part 1, *Kidokkyo sasang,* no. 309 (March 1984), pp. 177–93, part 2, no. 310 (April 1984), pp. 185–99.

Yi Yŏnghŏn. *Han'guk Kidokkyosa* [A history of the Korean church]. Seoul: Concordia ch'ulp'ansa, 1978.

YMCA. *Simin nondan* [Citizens' forum]. Seoul: YMCA, 1973.

Yu Kyŏngsang. "Saehoejuŭija Yesu" (Jesus: A socialist). *Ch'ŏngnyŏn,* vol. 3, no. 7 (July–August 1932), pp. 32–37.

Yu Tongsik. *Han'guk chonggyo wa Kidokkyo* [Korean religions and Christianity]. Seoul: Taehan kidokkyo sŏhoe, 1965.

———. *Han'guk sinhak ŭi kwangmaek—Han'guk sinhaksa sŏsŏl* [Patterns of theology in Korea—A history of theology in Korea: An introduction]. Seoul: Chŏnmangsa, 1982.

——— et al. *Kidokkyo wa Han'guk yŏksa* [Christianity and Korean history]. Seoul: Yŏnse taehakkyo ch'ulp'anbu, 1996.

Yu Yŏng'ik (Lew, Young Ick) et al. *Han'gugin ŭi taemi insik—yŏksajŏk ŭrobon hyŏngsŏng kwajŏng* [Korean view on America—A historical study on its formation]. Seoul: Minŭmsa, 1944.

Yu Yŏng'yŏl. *Kaehwagi ŭi Yun Ch'iho yŏn'gu* [A study of Yun Ch'iho during the time of enlightenment]. Seoul: Han'gilsa, 1985.

Yun Ch'unbyŏng. *Han'guk Kidokkyo sinmun chapchi paengnyŏnsa* [Christian newspapers and periodicals in 1885–1985: A history]. Seoul: Taehan Kidokkyo ch'ulp'ansa, 1984.

Yun Kyŏngno. *Han'guk kŭndaesa ŭi Kidokkyosajŏk ihae* [Modern Korean history from the perspective of history of Christianity]. Seoul: Yŏngminsa, 1992.

———. "Paegoin sakŏn ŭl t'onghaebon sinminhoe yŏn'gu" (A study of the Sinminhoe through examining the case of the 105 Men). Doctoral thesis, Koryŏ taehakkyo, 1988.

Yun Pyŏngsŏk, Sin Yongha, and An Pyŏngjik, eds. *Han'guk kŭndaesaron* [Historical essays on modern Korea]. Seoul: Chisik sanŏpsa, 1977.

Yun Sŏngbŏm. "Hwanin, Hwanung, Hwan'gŏm ŭn got Hananim ida" (Hwanin, Hwanung and Hwan'gŏm—Truly God). *Sasanggye,* vol. 5, no. 5 (May 1963), pp. 258–71.

———. *Kidokkyo wa Han'guk sasang* [Christianity and Korean thought]. Seoul: Taehan Kidokkyo sŏhoe, 1964.

English Language

Ahlstrom, Sidney E. "Theology in America: A Historical Survey." In *The Shaping of American Religion,* ed. James W. Smith and A. Leland Jamison. Princeton, N.J.: Princeton University Press, 1961, pp. 232–321.

Allen, Horace N. *Korea: Fact and Fantasy.* Seoul: Methodist Publishing House, 1904.

Anderson, Gerald H., ed. *Asian Voices in Christian Theology.* Maryknoll, N.Y.: Orbis Books, 1976.

Baird, Annie L. A. *Daybreak in Korea: A Tale of Transformation in the Far East.* New York: Fleming H. Revell Co., 1909.

Baird, William M. "Notes on a Trip into Northern Korea." *The Independent,* May 20, 1897.

Baker, Donald L. "Confucians Confront Catholicism in Eighteenth-Century Korea." Ph.D. diss., University of Washington, 1983.

———. "The Martyrdom of Paul Yun: Western Religion and Eastern Ritual in 18th Century Korea." *Transaction of the Royal Asiatic Society,* vol. 54 (Korea Branch, 1979), pp. 33–58.

Baldwin, Frank. "The March First Movement: Korean Challenges, Japanese Response." Ph.D. diss., Columbia University, 1969.

———. "Missionaries and the March First Movement: Can Moral Men Be Neutral?" In *Korea Under Japanese Colonial Rule,* ed. Andrew C. Nahm. Kalamazoo, Mich.: Western Michigan University, Center for Korean Studies, 1973, pp. 193–219.

———. *Without Parallel. American-Korean Relationship Since 1945*. New York: Pantheon Books, 1973.

Bark, Dong Suh. "The American-Educated Elite in Korean Society." In *Korea and the United States: A Century of Cooperation,* ed. Young-nok Koo and Dae-suk Suh. Honolulu: University of Hawaii Press, 1984, pp. 263–80.

Baumer, Franklin L. *Modern European Thought: Continuity and Change in Ideas, 1900–1950*. New York and London: Macmillan Publishing Co., 1977.

Bays, Daniel H., ed. *Christianity in China: From the Eighteenth Century to the Present.* Stanford, Calif.: Stanford University Press, 1996.

Bennett, John C. *The Radical Imperative.* Philadelphia: Westminster Press, 1975.

Benson, Purnell Hardy. *Religion in Contemporary Culture: A Study of Religion Through Social Science.* New York: Harper and Brothers, 1960.

Bikle, George B., Jr. *The New Jerusalem: Aspects of Utopianism in the Thought of Kagawa Toyohiko.* Tucson: University of Arizona Press for the Association for Asian Studies, 1976.

Bishop, Isabella. *Korea and Her Neighbors.* London: John Murray, 1898.

Brown, Arthur J. *The Mastery of the Far East.* New York: Charles Scribner's Sons, 1919.

Cary, Otis. *A History of Christianity in Japan.* 2 vols. New York: Fleming H. Revell, 1909.

Chandra, Vipan. *Imperialism, Resistance, and Reform in Late Nineteenth Century Korea: Enlightenment and Independence Club.* Berkeley: University of California, Institute of East Asian Studies, 1988.

———. "Nationalism and Popular Participation in Government in Late Nineteenth-Century Korea: The Contribution of the Independence Club (1896–1898)." Ph.D. diss., Harvard University, 1977.

Chapman, Gordon H. "Japan: A Brief Christian History." In *The Church in Asia,* ed. Donald E. Hoke. Chicago: Moody Press, 1975, pp. 302–27.

Cho, Soon Sung. *Korea in World Politics, 1945–1950.* Berkeley: University of California Press, 1967.

Choe, Ching Young. *The Rule of the Taewon'gun, 1864–1893: Restoration in Yi Korea.* Cambridge, Mass.: East Asian Research Center, Harvard University, 1972.

Chun, Sung-chun. "Schism and Unity in the Protestant Church in Korea." Ph.D. diss., Yale University, 1959.

Chung, David. "Religious Syncretism in Korean Society." Ph.D. diss., Yale University, 1959.

Clark, Allen D. *A History of the Church in Korea.* Seoul: The Christian Literature Society, 1971.

Clark, Charles A. *The Korean Church and the Nevius Methods.* New York: Fleming H. Revell Co., 1930.

Clark, Donald N. *Christianity in Modern Korea.* Lanham, Md., New York, and London: The Asia Society/University Press of America, 1986.

———. "Yun Ch'i-ho (1864–1945): Portrait of a Korean Intellectual in an Era of Transition." *Occasional Papers on Korea,* University of Washington, no. 4 (September 1975), pp. 36–76.

Cone, James H. *A Black Theology of Liberation.* Philadelphia and New York: J. B. Lippincott, 1970.

Conn, Harvie N. "Korean Theology: Where Has It Been? Where Is It Going?" *Sinhak chinam,* vol. 39, no. 2 (Summer 1971), pp. 52–81.

Conroy, Hilary. *The Japanese Seizure of Korea, 1868–1910: A Study of Realism and Idealism in International Relations.* Philadelphia: University of Pennsylvania Press, 1960.

Cook, Harold H. *Korea's 1884 Incident: Its Background and Kim Okkyun's Elusive Dream.* Seoul: Royal Asiatic Society, Korea Branch, 1971.

Cox, Harvey. *The Secular City.* London: SCM Press, 1965.

Cumings, Bruce. "American Policy and Korean Liberation." In *Without Parallel: American-Korean Relationship Since 1945,* ed. Frank Baldwin. New York: Pantheon Books, 1973, pp. 39–103.

———. *The Origins of the Korean War: Liberation and the Emergence of Separate Regimes, 1945–1947,* vol. 1. Princeton, N.J.: Princeton University Press, 1981.

———. *The Origins of the Korean War: The Roaring of the Cataract, 1947–1950,* vol. 2. Princeton, N.J.: Princeton University Press, 1990.

Cunliffe-Jones, Hubert. *Christian Theology Since 1900.* London: Gerald Duckworth and Co., 1970.

Davies, J. G. *Christians, Politics and Violent Revolution.* New York: Orbis Books, 1976.

Deuchler, Martina, *Confucian Gentlemen and Barbarian Envoys: The Opening of Korea, 1875–1885.* Seattle: University of Washington Press, 1977.

Drummond, Richard H. *A History of Christianity in Japan.* Grand Rapids, Mich.: William B. Eerdmans Publishing Co., 1971.

Eckert, Carter J., et al. *Korea, Old and New: A History.* Seoul: Ilchokak for Korean Institute, Harvard University, 1990.

Feuer, L. S., ed. *Basic Writings on Politics and Philosophy.* Garden City, N.Y.: Doubleday Press, 1959.

Fierro, Alfred. *The Militant Gospel.* New York: Orbis Books, 1977.

Fisher, J. E. *Democracy and Mission Education in Korea.* New York: Teachers' College, Columbia University, 1928.

———. *Pioneers of Modern Korea.* Seoul: The Christian Literature Society of Korea, 1977.

Forman, Charles W., ed. *Christianity in the Non-Western World.* Englewood Cliffs, N.J.: Prentice-Hall, 1967.

Gale, James S. *Korea in Transition.* New York: Eaton and Mains, 1909.

Gatewood, William B., Jr., ed. *Controversy in the Twenties—Fundamentalism, Modernism, and Evolution.* Nashville, Tenn.: Vanderbilt University Press, 1969.

Gilfford, Daniel L. "The Influence of Missionary Work Upon the Life of the Koreans." *The Student Missionary Appeal.* (Addresses at the Third International Convention of Student Volunteer Movement for Foreign Mission, Cleveland, Ohio, February 23–27, 1898.) New York: Student Volunteer Movement, 1898, pp. 361–64.

Gilmore, George W. *Korea From Its Capital.* Philadelphia: Presbyterian Board of Publication and Sunday-School Work, 1892.

Gouldner, Alvin. *The Future of Intellectuals and the Rise of the New Class.* New York: Seabury Press, 1979.

Grayson, James Huntley. *Korea: A Religious History.* Oxford: Clarendon Press, 1989.

Han, Bae-ho, and Kim, Kyu-t'ae. "Korean Political Leaders (1952–1962): Their Social Origins and Skills." *Asian Survey,* vol. 2, no. 7 (July 1963), pp. 305–23.

Han, Sungjoo. *The Failure of Democracy in Korea.* Berkeley and London: University of California Press, 1974.

Han, Woo-keun. *The History of Korea.* Trans. Kyong-shik Lee. Honolulu: University of Hawaii Press, 1971.

Harrington, Fred Harvey. *God, Mammon, and the Japanese: Dr. Horace Allen and Korean-American Relations, 1884–1905*. Madison: University of Wisconsin Press, 1944.

Henderson, Gregory. *Korea: The Politics of Vortex*. Cambridge, Mass.: Harvard University Press, 1968.

Hoke, Donald E., ed. *The Church in Asia*. Chicago: Moody Press, 1975.

Hong, Harold, Won Yong Ji, and Chung Choon Kim, eds. *Korea Struggles for Christ*. Seoul: Christian Literature Society of Korea, 1966.

Hudson, Darril. *The Ecumenical Movement in World Affairs*. Washington, D.C.: The National Press, 1969.

Hudson, Winthrop S. *American Protestantism*. Chicago: University of Chicago Press, 1961.

Hunt, Everett N., Jr. *Protestant Pioneers in Korea*. Maryknoll, N.Y.: Orbis Books, 1980.

Inglehart, Charles. *A Century of Protestant Christianity in Japan*. Tokyo: Charles E. Tuttle Co., 1952.

Johnson, David, ed. *Uppsala to Nairobi*. Geneva and New York: WCC, 1975.

Jones, George Herber. "Open Korea and Its Methodist Mission." *The Gospel in All Lands,* September 1898, pp. 391–96.

Kang, Wi Jo. *Religion and Politics in Korea under the Japanese*. New York: Edwin Mellon Press, 1987.

Kim, C. I. Eugene, and Han-kyo Kim. *Korea and Politics of Imperialism, 1876–1910*. Berkeley and Los Angeles: Univeristy of California Press, 1967.

Kim, Hyung-chan. *Yun Ch'i-ho, 1865–1945—Letters in Exile: The Life and Times of Yun Ch'i-ho*. Covington, Ga.: Rhoades Printing Co., 1980.

Kim, Key-Hiuk. *The Last Phase of the East Asian World Order: Korea, Japan, and the Chinese Empire, 1860–1882*. Berkeley and Los Angeles: University of California Press, 1980.

Kim, Nyung. "The Politics of Religion in South Korea, 1974–89: The Catholic Church's Political Opposition to the Authoritarian State." Ph.D. diss., University of Washington, 1993.

Kim, Yong-bock, ed. *Minjung Theology: People as the Subjects of History*. Singapore: The Christian Conference of Asia, 1981.

Kim, Yung-Chung. *Women of Korea: A History from Ancient Times to 1945*. Seoul: Ewha Womans University Press, 1976.

Koo, Young-nok, and Dae-sook Suh, eds. *Korea and the United States: A Century of Cooperation*. Honolulu: University of Hawaii Press, 1984.

Lee, Chong-sik. *Korean Workers' Party: A Short History*. Stanford, Calif.: Hoover Institute Press, 1978.

———. "Politics in North Korea: Pre–Korean War State." *China Quarterly*, no. 14 (April–June 1963), pp. 3–16.

———. *The Politics of Korean Nationalism*. Berkeley: University of California Press, 1963.

Lee, Kun Sam. *The Christian Confrontation with Shinto Nationalism*. Philadelphia: The Presbyterian and Reformed Publishing Co., 1966.

Lehman, Paul. *The Transfiguration of Politics*. New York: Harper and Row, 1975.

Li, Lincoln. *Student Nationalism in China, 1924–1949*. Albany, N.Y.: State University of New York Press, 1994.

Loetscher, Lefferts A. *The Broadening Church: A Study of Theological Issues in the Presbyterian Church Since 1868*. Philadelphia: University of Pennsylvania Press, 1954.

Mallalieu, W. F. "Mission in Korea." *The Korean Repository*, vol. 1, no. 9 (September 1892), pp. 286–87.

Marsden, George M. *Fundamentalism and American Culture: The Shaping of Twentieth-Century Evangelicalism: 1870–1925*. New York and Oxford: Oxford University Press, 1980.

Marty, Martin E. "Forward." In Hunt, Everett N., Jr., *Protestant Pioneers in Korea*. Maryknoll, N.Y.: Orbis Books, 1980, pp. ix–xi.

Masao, Maruyama. *Thought and Behaviour in Modern Japanese Politics*. London and New York: Oxford University Press, 1969.

McFadden, Thomas H., ed. *Liberation, Revolution, and Freedom*. New York: The Seabury Press, 1975.

McGiffert, Arthur C. *The Rise of Modern Religious Ideas*. New York: Macmillan Publishing Co., 1921.

McKenzie, F. A. *Korea's Fight for Freedom*. New York: Fleming H. Revell Co., 1920.

Mitchell, Richard H. *Thought Control in Prewar Japan*. Ithaca, N.Y.: Cornell University Press, 1976.

Moffett, Samuel H. *The Christians of Korea*. New York: Friendship Press, 1962.

———. "Korea." In *The Church in Asia*, ed. Donald E. Hoke. Chicago: Moody Press, 1975, pp. 369–83.

Moltmann, Jurgen. *Theology of Hope: On the Ground and the Implications of a Christian Eschatology*. New York: Harper and Row, 1967.

Moore, S. F. "An Incident in the Street of Seoul." *The Church at Home and Abroad*, vol. 16, no. 8 (August 1894), pp. 119–20.

Nahm, Andrew C. "The Emergence of the 'Democratic' People's Republic of

Korea." In *The Politics of North Korea,* ed. Jae Kyu Park and Jung Gun Kim. Seoul: Kyŏngnam University Press, 1979, pp. 37–59.

———, ed. *Korea Under Japanese Colonial Rule.* Kalamazoo, Mich.: Western Michigan University, Center for Korean Studies, 1973.

Neill, Stephen. *Colonialism and Christian Mission.* New York: McGraw-Hill Book Co., 1966.

Nelson, M. Frederic. *Korea and the Old Order in Eastern Asia.* New York: Russell and Russell, 1945.

O'Dea, Thomas F. *Sociology and the Study of Religion.* New York and London: Basic Books, 1970.

———. *The Sociology of Religion.* Englewood Cliffs, N.J.: Prentice-Hall, Inc., 1966.

Oh, Se Eung. *Dr. Philip Jaisohn's Reform Movement, 1896–1898: A Critical Appraisal of the Independence Club.* Lanham, M.D.: University Press of America, 1995.

Oothuizen, G. C. *Theological Battleground in Asia and Africa.* London: Hurst Co., 1972.

Paige, Glen D. *The Korean People's Republic.* Stanford, Calif.: Stanford University Press, 1966.

Paik, George L. *The History of Protestant Missions in Korea, 1832–1910.* P'yongyang: Union Choson Christian College, 1929; Yonsei University Press, 1970, reprinted.

Palais, James B. *Confucian Statecraft and Korean Institutions: Yu Hyŏngwŏn and the Late Chosŏn Dynasty.* Seattle and London: University of Washington Press, 1996.

———. "Democracy in South Korea, 1948–1972." In *Without Parallel: The American-Korean Relationship Since 1945,* ed. Frank Baldwin. New York: Pantheon Books, 1973, pp. 318–57.

———. "Human Rights in the Republic of Korea." In Asian Watch Committee, *Human Rights in Korea.* Washington, D.C.: Asian Watch, 1986, pp. 1–339.

———. "Korea on the Eve of the Kanghwa Treaty, 1873–1876." Ph.D. diss., Harvard University, 1968.

———. "Political Participation in Traditional Korea, 1876–1910." *Journal of Korean Studies,* vol. 1, no. 1 (1979), pp. 73–121.

———. *Politics and Policy in Traditional Korea.* Cambridge, Mass.: Harvard University Press, 1975.

———. "A Search for Korean Uniqueness." *Harvard Journal of Asiatic Studies,* vol. 55, no. 2 (December 1995), pp. 409–25.

Palmer, Spencer J. *Korea and Christianity: The Problem of Identification with Tradition.* Seoul: Hollym Corporation, 1967.

Park, Chung-shin. "Protestant Christianity and Historical Change in Modern and Contemporary Korea." *Cambridge History of Korea,* vol. 4. Cambridge and New York: Cambridge University Press, forthcoming.

———. "Protestant Christians and Politics in Korea, 1884–1980's." Ph.D. diss., University of Washington, 1987.

———. "Protestantism and Progressive Reform Politics in Late Confucian Korea." *Sungsil sahak,* no. 8 (1994), pp. 53–94.

———. "Protestantism in Late Confucian Korea: Its Growth and Historical Meaning." *Journal of Korean Studies,* vol. 8 (1992), pp. 139–64.

Park, Jae Kyu, and Jung Gun Kim, eds. *The Politics of North Korea.* Seoul: Kyŏngnam University Press, 1979.

Park, Yong-shin. "Protestant Christianity and Social Change in Korea." Ph.D. diss., University of California (Berkeley), 1975.

Peter, Victor W. "What Korean Young People Are Thinking." *The Korean Mission Field,* vol. 28, no. 5 (May 1932), pp. 92–95, and no. 6 (June 1932), pp. 129–32.

Quinley, Harold E. *The Prophetic Clergy: Social Activism Among Protestant Ministers.* New York: John Wiley and Sons, 1974.

Ro, Bong-Rin, and Martin L. Nelson, eds. *Korean Church Growth: Explosion.* Taichung, Taiwan: World of Life Press, 1983.

Roberts, J. Deotis. *A Black Theology.* Philadelphia: Westminster Press, 1974.

Robinson, John. *Honest to God.* Philadelphia: Westminster Press, 1963.

Robinson, Michael E. *Cultural Nationalism in Colonial Korea, 1920–1925.* Seattle and London: University of Washington Press, 1988.

———. "Ideological Schism in the Cultural Nationalist Movement, 1920–1930's: Cultural Nationalism and the Radical Critique." *Journal of Korean Studies,* vol. 4 (1982–1983), pp. 241–68.

———. "The Origins and Development of Korean Nationalist Ideology, 1920–1926: Culture, Identity, National Development and Political Schism." Ph.D. diss., University of Washington, 1979.

———. "Sinsaenghwal and the Early Korean Marxism." Paper presented at Korean Seminar, University of Washington, May 17, 1985.

Rogin, Michael P. *The Intellectuals and McCarthy: The Radical Spector.* Cambridge, Mass., and London: M.I.T. Press, 1967.

Russell, C. Allyn. *Voices of American Fundamentalism: Seven Biographical Studies.* Philadelphia: The Westminster Press, 1976.

Ryu, Jae Poong. "From Chosen to Taehan: Social Change in Twentieth Century Korea." Ph.D. diss., University of Minnesota, 1972.

Ryu, Tongshik (Yu, Tongsik). "Rough Road to Theological Maturity." In *Asian Voices in Christian Theology,* ed. Gerald H. Anderson. Maryknoll, N.Y.: Orbis Books, 1976, pp. 161–77.

Scalapino, Robert A., and Chong-sik Lee. *Communism in Korea. Part I: Movement.* Berkeley: University of California, Center for Japanese and Korean Studies, 1972.

Scheiner, Irwin. *Christian Converts and Social Protest in Meiji Japan.* Berkeley and Los Angeles: University of California Press, 1970.

Shaw, Joseph M., R. W. Franklin, Harris Kaasa, and Charles W. Busicky. *Readings in Christian Humanism.* Minneapolis: Augsburg Publishing House, 1982.

Shearer, Roy E. *Wildfire: Church Growth in Korea.* Grand Rapids, Mich.: William E. Eerdmans Publishing Co., 1966.

Smelser, Neil J. *Theory of Collective Behavior.* New York: Free Press, 1963.

Smith, James Ward, and A. Leland Jamison, eds. *The Shaping of American Religion,* vol. 1 of *Religion in American Life,* and *Religious Perspectives in American Culture,* vol. 2 of *Religion in American Life.* Princeton, N.J.: Princeton University Press, 1961.

Soltau, T. Stanley. *Korea: The Hermit Nation and Its Response to Christianity.* London: World Dominion Press, 1932.

Suh, Dae Sook. *The Korean Communist Movement, 1918–1948.* Princeton, N.J.: Princeton University Press, 1967.

Sunoo, Harold Hakwon. *Repressive State and Resisting Church: The Politics of CIA in South Korea.* Fayette, Missouri: Korean American Cultural Association, 1976.

Swallen, W. L. "Polygamy and the Church." *The Korean Repository,* vol. 2, no. 8 (August 1895), pp. 289–94.

———. *Sunday School Lesson on the Book of Exodus.* Seoul: Religious Tract Society, 1907.

Thomas, George. *Christian Indians and Indian Nationalism, 1885–1950: An Interpretation in Historical and Theological Perspectives.* Frankfurt am Main, West Germany: Verlag Peter D. Lang, 1979.

Tilly, Charles. *From Mobilization to Revolution.* Reading, Mass., and London: Addison-Wesley Publishing Co., 1978.

Treadgold, Donald W. *A History of Christianity.* Belmont, Mass.: Norland Publishing Co., 1979.

Vinton, C. C. "Presbyterian Mission Work in Korea." *The Missionary Review of the World,* vol. 6, no. 9 (September 1893), p. 671.

Wagner, Edward W. "The Civil Examination Process as Social Leaven—The

Case of the Northern Provinces in the Yi Dynasty." *Korea Journal*, vol. 17, no. 1 (January 1971), pp. 22–27.

———. "The Ladder of Success in Yi Dynasty Korea." *Occasional Papers on Korea*, University of Washington, no. 1 (April 1974), pp. 1–8.

Wakabayashi, Bob Tadashi, ed. *Modern Japanese Thought*. Cambridge: Cambridge University Press, 1998.

Weems, Benjamin B. *Reform, Rebellion and the Heavenly Way*. Tucson: University of Arizona Press, 1963.

Wells, Kenneth M. *New God, New Nation: Protestants and Self-Reconstruction Nationalism in Korea, 1896–1937*. Honolulu: University of Hawaii Press, 1990.

White, Ronald C., and C. Howard Hopkins. *The Social Gospel: Religion in Changing America*. Philadelphia: Temple University Press, 1978.

Wood, Gordon S.. "Intellectual History and the Social Sciences." In *New Directions in American Intellectual History*, ed. John Higham and Paul K. Conkin. Baltimore and London: The Johns Hopkins University Press, 1979, pp. 27–41.

Yamaji, Aizan. *Essays in the Modern Japanese Church: Christianity in Meiji Japan*. Ann Arbor, Mich.: Center for Japanese Studies, University of Michigan, 1999.

Yi, In-soo. "Competing Korean Elite Politics in South Korea After World War II, 1945–1948." Ph.D. diss., New York University, 1981.

Yi, Young-suk. "Liberal Protestant Leaders Working for Social Change: South Korea, 1957–1984." Ph.D. diss., University of Oregon, 1990.

Yip, Ka-che. *Religion, Nationalism, and Chinese Students: The Anti-Christian Movement of 1922–1927*. Bellingham: Western Washington University, 1980.

Yonhap News Agency. *Korean Annual 1981*. Seoul: Yonhap News Agency, 1981.

Yun, Ch'iho. "A Synopsis of What I Was and What I Am." *The Gospel in All Lands*, June 1887, pp. 274–75.

NEWSPAPERS AND PERIODICALS

Asian Languages

Ch'ŏngch'un [Youth], Keijō.

Ch'ŏngnyŏn [Youth], Keijō.

Chosŏn ilbo [Chŏson Daily], Keijō and Seoul.

Chugan Han'guk [The Korean times weekly], Seoul.

Chung'ang ilbo [Central daily news], Seoul/Chicago.
Han'guk ilbo [The Korean times], Seoul.
Hyŏpsŏng hoebo [Newsletter of Hyŏpsŏng Society], Hansŏng.
Kidok sinbo [Christian messenger], Hansŏng and Keijō.
Kidok sinbo [The Christian times], Seoul.
Kidokkyo sasang [Christian thought], Seoul.
Kŭrisŭch'an [Voices of Christians], Seoul.
Kŭrisŭdo sinmun [Christian news], Hansŏng.
Kŭrisŭdoin hoebo [Christian advocate], Hansŏng.
Miju Tong'a ilbo [The Tong'a daily news, Los Angeles edition], Los Angeles.
P'yehŏ [Ruins], Keijō.
Samyŏng [Mission], Keijō.
Sasanggye [World of thoughts], Seoul.
Sinang saenghwal [Christian life], Keijō.
Sinsaenghwal [New life], Keijō.
Taehan maeil sinbo [Korea daily news], Hansŏng.
Tong'a ilbo [East Asia daily], Keijō and Seoul.
Tongnip sinmun [The Independent], Hansŏng.
Wŏlgan Chosŏn [Chosŏn monthly], Seoul.
Wŏlgan Chung'ang [Chung'ang monthly], Seoul.
Yesugyo hoebo [The Christian news], Hansŏng.

English Language

The Church at Home and Abroad, U.S.A.
The Foreign Missionary, U.S.A.
The Gospel in All Lands, U.S.A.
Korea Communique, Japan.
Korea Scope, U.S.A.
Korea/Update, U.S.A.
The Korean Mission Field, Korea.
The Korean Repository, Korea.

INDEX

www.ingramcontent.com/pod-product-compliance
Lightning Source LLC
LaVergne TN
LVHW050257080826
844660LV00012B/652

* 9 7 8 0 2 9 5 9 9 5 7 2 4 *